CARGOES, EMBARGOES, AND EMISSARIES

CARGOES, EMBARGOES, AND EMISSARIES

The Commercial and Political Interaction of England and the German Hanse 1450-1510

JOHN D. FUDGE

UNIVERSITY OF TORONTO PRESS

Toronto Buffalo London

ISBN 0-8020-0559-4

HF455
.F83
1995

Printed on acid-free paper

Canadian Cataloguing in Publication Data

Fudge, John D., 1950–
    Cargoes, embargoes and emissaries : the commercial
    and political interaction of England and the German
    Hanse, 1450–1510

    Includes bibliographical references and index.
    ISBN 0-8020-0559-4

    1. Great Britain – Commerce – Hansa towns – History.
    2. Hansa towns – Commerce – Great Britain – History.
    3. Great Britain – Foreign relations – Hansa towns –
    History.   4. Hansa towns – Foreign relations –
    Great Britain – History.   I. Title.

    DA47.2.F83 1995   942.05 1   C94-931869-8

University of Toronto Press acknowledges the
financial assistance to its publishing program
of the Canada Council and the
Ontario Arts Council.

For Edna and Lilly

CONTENTS

FOREWORD

It is now almost half a century since Professor Michael Postan brought together the many strands of research on the late medieval history of the Hanse in his classic chapter 'Trade of the North' in the second volume of the *Cambridge Economic History of Europe*.[1] His encyclopaedic knowledge and brilliant analytical approach to the subject, which revealed a period when contracting commodity exchanges resulted in the largely successful Hanseatic use of political power to exclude rivals and cartelize commercial activity, has ensured that this interpretation of the late medieval Hanseatic trade remains as fresh today as when it was published in 1952. It has also, since that time, encouraged research to concentrate on the subsequent period encompassing the years 1500 to 1800.

Most of this later work has focused on the sixteenth century, revealing that the towns of the Hanseatic League underwent a protracted period of political decline; their commerce, although steadily expanding, proportionately ceded ground to Netherlands and English competitors. Indicative of these changes were the alterations in the fortunes of Danzig and Lübeck merchants. The intra-Baltic commerce of these towns at this period increased some two to three and one half times, while traffic between western Europe and the Baltic, passing eastward through the Sound, increased almost six-fold.[2] During the 1490s Danzig and Lübeck ships entering Baltic ports had each equalled or even surpassed in number those arriving from western Europe. A century later they were heavily outnumbered.

During the sixteenth century the Danzigers, like their Lübeck counterparts, had thus enjoyed a steady if unspectacular expansion in what remained essentially a 'traditional' intra-Baltic commerce. As that century drew to a close, the much greater part of their activity (eighty per cent) still involved the transportation of bulk cargoes from the city's maritime hinterland to their home ports for processing. These processed commodities, together with imported Swedish wares – copper, iron, and butter – were then exported eastward to Livonia and the ports of the Gulf of Finland, whence the ships returned with cargoes of hides and furs. Only about twenty per cent of Danzig's intra-Baltic commerce, however, involved such long distance activity. In the course of the sixteenth century, moreover, that intra-Baltic commerce was eclipsed by the bulk carrying trade from Prussia and Poland to the West.[3] Native Danzigers were also progressively displaced from the bulk carrying trade by western merchants as the century progressed, and the Lübeckers were virtually totally excluded.[4] Increasingly ousted from participation in the dynamic bulk trade between Danzig-Elbing and the West and confined to the much more slowly growing traffic within intra-Baltic commercial systems, merchants of the Hanse yielded both political and commercial influence to western rivals during the sixteenth century.

In the light of new research, therefore, Baltic commerce can be perceived in terms of two independent commercial systems centred on Danzig and Lübeck. Through a series of local trade networks their merchants gained entry to the full range of Baltic ports. By means of the links between Danzig-Antwerp and Lübeck-Leipzig,[5] which had been forged in the 1490s, they also gained access to western and central European commercial and financial systems and experienced the economic fluctuations of varying duration emanating from that source. Such fluctuations were induced in large part by fundamental changes taking place on the exchange markets of west-central Europe, which affected the tempo of commercial activity through variations in the cost of trade credit.[6] For a brief period from 1497 to 1504, the two Baltic trading systems were linked into a unitary capital market structure, but thereafter movements in the price of commercial credit at Leipzig and Antwerp fluctuated inversely. At first, between 1505 and 1526, Antwerp's Baltic trade felt the benefits of cheap money, before a fall in rates at Leipzig from 1527 to 1542 favoured Lübeck. Each displacement in activity between the two bourses in the years up to about 1542, however, saw interest rates on the exchange fall to a lower level than before and the volume of commercial activity through these centres increase. Nor did this pattern of spatial displacement in activity subsequently change. Periods of intense activity through Leipzig-Lübeck (in 1545–55 and 1565–95) continued to alternate with similar phases through Antwerp-Danzig (in 1542–5 and 1555–65). But now, in so far as activity was related to conditions on central European exchange markets, it took place in conditions of rising interest rates. Between 1542 and 1595 at Leipzig-Lübeck commercial activity was played out against a background of long-term rising interest rates. At Antwerp, on the other hand, the situation was somewhat different. Here in 1527/8 both conjunctural and structural changes in the city's money markets presaged a similar fate. Nevertheless, the integration of the city into the new financial system of Seville-Medina del Campo prevented Antwerp's suffering the same long-term fate that befell Leipzig. Henceforth, the changing fortunes of the Indies fleet dominated exchange operations in the city, and the influence of central European mining activity weakened. As trade cycle followed trade cycle (in 1527–42, 1537/42–65, and 1565–95) potentially the stage seemed set for a long-term fall in interest rates and an increase in commercial activity.

From its inception, however, the new system was subject to major changes, which initially altered its structure and ultimately brought about its demise. As the Spanish-Netherlands exchanges began to move to the new forces that were transforming activity at Medina del Campo, continuing Habsburg intervention on the Antwerp bourse crippled that city's money market and resulted in a displacement of financial activity elsewhere, bringing new life to centres like London. Yet the effects of the American silver boom were not confined to a geographical restructuring of European capital markets; as increasing supplies were transported to Spain, local specie markets were flooded, interest rates fell below the specie-export point, and supplies were transhipped elsewhere. Even before the Iberian trade boom of 1537/42–65 ran its course, the massive inflow of Spanish American silver began to create inflationary pressures within the European economy and alter the international balance of specie stocks, thereby transforming the structure of international money markets. Henceforth a new trend was superimposed upon the existing pattern of interest rates, as lenders attempted to protect their assets by enhancing rates in line with regional price increases and as greater margins on specie transfers increased the cost of commercial credit. All over Europe those with money to lend were forced to adjust to a very different market situation. Yet in most instances they seem to have responded in much the same way, with 'monetary' rather than 'real' factors exerting a dominant influence on their decision-making. Finance costs, including those for commercial credit, rose and from 1554 to 1565 trade declined, ushering in a crisis that marked the end of one age and the beginning of another. Henceforth central European commercial activity centred on Leipzig continued as before but at a much reduced level. Trade had shifted elsewhere – to Amsterdam and London, which now displaced Antwerp as the financial and commercial centres of the West. Here the transformation of domestic capital markets now attracted merchants to these cities to avail themselves of cheap commercial credits. Effective bullion markets, tapping the wealth of the Indies, also afforded them the opportunity to acquire a prime exportable commodity – specie. Thus a new trade emerged, particularly in the Baltic, which had suffered acute specie shortages since around 1540. In conditions of differential purchasing power of specie in East and West, it became highly advantageous to export the precious metal to obtain 'cheap' commodities; as a result Anglo-Dutch trade expanded rapidly but always to the tempo of American specie production and trade.

In the historiography of Baltic–North Sea trade there has thus been a tendency to contrast conditions in the late medieval and early modern periods. The former has been characterized as a time when contracting commodity exchanges resulted in the largely successful Hanseatic use of political power to exclude rivals and cartelize commercial activity. The latter period, on the other hand, is seen as a time of commercial expansion during which the Hanseatic League underwent a protracted period of political decline as their commerce, although steadily expanding, proportionately ceded ground to Netherlands and English competitors, who exchanged specie against 'cheap' commodities. How the transition between these two periods was made, however, has until now remained obscure. It is one of the great strengths of John Fudge's book that it traces for the first time, from an English perspective, how the denizens of the Steelyard assimilated in the period 1465–1509 the medieval practices associated with their east-coast trade with those of the new commerce along the London-Antwerp-Frankfurt trade axis. His analysis of this situation, in assuming an older tradition of political economy, moreover, sets a new research agenda concerning the political

response of the Hanse to its changed situation – a subject sadly
neglected by historians of the *Neuzeit*. For those who wish to savour the
best aspects of present-day Hanseatic history, read on.

Ian Blanchard
The University of Edinburgh

NOTES

1 M.M. Postan, 'The Trade of the North,' in *The Cambridge Economic History
of Europe*, vol. 2, *Trade and Industry in the Middle Ages*, ed. M.M. Postan
and E.E. Rich (Cambridge, 1952).

2 (a) Danzig 1490–2 Wojewodskie Archiwum Państwowe w Gdańsku,
Komora Palowa, Pfahlkammerrechnung. 300, 19/7; 1583 ibid 19/12.
Lübeck 1492–6, F. Bruns, 'Die Lübeckischen Pfundzollbücher von
1492–1496,' *Hansische Geschichtsblätter*, XI (1904–5), 109–31; XIII (1907),
457–99, and XIV (1908), 357–407. 1579–81, P. Jeannin, 'Le commerce de
Lübeck aux environs de 1580,' *Annales. ESC.*, XVI, 1 (1961), 36–65.
(b) Traffic through the Sound. N.E. Bang, *Tabeller over Skibsfart og Vare-
transport gennen Øresund*, 1497–1660, 2 vol. in 3 (København and Leipzig,
1906–33); and P. Jeannin, 'Les comptes du Sund comme source pour la
construction d'indices généraux de l'activité économique en Europe
(XVIᵉ–XVIIIᵉ siècle),' *Revue Historique*, no. 470–1 (1964).

3 A. Maczak, 'Der polnische Getreideexport und der Problem der Handel-
bilanz (1574–1647),' in I. Bog, *Der Aussenhandel Ostmitteleuropas
1450–1650. Die ostmitteleuropäischen Volkswirtschaften in ihren Beziehungen
zu Mitteleuropa* (Köln-Wien, 1971) and A. Attman, *The Russian and Polish
Markets in International Trade, 1500–1650* (Göteborg: Meddelanden från
Ekonomisk-historiska institutionen vid Göteborgs universitet, no 26,
1973).

4 At Königsberg, for instance, the Lübeckers constituted only 7% of the
total trade and 1% of the salt trade. P. Jeannin, 'L'activité du port de
Koenigsberg dans la second moitié du XVIᵉ siècle,' *Bulletin de la Société
d'histoire moderne*, 12ᵉ série (1958). Their activity was largely confined to
the import of high-value wares of central German and Mediterranean
origin.

5 On Lübeck's trade with Leipzig and Nürnberg, see, e.g., C.L. Nordmann,
'Nürnberger Großhändler in spätmittelalterlichen Lübeck,' *Nürnberger
Beiträge zu den Wirtschafts- und Sozialwissenschaften*, XXXVII–XXXVIII
(1938), and E. Westermann, 'Zu den verwandtschaftlichen und geschäft-
lichen Beziehungen der Praun, Froler und Mulich von Nürnberg, Erfurt
und Lübeck in der zweiten Hälfte des 15. Jahrhunderts,' in N. Bestmann,

F. Irsigler, and J. Scheider, eds. *Wirtschaftsgeschichte und Personenge-schichte. Festschrift für Wolfgang von Stromer* (Trier, 1987). On Danzig's trade with Antwerp, see P. Jeannin, 'Les relations économiques des villes de la Baltique avec Anvers au XVIe siècle,' *Vierteljahrschrift für Sozial- und Wirtschaftsgeschichte*, Bd. 43, Heft 3–4 (1956).

6 Preliminary findings on this aspect of the subject will be found in I. Blanchard, 'Credit and Commerce: From the Mediterranean to the North Sea Economies in the Early Sixteenth Century,' in H. Diederiks and D. Reeder, eds. *Cities of Finance* (Amsterdam: Royal Netherlands Academy, in press). That article may be set in a broader context by reference to the same author's 'International Capital Markets and Their Users,' in I. Blanchard et al., eds. *Industry and Finance in Early Modern History* (Stuttgart: Vierteljahrschrift für Sozial- und Wirtschaftsgeschichte, Beihefte 98, 1991).

century. Among other things, Jenks argues that Anglo-Hanseatic relations began to reflect a weakening of the Hanse no later than 1420. Since the publication of M.M. Postan's 'The Economic and Political Relations of England and the Hanse from 1400 to 1475,' well over fifty years ago, historians writing in the English language have had very little to say about the Hanse or how it interacted commercially and politically with England. Postan's interpretation has now been reassessed, though, by T.H. Lloyd. Lloyd's *England and the German Hanse, 1157–1611* offers a survey of relations between the Hanse and England for the entire period of their contact – a temporal scope that unfortunately precludes extensive discussion of the late fifteenth and early sixteenth centuries. A number of themes therefore remain largely unexplored. How did extraneous economic and political pressures contribute to the institutional deterioration of the Hanse in the late 1400s and early 1500s? How was the overland and seaborne commerce of northern Europe affected by Anglo-Hanseatic diplomacy or by Tudor-Hapsburg trade disputes? Moreover, to what extent did changing patterns within the greater European economy – especially the commercial ascendancy of Antwerp – affect English and Hanseatic trade? These are among the questions addressed in this present study. It attempts to incorporate much of the existing scholarship and to introduce to the anglophone reader some interpretations of archival evidence that will, in turn, constitute a worthy contribution to that body of scholarship.

The period under review spans the years 1450 through 1510. Lines of demarcation within the chronological framework are provided by two pivotal crises in Anglo-Hanseatic relations – the seizure of the Hanseatic salt fleet in 1449 and the general arrest of Hansards in England in 1468 – and a third, the disruption of the Anglo-Lowland trade in the 1490s, in which the Hansards were unavoidably caught up, and which followed closely on the heels of the articulation of the Anglo-Hanseatic status quo in 1491. Within each successive interval both the impact of the crises and their aftermaths can be identified by monitoring change in the structure of the trade and by fitting domestic and international political developments into the economic framework. Through this an assessment is possible of Anglo-Hanseatic 'relations,' which in turn reflect both economic and political change within the German Hanse.

A clearer picture also emerges of the scope and character of the Hanseatic trade in individual English ports and the degree to which it was affected by the ebb and flow of diplomatic relations. Likewise, the English commercial presence in the Baltic region, another subject somewhat muddied by historiographical orthodoxy far too reliant on the recorded complaints of restrictions there, is clarified through examination of English activity within the Anglo-Hanseatic network.

With regard to orthography and other usage, the German spelling of place-names has been followed except for well-known Anglicized variations, such as Cologne, Prussia, Lithuania, etc. Also, for the purpose of this study the convenient term 'Esterling' is used to distinguish the Hansards of the North Sea ports and the Baltic territories from those of Cologne and the lower Rhineland. Though not overly precise, this general definition is indeed common in contemporary English documents of the mid-fifteenth century, albeit less so by the early sixteenth. I use the terms 'Lowlands' and 'Low Countries' interchangeably for the various territories consolidated under the dukes of Burgundy in the late fourteenth and early fifteenth centuries. They include the duchy of Brabant and the counties of Zealand, Flanders, Artois, Holland, and Hainault. Finally, all monetary sums are expressed in English pounds sterling unless otherwise noted.

ACKNOWLEDGMENTS

The following study could not have been seen through to its conclusion but for the generous assistance of various institutions and the helpful counsel of numerous individuals. For the funding that made possible the research I am most grateful to the Faculty of Arts of the University of Edinburgh and the Committee of Vice-Chancellors and Principals of the Universities of the United Kingdom. I would like to extend my special thanks also to the courteous and helpful staffs of the libraries and archives in which I researched, particularly those of the Public Record Office, the Historisches Archiv der Stadt Köln, and the Algemeen Rijksarchief in Brussels.

For their unfailing encouragement, salutory criticism, and guidance I extend my thanks to Ian Blanchard, Tony Goodman, and Professor Kenneth Fowler, who directed my dissertation at Edinburgh. I am indebted also to Professor Klaus Friedland, and to Dr Gustaaf Asaert, whose invitation to consult his notes greatly assisted my investigation of the aldermen's registers at Antwerp. Likewise, my appreciation is extended to James Bolton, who kindly made available to me his dissertation on England's foreign merchants. The many helpful suggestions of Malcolm Burnett about translations, and those of Diana Greenway regarding palaeographical problems were invaluable. So, too, were the perceptive comments of David Ditchburn. Finally, to Gerrit van de Hoef also, for his immeasurable assistance with the preparation of the typescript, I wish to express my sincerest thanks.

J.D.F.

CARGOES, EMBARGOES, AND EMISSARIES

CHAPTER I

*T*INTRODUCTION: RADE, POLITICS, AND PIRACY 1400–49

Networks and commodities

By the middle decades of the fifteenth century the major commodity markets of northern Europe were linked by constituent land and sea transportation networks that facilitated the distribution of goods over vast distances. The primary axis of the long-distance seaborne trade stretched from the Baltic Sea in the north-east to Lisbon in the south. On the Atlantic seaboard it transected the main east-west axis of the continental trade at the Low Countries, which were now consolidated politically under the Burgundian ducal house. There, the Flemish entrepôt of Bruges and its Brabantine counterpart, Antwerp, were the gateways to a vital commercial corridor that connected England and the Lowlands with major European markets distant from the sea. The inland trade routes, in turn, provided economic congruity within Europe by interconnecting diverse regional economies. And they linked them not only with the northern maritime network, but also with a second great sphere of seaborne commerce – the Mediterranean.

Although it by no means lacked diversity, the commodity structure of Europe's long-distance trade was relatively uncomplicated and at the same time illustrative of the commercial interdependence of various regions. High-value woollen cloth, much of it manufactured in the Lowlands, England, and Tuscany, was the most important common component. Markets for woollen textiles were to be found throughout much of continental Europe, well beyond the regions where they were produced on a large scale. English cloth, for example, was shipped across the Narrow Seas to Zealand and Brabant, and transported overland from there to Frankfurt, Leipzig, and Venice. Textiles of both English and Lowland manufacture also were carried to markets all along the Atlantic/Baltic maritime network. Products directly connected with the cloth industry were hardly less important than the finished article. Manufacturers in the Low Countries were heavily dependent on supplies of imported Spanish and English wool, the latter available almost exclusively at England's wool staple at Calais. Equally vital for industries on both sides of the Channel were dyestuffs and mordants – from France, the lower Rhineland, and the Mediterranean. The organizational framework of long-distance commerce was further defined by the trade in grain, fish, and salt. Especially important was salt from Bourgneuf, Brouage, and La Rochelle on the Bay of Biscay (i.e., Bay salt), where Gascon wine could also be purchased. Salt was available as well, together with Iberian fruit and wine, from points as far south as Setubal. It was shipped north to England and the Low Countries, and to the fish-curing industries in Scandinavia. Other fleets brought Bay salt all the way to the eastern Baltic, to ports like Danzig, Riga, and Reval, for redistribution to the hinterland regions of Prussia, Poland, and Livonia. In return, these areas supplied grain – wheat, rye, and barley – to western consumer markets, especially in the densely populated Burgundian Lowlands. Also integrated with the trade in salt and grain were the North Sea fisheries. Cargoes of fish and fish products from Skania, the Hanseatic-controlled Norwegian fisheries, and Iceland were offloaded at ports in England and along the Atlantic seaboard. The last essential element in this maritime trade was the movement of relatively cheap bulk commodities from northern regions to English and Atlantic markets. Baltic centres, in particular, furnished western markets not only with grain, but also with vast quantities of lumber, pitch, iron, flax, and wax.

Functioning as depots, transit centres, and provisioning stations for merchants and shippers engaged in this seaborne traffic were various ports in Zealand: Middelburg, Arnemuiden, and Veere. They also were part of the conduit that connected England with the Lowland entrepôts and inland markets. It was here that the Atlantic/Baltic network linked with the flourishing cross-Channel trade. In addition to woollens, the ships arriving from England brought lead, pewter, hides, cheese, and occasionally grain. Those departing the Zealand quays for English ports were laden with dyestuffs and a diverse assortment of manufactured wares ranging from Cologne silk and high-quality steel to pins and straw hats. They also trans-shipped more costly exotic wares, especially spices, which originated within the Italian-dominated Mediterranean trade network. England remained largely self-sufficient in food production, and seldom needed to import grain, except to compensate for an occasional poor harvest or to provision an army. On the other hand, the kingdom did represent a substantial consumer market for imported fish, manufactured wares, and bulk raw materials. The same inland distributive routes that brought dyestuffs, spices, and manufactured wares to the Lowland entrepôts and thence to England, carried finished cloth and North Sea fish to the markets of Westphalia, the Rhineland, and points farther south and east.

Prior to the mid-fourteenth century the export sector of England's overseas trade had relied almost exclusively on shipments of high-quality wool to the Continent. Thereafter, exports of wool began to decrease, as more was consumed by England's own burgeoning textile industries. The manufacture of English woollens accelerated, and Flemish production declined correspondingly. During subsequent decades England's export trade developed a new dependency on cloth. English cloth exporters were dependent, in turn, on cross-Channel distribution points, since they lacked consistent direct access to more northerly continental markets. Together with the narrowness of the commodity base, this meant that both producers and retailers were vulnerable to protracted interruptions in the cloth trade. Serious interruptions occurred in the mid-fifteenth century with the loss of England's territorial possessions in France and a series of disputes involving two of the kingdom's most important commercial links: the Burgundian Lowlands and towns of the German Hanse. Unable to significantly diversify their export products, English merchants were faced with the alternative – trying to either expand existing markets for cloth or develop new ones. At the heart of the problem was access to distant markets along the Atlantic/Baltic axis or within the continental network east of Antwerp.

The commodity base of northern Europe's long-distance maritime trade did not change fundamentally during the fifteenth century. There was, however, some diversification, particularly within the foodstuff sector. Fish, salt, and grain remained central to the trade, but Hanseatic shippers from Hamburg and the Baltic increasingly brought beer with their grain and bulk freight cargoes, and English cloth shipments to the Continent were supplemented more regularly with consignments of cheese and dairy products. As the international merchant communities at the Lowland entrepôts expanded, so, too, did the selection of commodities available there. This necessarily translated into increased availability along the northern shipping routes as well. By the end of the century Hanseatic skippers, and others from Holland, Zealand, and Brabant who had loosened the Hanse's control of Baltic commerce, sailed for northern waters with cargoes that included not only cloth, salt, and Gascon wine, but also Iberian wines, imported fruits, and sugar from Madeira. Within the continental network, any of these commodities, together with beer from Hamburg or Wismar, might also augment the cloth, fish, and salt cargoes being carted overland from Brabant to Cologne, Frankfurt, and beyond.

Situated near the far end of the Atlantic/Baltic axis, the Prussian port of Danzig ascended to international commercial prominence during the fifteenth century, and emerged as both the leading trade centre in the eastern Baltic and the foremost supplier of cereals and forest products to western Europe. Distant markets in England and the Lowlands were of central importance. The Prussian hinterland, source of many of the exportable raw products, was jealously guarded by Danzig's merchant community and by successive Grand Masters of the Teutonic Order, who ruled Prussia and Livonia. Foreign access was actively discouraged. The only significant English import in the eastern Baltic was woollen cloth – trans-shipped over Hamburg and Lübeck or brought directly via the Danish Sound – with much of it destined for interior regional markets monopolized by agents of the Order and intermediaries from Danzig. The westward transport of bulky export products also depended on this *Umlandfahrt* around the Danish peninsula.

Often partners in this bulk carriage trade were the merchants of Lübeck, who also were important distributors of woollen cloth in the Baltic region, and therefore wary of foreign competitors. Hence, in addition to Danzig and Hanseatic ports farther to the east, Lübeck and other towns of the Hanse's Wendish sector – Stralsund, Lüneburg, Wismar, and Rostock – also favoured some restriction of the trade of English and Lowland merchants in the Baltic sphere. Although their motives varied superficially according to the character and commodity structure of the trade in each geographical area, they did not differ in any fundamental sense. Both Lübeck's attitude and that of Danzig were dictated by the self-interest of specific regional and civic merchant communities.

Portentous depredations[1]

Hansards in the Baltic ports often employed carriers from the Lowlands for the transport of wood and grain to the Atlantic seaboard, and ordinances intended to limit foreign participation in direct trade were not always effective. In 1422 Hollanders were prohibited from residing in Prussia. The following year they were forbidden to trade to Livonia, where the merchants of Reval, Riga, and Dorpat had supplanted those of Lübeck and Visby as the Hanseatic intermediaries for the trade to Novgorod and Russia.[2] These restrictions accomplished little, but did lead to a sustained campaign of obstruction and piracy by the Hollanders during Dano-Wendish hostilities, which lasted from 1426 to 1435. Moreover, shippers from Holland persisted in defying an attempted Wendish blockade of the Sound during this conflict. Fully cognizant of the potential commercial repercussions, the Order granted the merchants of Holland, Zealand, and England access to Prussia in 1428.[3] While the Wendish ports advocated the expulsion of foreigners, the Grand Master attempted instead to restrict his guests once they had entered Prussian territory. Lübeck and the Wendish towns did succeed in diverting some commercial traffic to old overland and coastal routes, but Prussia's seemingly irresolute attitude toward interlopers from the west muted the effectiveness of blockades. Mercantile and shipping interests in Holland continued to challenge Hanseatic control of the Baltic trade. A series of piracies exacerbated tensions to the point where the assembly of representatives from Hanseatic towns (the *Hansetag*), resolved to suspend commerce with Holland in 1436.[4] Again the eastern Baltic towns rejected such a severe restriction, but antagonism in the west eventually resulted in a state of war between Holland and the Wendish towns, which lasted from 1438 to 1441.

Meanwhile, an equally contentious issue was that of reciprocal trading privileges for English merchants in Prussia and Livonia. Hansards had long enjoyed a privileged status in England, by virtue of a series of charters granted in the late thirteenth and early fourteenth century, including Edward I's *Carta Mercatoria*.[5] A great many of their freedoms originally applied to other alien merchant groups in England as well, but the Hansards had managed to successfully defend their entitlements on into the fifteenth century, while others had not. In London they formed an established corporate body with various rights of jurisdiction over members. At least as early as 1170 Cologne merchants had maintained their *Guildhalla Teutonicorum* in London, which later became the enclave of the Hanseatic merchants – known from 1384 onward as the Steelyard. Hansards also were supposed to be free to move throughout the kingdom and to transact business with both foreign and denizen merchants.[6]

Hansards played a central role in both the import and export sectors of England's overseas trade. They were the main foreign suppliers of wood, wax, and other essential bulk commodities, and in any given year could also account for up to one third of England's aggregate cloth exports. Their competitive edge in England stemmed from differential rates for royal customs and the later Hanseatic exemption from subsidies. Woollen cloth was the principal export item.[7] For all merchants the duties were highest for 'in grain' (*in grano*) cloths of assize, coloured with expensive scarlet dye from the Mediterranean, followed by the 'half grain' or 'part grain' varieties. Most woollen exports, however, were without grain, dyed instead with cheaper colourants such as madder. Hansards paid a duty of 12d on each cloth without grain (*sine grano*), while denizens paid 14d. For non-Hanseatic aliens the rate was 2s 9d per cloth. Cheaper or undersized textiles like russets, straights, and friezes usually were categorized with miscellaneous goods paying the *ad valorem* poundage subsidy and the 3d custom. Worsteds, of little overall importance in the Hanseatic trade, were assessed by the piece according to set rates.[8] Most other commodities, both imported and exported, were assessed *ad valorem*. The poundage subsidy of 12d on the pound sterling applied to the merchandise of denizens and aliens, but Hansards secured exemption from it in 1437.[9] The petty custom of 3d on the pound was paid by all non-denizens, including Hansards. The application of the *ad valorem* rates can be illustrated with any of the common imports – for example, pitch and tar, consistently valued in the particulars of accounts at 20s per last throughout the second half of the century. After they were exempted from the poundage subsidy in 1437, Hansards freighting a single last would pay a petty custom charge amounting to 3d, while denizens would have to pay 12d poundage. Other aliens would be charged both the custom and the subsidy for a total of 15d. Separate fixed duties applied to exports of leather and hides, as well as to wool and wool-fells, although the latter were not of central importance to the Anglo-Hanseatic trade. Wax imports were far more significant, and Hansards were the principal suppliers. The duty on wax was one shilling on every hundredweight (quintal). Finally, the tunnage subsidy of 3s per tun of wine was paid by alien merchants.[10]

Oral declarations and certificates attested to the value of a merchant's goods at point of purchase, although customs records suggest that by the fifteenth century standard valuations may have been assigned to most commodities of a standard quality. In any event, throughout the second half of the century, variations in the values attached to most types of merchandise except foodstuffs were modest. These values, recorded for customs purposes, bear little relation to actual market prices in England.[11]

Differential duties gave Hansards some economic advantage in England, but their English counterparts enjoyed no such preferential treatment in Hanseatic towns. Even so, although English merchants frequently complained of arrest and harassment in Wendish ports,[12] they evidently did not fare so badly elsewhere. By the late fourteenth century they were well established at Königsberg, Elbing, and Danzig, and were engaging in wholesale and retail trade with other foreigners as well as Prussians. In Danzig they had formed a society with an elected governor[13] – an organization that seems to have been tolerated until the turn of the century, when Hansards trading to England (*Englandfahrer*) objected to changes in English customs regulations. The Prussian ports responded by prohibiting Englishmen from trading with non-Hansards and restricting their rights of residence, before eventually expelling them outright in 1403.[14] However, the effectiveness of a subsequent trade boycott, initiated in response to numerous English attacks on Hanseatic shipping,[15] was undermined by a lack of consensus and cooperation within the Hanseatic confederation. Also, the Hansards could do nothing to prevent English cloth being offered at key cross-Channel outlets in the Burgundian Lowlands.

In 1405 Henry IV's ambassadors and envoys of the Grand Master reached agreement in principle on reciprocal trading privileges for English merchants.[16] A number of Englishmen were ordered to make restitution for illegal distraint of Hanseatic ships and cargoes, and a commission was appointed to hear disputes involving merchants of the Hanse, Prussia, and Holland. But the 'divers homicides, depredations of goods and merchandise and other damages' perpetrated on and by the Hansards and Hollanders continued.[17] As a consequence, the situation of English traders attempting to return to the Baltic remained precarious. Unlike their Hanseatic counterparts in England they were not a corporate body with elected officials, and so they remained entirely subject to the jurisdiction of the Order and the Prussian municipalities. Another accord, agreed to in 1409, did little to moderate the enmity, and the piracy and commercial reprisals continued unabated. The next decade saw no end of claims and countercharges. Merchants of the Hanseatic *comptoir* at Bergen in Norway were accused of the robbery and murder of Englishmen. The Hanseatic *Englandfahrer* complained of tolls in England that ran contrary to the composition of charters previously granted by the Crown.[18]

Several Englishmen did, however, return to the Baltic ports, their transactions with hinterland markets soon drawing the ire of their Prussian rivals. As many as fifty-five English merchants were active in the trade to Danzig when renewed persecution again curtailed their commercial activity in 1422. New decrees limited the length of their stay in Prussian territory, and together with all other non-Hanseatic guests they were denied direct trade with the interior. This further provoked England's mercantile sector, which, enjoying solid representation in the Commons, lobbied during the 1420s to curtail the privileges of foreign merchants.[19] Meanwhile, the war between Holland and the Wendish towns was a welcome opportunity for protectionists in the Baltic centres to stifle England's trade there, as well as that of the Hollanders, by blockading the Sound. But numerous attacks on English shipping only led to renewed tension, and while privateers from Holland, England, and the Wendish towns clashed on the high seas, the pleas heard at Westminster and Danzig became as predictable as they were frequent. Hansards complained of harassment by sheriffs in London, and sued for discharge from local customs dues. In Prussia, delegations of English traders repeatedly appeared at the court of the Grand Master to complain of depredations, and to request permission to elect aldermen and occupy a common house. The Grand Master's ruling that English merchants should have 'alle recht und gewonheid als ander geste ...

haben' [all the rights and customs that other guests have] merely reaffirmed the status quo.[20]

Given the relative commercial freedom of Hanseatic merchants in England, demands for reprisals against them were to be expected, in order to emphasize the struggle for reciprocity. At the same time, the Hanse's important contribution to the overall mercantile prosperity of the kingdom could not be overlooked. The government itself recognized that the uneasy relations were indeed affecting trade, and that Hansards now 'abstained from coming to the realm as they used to do, fearing that hindrance or arrest might be laid upon them.' Royal decrees issued in 1430 therefore called for a halt to the harassment of Hansards and their ships.[21] In Henry VI's England, however, proclamations hardly constituted effective law, and they by no means guaranteed redress. Reported instances of piracy were numerous, and complaints multiplied. When requests for the return of a captured English vessel failed to induce a response from the Wendish towns in 1432, the king and his council, at the urging of the Commons, authorized the arrest of ships belonging to the merchants of Lübeck, Rostock, Hamburg, and Wismar. In England, Hansards already were vexed by increased subsidy rates. By the mid-1430s, despite intermittent diplomatic exchanges, relations had degenerated to the point of impasse.[22] Hanseatic merchants in London suspended their trade there in April 1434, and the *Hansetag* at Lübeck considered a boycott of English cloth to protest the introduction of an ordinance requiring merchants to value their goods for royal customs and subsidies according to their worth in England. The Grand Master threatened the expulsion of all Englishmen from Prussia if old privileges in England were not restored within six months.[23]

At this point, difficulties with England's main cross-Channel trade link, the Burgundian Lowlands, also came into play. Protectionist ordinances already prohibited the sale of English cloth in Flanders. In June 1434, Duke Philip the Good of Burgundy extended the ban throughout his territories, effectively closing the entire Lowland corridor to English traffic.[24] With Anglo-Hanseatic relations already strained, England's vital wool and cloth trade, on which the national economy was so dependent, was necessarily at risk. The situation immediately prompted a shift in the attitude of the Crown toward the Hanse. By mid-June the council had reversed its policy and rescinded the letters patent that had been sent to customs collectors regarding the valuation of merchandise. Exports from England were again to be valued according to their worth 'betwix marchant and marchant' and imports valued according to their worth at place of purchase overseas.[25] Still, the Burgundian restrictions on English cloth and wool remained in effect. Moreover, the reconciliation of Franco-Burgundian differences in September 1435 (the Treaty of Arras) opened the way for Duke Philip's intervention in England's ongoing war with the French. Again the implications for England's overseas trade were profound, and as a result, bargaining with representatives of the Order and the major Hanseatic towns continued. These negotiations culminated in 1437 with another apparent compromise on the issue of reciprocal trading rights. By the terms of a new treaty English merchants in Hanseatic towns were not to be charged duties that were not of ancient and continuous usage. This was the quid pro quo for the exemption of Hansards from subsidies in England.[26] While shifting allegiances on the Continent temporarily eliminated the Lowland markets, and dealt English military ambitions in northern France a serious blow, the accord with the Hanse attempted to make the other principal continental market for cloth more secure. But the agreement actually had little effect on English merchants trading to Prussia. The Grand Master, under pressure from Danzig, would not ratify it, and Englishmen remained subject to existing taxes and the stringent commercial regulations that affected all foreigners at the Prussian staple.[27]

Notwithstanding Danzig's attitude on reciprocity, the Crown already had established a precedent for the keeping of the seas, which tended to undermine any gains that the English interpreted in the 1437 agreement. Indeed, it was a policy that brought the kingdom even closer to confrontation with the Hanse. Piracy in the Narrow Seas, exacerbated by England's continuing war with France, had played a significant role in Anglo-Hanseatic politics up to 1430. In the middle decades of the century it would come to displace England's clamour for reciprocity in the Baltic as the dominant issue. By 1436 England's continental foothold at Calais was not secure, but ships of the wartime fleet established by Henry V to ensure a successful defence of his French possessions had been sold off during the 1420s to pay royal debts. Until the mid-1430s the Crown relied on indentured captains to keep the sea. But in 1436 licences were issued to ordinary merchants and shipowners to 'resist the king's enemies on the sea' at their own expense. Captured 'enemy' ships and cargoes became property of the licensees. Coupled with the suspension of statutes that made violations of safe conducts at sea and receipt of pirated goods treasonable offences, this mercenary legislation only aggravated the already volatile situation with the Hanse. Shipowners petitioned for and received licences in London and various other familiar ports of call for foreign ships, including Hull, Ipswich, and Lynn. Eventually as many as thirty of them went to sea, predominantly in the busy shipping lanes off France and Flanders. The official recognition of the profit motive in sea keeping was tantamount to licensing piracy.[28]

In attempting to govern a nation economically drained by a century of intermittent war with France, and further weakened by the infighting of a self-seeking aristocracy not easily amenable to law, the Crown was frequently unwilling or unable to police the activity of the seafaring population. Preoccupation with the wars in France resulted in more neglect of the problems of lawlessness and disorder. Before its dispersal, even Henry V's fleet had been used primarily for the transport of troops rather than for any concerted campaign against pirates. Under young Henry VI, who held virtually no control over the aristocracy, perversion of the law by those who enjoyed the favour of the ruling council increased. In England's harbour towns there was no shortage of individuals willing to receive stolen goods, and law of the sea was meaningless to influential offenders who routinely threatened plaintiffs, paid off government officials, and bribed juries. Anarchy on the high seas could flourish because there was no central government in England strong enough to stop it.[29] Licences were granted infrequently after 1436, and in 1442 the Commons pressed for, and succeeded in establishing a small fleet of privateers to keep the sea. Nevertheless, attacks on Hanseatic and Lowland ships continued with striking regularity. It was not unusual for them to be plundered while at anchor in English harbours.[30]

The Commons ushered in the 1440s with new restrictions against foreigners that further reflected the temperament of the merchant community and its influence in political affairs. When Parliament granted the king his subsidies in 1440, an alien subsidy on foreign merchants was included.[31] The Hansards maintained their exemption, and this enabled their enemies in Parliament to play on the biases of an expanding merchant class in order to sharpen the focus of anti-Hanse sentiment. The already familiar requests for reciprocity became more common, and were given added emphasis with complaints of new taxes, extortion, robbery, and imprisonment in the Baltic ports of Stettin and Danzig. Again the king protested to Lübeck and the Grand Master over the unfair treatment of Englishmen trading to Hanseatic towns, and again in 1442 a parliamentary petition demanded the revocation of Hanseatic privileges in England if the situation were not soon remedied.[32]

Hindered it may have been, but English trade at Danzig continued nevertheless. The three-year war between Holland and the Wendish towns had not deterred the rapid re-establishment and growth of English trade in the region, despite Lübeck's attempt to blockade the Sound. Complaints by Danzig merchants at the turn of the decade indicate that in spite of restrictions Englishmen in that town were trading with non-Hansards and keeping their warehouses open all day to the alleged detriment of local businessmen.[33] When the Wendish dispute with Holland ended with the Peace of Copenhagen in 1441, ships from Holland, Zealand, and England returned to the Baltic in increasing numbers. In England, however, the controversy over reciprocity provided a certain rationale for the proposed revocation of Hanseatic franchises and to some extent for piratical attacks on Hanseatic shipping. Petitions in Parliament followed one after another, until finally Henry VI agreed to present the Hanseatic towns with an ultimatum. They were to acknowledge the reciprocal trading rights of English merchants by Michaelmas 1447 or else the immunities enjoyed by Hansards in England would be suspended. Tension was heightened further with the distraint of some Cologne merchants in Colchester. Reacting to the arrests and the threatened revocation of freedoms in England, a *Hansetag* at Lübeck contemplated the apprehension of Englishmen in Hanseatic territory. The Order and the Prussian towns demurred, however, again preferring to have their own representatives clarify the situation in England before taking action.[34] But it was the intent of the English government to force the Grand Master's acceptance of the reciprocal terms of the 1437 treaty. To this end, the Crown was not prepared to accept the equivocal response of the Prussian emissaries who arrived in the summer of 1447. The king's ultimatum lapsed, and at the end of September the privileges of Hansards in England were rescinded.[35]

By this time the lack of consensus within the Hanse was clearly evident to the English, but the political leverage achieved with the suspension of Hanseatic charters was tempered by another Burgundian boycott. Then it was rendered even less effective by the resumption of war with France in 1449. Should the Hansards now impose sanctions of their own or close the eastern Baltic to English trade – and there was considerable agitation from within the Wendish sector to do just that – then England's economic isolation might be grave indeed. Moreover, a significant disruption of Anglo-Hanseatic trade would result in the loss of yet more customs revenue crucial to the war effort. Consequently, by early 1449 Henry VI had dispatched an embassy, headed by Dr Richard Caunton, to Lübeck for the purpose of establishing a dialogue with the Hanseatic towns and the Grand Master. Although a number of proposals were exchanged, little progress was made on the question of English rights in Prussia or the reinstatement of Hanseatic privileges in England. A new round of talks was set for May 1451 at Deventer.[36] The discussions at Lübeck had not yet concluded, however, when Parliament renewed its grant of tunnage and poundage to the king, with the stipulation that Hansards should not be exempted from payment.[37] Moreover, within a matter of weeks any hopes for an amicable solution were dashed by the most astounding privateering feat to date. Commanded by the sometime mayor of Dartmouth, Robert Wenyngton, and at sea under official sanction, English freebooters captured in May a huge fleet of ships belonging to Lowland and Hanseatic ports, as it returned north from the Biscay coast. The prizes, laden with salt and wine, were taken to the Isle of Wight. Had the time now come 'to trete for a fynell pese' with the Hansards, Hollanders, and Flemmings, as Wenyngton speculated? The non-Hanseatic carriers were soon ordered released, but the Prussian and Wendish vessels, including sixteen from Lübeck, were not. Another escalation of the Anglo-Hanseatic controversy was assured.[38]

The Hanse in Northern Europe
ca. 1450

• Major Hanseatic Towns

○ Major non-Hanseatic Towns & Towns frequented by Hansards

⊕ Hanseatic Comptoir

— Limits of the Empire and the Teutonic Possessions

0 50 100 150 200 250 300 km

Scale 1:6000000

J.D.F. 1987

BALTIC SEA

Stockholm

Visby

Bornholm

Stettin

Revel

Narva

Novgorod ⊕

Dorpat ○
Pernau

Riga

LIVONIA

Königsberg

Danzig   Elbing

PRUSSIA

Kulm

Thorn

LITHUANIA

POLAND

Posen ○

Warsaw ○

Breslau ○

Cracow ○

Prague ○

CHAPTER II
DIPLOMACY AND MERCANTILE ENTERPRISE
1450–68

It would be difficult to find a more important or representative reflection of the Anglo-Hanseatic controversy in the mid-fifteenth century than the seizure of the Bay fleet in 1449. It was a pivotal incident in the course of relations between the Hanse and England, in that it broadened the dimensions of the existing conflict, and remained a source of bitter enmity for two decades. The long-term repercussions were both political and economic. In particular, responses from within the Hanseatic membership came to reflect a number of the fundamental contradictions that would characterize internal Hanseatic politics throughout the second half of the century. From this point onward the Hanse's relations with England consistently accentuated commercial and political alignment within the confederation itself.

Anglo-Hanseatic political relations in the mid-fifteenth century

Considering the chaotic state of English royal administration at the time, it is not inconceivable that some of Henry VI's councillors condoned Wenyngton's initiative or even profited from it.[1] Wenyngton was pardoned in 1452. Within the Hanseatic community Esterling merchants from the Wendish ports and Prussia had incurred the heaviest losses, with Lübeckers claiming £18,000 in damages. Englishmen did not frequent Lübeck, so unlike Danzig, the town was unable to compensate merchants immediately by confiscating English ships or goods in the Baltic.[2] There was, therefore, little doubt that the Lübeckers would resist any sort of compromise with England. At the *Hansetag* that convened at Bremen in July Lübeck attempted to align other member towns in support of compensation claims against England, but with little success.[3] Cologne and the Prussian towns were far more interested in gaining relief from the poundage subsidy. They were clearly unwilling to sacrifice their lucrative English trade for a dispute between England and the Wendish towns over the Bay fleet incident. In a prelude to what was to follow in the 1460s, Cologne's envoys in Flanders hastened to clarify the town's status vis-à-vis England with English officials.[4]

The decision of the non-Wendish towns not to escalate the tensions ultimately paid dividends, because the English government also was keen to deflect attention away from the compensation issue and refocus instead on the terms of the 1437 treaty. An Anglo-Hanseatic summit was proposed for the summer of 1451 at Utrecht, and by early October 1449 Hansards trading to England were freed once again from the offending poundage subsidy. Two months later the Crown made it clear that this exemption did not apply to Wendish merchants or to those from Danzig.[5]

Frustration in Lübeck peaked in the summer of 1450, when the Crown presumed to negotiate a settlement of differences with Danzig and the Order. English envoys, headed by the king's secretary, Thomas Kent, and London merchant John Stocker, took ship for Prussia. They were intercepted at sea by Wendish Bergenfahrer (skippers trading to Norway), taken to Lübeck, and there placed under house arrest.[6] This was an obvious affront to Danzig and to the Grand Master, under whose safe conduct the delegation was travelling. His expressed willingness to receive the English envoys had raised the possibility of an Anglo-Prussian compromise, and thereby challenged the position taken by Lübeck. At any rate, when news of the capture reached England, Hansards and their goods were arrested, and worst affected were the Prussians and Cologners.[7] Thomas Kent's subsequent flight from Lübeck in the spring of 1451 aggravated the volatile situation, sowing the seed of mistrust and rendering prospects for an immediate accord most unlikely.[8]

Nevertheless, Lübeck's claims against England headed the agenda of the diet convened at Utrecht in May 1451, and authorities in the major English ports were instructed to make proclamation ensuring the physical protection of Hansards until that time.[9] The mandate was issued amid a rash of illegal attacks on Flemish, Hanseatic, and Italian shipping during 1450 and 1451, and not surprisingly the session at Utrecht produced no agreement. From the outset Lübeck refused to treat with Thomas Kent, who had reappeared as a member of the English contingent. Delegates from the eastern Baltic, still determined to restrict expansion of English trade to the hinterland, preferred to ease the tension by offering short-term safe conducts for English traffic. Before the meeting Cologne again distanced herself from Lübeck's cause, and her representatives and those from Hamburg, Bremen, and Prussia were able to achieve a continuance of trade.[10] Lübeck's refusal to endorse the new arrangement, and her subsequent attempts to obstruct the maritime and overland shipment of English cloth, compounded confusion and resentment within the Hanse. The position of Cologne cannot be too highly stressed in this regard. Cologne merchants trading to England went so far as to request official letters from their civic council dissociating them from Lübeck.[11]

The Lübeckers had become isolated from much of the rest of the Hanse on the compensation issue, and they could not command the compliance of recalcitrant members.[12] The Prussian and Livonian towns, Cologne, and even Hamburg and Bremen rejected Lübeck's uncompromising attitude, and instead welcomed subsequent extensions of the safe conduct agreement with England. King Henry reciprocated by freeing Hansards from the poundage subsidy when it was granted to him for life in 1454. Danzig was now included in the exemption, but Lübeck was not. Indeed it was not until 1456 that Lübeckers agreed to a new eight-year safe conduct pact and thereby gained relief from the subsidy.[13] Lacking the unanimous support of other major towns within the confederation, Lübeck was incapable of pressing the issue of compensation. New commercial relationships were evolving in northern Europe, and old ones were being strengthened. Both the presence of Hollanders and Englishmen in the Baltic and Cologne's close links with England now encouraged regional particularism. Estrangement within the Hanseatic sphere and the challenge to Lübeck's political authority can be seen as but two manifestations of this larger and more fundamental process.

In the eastern Baltic a state of war now existed between the kingdom of Poland, the Prussian towns, and the Teutonic Order, increasing the danger to foreign shipping. The defeat of the Teutonic knights at Tannenberg in 1410 had effectively ended German expansion in the eastern Baltic, and was a grim prologue to an era of political instability fatal to the Order and profoundly important to the political destiny of the Hanse. Thereafter, the towns east of the river Oder had an ever greater share in state affairs, and in 1440 the estate owners and some twenty towns, including the prominent trading centres of Danzig, Elbing, and Thorn, confederated to protest the Order's abusive taxation. Fourteen years later, in 1454, this league allied with Poland in an attempt to break the power of the knights.[14] A brutal war would devastate much of rural Prussia and disrupt trade in the Baltic for the next thirteen years.[15] As this conflict was played out in the east, the quarrel in the west with England worsened steadily.

In England the demands for trading rights in Prussia had long since become little more than a pretext for piracy, and the government, shaken by dynastic uncertainties that soon would engulf the country in the Wars of the Roses, was powerless to stem the tide of maritime violence and indiscriminate attacks on foreign shipping. Despite the declared new friendship between the English king and the Hanse, a Danzig ship bound for Hull in 1453 was diverted to Newcastle, where its grain cargo was seized and disposed of. The following year a kog from Middelburg was taken, and another hijacked while at anchor off Coldwater.[16] By 1456 Hansards in Ipswich dared not leave port, claiming 'Subjects of the king in ships of war intend to spoil [Hansards] of goods and merchandise shipped in their ships ... under colour of search, asserting that the goods are not customed, contrary to the friendship between the king and them of the Hanze.'[17] The earl of Warwick – self-styled 'kingmaker,' privateer, and governor of Calais – instigated an attack on another Hanseatic salt fleet in July 1458. His minions seized eighteen of Lübeck's ships and, in so doing, quickly revived animosities in the Wendish sector of the Hanse.[18] Yet despite this and other attacks on shipping, other towns of the Hanse again offered the Lübeckers only scant support for any retaliatory action in the North Sea. Lübeck's privateers continued to prey on English shipping, but opportunities for reprisal were, on the whole, limited. The English presence in Baltic waters had been diminished already, due to the war in Prussia and Poland and the danger it posed to foreign shipping.

The Hansards and Edward IV

While the easily defined perimeters of dynastic epochs do not necessarily bear direct relation to developments affecting mercantile concerns, the crowning of Edward IV in 1461 did mark the beginning of an important new era in relations between England and the Hanse. The imprint of the early years of the reign is not to be found in an altered commodity structure, or even in the fluctuating volume of trade. Rather, the 1460s must be assessed primarily within the context of an uneasy Anglo-Hanseatic dialogue, which delineated and galvanized economic and political interests inside the Hanse. This did not, however, alleviate piracy or satisfy Lübeck. As a result, the end of the decade would see Anglo-Hanseatic relations ultimately consumed by political crisis.

The quarrel between England and the Wendish towns was still simmering when the new king came to the throne. English access to the Baltic via the Sound had been made difficult, and the denizen merchant community strongly opposed the renewal of Hanseatic franchises, again citing what it perceived as the denial of reciprocal rights in Prussia. Mindful that much of the discontent emanated from the prosperous livery companies in London, and that the capital was one of the corner-stones of his political support, Edward immediately embarked on a policy designed to remove any complacency the Hansards might have had regarding their status in England. He ensured that, henceforth, England would take an active role in defining Anglo-Hanseatic issues and their order of priority. When the Hansards in London first peti-tioned for confirmation and extension of their ancient liberties, Edward demanded to know which towns were Hanse members, how his sub-jects were treated in those parts, and for what reasons he should grant the Hansards special status in his kingdom. The Hanseatic reply appar-ently satisfied the Crown for the time being, but hardly pacified the burgesses of London, who had a commission ready to present argu-ments against the Hanse in the coming Parliament. The extension of Hanseatic privileges was granted, initially for only a few months, and then again until midsummer 1465. But there was an important condition attached. Before the renewal expired, the Hanse was required to send a fully accredited diplomatic embassy to England to negotiate a solution to the outstanding differences. The talks were also to include represen-tatives from Denmark.[19]

The stipulation was crucial, since the extension was granted largely through the efforts of Cologne and Nijmegen merchants in London. Lübeck remained alienated, and initially refused to approach the English government on any issue other than reparations. And, although Danzig was anxious not to have Hanseatic privileges in England revoked, the war in the eastern Baltic cast doubt on whether the Prussian towns could or would agree to send a delegation. Nevertheless, the Steelyard merchants soon prepared their list of grievances for presentation – including numerous charges of harassment, false arrest, and extortion by officials in London and the Cinque Ports – and set about laying the groundwork for the promised negotiations. After several delays the talks were convened, though not in England. Instead, English delegates attended the *Hansetag* at Hamburg in the summer of 1465.[20]

The ensuing discussions marked another pivotal turn in Anglo-Hanseatic diplomacy because, although Lübeck participated, political alignment within the Hanse now allowed the English to weather a period of potentially grave economic vulnerability. To some degree England actually enhanced its position *vis-à-vis* future discussions on reciprocity in the Baltic.

Notwithstanding the Hanse's compliance with England's request for the meeting, by the summer of 1465 England's position was not entirely favourable, and could have been extremely serious, had the Hanseatic confederation been able to display some semblance of unity. In 1463 Edward IV had attempted to protect English textile producers by imposing a prohibition on imported cloth. The ban was aimed at and was detrimental to the already struggling drapery industries in Flanders. Philip the Good responded with a boycott of English woollens in October 1464,[21] and Edward then countered in January 1465 with a ban on all Burgundian goods except foodstuffs. The closing of the Burgundian dominions to English textile imports crippled the trade that English merchants had established at the Brabantine entrepôt of Antwerp, and once again made friendly relations with the Hanse almost imperative.[22] Hanseatic merchants were specifically exempted from the prohibitions in England, and the Crown might have been forced to re-evaluate its options still further, had it been confronted by a united Hanse and, therefore, the possibility of virtual exclusion from the northern continental trade. Such a difficult situation did not present itself, however, as Lübeck's demands obviously were not consistent with the wishes of the other principal Hanse members. Fully aware of this division, the English delegates at Hamburg took a calculated risk and refused to discuss Lübeck's claims seriously. Moreover, they offered another five-year extension of Hanseatic privileges only on the condition that the Hansards agree to meet with them again within two years. The diet duly adjourned without agreement, although the extension and the proviso were in fact proclaimed in the summer of 1466, with the term to commence on 24 June.[23]

On the surface, then, Anglo-Hanseatic diplomacy seemed to be plodding along at a familiar pace. The rank and file of the Hanseatic membership apparently would be satisfied with a reconfirmation of privileges in England, and the English pacified with a promise of further discussions and another opportunity to air their views again on reciprocity. An Anglo-Danish treaty also was proclaimed by early autumn, which further isolated Lübeck.[24] On the question of access to the Baltic for his merchants, Edward IV could now deal directly with the Danes and the Prussians. Supported only by some of their Wendish neighbours on the question of compensation, the Lübeckers surely would not continue to jeopardize the interests of other towns that maintained a commercial presence in England. Hopefully, the issue would fade from the forefront unresolved, to the satisfaction of both the English government and Cologne, Hamburg, and the Prussian towns, whose trade with England was by now considerably more significant than Lübeck's.[25]

Yet it was this very absence of strong commercial ties between Lübeck and England that likely helped shape an entirely contrary Wendish response. Quite simply, since the Lübeckers no longer had a particularly substantial English trade to protect, their claims against England continued to take precedence over the comprehensive interests of other Hanseatic merchant groups who did. It is open to question which groups better represented 'Hanseatic' interests at this juncture. To again let the English government's responsibility for Warwick's provocations go unchallenged would severely undermine the Hanse's ability to deter or counter any similar development in the future. On the other hand, an obvious lack of consensus necessarily called into question the political credibility of the entire confederation and its leadership. Lübeck now steadfastly refused to send delegates overseas to discuss a truce or Hanseatic privileges, insisting instead that negotiations with the English focus on the reparations issue, and that they not take place in England. Rostock, Wismar, Stralsund, and Bremen all concurred with this view.[26]

So another winter passed with no confirmation of the Hanse's intent to enter into further discussions. Meanwhile, negotiations for renewal of a mercantile treaty between England and Burgundy had been under way for some time, and by the spring of 1467 word reached the Steelyard of the growing displeasure among royal advisers over the silence of the Hanse. The Steelyard men knew well the significance of the proviso attached to the latest renewal of their privileges. They implored Cologne to intercede with Lübeck, and hastily dispatched their secretary, Hermann Wanmate, to Hamburg and Prussia to look for ways to bring pressure to bear on Lübeck and the Wendish towns. Only after a summer of apparently feverish intra-Hanse diplomatic activity was a compromise coaxed from Lübeck and her allies. With considerable relief Hamburg was able to write to King Edward on 4 November 1467 that Lübeck and all the principal Hanseatic towns except Bremen had agreed to a five-year truce with England, and to a meeting with English ambassadors, provided the venue was on German soil and the discussions included the question of compensation.[27]

By the end of the month a new course in Anglo-Burgundian relations rendered Lübeck's compliance almost academic, and cast serious doubt on the immediate resumption of talks. Charles the Bold had succeeded his father, Philip, as duke of Burgundy, and he now allied himself with Edward IV against Louis XI of France.[28] A new commercial treaty also was concluded. The Burgundian embargo on English goods was rescinded, and with it disappeared a principal device from which the Hanse had indirectly drawn economic leverage in its dealings with England. Although the Hanse's privileged status in England was extended for a further year in March 1468[29] on the basis of the correspondence received from Hamburg, the English government had now effected an important shift in foreign trade policy. It had eased the dependence on the Hanseatic trade link by virtue of the agreement with Burgundy, and had firmly established that the special status of Hansards in England was conditional upon certain terms, albeit modest ones, set down by the king.

Once again in the mid-1460s English ships were plying routes that would take them to the Baltic. They also frequented Iceland, in deliberate defiance of the 1465 Anglo-Danish agreement that prohibited unlicensed trade there. It was not long before the behaviour of fishing crews from Bristol and Lynn touched off a series of recriminations eventually leading to a trial of strength with the Hanse. In 1467 they robbed and burned several houses on the island, and murdered the Danish governor.[30]

June of the following year saw a handful of English merchant ships riding at anchor in the Sound, waiting to pay tolls to the Danes before sailing on to Prussia. They went no farther. Encircled by a squadron of eight vessels, including two from Danzig, the English skippers were obliged to surrender their ships and cargoes without offering resistance. English accounts of these and subsequent events include stories of Danzigers dividing up the merchandise in Copenhagen, and of English cloth being offloaded in Danzig under cover of darkness.[31] The Danish king claimed that the confiscations were in response to the atrocities committed in Iceland the previous autumn. It was also rumoured in Denmark that the king had received a letter from Edward IV suggesting that he 'take and do his beste whit Englisshmen.'[32]

Among those identified as leaders of the adventure were three Prussian captains, Heinrich Sterneberch, Vincent Stolle, and Michael Ertmann. Their participation in the seizure could not be denied, although their affiliation with Danzig at this time was perhaps not so obvious as the English testimony implied. They were among several who, having served on the side of Danzig and Poland in the war against the Order, were faced with a somewhat difficult transition to peaceful maritime enterprise upon its recent conclusion. Instead, they chose to serve the king of Denmark in his continuing disputes with the Swedes. They did so against the wishes of Danzig's council, and as a result were supposed to have forfeited citizenship of the town. When Ertmann returned there in September he was indeed imprisoned briefly. Danzig argued, then, that responsibility for the Sound incident rested with the Danish monarch and a few Prussian expatriates. However, English depositions also implicated several other citizens of Hanseatic towns, including two from Lübeck and eight more from Stralsund.[33]

While various circumstances suggest the possibility of some sort of conspiracy, motives and the degree to which Hansards actually were involved are entirely open to speculation. Four of the ships, from Lynn and Boston, were carrying almost all of the aggregate yearly woollen exports from the ports of the Wash. The Hanseatic share in these cargoes was insignificant.[34] At least one Lynn merchant later testified that he had been forewarned by a Danzig associate that he would be wise to dispose of his goods cheaply before the ships sailed for the Baltic. In addition to the rumours in Denmark of King Edward's alleged complicity in the affair, the purser aboard one of the captured vessels claimed to have been told that the English were 'solde longe tyme before' they ever reached the Sound. Also, although the Steelyard merchants emphasized that the mercenaries were banished from Danzig, Hansards and Englishmen alike attested to their presence there both before and after the incident.[35]

King Christian's acknowledged responsibility for the arrest of the English ships, and his insistence that they were sequestered in retaliation for the raid in Iceland, did not soothe injured English pride or pacify the indignant members of the denizen merchant community, who clamoured for redress.[36] Edward's protests to Copenhagen brought no satisfaction, and the absence of Danish ships and goods in England virtually ruled out the possibility of reprisals against Denmark. As a result, the involvement of the Danzigers assumed an exaggerated importance. The Sound incident would now precipitate a wave of persecution in kind, and so render prophetic a remark attributed to one of the accused, that 'there shuld a 1000 and 1000 menn of the Hans wyssh, that they had never been boren for the seid werk.'[37] Casual commercial violence had plagued relations between England and the Hanse for more than half a century. Now, as royal advisers pressed the king for harsh reprisals, the audacious spirit of the more militant elements within England's mercantile sector was channelled anew into anti-Hanse prejudice. The most serious and protracted disruption of Anglo-Hanseatic relations was about to begin.

Hanseatic merchants in England

In addition to the political context of this impending conflict, there is, of course, an underlying economic one. To establish this frame of reference, it is imperative to look in some detail at the principal elements of Anglo-Hanseatic commerce. The English export trade of the mid-fifteenth century relied almost exclusively on wool and woollen cloth. Little else was shipped abroad except hides and some tin from south- and east-coast ports, although fragmentary customs records also show occasional shipments of barley and corn from Lynn in the 1450s and 1460s, as well as some lead exports from Hull.[38] Except by special licence, almost all English wool exports reached continental markets via the Calais staple, where the trade was monopolized by English staplers.[39] The Hanseatic role was not significant. But the lifeblood of overseas commerce was the export of woollen cloth, and in this sector the Hansards were an essential link to northern European markets.

England produced and exported a wide range of woollen cloths, from heavy double worsteds and finished cloths of assize to coarser and cheaper varieties such as kerseys, straights, friezes, and stockbreds. They were identified according to colour, type, and place of manufacture. In the Baltic, for instance, woollens from London, Lynn, Colchester, Beverley, and Norwich were distinguished from simple 'English' cloths and kerseys.[40] Much of the cloth manufactured for the export market actually came from Yorkshire, Gloucestershire, Coventry, London, and East Anglia. Merchants of the Steelyard, or for that matter anyone exporting textiles from the capital, undoubtedly purchased a good deal of their cloth directly or by sample at London's main woollen exchange, Blackwell Hall, where clothmakers from diverse areas of England wholesaled their wares.

It was common for exporters to buy cloth on credit in London, and at least some bills were payable in Flemish money at Bruges or at the trade fairs across the Channel at Antwerp and Bergen op Zoom. A record of outstanding loans in London's Dowgate ward, where the Steelyard was located, shows that in the late 1450s Hansards borrowed considerable sums of money from several prominent London mercers and drapers, presumably to finance cloth purchases. Also, in 1468 the clothmen of Gloucestershire would lament that imprisoned Hanseatic merchants owed them more than £5,000. But the Hansards also extended credit to their English associates, as records of the Mayors' Court show several cases of Hansards suing Londoners for unpaid obligations.[41] Certainly, too, much of the cloth bought by foreign merchants was paid for in cash or in kind, and some of it was made to order.[42]

Throughout the 1450s and 1460s Hansards exported about 8,600 cloths of assize each year from England. Occasionally small quantities were customed for shipment from Southampton and Bristol, as well as from Sandwich and Yarmouth in the early 1460s. But aside from these rare instances, the Hanseatic cloth trade, at least in so far as it is reflected in customs returns, was concentrated almost entirely at Hull, Ipswich,

Lynn, Boston, and especially London.[43] Published totals from the extant Exchequer customs enrolments, used previously by H.L. Gray in a study of English exports, verify that the cloth export trade already was depressed well before the disputes with the Hanseatic towns erupted into open conflict.[44] Renewed fighting in France from 1448 to 1453 and civil strife in England a decade later contributed to the decline, reducing yearly volume to about 75% of the pre-1448 level.

Fluctuations or trends in English woollen exports were but one facet of a much larger and more intricate system of trade. Aside from the wool trade, exports to overseas markets were not so vital to many of England's east-coast towns as the flourishing coastal traffic. Newcastle, for example, sent coal, lead, salt, and salmon southward to London and the East Anglian ports, whence it could be reshipped. The ports of Yarmouth and Lynn sent herring and grain to the north-east. The foreign trade of London created a demand for extra tonnage, and thus provided employment for coastal vessels, while the herring fisheries off Yorkshire, south Lincolnshire, and Norfolk continued to prosper also.[45]

The Hanseatic role in England becomes clearer, then, if the distinction is drawn between the local economies of the eastern coastal towns and that of southern England and London, which commanded the lion's share of England's cloth exports. The woollen trade, centred in the capital and served by cross-Channel shipping to the Low Countries, attracted many Hansards, and especially the merchants of Cologne. But the business of importing products into other parts of England was not dictated by the cloth trade. In East Anglia and ports to the north like Hull and Newcastle, the exporting of English woollens by Hanseatic merchants often was incidental to the importation of commodities, particularly from the Baltic. The Esterlings came to these areas not primarily as buyers of cloth, but rather as sellers of the timber, iron, and naval supplies essential to eastern England's fishing and shipbuilding industries and the coastal trade.

The Hanse's export trade to England was very diversified, but of central importance was the Danzig staple, which supplied the bulk commodities of the Prussian and Lithuanian hinterland. These included wood and by-products of the lumber industry, which were in fairly constant demand in England, both for domestic building purposes and ship construction. Also important were ashes, used for dyeing cloth and for the manufacture of soap. Other Baltic products included cereals, peltware, canvas, cable and cordage, various other naval supplies, bowstaves, and finished articles like tables, counters, and cutting boards. In addition, the Prussian staple supplied hemp, flax, yarn, and Swedish bog iron called osmund, and Danzig ships arriving in England during the 1450s and 1460s almost invariably offloaded high-bulk cargoes of lumber, pitch, and tar.[46] Despite temporarily depressed wood prices in England in 1450, a business agent of the Order could confidently report that most of the products in demand there came from Prussia.[47]

Merchants from Lübeck, Hamburg, Westphalia, and Cologne also participated in the redistribution of bulk commodities, either directly from the Baltic, or via Hamburg, Amsterdam, Antwerp, or the ports of Zealand. On occasion Cologners even used English carriers to freight their cargoes from Danzig. However, the English trade of merchants from Cologne, the lower Rhineland, and Westphalia was generally more concentrated in high-value, low-bulk manufactured wares. To England they brought costly silk, linen, thread and buckram, Osnabrück cloth, fustian from Augsburg and Ulm, and fine steel from Siegerland. Merchants from Cologne, who were concentrated in London and Ipswich, also offered dyestuffs, furs, wire, and a wide range of manufactured wares.[48] The basic commodity structure illustrates another fundamental distinction between England's Baltic trade links and those with Westphalia and the lower Rhineland.

To delineate the Hanseatic trade in England still further, it is necessary to venture briefly into the statistical morass of surviving customs records. The petty custom of 3d on the pound applied to all Hanseatic imports into England save wax and wine, as well as to exports except cloth, and Exchequer enrolments record the annual totals for the value of all non-denizen merchandise subject to this *ad valorem* tariff. Although corresponding particulars of accounts are too fragmentary to permit a precise evaluation of the Hanseatic share in the alien trade of English ports over the long term, some delineation for shorter periods is possible. Together with totals for woollen exports, which do distinguish Hanseatic shipments from others, the petty custom totals (already published for years up to 1482) shed much light on the character and volume of trade in individual ports throughout the second half of the fifteenth century.[49]

a. Lynn

During the eighteen-year period from Michaelmas 1449 to November 1467 woollen exports from the port of Lynn totalled 10,353 cloths. The average yearly volume, therefore, was about 575, though annual totals for the second half of the period decreased significantly. The Hanse's share in this admittedly marginal trade varied from year to year, but accounted for approximately 23% of the aggregate and averaged 132 cloths annually. The remainder was in the hands of denizen traders. Other alien merchants played no significant role. In the Exchequer year 1467–8 Lynn's exports peaked at 963 cloths. The Hanseatic share plummeted to a mere 5%. Denizen merchants exported 911 cloths, all of which were freighted in the English ships seized at Helsingor *en route* to the Baltic.

In the same eighteen years prior to the autumn of 1467 the value of merchandise paying the petty custom at Lynn was £13,689, an average of about £740 per year. Particulars of accounts are not continuous for the entire period, but do survive for certain years. A nineteen-month stretch ending in January 1457 saw Hansards account for 39% of the alien merchandise customed at Lynn. In a two-year span from Michaelmas 1459 to November 1461 they owned 62% of slightly more than £2,000 worth of non-denizen goods. One final example, the account for 1467–8, shows a below average 3d custom total of only £497 worth of goods, with Hansards still accounting for 62%. For these last two example periods imports and exports are easily distinguishable. Merchandise imported into Lynn by Hansards was valued at £1,245, while exports, except for cloths and worsteds not subject to the petty custom, were worth less than £100. The vast majority of Hanseatic cargoes were carried to Lynn by Danzig ships.[50]

b. Boston

In neighbouring Boston there also were significant fluctuations in annual woollen exports and 3d custom totals. In a nine-year span beginning at Michaelmas 1449 denizens exported 2,061 cloths. The Hansards' total was half that, and they shipped no cloth from Boston between September 1450 and Michaelmas 1454. During the same nine years the sum value of merchandise paying the petty custom was close to £5,000. Again, however, a yearly average of £538 is entirely unrepresentative, since less than £900 worth of alien goods was exchanged during the first five years of this period. This in itself represents a drastic reduction in the value of the alien trade from what it had been during the preceding five years. This is no doubt partly attributable to strained relations with Lübeck, and the absence of the Wendish *Bergenfahrer* from Boston in the early 1450s.[51] The *Bergenfahrer*, primarily Lübeckers and Hansards from the other Wendish ports, controlled the Norwegian cod fisheries through the Hanseatic *comptoir* at Bergen. The distributive fish trade with England and, hence, Lübeck's central economic interest there, was concentrated largely at Boston. As yet, the English dependency on the Bergen *comptoir* was circumvented only periodically through direct trade, by licence, to Iceland.[52]

A gap in Boston's customs records occurs in the late 1450s, but figures are complete for roughly eight successive Exchequer years up to October 1467. Woollen exports totalled about 4,428 cloths, and Hansards accounted for 63% of the trade. The Hanseatic portion of the annual total fell to under 10% in 1467–8, the same year that at least 344 of the 576 cloths shipped abroad by native merchants were confiscated aboard English vessels at the Sound. The post-1459 period also saw the alien trade in miscellaneous merchandise recover to an average annual value of £932, and again the importance of the *Bergenfahrer* is apparent. In the first twenty-two months of this period Hanseatic merchandise exchanged at Boston represented 90% of the alien total. Moreover, two thirds of these Hanseatic goods consisted of fish cargoes imported by the *Bergenfahrer* in ships from Stralsund and Danzig. A similar pattern continued on the eve of the Anglo-Hanseatic conflict. From March 1467 to March 1468 the value of alien goods was only £452, but the Hanseatic share was still a full 72%, and included fish imports worth £200. Hanseatic vessels usually carried the large cargoes of fish and bulk raw materials to Boston, though Hansards employed some alien shipping as well, and occasionally exported small quantities of grain from the port.[53]

c. Hull

In the north-east, Hull customs records, which also incorporate totals from Scarborough, indicate a decline in the cloth trade during the 1460s. From 1458 through 1467 fewer than 10,000 cloths were exported from Hull, though twice that number were shipped during the previous nine years.[54] While annual Hanseatic exports declined slightly, those of denizens were halved. Despite this marked decline in overall volume, the cloth trade from Hull continued to be controlled by the denizen merchant community. For the entire eighteen-year period Hansards accounted for only 9% of Hull's cloth exports, and the share of other aliens was negligible. Most of the Hanseatic cloth was freighted in Danzig ships. As in other east-coast ports, total exports recovered temporarily in 1467–8 to 1,663 cloths, while the Hansards accounted for 11%. Again, a substantial portion of the denizen woollen exports, belonging to merchants from York and Hull, was confiscated on the way to the Baltic in the summer of 1468.

Hull was important for both coastal and overseas commerce. Ships from Flanders and ports in Zealand called there regularly, as did others from London, Dartmouth, North Berwick, and Leith. An alien trade in miscellaneous goods worth £18,544 was recorded at Hull between December 1449 and Michaelmas 1467, and again the Hanseatic element had a distinctly Baltic character. Four Danzig ships called at Hull in the summer of 1453, and a decade later, when petty custom merchandise was valued at slightly less than £2,000, three Hanseatic vessels, all from Danzig, offloaded cargoes worth £645. In the Exchequer year 1464–5 three Danzig ships delivered Hanseatic goods representing 44% of the alien total. Two years later the £249 worth of Hanseatic goods exchanged at Hull represented only one quarter of the alien total, but included £40 worth of lead exports. Most of the bulk imports, as well as the lead cargo, were freighted by Danzig shipper Derick Schach, although Hamburg shipper Claus Scult also delivered a consignment of pitch, tar, and boards. The following summer both of the Hanseatic ships arrested at Hull had arrived from Danzig, and perhaps a third had already cleared the port when the others were impounded.[55]

d. Ipswich and Colchester

In contrast to Hull and the ports of the Wash, where Baltic merchants were the key Hanseatic participants in the woollen trade, the greater share of cloth exports from Ipswich belonged to Cologne merchants of the London Steelyard. In 1458–9, for example, Cologners and their agents shipped at least two thirds of the Hanseatic total. Other Hansards active in the Ipswich woollen trade came from Lübeck, Hamburg, Duisburg, and Nijmegen, and were resident in London. Non-Hanseatic aliens were of comparatively minor importance in the overseas traffic in cloth from Ipswich or from neighbouring Colchester, whence much of the cloth was actually shipped. For customs purposes the port of Colchester came under the jurisdiction of the collectors at Ipswich. From midsummer 1449 until Michaelmas 1467 almost 38,000 cloths were exported from Ipswich/Colchester – an average of slightly more than 2,100 per year – and Hansards shipped 72% of the total. Many of their exports left port in English or other non-Hanseatic vessels bound for the Lowlands. Though an annual average for denizens would be 572 cloths, actual exports exceeded 500 units in only two years after 1458. Hansards maintained their volume of about 1,500 more consistently, except for a sharp variation at the end of the period. The Hanseatic total of 4,500 cloths shipped in 1465–6 fell to just over 600 the following year, and improved only slightly the year after that. This is hardly surprising, since the ports' aggregate output in 1467–8 was less than 1,400 units.

During the 1449–67 period the value of miscellanea exchanged at Ipswich/Colchester by non-denizens averaged £2,211 per year for a total of almost £40,000. The Hansards were conspicuous if not preponderant. Petty custom goods with an aggregate value of only £1,375 were recorded in 1458–9, but Hanseatic merchandise none the less accounted for 80%. In 1465–6, when Hansards were responsible for 95% of the ports' cloth exports, they also owned 86% of the more than £3,000 worth of alien merchandise paying the 3d custom. The ratio of import to export values is noteworthy. Customed Hanseatic imports that year were valued at £2,534, while exports were worth only £172. Much of the bulk cargo, plus twenty-nine quintals of wax not subject to the petty custom, was imported into Ipswich/Colchester for merchants from Hamburg.[56]

e. London

Cloth exports from London far surpassed those of any other port in the kingdom. From March 1450 until Michaelmas 1467 more than 284,000 cloths were customed for export from the capital. Half of them belonged to denizens, but 41% were Hanseatic. The last nine years of this period saw a trend toward slight growth in the total volume, largely attributable to a modest increase in denizen and alien shipments. In 1467–8, though, while the Hanseatic total of 6,437 cloths was consistent with the yearly average, denizen and alien totals doubled to 15,052 and 3,986 respectively. Yet, while customs returns clearly illustrate London's dominance as the hub of southern England's cloth export trade, they cannot necessarily be taken as an accurate reflection of the overall volume of shipping and subsidiary activity. Large consignments of woollens customed in London could be and were carted to Dover for shipment overseas,[57] and cargoes from London likely were shipped from other ports in Kent, Essex, and Suffolk as well. Imported goods destined for London, on the other hand, were customed at port of entry and their values therefore are absorbed in petty custom and poundage figures for Sandwich and perhaps Ipswich.

During the eighteen-year period ending Michaelmas 1467 almost 75% of all Hanseatic cloth exports from England originated in London. Woollen shipments from London and Ipswich/Colchester combined represented a full 93% of the Hanseatic cloth export trade. Particulars of accounts for the 1450s and 1460s are too fragmentary to provide any insight into the Hanseatic share of petty custom merchandise. Enrolments indicate that £374,418 worth of alien goods were customed at London in the eighteen years commencing in March 1450, with a trend toward higher average yearly totals in the 1460s.[58] The most active Hanseatic dealers in English woollens were the merchants of Cologne, though the Steelyard community also included traders from Dinant, Nijmegen, and Duisburg, the Westphalian towns of Soest, Münster, and Dortmund, and Esterlings from Danzig, Lübeck, and Hamburg. They employed Baltic carriers as well as English and foreign vessels making regular crossings to Zealand and Brabant.

f. Other ports

Finally, the fragmentary records of other English ports where the Hanseatic presence was limited or intermittent again reflect the somewhat itinerant nature of the trade of the Baltic Hansards. For example, Kersten Kosseler, a skipper from Danzig, delivered more than £200 worth of bulk freight to Bristol in November 1467. Evidently, this was the primary purpose of the venture, since the corresponding customs enrolments indicate that Hanseatic merchants exported fewer than a dozen cloths from Bristol during the Exchequer year 1467–8 – their first woollen shipments from that port in more than half a decade.[59] Likewise, at Yarmouth (i.e., Blakeney, Dunwich, and Yarmouth) another £200 worth of Hanseatic imports, including substantial quantities of wood, flax, pitch, tar, skins, osmund, and fish oil, were customed in

1464–5. Again, though, only a few cloths and a small grain consignment were shipped out of the port by Hansards.[60]

Another illustration of the Anglo-Hanseatic commodity structure, which in turn reflects the role of the two principal Hanseatic groups in England, is provided by the customs records of Southampton, where again there is little evidence of sustained Hanseatic activity. In 1463, Kosseler offloaded another £174 worth of Baltic cargo at Southampton, wintered in England, and departed with the only Hanseatic woollen cargo for the Exchequer year 1463–4 – a mere nineteen cloths of assize. In April another £240 worth of fustian and thread, belonging to Cologne merchant Johann van Bryle and likely destined for London, was brought to Southampton from the Lowlands in two Venetian galleys.[61]

As with Ipswich/Colchester, the foreign trade of Sandwich (i.e., Dover, Sandwich) was closely linked to that of the capital. Hansards – mostly Cologners from the London Steelyard – exported 469 cloths in 1462–3, while their imports, which consisted primarily of furs and thread, were worth at least £333. Two years later, the minimum value of Hanseatic imports at Sandwich, including furs, dyestuffs, alum, fustian, and thread, exceeded £750, yet the Hansards had fewer than a dozen cloths customed for export. Again, Italian galleys, as well as English and other foreign vessels, were used as the carriers. In the turbulent year 1467–8 Hansards had no cloth customed for export from Sandwich, but Cologners and Westphalian merchants imported vast quantities of furs, thread, and fustian valued at almost £1,700.[62]

In some instances it is possible to evaluate the Hanse's contribution to England's foreign trade through balances of trade, although calculations of Hanseatic balances in any English port necessarily depend upon an estimated value for cloth exports. The vast majority of Hanseatic cloth exports, and virtually all those from ports other than London, consisted of cloths without grain (*sine grano*).[63] Under normal circumstances Hansards would pay a custom of 12d for each cloth of this quality, irrespective of purchase price, and usually the particulars of accounts contain only a tally of the cloths in each shipment. Occasionally, however, the poundage subsidy of 12d on the pound was calculated on Hanseatic goods, including woollen exports, before official renewals of the Hanseatic exemptions reached local collectors. In these instances values were recorded. Some Lynn and Hull accounts for the 1460s show Hanseatic cloth exports rated at £1 each, while still others for Boston and Lynn give a value of £1 6s 8d. Later accounts for Ipswich also use this second value. Both rates found in the particulars of accounts are lower than the one used by H.L. Gray, who estimated at £2.[64] It must be stressed, of course, that such low valuations bear scant relation to retail values. Throughout the second half of the century some types of English cloth retailed for upwards of £3 each. But retail prices for other diverse commodities, including wax, dyestuffs, and pitch, also were as much as double the values entered in customs particulars.[65] The minimum cloth values recorded by customs officials are at least consistent, then, with the equally low values applied to other Hanseatic goods paying the petty custom. On this premise only, therefore, the second value of £1 6s 8d is as appropriate as any on which to base a cursory evaluation of the Hanseatic cloth export trade in years for which corresponding 3d custom figures survive.[66]

To determine the combined worth of Hanseatic exports, the value of russets, friezes, coverlets, and all other petty custom exports must be added. Worsteds, which paid a separate rate, were of no significance outside of London. The only conspicuous Hanseatic imports to which separate duties applied were wax and wine. But like worsted shipments, wine cargoes offloaded for Hansards at ports other than London were negligible, and therefore do not affect trade balance calculations for the east-coast ports. Wax cargoes were important, though, and values are recorded.

Estimated trade balances for various years during the pre-1468 period again mirror certain basic characteristics of the Hanseatic trade outside of London. And again, the importance of the Baltic connections for the east-coast ports is very evident. In the mid-1450s at Lynn, for example, Hanseatic export values were approximately equal to imports. But by the end of the decade, when dangers to shipping prevented English carriers from hauling bulk supplies from Danzig, and there was a decrease in the demand for English woollens in the eastern Baltic ports, the value of Hanseatic imports at Lynn exceeded exports sevenfold. Devaluation of the English pound sterling briefly stimulated cloth exports in 1464–5, so that the Hanseatic trade balance at Lynn slightly favoured exports out of the port. However, during the period from November 1465 to November 1468 the £1,230 worth of goods brought to Lynn by Hanseatic merchants would have been double the estimated value of their exports.

At Boston, where the Wendish *Bergenfahrer* were most active, totals varied quite radically, but there is little indication of any great discrepancy in the value of imports and exports. In twenty-two months beginning in December 1459 Hanseatic cargoes exported from Boston would have had a value of £1,767 and imports at least £1,583. For a two-year period ending in March 1467 the figures are £725 and £713 respectively. A final example, the fiscal year 1467–8, reflects the controversy of the summer of 1468. Hanseatic exports from Boston would have had an estimated value of only £134, but £324 worth of Hanseatic goods had already been offloaded before trade was suspended in August.

The value of yearly Hanseatic imports at Hull usually exceeded that of exported wares. In 1452–3, however, Hanseatic woollen shipments totalled close to 400 cloths, and therefore the value of exported cargoes would have surpassed imports by £163. As in Lynn, totals for 1461 were drastically reduced, and in three subsequent years prior to Michaelmas 1468, for which particulars of accounts survive, the value of imports exceeded exports. In the fiscal year 1464–5 the ratio of Hanseatic import to export values at Hull was 3.5 to 1.

To the south, at the cloth exporting centres of Ipswich and Colchester, the situation was quite different, though customs particulars provide only two sample periods. Hansards were the predominant alien importers, but Hanseatic exports from Ipswich/Colchester in 1458–9 still would have been worth £1,676 and imports less than £1,100. In 1465–6, when Hansards shipped more than 4,500 cloths, the value of exports would have surpassed imports by £3,500.

The Hanseatic traffic to and from Ipswich/Colchester was an extension of the trade in London, although Hansards did not dominate the alien trade to such a degree in the capital. London Hansards imported a variety of merchandise into England, ranging from silk and harp strings to raw iron, alum, and wood. They shared in the long-distance carriage trade from the North Sea and Baltic ports and in the continuous traffic to and from the Lowlands, which employed alien, English, and Hanseatic carriers. Many imports reached England via Bruges, Antwerp, and Bergen op Zoom. The majority of cloth exports to the Continent originated in London. From the Lowland ports cloth could be moved coastwise to Hamburg and thence to Lübeck and the Baltic or, as was the case with much of the cloth exported by Cologners, carried to the trade fairs at Frankfurt and Leipzig. Though it was not unusual for merchants of the Steelyard to travel outside London or even to accompany cargoes across the Narrow Seas, perhaps thirty to forty Hansards plus their servants resided in southern England on at least a semi-permanent basis. Several more than that were charged duty on cloth exports from London between Michaelmas 1461 and 20 May 1462, but not all of them need have been in the English capital. Resident factors could transact business on behalf of any number of merchants. Thirty-four Hansards had gathered at the Steelyard in February 1447 to endorse new regulations for their fellowship. Arrests at London in 1468 netted at least thirty-two, several of whom had one or more servants.[67]

From the extant English customs records, the general pattern of the Hanseatic trade is, then, clearly discernible. At Hull or either of the ports of the Wash Hanseatic merchants could account for anywhere from one quarter to 90% of the alien trade in miscellaneous goods in any given year. They also were the only significant non-denizen group active in the cloth export trade. Both the import and the export trade of the Hansards at these ports was served primarily by vessels from Danzig and Hamburg. The Wendish *Bergenfahrer* also linked Boston to the Norwegian fisheries. During the 1460s the volume of this trade fluctuated from year to year, but severe trade imbalances evidently were the norm, except perhaps at Boston. They did occur at Hull and Lynn from the mid-1460s onward, when the aggregate value of Hanseatic imports far surpassed that of exports. In comparison to the Hansards most active in London and Ipswich/Colchester, then, the Hanseatic men in these eastern and northern ports managed a more itinerant import trade in low-value bulk commodities. Aside from cloth, exports usually were confined to occasional shipments of grain, pewter, hides, and lead. For the most part, Hansards bringing fish and bulk freight to Hull, Lynn, and Boston reinvested their profits in English cloth or used their cash elsewhere – perhaps at London or anywhere along the Atlantic seaboard as far south as La Rochelle – to buy other cargo.

Anglo-Baltic commerce and the Bay salt trade

For ports in northern and eastern England the Hanseatic trade had a distinctively Baltic orientation. It was centred on the Prussian staple at Danzig. Hence, the supply and distribution networks that led to and from that port were of considerable importance to the Anglo-Baltic trade. At Danzig the principal imports consisted of salt, herring, and cloth.[68] A main source for salt was the Bay of Bourgneuf. The herring fisheries that supplied the Baltic region were as yet controlled by Hollanders and the Hansards themselves. The supply of cloth, however, was tied to the woollen industries of the Low Countries and England.

Though it dates from 1460, when Baltic commerce was disrupted by war between Poland, the Prussian towns, and the Teutonic Order, the earliest surviving record of shipping at Danzig for this period neverthe-less illustrates some of the essential characteristics of the seaborne trade.[69] First of all, the majority of Danzig's high-value cloth imports came via Lübeck. Although cloth was the only cargo aboard four ships arriving 'uth Engelant' in 1460, the quantities were small and one of the ships apparently carried no cargo at all. From the Bay and the Lowland ports only twenty-two ships reached Danzig either in ballast or laden almost exclusively with salt. It is very apparent, too, that many of the same merchants importing salt and cloth from Lübeck also shared in cargoes brought from England and the Atlantic seaboard. Occasionally these same merchants imported bulk goods from Reval and Stockholm. However, they were not active in the brisk coastal traffic to and from the Wendish ports of Rostock and Stralsund, nor in another important facet of intra-Baltic commerce, the substantial trade in Danish meat and butter. Within the port's mercantile community as a whole, however, there was wide participation in the seasonal importation of herring from Skania. The traffic in cloth and Bay salt therefore was tied to a fairly well-defined core of men within Danzig's mercantile sector, whose trade had a distinctly western focus, with Lübeck as a major transit point. The next surviving Danzig record of seaborne imports indicates this same basic pattern again in 1468. The volume of shipping from west of the Sound had greatly increased, but many large consignments of cloth continued to reach Danzig distributors via Lübeck.[70]

Another crucial link in this trade is revealed in a 1465 account, which shows that most of the merchants who imported from Lübeck and beyond were heavily implicated in the exchange of salt, herring, and cloth for the grain and forest products reaching Danzig via Thorn and the river Vistula.[71] Staple regulations restricted direct foreign contact with hinterland markets, and merchants from Danzig and Thorn con-trolled the trade in timber and forest products by paying producers well in advance for consignments delivered in spring, when the Vistula was navigable.[72] From northern and eastern Mazovia and Podlasia wood was floated to the Baltic via inland waterways. Some also came from Lithuania, where Kovno was an important transit centre. Baltic shipyards took a substantial portion of the timber, but great quantities were shipped westward. Sawn lumber was graded according to type and quality. Particularly common in the trade to England were wainscots (*Wagenschoss*) – broad oaken beams or sawn planks sold by the long hundred – used extensively for wall and ceiling panels, as well as for ship construction. Poorer quality oak and beechwood was cut into shorter clapholts (*Klappholz*) for use by coopers and carpenters. Numerous other varieties, including ships' masts and coniferous softwoods for scaffolding, also were shipped to England. So, too, were yew bowstaves (*Bogenholz*).[73]

In the pitch and tar trade along the Vistula merchants from Thorn were important middlemen. Ashes from Mazovia were also transported along this route, or from Lithuania over Kovno, while Hungarian iron and copper augmented the principal overland imports, reaching the Baltic via Cracow and Thorn. Two other commodities were crucial to Danzig's overseas trade: grain and wax. Cereal exports from Mazovia and greater Poland, especially barley, rye, and wheat, were redirected to western Europe through Danzig or Lübeck. Shipments to England were intermittent, however, and apparently coincidental with English shortfalls. By contrast, consignments of wax reached English harbours in Danzig ships on a regular basis. The major sources were in Lithuania, and again Kovno was one of the main outlets. Wax usually was shipped to western markets in large blocks (*Stro*) weighing up to several hundred kilograms.[74]

The western orientation of Danzig's salt and cloth importers also applied to their export trade, which depended on the long-distance carriage of low-value bulk commodities. Though variations were numerous, there were two predominant patterns in Hanseatic shipping between the Baltic and England: regular, uninterrupted voyages originating in Danzig, and annual visits to English ports by ships integrated into the Bay salt trade and commerce with the Lowlands. There was considerable direct sea traffic between Danzig and eastern England, a voyage that could be accomplished two or three times in a calendar year. An example is provided by the accounts of Lynn and Danzig for 1467–8.[75] Danzig shipper Paul Roole, who regularly called at Lynn during the mid-1460s, docked there in December 1467. He sailed for Danzig, laden with cloth, at the end of February 1468, and was back in Lynn offloading wood, osmund, and canvas by the second week in May. At Whitsuntide he was anchored at Helsingor on his way back to Danzig,[76] and he entered the port of Lynn again on 11 August, apparently unaware of the fate of other Hansards in England, with another shipment of boards, oars, tar, and iron. Two return trips between England and the eastern Baltic, including the offloading and refreighting of cargo, were completed in slightly more than five months, and there would have been plenty of time for Roole to return to his home port again in 1468 had not the general arrest of all Hansards in England prevented him. Another Danzig shipper involved in this direct trade was Jesse Bunde, master of one of the ships returning home from England in 1460. He refreighted his ship with oars, tar, wood, and iron, and had arrived back in Lynn by mid-October of that same year.[77]

Other Baltic skippers disposed of bulk cargoes in eastern England, though not necessarily in exchange for English cloth. They were more closely linked to the Bay salt trade. One of them was Hildebrand van der Wald of Danzig, who brought wood, ashes, osmund, and tar to Lynn at the end of November 1459. English particulars of accounts record only ships with taxable cargoes, and when there is no reference to a vessel leaving port, it may be presumed that it departed in ballast. There is no record of van der Wald leaving Lynn, but the 1460 Danzig account shows him returning to the Baltic from the Bay, laden with salt. He sailed back to Lynn later in the year with Jesse Bunde.[78] Among the other Baltic Hansards trading to England and to other ports along the Atlantic seaboard was Derick Schach, master of the *George* of Danzig. He brought iron, wood, and canvas worth £150 to Hull in June 1467, and departed there on 19 July with a cargo of cloth and lead. His subsequent return to Danzig in 1468 'uth der Baije' with a cargo of salt[79] is illustrative of the integrated trade of merchants and shippers who disposed of their Baltic cargoes in England and were also active in hauling salt from the Bay of Bourgneuf.

The traffic in cheap Bay salt was an integral feature of the northern European trade structure. The demand for salt in the eastern Baltic far exceeded the supply from indigenous sources, so large convoys of ships from the Lowland and Baltic ports weighed anchor for the Biscay coast each year, perhaps carrying fish, grain, or cloth, and returned to northern waters laden with salt. Some also brought back wine cargoes from La Rochelle, while still others sailed on to Setubal and Lisbon for salt, spices, fruit, and sugar.[80] Though some salt was offloaded in England and the Lowland ports, the Hanseatic hulks and other vessels chartered in Holland and Zealand brought large shipments to the Baltic. There it was trans-shipped from Lübeck to the Bergen *comptoir*, Riga, and Reval, and from Danzig to the markets of the Prusso-Polish hinterland. In 1468 sixty ships reached Danzig with salt and wine cargoes from the Bay. Other fleets, including those from Holland, often sailed directly to Königsberg, Memel, Riga, and Reval.[81]

This annual transfer of bulk cargo over vast distances lent itself to a variety of auxiliary or tangential trading activities, among them the Hanseatic trade to England, and in particular the traffic in bulk goods from the Baltic. Baltic skippers like Schach and van der Wald would not return home during the winter, but a ship offloaded in England before late autumn could then depart, either in ballast or laden with cloth, for winter service in more southerly waters. Cloth could be disposed of in the Low Countries or elsewhere along the route to the Bay or Lisbon. Vessels freighted with salt during the winter could then return to England, the Lowland ports, and/or sail on to the Baltic in the spring.

Some Hanseatic shippers did in fact haul Bay salt back to England, for both Hanseatic and English merchants. Hans Schomaker brought a cargo of wainscots and pitch to Yarmouth in October 1451, returned there with salt the following spring, and left again carrying cloth. In October 1458 he again brought ninety charges of 'sal de bay' worth £60 to London. In the early 1460s Hanseatic and alien skippers also delivered salt and wine cargoes to Ipswich for Cologne merchant Johann van Ae,[82] and in December 1457 Baltic shipper Gasper Sculte brought a cargo of Bay salt to London for John Warnes. Sculte also agreed to freight seventy charges of Bay salt to England for Winchelsea merchant John French, only to discover on his arrival at the Bay that the Englishman had not the means to pay for a cargo. The resultant confusion caused the ship to be delayed at the Bay some eight weeks. After securing a loan of 94 marks on behalf of French, the skipper freighted the cargo and brought it to the Thames, where he was delayed at least another twenty-four days waiting for payment, and again forced to 'abide behynd other hulkes of his contre in grete perell.'[83]

The Hanseatic kogs, hulks, and later caravels were the main carriers in this long-distance trade. It is not easy to distinguish precisely one type from another, though prior to mid-century kogs were single-masted klinker-built vessels. Generally they were smaller than the later types, which featured forecastles and aftercastles, as well as sternpost rudders. Three masts eventually became more common, and a typical hulk of the later fifteenth century may have had a keel length of about seventeen metres and a beam of almost six. However, much larger caravel-built vessels were being constructed in Danzig by the 1480s. Up to a dozen or more partners shared ownership of the large Hanseatic ships, which, when they did leave port for England, the Lowlands, or the Bay, were crewed by Hansards.[84] As the Bay fleets indicate, they frequently – though not always – sailed in convoys. Baltic shipping, however, was required to close down between 11 November and 22 February each year.[85]

The Hanse, England, and the Brabant fairs

Within the broad Hanseatic commercial network the trade of the Cologners, Westphalian merchants, and other Hansards resident at the London Steelyard was somewhat different, though not entirely separate from those primarily concerned with the Anglo-Baltic trade. As it was in the Lowlands, the trade of this group was closely linked to the textile manufacturing industries. This is not to say that it was concerned exclusively with the purchase and redistribution of woollen cloth. Merchants at the Steelyard were, together with the Italians, the main foreign suppliers of soap, mordants, and essential dyestuffs like woad, litmus, and madder. Although Zealand was a principal source for madder, there was also some dependence on more distant regions in France and the upper Rhineland areas around Speyer and Worms. Litmus and woad were obtainable throughout the Maas-Rhine delta region, as well as in Picardy and Normandy. Distribution of these dyestuffs along the Atlantic seaboard and to England was keyed to the markets of Bruges, Antwerp, and Bergen op Zoom, where again the merchants of Cologne assumed an integral role.[86]

Industries in or near Cologne also supplied a variety of manufactured wares for export, such as wire, 'Cologne thread,' and inexpensive linens, and the Cologners also linked England to the steel manufacturing centres of Siegen and Breckerfeld. Still other consignments of raw materials and finished goods, which eventually found their way to England via Cologne, were purchased by the Steelyard merchants or their agents during regular visits to the trade fairs at Frankfurt. Precious metals, furs, potash, wax, and grain from Poland were available also at the Leipzig market.[87]

Consignments of cloth purchased by Hansards in England were distributed to many of the same regions that served the Hanseatic import trade. English woollens were retailed to the south Germans at the Antwerp and Bergen op Zoom trade marts, or transported by river to Mainz and Frankfurt, whence they could be taken onward to Regensberg and Vienna. There were overland connections with Cracow and Breslau as well, via Nürnberg, Leipzig, and Posen. But these connections with the south and east were not the sole focus of the Cologners' distributive trade in English woollens, since they also redirected English cloth to the Baltic via Hamburg and ports in Zealand. The ship that transported Thomas Kent and John Stocker to the Baltic in 1450 was carrying at least five 'terling' of English cloth belonging to Cologners. In 1452, the diversion of other shipments over Hamburg and Neustadt, intended to avoid Lübeck's embargo on English goods, greatly annoyed Cologne and Danzig merchants of the London Steelyard.[88]

Both the trade in English woollens and the traffic in dyestuffs and low-bulk imports relied to a great degree on non-seasonal shipping to and from ports like Middelburg, Dordrecht, Veere, and Antwerp, and were by no means confined to Hanseatic carriers. And, in contrast to the majority of shipments from the Baltic, which usually belonged exclusively to Hansards, combined cargoes belonging to denizen, alien, and Hanseatic merchants were very common. In January 1459, for example, shipper Walter Hermansson arrived at Colchester with a large cargo for alien and denizen traders, as well as £500 worth of madder, litmus, woad, alum, 'holandcloth,' and other merchandise belonging to merchants of the Steelyard. Hermansson departed England in February, carrying 414 woollen cloths for Hanseatic merchants. At least 280 of these belonged to Cologners.[89]

The movement of cargo across the Narrow Seas was partly dependent on Antwerp's seagoing merchant fleet, which by the 1470s numbered about sixty vessels. Until mid-century Antwerp captains had regularly freighted English wool to the Mediterranean for Florentine merchants. But the closing of the Levant, after the fall of Constantinople, precipitated a decline in the Florentine cloth industry, and lessened the demand for high-quality English wool. Thereafter, when Anglo-Burgundian political squabbles did not prevent them, shippers from Antwerp increasingly turned to the Channel routes, hauling linen, dyestuffs, and mixed cargo to London and Colchester, and returning to the Brabant fairs with English cloth belonging primarily to Hansards and Englishmen.[90] Throughout the 1460s several Antwerp carriers were employed by the Steelyard merchants on a regular basis. Moreover, the commercial interests of the Hansards at Antwerp and London also extended to the realm of shipping. It was not uncommon for Antwerp shippers to purchase vessels from the same Hansards who regularly hired their services. Several merchants active in the seaborne trade to and from London, including Johann Dasse (Nijmegen), Arndt Stakelhusen (Cologne), Johann van Dorne (Cologne), and Everhard Clippinck (Cologne/Dortmund), numbered among the Hansards who sold vessels to Antwerp captains during the 1450s.[91] Unlike the shippers from Zealand and Holland, the Antwerp carriers were not yet particularly significant in the Bay salt trade, nor in the carriage trade to and from the Baltic. A Danzig-bound Antwerp ship, freighted with cloth at Coldwater, was captured by the Lübeckers in 1453. However, records of ships that tied up at Danzig in the 1460s do not specifically mention vessels from Antwerp.[92]

Restrictions on English cloth at Bruges, and the uncertainty of the Baltic market in the 1450s, meant that Hanseatic and English merchants alike required a transit/distribution point to link the London woollen trade with the vast German and Lowland markets. Dordrecht, ideally situated to serve both the Rhineland and North Sea traffic, was a logical choice, but stringent staple policies there were unpalatable, particularly to the Cologners. Antwerp and neighbouring Bergen op Zoom, on the other hand, welcomed the English cloth trade, since they had no significant textile industry to protect, and no close relationship with Brabantine drapery towns dependent on export industry. Moreover, the two towns already hosted great trading fairs twice yearly. Each autumn the international merchant community was drawn to the St Bavo mart (*Bamissmarct*) at Antwerp, followed by the Cold fair (*Coude Bergemarct*) at Bergen op Zoom. They returned in spring to Bergen's Easter mart (*Paessche Bergemarct*) and the Whitsun fair (*Pinxteremarct*) at Antwerp. Any industrial base that did exist in or around these centres was almost wholly dependent on the dyeing and finishing of cloth imports.[93]

English merchants had been doing business at Antwerp for decades, though English bullionist policies, requiring cash payment for wool at the Calais staple, triggered a series of Burgundian embargoes that periodically undermined their trade in the 1430s and 1440s. The lifting of the embargo in 1452, which reopened Antwerp to English trade, was followed within a year by the evacuation of the Bruges staple by the Hansards. The Hanseatic merchants went to Utrecht, while the English returned to Antwerp. The English presence there was sustained throughout the 1450s and early 1460s. Registers of the Antwerp aldermen, which constitute a partial record of contracts, debts, and litigations, frequently mention merchants from London and Colchester. Englishmen encountered not only Lowland merchants and Cologners, but also traders from Breslau, Cracow, Frankfurt, Hamburg, and the Baltic.[94] The reimposition of the Burgundian ban in 1464 again threatened English trade, forcing the temporary removal of the English community to Utrecht. By then the Hansards had officially returned to Bruges, and Utrecht, eager to accommodate a foreign merchant community, offered a series of attractive trading privileges that induced English merchants to remain there through 1466. Only the agreement between England and Duke Charles, concluded in the autumn of 1467, prompted their return to Antwerp.[95]

Already in the 1450s major woollen shipments from London and Ipswich/Colchester, owned by Hanseatic and English merchants, were timed to coincide with the trade fairs at Bergen op Zoom and Antwerp. Like their English counterparts, the Steelyard merchants, and particularly those from Cologne and the lower Rhineland, either attended the marts or were represented there by resident factors.[96] Money borrowed to finance cloth purchases was repaid during these fairs, and their importance is further confirmed by shipping patterns from the southern English ports. In 1458, for instance, with the St Bavo fair at Antwerp commencing in late September, more than 950 cloths belonging to Hansards, plus several hundred more owned by Englishmen, were shipped from London during the second week of September. The Exchequer year 1461–2, during which Hanseatic cloth exports from the capital exceeded 9,000 units, provides another example. Approximately 2,000 cloths were shipped between 9 October and 9 November, to arrive in time for the annual Cold fair at Bergen op Zoom. No further Hanseatic cloth shipments were recorded until mid-February 1462. From then until the beginning of March, however, another 2,000 cloths, likely bound for the Easter fair at Bergen op Zoom, were freighted for the Hansards. The final two weeks of April saw a further 1,900 cloths customed for export from London, almost certainly destined for the Whitsun fair at Antwerp. Unfortunately, the extant 1461–2 particulars of accounts for London do not extend to the end of the Exchequer year, but there can be little doubt that a fourth series of shipments was made again in early September, for the autumn fair at Antwerp. A similar pattern is also discernible in the accounts of Ipswich/Colchester.[97]

But the importance of Antwerp and Bergen op Zoom as expanding centres of international commerce and of the Hanseatic trade did not stem exclusively from their advantageous locations, or from unrestrictive policies *vis-à-vis* the transit trade in English woollens and manufactured wares and dyestuffs. Their situation on the easily navigable Scheldt-Honte channels, which had been deepened by great inundations in the late fourteenth and early fifteenth century, suited the Baltic trade as well. Bruges and her outport of Sluis were waging a losing battle against the silting of the Zwin estuary, and by mid-century, if not long before, cargoes from and for the Flemish staple were routinely handled at Middelburg and Arnemuiden roads. Likewise, to the north, Deventer and the Zuider Zee port of Kampen were increasingly less able to accommodate the deep-draft vessels from Prussia and their heavy cargoes. Again Antwerp, Bergen op Zoom, and their outports in Zealand were preferred. Baltic cargoes could be carried directly to the fairs, transferred to lighters in Zealand for onward transport, or offloaded at the quays of Middelburg, Veere, Vlissingen, or Zierikzee. They could be stockpiled for subsequent distribution or redirected to England either by Hanseatic shippers or by English and Lowland carriers serving the cross-Channel trade.[98]

During the 1450s and 1460s, then, a number of circumstances combined with political developments to favour the ascendancy of the Brabant fairs. The protectionist regulations at Bruges (based on ducal charters), which were aimed specifically at the increasingly competitive English textile industry, invited a shift in the distributive market for English woollens. Expansion to the Baltic was checked by Lübeck and the Danes, so Brabant became a principal conduit for textiles from England. Shipping patterns also altered, as more Antwerp shippers joined the cross-Channel routes. Moreover, although the Hansards had

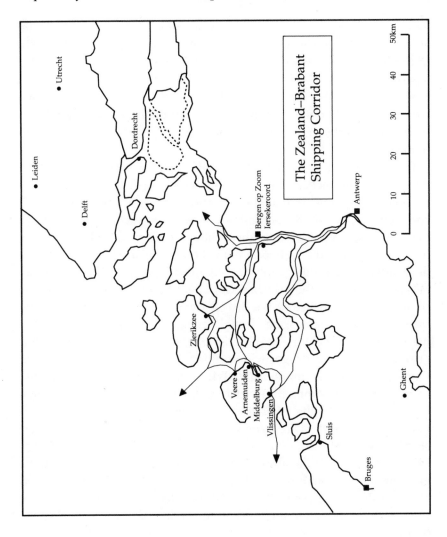

The Zealand–Brabant Shipping Corridor

evacuated the Bruges *comptoir* for a time, they could not contemplate abandoning the international fairs at Antwerp and Bergen op Zoom. In December 1457 they were granted free trading privileges at Antwerp for a period of twenty years.[99] Finally, the silting of the Zwin had begun to hinder the large Baltic hulks laden with cargo for Bruges, so that they were increasingly obliged to moor instead at the Zealand quays, which were the primary transit points for England's cloth export trade to Brabant.

The heightened significance of the fairs was not necessarily compatible with all entrenched economic interests within the Hanseatic sphere, however. Again it accentuated the political divergence between Lübeck and Cologne. For the seaborne trade of Lübeck, such English cloth as might be required for Baltic distribution could be freighted directly from London and the east-coast ports. Otherwise, the woollen industry in Flanders could still supply the comparatively static Baltic market. Hence, for Lübeck, the principal cloth distributor for Scandinavia, the continued maintenance of the Bruges *comptoir* seemed viable. But the merchants of Cologne were strongly connected to the more dynamic markets of upper Germany. Flemish production could not meet their growing needs, and Bruges was of little use in the woollen trade from England except for uninterrupted transit. Bruges remained a vital market for other commodities such as wool, alum, and Flemish cloth, but since the retailing of English woollens already had become an indispensable facet of Cologne's commercial interests, Cologne merchants now were turning to Antwerp and Bergen op Zoom. And logically so, for the fairs, in attracting more of the cloth trade, also lured a growing international merchant community. Had the Cologners failed to establish themselves in the English woollen trade in Brabant, there was an array of other foreign entrepreneurs capable of seizing the initiative.

CHAPTER III
CONFRONTATION, WAR, AND RECONCILIATION

Under Edward IV, provisos attached to the renewal of Hanseatic charters had led to an important delineation of key mercantile interest groups trading to England. Dealing extensively in high-value cloth, dyestuffs, and manufactured goods, and operating primarily out of the London Steelyard, were the merchants of Cologne, Westphalia, and the lower Rhineland. Although also active in the English capital, Esterlings from Hamburg and the Baltic supplied fish and bulk freight to east-coast ports as far north as Hull. During the mid-1460s the English government also had induced the Hansards to agree to reopen a dialogue that included the issue of reciprocal trading privileges for English merchants in Hanseatic towns. Coupled with a policy of conciliation with Denmark and the new duke of Burgundy, this had laid the foundation for a gradual though potentially significant eastern expansion of English mercantile interests. But this initiative, too, had been undone by a wantonly violent foray into Iceland, which immediately wrecked the Anglo-Danish peace. The depredations that followed at Helsingor, in themselves no more cowardly or illegal than those that precipitated them, provided a pretext for continued reprisals. The escalation of hostilities that followed ushered in another critical phase in the Anglo-Hanseatic conflict, which not only further sharpened divisions within the Hanseatic membership, but also significantly altered the volume and subsequent patterns of English overseas trade.

The crisis of 1468

Aside from the fervid complaints of injured Englishmen,[1] additional anti-Hanse agitation in 1468 originated from within London's merchant fraternities. Attitudes there were firmly rooted in the question of differential customs and subsidies favourable to German competitors, and the corresponding lack of reciprocal benefits. As an ever larger share of England's cloth export trade began to accrue to the capital during the middle decades of the century, little in the way of real or fancied injury was necessary for at least some of London's cloth dealers to unleash a torrent of pent-up ill will against the Hansards. The seizure of English ships at the Sound was more than they could tolerate. The Hansards were the most highly privileged foreign merchant group in the realm, and it seemed, during the emotion-charged days of late July at least, that the benefits they enjoyed were repaid only with the treachery of the Baltic skippers.

London had become a much more permanent centre of court and royal administration under Edward IV than it had been during the reign of his predecessor, and the young king routinely turned to the foreign and native merchant communities for financial assistance. The denizen merchant sector as a whole also maintained significant representation in Parliament.[2] Yet to this point Edward IV, himself a participant in overseas trading ventures, had not allowed mercantile pressures to interfere with political and diplomatic objectives. He had ensured that protectionist and nationalist commercial legislation did not unduly restrict the Hanseatic merchants in England. Their privileges had been confirmed over the objections of London, and in 1462 they were exempted from the provisions of a charter granted to the city, which introduced a new tax on foreigners. Throughout the 1460s Edward had countered anti-Hanse prejudice by confirming Hanseatic charters only for short periods, and had established a policy that recognition of Hanseatic liberties in England was now dependent upon continued dialogue on English claims to reciprocity.[3]

By the summer of 1468, however, the monarchy still was not secure. There remained the very real threat of Lancastrian insurrection backed by France, and Edward's secret marriage and the alliance with Burgundy had alienated his ambitious and powerful cousin, Warwick. Moreover, while the king's financial reliance on the London business community continued, resentment there was growing over the greed of the queen's family members and their influence at court. The recent indictment of a number of prominent London burgesses in a series of inconclusive treason trials had offended the wealthy merchant sector still further and exacerbated discontent. In consideration of the latest outrage on the high seas, then, it had become expedient for the Crown to agree to punitive measures, if for no better reason than to avoid the risk of increasing antipathy in the capital.[4]

Finally, in addition to the indignation of London's merchant sector, there was pressure for reprisals against the Hanse from within the king's council, where Richard Neville, earl of Warwick, quickly grasped the opportunity to turn public opinion to his own advantage. The interests of the anti-Hanse lobby now coincided with those of a faction centring around the Neville clan, whose involvement in the dispute with the Hansards stemmed from a curious combination of disregard for the foreign trading community, legitimate claims for damages at the Sound, and not a small measure of political brinkmanship.

The earl's personal contempt for the Hanse had been amply demonstrated off Calais a decade earlier, and he also may have had interests in the ships taken at the Sound. But unlike others who suffered material losses in 1468, his motives for seeking hasty action against the Hansards were essentially political. He favoured Louis XI of France, and schemed to undermine the new Anglo-Burgundian alliance. Now his political ambitions conveniently meshed with the immediate concerns of London's more militant merchant groups. Reactions out of all proportion to the seriousness of the original dispute could not help but cause embarrassment to King Edward in his new Burgundian alliance, and at the same time appease London's merchants. Furthermore, if the punitive action were severe enough to provoke an open confrontation with the Hanse, the resultant disruption of Narrow Seas shipping would stall a joint Anglo-Burgundian invasion of France. Warwick no longer dominated the man he had made king of England, nor did he control his sovereign's council, but there is little doubt he had his way on this occasion. Indeed, it would have been surprising if he had not, given the mood in London, and the fact that the circle of royal advisers in the capital at this time included his brother John, earl of Northumberland, who owned one of the confiscated ships. Present too, and among those who could be counted unfriendly to the Hanse, were John Wenlock and Thomas Kent.[5]

However, the English government could ill afford to obstruct Anglo-Hanseatic commerce completely, and the strong connections with the merchants of Cologne remained vital. Cologners supplied many essential imports, and were equally prominent in the Hanseatic share of London's cloth trade. They also borrowed money and bought cloth on credit in London, making their abrupt and total exclusion from the English trade not entirely desirable. It was the merchants of Cologne, moreover, who resisted the Hanse's artificial maintenance of the *comptoir* at Bruges, where Flemish woollen production was increasingly unable to meet the growing continental demand. The expanding cloth export industry of Holland and that of England had filled the void, but protectionist statutes prohibited the marketing of English cloth at Bruges. The Hanse also had granted the *comptoir* there a special tax (the *Schoss*), on goods purchased or sold in Zealand, Brabant, and Holland. Cologne's objections to the tax led to protracted arguments with Lübeck, both prior to the evacuation of the *comptoir* in the early 1450s and after the Hansards' return there in 1457.[6] Cologne's obvious disillusion with her northern Hanseatic neighbours regarding the Bruges *comptoir* and affairs in the Baltic, together with the town's strong trade links with England, certainly invited English exploitation of Hanseatic disunity. Already in 1441 a Commons' petition, which protested at length about alleged crimes by Hansards, had demanded suspension of Hanseatic privileges on condition that such measures should not apply to Cologners.[7] And, since the Cologners had dissociated themselves from Anglo-Wendish disputes in the middle decades of the century, the town's special relationship with England had to be taken into consideration by the English government in 1468.

On 23 July representatives from the Steelyard were summoned to the Star Chamber at Westminster to hear trumped-up accusations that the taking of the English ships had been part of a Dano-Hanseatic plot. The Hansards were alleged to have been motivated by fears that Hanseatic control of the traffic in 'Oesterschen guede' [eastern goods] would be threatened if the vessels reached Danzig. Although the allegations were hardly credible, the anticipated denials were rejected quickly, and the Hansards ordered to pay damages of £20,000 or face immediate imprisonment. The small delegation was, however, granted brief leave to consult with the rank and file of the Steelyard fellowship.[8]

The position of the Hansards was far from enviable. For the past three years their status in England had been confirmed on a short-term basis, and with the stipulation that representatives from distant Hanseatic towns unanimously consent to discussion of reciprocal status for

Englishmen. No such talks had yet convened, and the latest renewal of Hanseatic privileges had been for one year. The governor of the Steel-yard, Gerhard van Wesel, was in London when the new crisis arose, but many elder members of the fellowship, experienced in matters of diplomacy, were temporarily overseas. Not only that, at the time the Hansards were summoned before the king's council, both of their regular English proctors were away from London. According to van Wesel, the men of the Steelyard therefore agreed to find sureties for the sum of the damages rather than go to prison and have their property confiscated – at least until they could prove their innocence. Whereupon they understood that they would be allowed sufficient time to prepare documentation for that latter purpose. Shocked they professed to be, then, when on the afternoon of the 28th the mayor of London, accom-panied by sheriffs and aldermen, appeared at the Steelyard gates in the king's name, to arrest the inhabitants and seal the warehouses. The bewildered Hansards, many of them young servants and factors, were led away to Ludgate prison. Caught unawares and unable to warn their ships' captains, Hansards in Boston, Lynn, Hull, Ipswich, and Colchester also were arrested, and had their goods and ships impounded.

But almost immediately the Steelyard's chief representative was offered the opportunity to speak again with the chancellor, Robert Stillington, whose eventual line of enquiry all but betrayed the govern-ment's true intent. By asking about the composition of the Steelyard fellowship, Stillington first established that van Wesel was a Cologner. He then inquired how Cologne stood with the king of Denmark, at the same time hinting that he already had information of some ongoing dispute. Without further prompting, van Wesel told the chancellor what he apparently wanted to hear. Cologne, he replied, had been at odds with Denmark for some time. Turning to the recorder present, Stilling-ton ventured to suggest that this might be of interest to the king. And so, evidently, it was. Accompanied by legal counsel, van Wesel returned to Westminster within a day or two, ostensibly to present documents in defence of the Hansards. On this occasion, though, he was received by George Neville, the archbishop of York, who assured him that there was no immediate need for documentation, since the young servants from the Steelyard and all the merchants of Cologne were to be freed, on condition that they not leave England.

If the Cologners' version of events is believed, they had been pre-sented with a *fait accompli* that left them no choice but to accept what they had been offered.[9] The rest of the Hansards and their property would remain under arrest at least until the autumn, awaiting a definitive quasi-judicial ruling on the matter by the council. In the interim, would not the interests of the Hanse, to say nothing of the Cologners, be best served if some of the Steelyard merchants remained free to prepare a defence of the fellowship? In mid-November, however, after all the legal arguments had been heard, the 'sentence' of the council drove the wedge still deeper between the Cologners and their jailed colleagues. The property of the Cologne merchants was returned to them. That of other Hansards would be divided up to compensate injured Englishmen. The earl of Northumberland alone was awarded more than £1,250 for his losses at the Sound, and except for the Cologners, all the Hansards in England, including some young factors and mariners, remained incarcerated. Control of 'Hanseatic' commerce in England reverted exclusively to the merchants of Cologne.[10]

The preferential treatment accorded Cologne was as much another compromise, intended to appease powerful interest groups in and around London, as a stratagem aimed at further exploiting Hanseatic disunity. The penalty imposed on the other Hansards would avenge the merchants of London and the east-coast ports who had suffered losses at the Sound, but would leave intact another integral link in England's foreign trade. On the surface the immediate risks were minimal. Precedent suggested that the Cologners would opt for a privileged status that excluded other Hansards. They valued their English trade too highly to relinquish it by choice. But had they not, and had they elected instead to close ranks with the rest of the Hanse, there still would have been ample opportunity for serious negotiation.[11] However, the vindictive punishment meted out to the Esterlings was a serious and counter-productive departure from Edward IV's previous policy, in that it effectively subverted any real chance of Englishmen gaining a larger share of the Baltic trade. The incessant complaints about non-observance of the terms of the 1437 treaty, which the English interpreted as reciprocal, were less than convincing at the best of times. Now they were entirely meaningless.

English mercantile interests in the Baltic

What, then, was the erstwhile role of the English in the Baltic trade? The clamour for reciprocity invariably focused on Prussia, and there is no question that the most coveted market was that of the Danzig staple. Baltic Hansards, and especially Danzig shippers, were very important in the overseas commerce of London and England's east-coast ports, but direct trade between the Baltic and England was by no means the exclusive preserve of the Esterlings.[12] An organization of English businessmen still functioned in Danzig in the mid-fifteenth century, and no doubt these men were well acquainted with the central meeting place for merchants, the *Artushof*, which would evolve later as the town's international commercial hall. In 1447 at least three English ships called at Danzig. The number of resident Englishmen arrested there four years later is uncertain, but it is instructive that a plea for the release of a colleague was made in the name of the 'Alderleuute und der gemeyne couffman us Engelant, nu czu czeit czu Danczke in Preuwsen wesende' [Aldermen and common merchants of England presently at Danzig in Prussia].[13] One of this fellowship, Robert Parker, even requested permission to continue his trade there at least until the meetings at Utrecht had been concluded. Merchants from Lynn had shared in the cargo of a Holland ship captured by pirates on a voyage from Prussia to England in 1450. An English ship seized by the Danes on its return voyage from Prussia carried Londoner John West, factor of two Boston merchants, on whose behalf he negotiated the vessel's release.[14]

Letters that accompanied a shipment of woollens from Lynn aboard a Danzig ship in 1452 attest to the continued presence of a group of English business agents in Danzig, despite the turbulent state of Anglo-Hanseatic affairs. The cloth was to be received by William Yekes and Thomas Syndal, factors of two Lynn merchants, John Francis and Henry Berinckhem. Robert Parker also was named as agent for Robert Stocker, and Berinckhem's instructions for disposal of his portion of the cargo were addressed to yet another Englishman in Danzig, John Jacksall. In addition, some of the cloth was sent to Yekes under the seal of a Hansard. The Englishman was instructed to relay news of its arrival to a Danzig intermediary, who in turn would contact the intended recipient, a Danziger named Mekelfeldene. The parcel was for payment of a debt owed Mekelfeldene by Berinckhem.[15]

The English presence in Danzig was maintained throughout the mid-1450s. John Jacksall was still trading there in the spring of 1455, and in the interim London merchant Stephen Barry and his partners had been granted freedom to trade throughout Prussia for a period of twelve years. Barry already had been shipping English cloth to the Baltic as early as 1448.[16] In May 1457 Danzig issued additional safe conducts, valid until September of the following year, for three English ships from Hull and Lynn. The privilege applied to ten English merchants identified by name, together with 'al eren mannen und geselschopen' [all their servants and partners]. Included among them was Lynn merchant John Thorsby, who indeed purchased a ship in Danzig later in the year.[17] It is possible, perhaps even likely, that these individuals and others from Lynn already were established in the Baltic trade, and that their safe conducts simply confirmed the status quo. Lynn customs records indicate that a large bulk cargo consisting exclusively of Baltic commodities – grain, iron, pitch, tar, staves, and 'Revell fflaxe' – had been offloaded from an English ship for English merchants the previous autumn.[18] But the continued presence of Englishmen in the Baltic throughout the 1450s relied much less on trading privileges in Danzig than on Anglo-Danish relations. It also depended on the business acumen of individual entrepreneurs and their luck in avoiding the political quarrels that endangered seaborne commerce. The luck of the English ran out before the end of the decade, and the decisive blow probably was Lübeck's response to Warwick's attack on the salt fleet in 1458. Thereafter the situation of Englishmen attempting to trade to the Baltic became more precarious once again. Surviving evidence for the next half decade is limited and does not point to a sustained English presence in Danzig, although this is not to say there was none at all.

None of the four ships entering Danzig from England in 1460 was English, and of the names of cargo owners listed in the port's quayage records only one is easily identifiable as non-German, and is perhaps that of an Englishman. Moreover, surviving English customs particulars for the late 1450s and early 1460s show that Baltic ships discharging cargo in England did so almost exclusively for Hanseatic merchants.[19] Undoubtedly the Danes and Lübeckers were largely responsible for limiting English participation in the Baltic trade at this time. Henry VI appealed to Lübeck in early 1461 for the return of the *Maryeflour de Gernesay*, taken by Lübeck's raiders. Two years later another English vessel, fully laden at Danzig with wood, tar, and iron, was intercepted by Lübeckers on the homeward voyage to Lynn.[20]

If the risks to shipping were insufficient in themselves to curtail English activity, incentive for English merchants must have been further dampened by the generally unstable cloth market in the eastern Baltic. The reopening of the Bruges *comptoir* in 1457-8 had re-established ready access to the supply of Flemish woollens, and Lübeck, regardless of the disruption of intra-Baltic trade, remained the key traditional distributor to eastern regions. Lübeck's blockade of the Sound notwithstanding, the enhanced availability of Flemish cloth, together with complaints in Riga, Reval, and Dorpat regarding undersized and falsely packed English cloth, rendered the market for English woollens in Livonia rather unpromising. Though English cloth was still available there, it simply was not wanted.[21] So by the early 1460s, English trade to the Baltic, even in its broadest sense, was confined all the more to the Danzig staple. Yet even this link was threatened by the continuing war between Poland and the Teutonic knights. By 1465 Danzig had to warn English shippers to venture into the Baltic only in convoys, as no protection could be guaranteed for individual captains foolhardy enough to come alone.[22]

The decline of direct English participation in the Anglo-Baltic trade, which began after 1458, lasted until the mid-1460s, when it was remedied within a very short period by a series of timely economic and political developments. Introduced in 1464, in response to the difficulties in the Anglo-Lowland trade, a 25% devaluation of the English pound sterling attempted to strengthen English cloth on foreign markets and encourage exports. Indeed it was important enough to be worthy of note in the contemporary Danzig chronicle of Caspar Weinreich.[23] The following year saw England and Denmark temporarily set aside their long-standing hostilities and reach agreement on a commercial treaty. This effectively eliminated any extraneous support the Lübeckers could muster for obstruction of English shipping. The rest of the Hanseatic community had long since dismissed Lübeck's quarrel with England, and the recent meetings with English envoys at Hamburg merely emphasized this. The Sound was again open to English traffic. Within a year, too, the war against the Teutonic knights, which had played havoc with Baltic shipping, ground to its conclusion. In a remarkably short space of time the two principal risks to Anglo-Baltic trade had been removed, precisely when Anglo-Burgundian relations dictated some sort of initiative in England's export sector.

Whether or not a community of resident English merchants still existed in Danzig by the mid-1460s, this brief period of political stabilization after 1465 certainly provided the impetus for Englishmen to return there. And return they did. The *Raphael* of Bristol sailed home from Danzig in the autumn of 1467, freighted with lumber, tar, bowstaves, counters, and tables. Some sixteen English merchants and mariners were set ashore safely at Grimsby, Holderness, Hull, and Sandwich, before the vessel finally foundered off Kilkampton. Nor did all the Englishmen come home that year. At least one other merchant, William Wathyne of London, remained in Danzig through the winter of 1467–8.[24]

The changed political climate set the stage for the series of bizarre and dramatic events that followed in the summer of 1468. Circumstances obviously favoured a concerted attempt to penetrate the Baltic market, and if ever there was an opportunity to establish a stronger English presence in the region, surely this was it. But squandered opportunities were synonymous with England's Baltic experience in the last forty years of the century, and when the English ships set sail for Danzig in the spring of 1468, this latest chance had already been lost through the inexplicable behaviour of the English fishermen in Iceland some months before. Once again the king of Denmark had been offended and provoked, and he would not be long in exacting his price from an unsuspecting English fleet bound for the Baltic. And if advocates of protectionism in Danzig had been concerned seriously about an imminent English intrusion, then in one sense the antics of those English mariners in Iceland played directly into their hands. Experience with the Hollanders and Zealanders had already demonstrated that statutes alone were not enough to restrict foreigners in the Baltic trade, but a new English thrust could be checked if there was a reasonable pretext for limiting passage through the Sound. The English themselves had just created one. King Christian would, for his own reasons, initiate the capture of the English fleet, but circumstantial evidence of some complicity within the Hanseatic towns is not very surprising.

Yet, irrespective of protectionist currents in Danzig, it is scarcely plausible that the attack was condoned by the governing oligarchy there. The taking of an English fleet was sure to provoke reprisals that could, and ultimately did, jeopardize Danzig's access to the lucrative English market. Obvious targets for reprisals would be the Esterling shippers and merchants in eastern England, especially at Hull and Lynn, where the Danzigers formed the preponderant Hanseatic group. There were no precautionary measures to safeguard interests in these ports, such as the evacuation of individuals or goods in the spring of 1468. Instead, many of Danzig's *Englandfahrer* faced arrest by late July, and several others unwittingly called at Hull and Lynn in August and were promptly jailed. At least seven, and perhaps as many as nine Baltic ships were seized in England.[25] There is, perhaps, only slightly better reason to suspect some of the Wendish *Bergenfahrer* of collusion. They did of course resist the intrusion of Hollanders and Englishmen into the Norwegian and Icelandic fisheries, and this coloured their attitudes *vis-à-vis* neighbouring Denmark. The crimes of the English in Iceland would have been ample excuse for both the Danish king and troublesome individuals from the Wendish towns to escalate the violence. Economic risk to the Danes was minimal, as their trade with England was insignificant. That of the Wendish towns was concentrated largely in the fish trade at Boston. Coincidently, although a consignment belonging to the *Bergenfahrer* was discharged from an English ship in January 1468, no Wendish ships had called at the Lincolnshire port since 1465. Within a year of the trouble at the Sound Lübeck had also persuaded Denmark to impose severe restrictions on Hollanders and Englishmen trading to Iceland and Bergen.[26] But the north Atlantic fisheries were not the only issue. Relations between England and Lübeck had been strained for two decades, and the Crown's continued refusal to indemnify victims of Warwick's attack on the salt ships in 1458 was a source of lingering humiliation for the Lübeckers.

In the spring of 1468, three English ships – two from Newcastle and one from Southampton – had passed safely to Danzig. Of the seven others that were seized in mid-June at the Sound, five had weighed anchor at either Boston or Lynn, and their cargoes are recorded in the extant customs particulars for the Wash ports.[27] Small quantities of worsteds, cheese, lead, and Gascon wine were aboard, but of much greater significance were the extraordinary cloth cargoes. A total of 1,256 cloths were being carried from these ports to the Baltic for no fewer than three dozen English merchants. Rather unusual, too, was the Hanseatic tally of only 56 cloths aboard the English vessels, and an equally low number carried in Hanseatic ships. During the preceding three years, total combined cloth exports for Boston and Lynn fluctuated rather radically, but averaged around 1,000 units annually, with denizens accounting for only about 400 per year. The 1468 totals for Lynn indicate not only an enormous surge in woollen exports (963 units), but also that virtually all of the cloth was being shipped to the Baltic by indigenous English merchants. And in Boston, the 346 cloths sent to the Baltic by Englishmen represented well over half of the denizen total for that port.

It is possible that some cloth belonging to Hansards was being shipped through English intermediaries. Hans Barenbrock, an Esterling at the Steelyard, later claimed to have sent 84 cloths in the ships from Boston and Lynn and 13 more in a vessel from London, all through the agency of indigenous merchant William Wales. While Barenbrock is not listed in the appropriate accounts for the ports of the Wash, Wales is shown to have had 180 cloths customed in his name – far more than any other single English merchant – aboard ships later taken at the Sound.[28] This, of course, mitigates against any conspiracy by the Steelyard men. If any of them had been party to a plot to ambush the English ships, then sending merchandise under the seal of an Englishman was the last thing they would have contemplated.

Another ship, the earl of Northumberland's *Valentine*, had sailed from Newcastle to Hull before setting out for Danzig. Although no particulars of customs survive for these ports, complaints of the ship's capture refer to another rich cloth cargo. Still less is known of the seventh ship, the *George* of London, but several Londoners claimed damages after the vessel was seized. In all, sixty-eight English merchants from London, York, and Hull claimed shares in the captured cargoes.[29]

During the two decades immediately prior to the Sound incident English participation in the Baltic trade had been marked by three distinct phases, which together provide a context for the capture and indeed the very existence of such exceptional cargoes in 1468. After 1450 direct English involvement in trade to and from the Baltic, though limited, had continued, despite the obstinacy of Lübeck and various other threats to shipping. There is ample evidence that at least a small English merchant community functioned in Danzig until 1458. Thereafter, for a period of perhaps seven or eight years, English trade there was hindered by the vigorous obstruction of shipping by Lübeck and the Danes, and the escalation of the sea war in the eastern region. In addition to these problems of access, there was also a decline in the popularity of English woollens in Livonia, which in any case depended on Lübeck as a main supplier. Hence, by the mid 1460s, when the Anglo-Danish treaty and the cessation of war in the east created more favourable circumstances for increased trade, the English first needed to re-establish their presence in the region. The attempt to reconstruct strong commercial links with Danzig and ultimately lessen England's dependency on cross-Channel trade began in 1466. It was manifest in the safe passage of ships to Prussia the following year and the large number of English vessels bound for the Baltic in 1468.

The persistent protests of unfair restrictions at the Prussian staple must also be assessed within the context of the English role in the Baltic trade from 1450 to 1468. The sustained, albeit modest presence of Englishmen in Danzig had been interrupted not as the result of discriminatory statutes there, but because of extreme risks to shipping. Yet what English complaints invariably chose to ignore was the fact that access to Baltic markets hinged on passage through the Sound. In other words, it depended to a great extent on relations with Denmark. Lowland shippers had illustrated this throughout the 1450s and 1460s, by actively pursuing peaceful relations with the Danes in order to safeguard their long-distance carriage trade in salt and grain.[30] Notwithstanding disruptions in the eastern regions, they had demonstrated that if passage to the Baltic could be assured for prolonged periods, the effectiveness of regulatory ordinances in Lübeck, Danzig, and Riga was limited. The English, by contrast, were not primarily bulk carriers, and they certainly lacked the shipping tonnage to compete in that type of trade with the Hanseatic and Lowland shippers. But even if they had contemplated something less ambitious, such as the simple exchange of high-value woollens for bulk raw materials, the first prerequisite still would have been an Anglo-Danish relationship – and preferably one with Lübeck – that would enable consistent safe passage through the Sound. Without this, the question of restrictions or reciprocal rights was completely irrelevant. The pattern of the mid-1450s and of the period 1465–8 indicates that the Danzig staple could and did attract English merchants and shipping, regardless of statutes there designed to restrict them. The often predictable English protests were lodged at least in part, then, for rhetorical effect. The real issue was the widely resented privileged status of Hansards in England.

Intra-Hanse political alignment

In addition to the disputes with England, the Hanse's political relations

with the Burgundian territories also were anything but tranquil during
the middle decades of the century. There were complaints of violations
of Hanseatic trading privileges at Bruges, and the end of the war
between Holland and the Wendish towns in 1441 had scarcely affected
piratical attacks on North Sea shipping. Led by Lübeck, the Hanse had
resorted to a boycott of Flanders in 1451, and had transferred the
Bruges *comptoir* to the independent bishopric of Utrecht. The ban was
contravened routinely by merchants of several towns, including Duisburg, Soest, and Cologne.[31] Flemish cloth, purchased at Bruges and at
the Antwerp market, continued to be distributed throughout Hanseatic
territory as far east as Prussia. By 1457 Philip the Good's occupation of
the territories of the bishopric of Utrecht forced the Hansards to negotiate a return to Bruges and to lift their self-imposed embargo.[32]

Elsewhere, by 1466, King Casimir IV of Poland and the Prussian
towns had prevailed, and the war against the Teutonic Order had ended
with the second Treaty of Thorn. Poland gained full sovereignty over
all of western Prussia, and the king granted Danzig what amounted to
exclusive authority in matters of trade.[33] Already the busiest of the
Prussian ports, Danzig set out to ensure her long-term mercantile
ascendancy by forbidding transactions between foreign traders and
interior markets, except through the agency of one of her citizens. The
chronic disorder of the previous decade and the ultimate demise of the
knights had indeed allowed members of the trading community in the
eastern Baltic ports to preserve, consolidate, and enhance their commercial and political predominance. The landed estates, producers of many
of Prussia's exportable raw products, soon acquiesced to the authority
of Danzig's mercantile elite. Political cohesion within the Hanse by no
means improved with the collapse of the Order, for although the selfish
policies of the knights were removed, they were replaced by the equally
narrow particularism of Danzig's commercial bourgeoisie. Upon being
accorded full authority in affairs of trade by Casimir, Danzig continued
to attempt to restrict the activities of all foreign merchant groups.[34]

Throughout the fifteenth century the trading centres of Prussia and
Livonia had, like their Hanseatic neighbours to the west, adopted
attitudes of independent protectionism regarding diplomatic and commercial policy. This approach was manifest in open confrontation with
the Order, and in frequent disagreements with Lübeck regarding trade
with western markets through the Sound, and the protection of resource

bases and markets in the eastern European hinterland. Moreover, Lübeck had not supported Danzig against the knights. That would have entailed voluntary disruption of the town's important trade to Riga, and risked provoking the Danish monarch, who favoured the Order. Of the Prussian ports, only Königsberg was subject to the rule of the Order after 1466. The others stood at the vanguard of protectionism in the eastern Hanseatic sphere.

By 1468, unity within the Hanse seemed to exist only so far as it served individual interests. While some Lübeckers perhaps deluded themselves about their imagined political pre-eminence within the confederation, the changing realities of the European trading economy had begun to lead other prosperous towns such as Bremen and Hamburg, and particularly Danzig and Cologne, in diverse directions. In matters of considerable economic and political importance, each had adopted a particularism based on control of regional markets, centres of production, or specific foreign trade links. Cologne objected to the expensive maintenance of the Bruges *comptoir*, strengthened her hold on the trade in dyestuffs, metal products, and textiles, and openly cultivated a special relationship with England. Bremen, too, often remained detached from even the Wendish sphere, and strove to control grain transport on the Weser and along the North Sea coast. The town's quarrels with the duke of Burgundy during the 1440s resulted in separate peace agreements that did not always apply to the Hanse as a whole. Nor did indiscriminate attacks by Bremen's pirate fleet make it any less awkward for the rest of the Hanse to negotiate amiable relationships with England and Holland.[35] The town's refusal to treat with English officials after 1465, despite Lübeck's eventual consent, speaks volumes. Though still bound by the attitudes of the Wendish group, the burgesses of Hamburg also asserted themselves in opposition to Lübeck, and prospered through a flourishing trade with England and the Lowlands, and monopolistic ordinances relating particularly to the traffic in cereals.[36] Far to the north-east, Reval and Riga severely restricted access to the Livonian hinterland, and monopolized Hanseatic trade with the Russians at the Novgorod emporium. Finally, Danzig, aided by the demise of the Teutonic Order, had succeeded in dominating the trade of the Vistula and the Prusso-Polish interior, and now was the primary supplier of bulk raw materials to England and points along the Atlantic seaboard. These rising civic and regional powers each enforced their own trade regulations, not only against foreign nationals but also against other non-resident Hansards as well.[37]

The most obtrusive challenge to the Hanse's *raison d'être* culminated with Cologne's response to the release of her merchants in England in the summer of 1468. The town thanked King Edward, and advised Cologners not to lend money to other affected Hanseatic merchants or become involved in the conflict in any way.[38] Cologners duly assumed absolute control of the Steelyard, and for the next half decade England and the rest of the Hanse were embroiled in a sea war, perhaps a predictable, if not inevitable result of more than a half century of controversy.

England and the Hanse at war

In England a succession of insecure monarchs, and particularly the reign of Henry VI, had done little positive to affect the demeanour of the maritime trading community. The violence that marked the deterioration of Anglo-Hanseatic relations in the mid-1400s was symptomatic of acute political weakness within the realm. The warlike proclivities of the English did not stem entirely from the quest for reciprocity in Hanseatic territories. In London, English merchants were more interested in restricting or even revoking the trading privileges of their Hanseatic rivals than in achieving parity in Prussia for their colleagues from the other east-coast ports. In this context the anti-Hanse agitation in England can be seen, at least in part, as a struggle for more equitable application of royal customs and subsidies, whereby Hansards would forfeit their advantage, particularly in the highly competitive cloth export trade. English merchants trading abroad reinforced anti-Hanse sentiment with often legitimate complaints of exclusion from, or persecution in the Baltic region. But their arguments were offset as often as not by the epidemic of piracy for which the merchant community itself was largely responsible, and which the century of intermittent conflict with France had encouraged. During the middle decades the emergence of powerful mercantile interest groups, which included individuals schooled in commercial violence, combined with a belligerent aristocracy to challenge the authority of a government already handicapped by political turmoil and a perpetually exhausted treasury.[39]

Neither the Steelyard fellowship nor the Hanse as a whole could have anticipated the extraordinarily severe measures instituted against them in the summer of 1468. But dismayed and angered as they were, the delegates who gathered for the Hanseatic assembly at Lübeck in August could do little except initiate a diplomatic campaign for the prompt release of their imprisoned colleagues. Hence, prior to the council's verdict or 'sentence' in late autumn, the English government was deluged with appeals. The protest of the *Hansetag* was followed closely by separate letters from important towns such as Nijmegen, Kampen, Stralsund, Soest, and Duisburg. Typically, the pleas stressed that the piratical encounter that had precipitated the English reprisals was orchestrated by the king of Denmark, and that the Hanse could be implicated only in so far as a few Baltic pirates apparently had been willing accessories. The Steelyard Hansards, meanwhile, argued that their arrest violated letters patent, confirmed by Edward IV, which granted immunity from arrest and prosecution for transgressions committed by others.[40]

The prisoners in London also occupied themselves in soliciting support within the kingdom. Duisburg merchant Joris Tack later recounted: 'doe hadden wy gefangen gemeynlich al den lackenmackers int lant geschrieven to London to komen, omme ons bystant to doen ...'[41] The clothmakers of Bristol, Wiltshire, Somerset, and Gloucester responded with petitions reminding the government that the Hansards were and ever had been friends of England, and expressing considerable alarm at the harmful repercussions of their arrest and detention. Protested the men of Gloucestershire: 'your seid besechers been and have been deferrid and delaied of paiement of ther dettes owyng to theyme by the seid [Hanse] merchauntes whiche drawith among theyme to the summe of £5000 and more to their full grete damage and likly undoyng, if it this long shold stond.'[42] But the king's advisers were unmoved, and according to their command goods belonging to Hansards other than the merchants of Cologne were forfeited. The Esterlings remained in prison. In addition, the Crown forced a loan of £1,000 from the Steelyard merchants – Cologners and Esterlings alike.[43]

Another wave of diplomatic protests followed in the new year. Appeals from the emperor, the king of Poland, and several territorial princes had already reached London. Now came a plea from the archbishop of Cologne on behalf of the merchants of Nijmegen. A missive from the Four Members of Flanders (Ghent, Ypres, Bruges, Franc de

Bruges) admonished the English government, and William Caxton, then head of England's merchants in the Lowlands, also voiced support for the Hansards.[44] Yet it was not until late March 1469, following repeated requests by the duke of Burgundy, that Edward relented. Again the Crown reiterated the vague charges against the Hanse before releasing the Esterlings and requesting talks with Lübeck officials at Bruges in May or June.[45]

By this time the merchants of Cologne were irremediably split from the rest of the Hanse. Prior to the council's verdict they had attempted to purchase letters from the emperor on behalf of all the imprisoned Hansards. Wine was sent to the prisoners at Ludgate, and legal costs and gifts to English officials were paid for out of the Steelyard coffers.[46] But Cologne's early acceptance of exclusive status for her merchants, and the Crown's eventual decision to confirm it as well as the punishment of other Hansards, ultimately began to erode personal loyalties within the Steelyard fellowship. In December 1468 Hermann Wanmate wrote to Lübeck that the Cologners had become defensive and unhelpful, and quite rightly surmised they would not wilfully alter their current status in England. In February 1469 the king implicitly confirmed the new status quo by arranging to reimburse the Cologne merchants £516 for their portion of the £1,000 loan he had forced from the Steelyard.[47] The Cologners subsequently ignored the *Hansetag's* threat to suspend the Hanseatic privileges of any merchant who did not leave England by 24 June, and during the summer van Wesel and his lawyers made three visits to the king at Windsor and St Albans to have the charters of the Cologne merchants extended.[48]

The lengthy confinement of the merchants had hardened attitudes within the rest of the Hanseatic community, and England's refusal to retract charges of complicity in the Sound incident was an indignity that could go unchallenged no longer. Buoyed, perhaps, by the release of the hostages in England, the assembly that convened at Lübeck in the spring of 1469 not only recalled them to their home towns, but also issued a scathing rebuttal of the English allegations.[49] The secretary of the Bruges *comptoir* was instructed to reject any English claims and to press for nullification of the council's sentence. The Hansards now would settle for nothing less than full compensation for all damages resulting from the English reprisals. Predictably, the demands presented at Bruges were rejected, and subsequent political events in England quickly diminished still further any possibility of negotiated settlement. By the end of July Edward IV was prisoner of the disaffected earl of Warwick. With royal administration in the hands of the Neville faction, prospects of compromise with the Hanse all but vanished.

The significance of this turn of events was not lost on Duke Charles of Burgundy, to whom Edward's insecure reign was a source of appreciable concern. Cognizant that a protracted Anglo-Hanseatic dispute would disrupt the Narrow Seas and Channel trade to the likely detriment of the Burgundian treasury, and acutely aware of Warwick's French affiliations, Charles had urged restraint in England's quarrel with the Hanse. But an English administration friendly to France was of no political use to him, so the waning fortunes of his Yorkist ally now dictated a somewhat more sympathetic attitude toward the Hanse. The Hansards themselves must have realized the futility of further discussions with an English government alternately too preoccupied with political intrigue to deal responsibly with international mercantile disputes, or controlled by a faction openly hostile to the Hanseatic community. After a year of diplomatic initiatives, moderate inclinations, which ironically were particularly evident in the Wendish sector, gave way to more militant ones. Nothing more could be achieved through negotiation. The disagreement now would be settled on the high seas. In the autumn of 1469, without formal authorization from the *Hansetag*, the Hanseatic merchants in Bruges fitted out two privateers for action against English shipping. The vessels were commanded by captains from Danzig, Paul Beneke and Martin Bardewik, and operated out of Flemish ports with the tacit approval of Duke Charles of Burgundy.[50]

The privateers deployed in the Channel and the North Sea throughout the ensuing four years were essentially merchant ships manned by extra levies of soldiers. The refitting of a vessel for military service primarily attempted to create additional space for soldiers and their weapons, and accommodate whatever rudimentary cannon might be available.[51] Because they had to be revictualled frequently and were in constant need of repair, they remained at sea only for short periods, usually not exceeding two or three weeks. As might be expected, the owners and crews were as interested in profit as in forcing a settlement with England. There were skirmishes with French ships as well as English, and by the summer of 1470 a state of war also existed between the Hanse and France.

The first victim of the new Hanseatic initiative was the *Joen* of

Newcastle, taken on New Year's Day 1470, and it was not long before other privateering vessels were on their way from Danzig. One of them was captained by Eler Bokelman, a skipper well acquainted with both sea warfare and the Anglo-Baltic trade. After serving against the Order in the early 1460s, he had rejoined the Danzig/England route, and in the summer of 1468 his ship and a cargo belonging to several Hanseatic merchants were seized at Hull. In late May 1470 he and Bardewik were defeated by a far superior English flotilla off the coast of Scotland.[52]

English shipping subsequently incurred substantial losses during the summers of 1470 and 1471, even though Danzig and Hamburg appeared to be the only major Hanseatic towns interested in an active campaign.[53] An official boycott of English merchandise was instituted in autumn 1470. With this measure Danzig and the Polish king concurred, provided other Hanseatic towns were prepared to observe the sanction.[54] The *Hansetag* of August-September 1470 introduced trade restrictions aimed at strengthening the Bruges staple and isolating the merchants of Cologne. It also threatened the Cologners with expulsion from the confederation. Unswayed, the merchants remained in England, and the town was formally expelled from the Hanse in April 1471. The ships and goods of the turncoat Cologners then became fair game for the Hanseatic privateers. Moreover, attacks on other foreign ships soon rekindled old animosities in Holland. Eventually, as many as eighteen Hanseatic ships became actively involved in the disruption of maritime commerce, even though Duke Charles forbade his subjects to provision the Hanseatic raiders soon after Beneke's initial foray.[55]

In September 1470 the political turmoil in England had assumed a new magnitude, as Warwick forced Edward IV to flee the Realm. The fugitive king and his small following departed from Lynn, and were pursued closely by Hanseatic privateers *en route* to the Lowlands. Duke Charles's support for his brother-in-law's return to England was assured by February 1471, when Warwick concluded an alliance with Louis XI. The French had already begun their assault on Burgundian territory in December, and the new treaty amounted to a declaration of war by the English, rendering Edward IV's speedy restoration essential to the Burgundians. Prodded by the duke, and apparently hopeful that if Edward safely regained his crown he would make peace with the Hanse, the Esterlings actually provided a sizeable naval escort for his return from exile in March 1471.[56]

The crossing was uneventful, and Warwick's death at the battle of Barnet on 14 April, coupled with the defeat of Queen Margaret at Tewkesbury, at last removed the most serious threats to Edward's monarchy. Upon regaining his kingdom, however, his indebtedness to the Esterlings was set aside temporarily. Only the franchises of the Cologners were guaranteed for a further year,[57] thereby ensuring the continuation of the maritime conflict. Off the coasts of England Beneke and his raiders prowled unmolested, taking two more prizes and capturing the lord mayor of London aboard one of them. The boycott of English wares was tightened, and in August 1471 the *Grosse Kraweel*, a mammoth French-built caravel, sailed from Danzig to join the hunt, accompanied by a smaller ship captained by none other than the free-lance privateer Michael Ertmann.[58]

The *Grosse Kraweel* was actually the *Saint Pierre de la Rochelle*, which had come to the Baltic in 1462 as part of the Bay salt fleet and subsequently was left abandoned in Danzig as unseaworthy. In 1470 the civic authorities decided to refit the vessel, and when it finally left port a year later, commanded by Danzig councillor Bernt Pawest, it was armed with seventeen cannon, and carried a veritable army of more than three hundred men. Unwieldy, expensive to maintain, and barely seaworthy at the best of times, the caravel had a less than illustrious history under Pawest. He was plagued by foul weather in the winter of 1471–2, more than once the ship ran aground, and the crew was mutinous. Despite all its impressive physical credentials the *Grosse Kraweel* spent a good part of its early military career immobilized in the Zwin estuary, more a curiosity to visitors than a threat to English shipping. That would change in the summer of 1472, when Beneke assumed command.[59]

During the first two summers of the Anglo-Hanseatic War only Hamburg, Danzig, and to some extent Bremen had been inclined to underwrite expensive privateering ventures. A more reluctant, perhaps even indifferent attitude prevailed in Lübeck. One reason for this, suggested by F. Rörig, may have been that the privateering contracts of the Lübeckers offered too little incentive to ships' crews, while those of Hamburg's privateers, by contrast, presented good prospects for substantial personal gain.[60] In any event, it was not until May 1472 that Lübeck fitted out four vessels to join Beneke, Ertmann, and several other Hanseatic ships at Sluis for what promised to be a very lucrative if not decisive campaign.[61]

The devastation of English maritime commerce, which the addition of the Lübeck squadron might have ensured, was averted, in part, by the timely stabilization of the political situation in England. With the monarchy on a more secure footing and the menace of Warwick's private navy removed, the English were able to deploy at least eighteen fighting ships in the summer of 1472, probably under the overall command of John Howard. In early July, only two weeks after being severely mauled by a French squadron, the Hansards were surprised by the English flotilla and soundly defeated. The ships from Lübeck were captured and burned, and Ertmann was among the Hanseatic prisoners.[62]

With the Yorkists secure in England, Duke Charles's interest in the Anglo-Burgundian alliance, and therefore a solution to the Anglo-Hanseatic dispute, also was revived. In the autumn of 1472 a Milanese diplomatic agent reported home from Gravelines that the duke had undertaken to bring about an agreement between England and the Esterlings. Such an enterprise was by then all the more expedient, with rumours circulating that the Hansards were now in league with the French. Although attacks on neutral shipping had already prompted the duke to forbid the revictualling of privateers by his subjects, the Hansards continued to launch raids from harbours in Holland and Flanders.[63]

The Hanseatic threat remained, but the vital Anglo-Lowland trade was preserved. Within the Hanse the reversals of 1472, which included Bardewik's death off Calais, served to further accentuate diverse attitudes. In particular, the defeats dampened Lübeck's enthusiasm for confrontation, which had been no more than moderate to begin with. Already by July 1472 there had been preliminary peace overtures from both the Wendish sector of the Hanse and the English government.[64] But militants within the Hanse were not yet prepared to yield. Danzig's privateers did not return to the Baltic, and Hamburg continued to equip fighting ships. In the autumn a pair of English and Spanish ships sailing from Flanders were captured and taken to the Elbe.[65] Yet to be reckoned with also was the *Grosse Kraweel*, now commanded by perhaps the most resourceful and redoubtable of Danzig's captains.

During the winter of 1472–3 the *Grosse Kraweel* was purchased by three members of Danzig's civic council, Johann Sidinghusen, Tydemann Valand, and Heinrich Nederhoff. All three were prosperous merchants, and both Valand and Nederhoff had substantial trading interests in England. They duly instructed Beneke to continue his efforts against English shipping.[66] The conflict at sea then resumed in the summer of 1473, and culminated in the most celebrated of all Hanseatic privateering exploits. Beneke and his men, who had wintered near Hamburg, attacked two Burgundian galleys chartered by the Medici bankers in Bruges for a voyage from Zealand to Florence. Before making for the Mediterranean, the ships were supposed to discharge cargoes of alum in England and take on consignments of English wool. The remainder of their rich cargoes from the Low Countries consisted of woollens, linens, tapestries, and furs belonging to Italian and English merchants. Also aboard were two altarpieces intended for Florence, including Hans Memling's 'Last Judgment,' commissioned by a former manager of the Bruges branch of the Medici. Although the galleys flew Burgundian colours and the Hansards had been warned by the Burgundians to leave them alone, Beneke trailed them to the English coast. One galley sped on to Southampton, but the other eventually offered a fight, and after a fierce struggle resulting in numerous casualties, Beneke and the Esterlings won the day. They brought their prize back to the Elbe, where the booty was divided, and Memling's famous altarpiece eventually found its way to the church of St Mary in Danzig.[67] Even other Hanseatic towns were shocked at Beneke's daring. Hamburg and Lübeck, fearing reprisals by Duke Charles, hesitated to allow the offloading or transit of the Danzigers' spoils. The affected English merchants immediately sought the help of their king, but neither Edward's letter of protest to the duke, nor the outrage expressed by the Italian merchant community in Bruges could accomplish more than the belated and brief arrest of Hansards in Flanders.[68]

The depredations at sea continued,[69] but Beneke's notorious caper was essentially the last major engagement of the Anglo-Hanseatic War, and most certainly expedited a negotiated solution to the strife. The principals had in fact become weary of their costly and disruptive struggle. In England, Edward IV's consolidation of power had permitted him to become more independent of baronial factions, and indeed he had destroyed the enemies who once stood between him and an ambitious military alliance with the Burgundians. Such an agreement now took precedence over a maritime commercial dispute, which, in any case, had been reduced to stalemate. Royal interests now would be best

served if vessels attempting to defend English commerce against Hanseatic corsairs could be deployed exclusively against the French. Moreover, the speedy stabilization of England's national economy was
another essential preliminary to the impending struggle with France.
And, as it had been from the outset, resolve within the Hanse was also
in question. Danzig, a leading protagonist, was frustrated by non-
observance of the embargo on English goods by other Hanseatic towns.[70]
Elsewhere, and especially in Lübeck, the costs of maintaining privateers
and the defeats of the previous summer had also had a sobering effect.

The Treaty of Utrecht and internal Hanseatic divisions

Already in early 1473 English envoys had been instructed to coordinate
truces with both Denmark and the Hanse, and initiate discussions for
a new trade agreement with the Burgundians. A truce with the Danes
was agreed to in May, and by midsummer negotiations with the Hansards were set to begin. A small entourage headed by the king's secretary, William Hatclyff, first went to Bruges in an initially unsuccessful
attempt to conclude a new agreement with Burgundy, and then continued on to Utrecht and meetings with the Hansards. Waiting at
Utrecht was a Hanseatic delegation two dozen strong, led by Lübeck
Bürgermeister Heinrich Castorp. The towns of Hamburg, Deventer,
Danzig, Dortmund, and Münster also were represented, as were the
London, Bruges, and Bergen *comptoirs*.[71]

Discussions commenced on 14 July, and heated debate ensued almost
immediately. The Hansards demanded nullification of the sentence
imposed by the king's council. They protested once again that they had
been held accountable unjustly for crimes perpetrated by the king of
Denmark. Though they argued that the judgment was both legal and
just, the English envoys were understandably rather hard-pressed to
explain why the Cologners had been let off. They suggested instead that
discussions not dwell on the legality of the sentence, but rather concentrate on solutions to the situation at hand.[72] Although the initial Hanseatic request for the return of ancient privileges in England presented
no obstacle, the Esterlings also expected restitution totalling £20,000,
return of the Steelyard in London, and property for the establishment
of permanent facilities at Boston and Lynn. The Hanseatic delegation
was amenable to Hatclyff's proposal that recompense take the form of

exemptions from royal customs and subsidies, but the English ambassador insisted that he was not empowered to fix the sum. Nor would he make any commitment regarding the requests for 'houses' at Lynn and Boston, claiming such matters required parliamentary consent. His predicament was complicated still further by a Hanseatic stipulation that Cologne be excluded from all Hanseatic privileges in England until such time as the town might be readmitted into the Hanse.

Messengers were dispatched to England, and the talks were suspended during August, as English delegates awaited instructions regarding 'the 3 grete difficultes, the somme which was to excessive, the howses which wer other mennes and not the kinges, the Coloniers which had not offended.'[73] When the messengers returned and the negotiations resumed in early September, the Hansards were advised that the king's acceptance of terms would require the approval of Parliament, which would not be summoned before October. Troubled by this delay, the increasingly impatient Hanseatic contingent countered with a list of essential articles 'from which thay wold in no wise departe,' namely monetary compensation, the properties in England, and the exclusion of Cologne.[74] The particularly strong stand taken against Cologne reflects the resentment that the town's defection had caused within the Hanse: 'thay said finally in this wise: The citees of the Hanse be confedered and have advised among hem self to have no comune with the Coloniers ne to be joyned with thaim in no rome ne place ne to dwell, wher thay shuld enjoye as grete privilegges as thay have. They knew well that and thay abode in England and shuld have thaires or like privilegges, it wer certain, that thay shuld be destroyers of the Hanse.'[75] A truce extending to March 1474 was arranged, with the stipulation that the diet reconvene in January, by which time the English government was expected to have formulated a firm reply. The claims of the Hanse did not go unchallenged when the delegates finally did meet for a third time in February 1474. The exclusion of Cologne was resisted, but eventually the English consented to it and thereby managed to reduce the grant of customs exemptions to £10,000. The franchises of the Cologners in England were to be terminated by 1 August. With calculated reluctance Edward IV conceded to all the main Hanseatic demands. The English did manage to have clauses from the 1437 treaty upholding the principle of reciprocity inserted into the new agreement, but these were of little immediate importance, even though

Danzig's delegates balked at them. On the final day of February 1474 the agreement was concluded, signifying the end of the war between England and the Hanse.[76]

In the end, the Hansards had regained their ancient liberties in England, and they would not be long in re-establishing their integral place in England's overseas trade. The war had various broader implications. Modern scholarship, however, has devoted scant attention to the privateering campaigns, relying instead perhaps on E.M. Carus-Wilson's suggestion that the sea war was a 'half-hearted' exercise, and that prior to 1472 the English were too preoccupied with domestic political intrigue to carry the conflict to the Hansards.[77] In a somewhat similar vein, German scholars have, until quite recently, consistently emphasized what they viewed as a unifying and hence positive effect of the war on the Hanseatic confederation as a whole. This interpretation was pioneered by W. Stein at the turn of the century, and since then the premiss that the quarrel strengthened Hanseatic resolve and resulted in an aggressive and united campaign against the English has attracted several adherents.[78] However, in view of the numerous instances of maritime violence prior to 1468 and the obvious divisions within the Hanse that Anglo-Hanseatic disputes already had revealed, the resolve of both the English government and the Hanseatic membership remains a central interpretive issue.

There is little question that Edward IV acquiesced to the will of the Neville faction and the grievances of London's merchant community in the summer of 1468. Notwithstanding the dictates of domestic politics with which the king was confronted, the measures adopted against the Hansards lacked the coherence and perspective of previous policy. They reflected an astonishing insensitivity to the probable long-term repercussions. Surely it was apparent at the time to Edward's advisers and to those in the mercantile sector that the imposition of the council's severe sentence would provoke rather than discourage further confrontations with the Prussian and Wendish shippers. The special treatment accorded Cologne virtually guaranteed that it would. Yet this was not of particular concern to militant English merchants whose focus evidently did not extend beyond the long-sought opportunity to curtail the activity of some of their privileged foreign rivals. Initially at least, the denizen merchant community seemed content enough just to be rid of the Esterlings. Warwick and his adherents hardly intended to test the maritime prowess of the Hanse either. The earl would be well enough served if retaliation by the Esterlings destabilized North Sea commerce and ultimately diverted the attention of both Edward and Duke Charles away from France. When the inevitable Hanseatic challenge did arise early in 1470, the Crown was woefully ill-prepared. Edward was hamstrung by the renewed Lancastrian threat and Warwick's aborted insurrection.

The earl had escaped from England in the spring with several ships commandeered from ports in Devon and, upon being turned away from Calais by Wenlock, had set about attacking Burgundian and Breton shipping in the Channel. He was soon joined by Thomas Fauconberg with several more vessels. Such naval forces as Edward was able to muster were necessarily deployed against the fugitive earl and his menacing fleet.[79] Earl Rivers and Howard had chased Warwick to Honfleur by mid-June and, together with a Burgundian squadron, were blockading the bay of the Seine as Neville and Louis XI plotted the restoration of Henry VI. Only after his primary adversary was holed up in Honfleur could Rivers withdraw to the East Anglian coast to engage the marauding Esterlings. Warwick was then able to slip away to safer anchorages at Barfleur and La Hogue. Although the Anglo-Burgundian blockade of the Norman coast resumed later in the summer, it had to be lifted again in early September due to storms. By then, the Hanseatic privateers were attacking English shipping with impunity, and the 'kingmaker' still possessed a substantial navy with which to launch his successful invasion of England.[80]

The Hanseatic privateers had things much their own way throughout the next year, as Edward IV was not fully re-established in the English capital until late May 1471. But within a year his consolidation of political power did foreshadow a change in attitude toward the Hanse. The monarchy no longer was entirely susceptible to the whims of baronial factions, and there was a conscious effort to bring the conflict with the Hanse to its conclusion. Early in 1472 peace overtures were made. Howard's fleet then drove the Hanseatic privateers temporarily from the Flemish coast and eased pressure on English shipping. The English victory also caused some of the less militant elements within the Hanse to become even more amenable to a peaceful settlement. Yet Howard's success and that of other armed English merchant ships[81] was by no means decisive. Hanseatic privateers continued to operate with or without the expressed consent of their home ports, and so long as there was no agreement between England and the Hanse, harassment of English shipping could go on almost indefinitely. Moreover, at Westminster the French again were perceived as England's real enemy, and not simply in terms of European geopolitics. During the summer of 1472 French privateers were said to have captured more than twenty English ships returning to England from northern waters with valuable fish cargoes. The Hansards had made their peace with France by the end of August the following summer.[82] So, by the time Hatclyff began bargaining with Hanseatic representatives at Utrecht, peace with the Hanse had re-emerged, together with the Anglo-Burgundian alliance, as a main priority of the English government. Although realistically there could be no sustained attempt to engage the Esterlings at sea until 1472, the peace initiatives of that year, Howard's efforts, and the subsequent negotiations at Utrecht were anything but half-hearted. They reflected an earnest attempt to end the conflict quickly and by whatever means possible – either militarily or through negotiation.

Professor Postan's conclusion that the Hanse's rift with England was 'a joint concern of all the Hanseatic towns from Westphalia to Livonia'[83] essentially reiterates an interpretation that became part of Hanseatic historiography in the early decades of this century. Yet by no means does the evidence relating directly to reactions within the Hanse confirm this supposition. By 1468 the major Hanseatic trading centres east of Danzig had already demonstrated their independence with protectionist legislation regarding foreign contact with the Livonian hinterland. Riga, Dorpat, and Reval were involved only nominally in direct trade with England, and were largely unaffected by the arrests there. All three towns specifically refused to participate in the distant privateering war, and Dorpat showed little interest in a Hanseatic embargo on English cloth either. Livonian representation at Utrecht was negligible, and Riga's refusal to ratify the new pact with England illustrates still further the relative insignificance of the Anglo-Livonian connection. Riga objected to any notion of reciprocity for English merchants, and was quite indifferent to the stipulation that towns declining to endorse the treaty were to be excluded from Hanseatic privileges in England. Riga's ratification came only a quarter century later, in 1500.[84]

The initial reluctance of the Wendish towns to resort to military means stemmed primarily from the nature of their trade and the political rift with Cologne. Unlike the attacks on the Bay fleets in 1449 and 1458, the arrests in England in 1468 had not affected a fundamental link in the seaborne commerce of the Wendish towns. True, Lübeckers were important middlemen in the Norwegian and Icelandic fishing industries for which England remained a market, but the controversies of the 1450s already had diminished severely any comprehensive trade with England. Indeed, a principal Lübeck delegate at the Utrecht negotiations discouraged participation in an elaborate and ritualistic return of the Hansards to London, since Lübeck had no great trade there. The town's distributive trade in woollens remained keyed primarily to the Flemish market and the Bruges *comptoir*. Relations with Denmark and the vital Bergen *comptoir* also dictated responses within the Wendish community. During 1469, for example, mediation of the Dano-Swedish war was a priority.[85] Finally, though, the Lübeckers knew all too well the difficulty of trying to force a naval commitment against England from the rest of the Hanse, especially when the Cologne/England connection remained so strong. Lübeck's hard line against the English throughout the previous two decades had attracted markedly little support from within the confederation. When the new crisis arose, Lübeckers hesitated to commit themselves to a costly naval struggle, even though some of them no doubt realized that a resolute response to the English was probably essential. The conservative and initially indecisive course that they did adopt not only failed to impress the as yet unstable English government, but also drew contemptuous criticism from the town's strong-willed detractors within the Hanse itself.[86]

Hamburg, on the other hand, carried the war to the English with belligerent enthusiasm, as the town's proximity to the crowded North Sea shipping lanes rendered excellent the prospects for profitable privateering ventures. What is more, Hamburg's merchants and shippers had been active in the trade to England and were affected by the arrests there in 1468. They sought to recoup their losses, and stood to gain further if an advantageous peace could be imposed on the English. Shippers from Bremen, already notorious for their indiscriminate provocations, also joined the fray. That they too attacked English vessels is not surprising, although theirs was ostensibly an extraneous dispute with Antwerp, and the main focus of their campaign was Brabantine shipping.[87]

Most seriously affected by the arrests in England were the merchants of Danzig.[88] But even if they were banished from England, a modicum of versatility within the framework of their bulk carriage trade enabled them to dispose easily of more of their timber, iron, grain, and flax in Zealand, Holland, and Brabant. Supported by the neighbouring towns of Elbing and Thorn, Danzigers fought the English essentially to recover their losses and avenge the council's sentence. If privateers could eventually force England to negotiate a favourable peace, all the better. Then Danzig could well expect to recover the lucrative English market for Baltic products, and still limit reciprocal privileges for English merchants trading to Prussia.

Finally, as far as the military aspects of the war were concerned, the participation of the Westphalian towns, many of them with close trade links to Cologne, was negligible. And, if there was no unanimity regarding the use of force, its absence was exemplified still more by the apparent failure of the other standard Hanseatic weapon, the embargo on English woollens. Dortmund resisted it outright, and Danzig repeatedly complained that significant quantities of English cloth reached Breslau during the war years through the complicity of Hanseatic towns in Westphalia.[89]

This range of responses, therefore, does not indicate that by the spring of 1469 the Hanse was 'bis auf Köln wieder einig' [once more united except for Cologne].[90] Nor does it substantiate Postan's similar claim that Cologne's defection and the subsequent controversy 'restored cohesion and unity among the Hanse's other parts.'[91] Actually, nothing of this sort occurred. While Cologne's estrangement and England's challenge may have afforded the opportunity for consolidation within the rest of the Hanse, subsequent events merely demonstrated the confederation's inability to unite in the face of crisis. Except for Lübeck's disastrous participation in 1472, the sea war was fought by privateers from Danzig and the North Sea ports, as much intent on profiting from commercial violence as forcing a settlement with the English. Other Hanseatic towns watched quietly from a distance. Moreover, the internal divisions, now based on rather clearly defined economic concerns and political allegiances, had accentuated a serious element of artificiality in the Hanseatic confederation that was not easily erased by the Peace of Utrecht. Two years passed before Cologne was reinstated as a member town of the Hanse, thereby regaining, through renewed eligibility for Hanseatic privileges in England, her competitive capacity in the vital English trade. And it was not until 1476, also, that Danzig finally consented to ratify the treaty agreed upon at Utrecht.[92]

The altered commercial network

The economic effects of the dispute between the Hanse and England were not necessarily all pervasive either in England or within the Hanseatic community. The most obvious impact was felt in England's east-coast ports, where the absence of the Esterlings resulted in severely diminished woollen exports. The merchants of Cologne, however, continued to trade and maintain a high profile in southern England, especially in London and Ipswich/Colchester.

In 1468–9, when other merchants of the Hanse were imprisoned, and the status of the Cologners both within the Hanse and in England was the subject of much controversy, 'Hanseatic' cloth shipments out of London constituted less than 3% of total woollen exports from the capital. However, throughout the ensuing five-year period, which included a Hanseatic boycott of English textiles, Cologne's eventual expulsion from the Hanse, and the constant menace of Hanseatic and French privateers, the merchants of Cologne exported an average of 3,400 cloths each year from London. Although this was only about half the annual Hanseatic average for the immediate prewar period, it was, under the circumstances, a considerable achievement. During 1472–3, twenty-three different Cologne merchants had cloth customed in their names for shipment abroad from the Steelyard.[93]

Most of this English cloth would have been shipped initially to the Brabant fairs, as Cologne's primary distribution network remained relatively unchanged. There is no doubt that ports in Zealand, such as Middelburg and Veere, continued to be utilized extensively to link much of London's woollen trade to Lowland markets. In April 1472 Johann van Ae the Younger hastened to inform the Steelyard that several cargoes sent from Colchester, including those freighted in 'unsse drije smaelle scheppen' [our three small ships] had arrived safely in Zealand, and that two more vessels would shortly be ready to depart thither. By summer's end another cloth shipment destined for Zealand, and owned by the Steelyard Cologners, was robbed *en route* by French pirates.[94] The correspondence of van Ae, together with other references to the presence of business agents in Colchester,[95] assigns a significance to that port not readily discernible from customs figures. Between Michaelmas 1468 and Michaelmas 1474 only about 600 cloths were customed for export from Ipswich/Colchester by Cologne merchants, albeit these were virtually the only such shipments from any port other than London. It is entirely possible, however, that some of the woollens customed at London were initially transported overland or coastwise to Colchester, and then sent to Zealand and Brabant with the cross-Channel convoys.

Scattered particulars of accounts for the 1468–74 period do not indicate any significant change in the basic commodity structure of the Cologne/England trade. The Cologners did not, for instance, assume a much greater role in the trans-shipment of bulk iron, wood, and flax to England. While traffic in these commodities remained a part of their trade in raw materials, the movement of dyestuffs was still of greatest importance. Finished wares, such as fustian, buckram, linen, and steel also were essential to the trade. Antwerp shippers making regular calls at London during 1472–3 usually carried consignments of madder, soap, and steel for Cologne merchants, and the same was true of those who came to Ipswich and Colchester.[96] There was also an extremely rare instance of a Cologner, Simon Clementz, sending a cargo to Hull. It, too, was brought in an Antwerp ship, in the spring of 1471, and consisted of litmus, ashes, madder, oil, hops, and herring valued at £43.[97]

In addition to a reduction in the cloth export trade from eastern England, there was also, of necessity, a partial restructuring of the distributive trade in bulk freight from the Baltic. Direct shipments to English ports had ceased. Cargoes of wood, tar, osmund, ashes, and flax, owned for the most part by Baltic Hansards, were now offloaded instead at Middelburg, Veere, and Arnemuiden, or transferred there from Sluis. Large consignments of these bulk commodities, customed to Englishmen, were then reshipped from the same quays in English vessels.[98] Also, throughout 1472–3 at least, bulk cargo belonging to Zealanders was freighted to England by shippers from Veere. The inclusion of ashes, wainscots, and chests 'de Prucya' leaves no doubt as to the source of supply.[99] Aside from the obvious immediate opportunity for expanded commerce, there were other inducements to attract the Zealanders. Zealand shippers already were established in the trade to eastern England, and Veere merchants benefited from certain customs privileges there. There were reciprocal privileges for Englishmen in Veere, and in November 1471 exemption from tariffs in England was extended to merchants from Middelburg.[100]

The trans-shipment of Baltic freight via the Zealand outports certainly was not new. English merchants were active in Middelburg long before 1468, and it was not unusual for Hansards to redirect cargoes to England from the Zealand quays.[101] However, the disruption of direct Anglo-Baltic trade, which the Anglo-Hanseatic political dispute had precipitated, forced an increased reliance on this link, thus placing a new emphasis on flexibility within the distribution network. And obviously the political key to commercial flexibility in this instance lay with the Hanse's relations with Duke Charles and the counts of Holland and Zealand.

By 1472, then, the movement of Baltic wood, iron, and flax to England was not totally restricted. Though the overall volume of the trade in these products to English ports was reduced, Baltic freight was readily available in the Lowlands. The 1472–3 toll records for the Zealand quays show that shippers from Lynn, London, Hull, and Newcastle, who offloaded hides, lead, and English cheese, were supplementing their homeward-bound wine and fruit cargoes with bulk freight, especially iron and osmund. Significantly, the value of alien and denizen merchandise paying the poundage subsidy at Hull and Lynn that year far surpassed that of previous years, while at Boston and Ipswich recovery was only marginal. The majority of other consignments not intended for north-eastern England were likely carried via the shortest and perhaps safest sea route directly to London. There, too, poundage totals far exceeded even the prewar average. And only in London and Hull were there appreciable increases in the value of alien merchandise paying the petty custom. The non-denizen trade in East Anglian ports remained severely depressed.[102]

A curious entry in the Middelburg toll records also suggests that, notwithstanding the self-imposed embargo on English goods, some direct commercial contact with England may have been maintained by Hansards other than the merchants of Cologne. In December 1472, Danziger Albrecht Valand, who had been arrested at the Steelyard in 1468, was listed as the merchant on whose account a cargo of eight sacks of litmus was sent to England.[103]

Valand and fellow Esterlings also shipped textiles directly from the

Zealand outports, though obviously none of English manufacture until 1474. In 1469, well before the imposition of the Hanseatic boycott, an Enkhuizen ship had taken four 'engl laken' (sic. English cloths) to the Baltic,[104] but thereafter the records of vessels arriving and departing Danzig make no specific mention of English woollens. The likely beneficiaries of the ban were the clothmakers of Brabant, Holland, and Flanders. In addition to textiles of unspecified origin, cloth from Kampen, Amsterdam, Hoorn, Deventer, Leiden, Dordrecht, and Flanders was carried to Danzig during the war years. While most major consignments still reached the eastern Baltic via Lübeck, there were several important shipments in 1472 arriving 'uth Seeland.'[105] In addition to the increased dependence on the Zealand quays, it is also likely that the Danzigers made more frequent use of ports in Holland. According to one contemporary chronicle, fifty of Danzig's merchant ships were in Holland in the spring of 1473.[106]

Whether or not any other goods of English origin reached the Baltic is largely a matter for speculation. The most likely possibility is lead, although seaborne lead imports into Danzig from 1468 to 1472 could hardly be termed significant. The quayage records offer a hint of some trade, but no hard evidence. In 1472 the merchants of Hull brought large consignments of lead to Veere, and coincidently the only lead shipments entering Danzig during that year or the previous one arrived in ships from Zealand. The lead formed part of mixed cargoes that also included salt, wine, and cloth from Flanders and Dordrecht. One of the shippers had traded to Hull and Lynn in the mid-1460s.[107]

The importance of the Lowland shippers and, in turn, the integral function of the Zealand quays as transit points, depots, and revictualling stations for the Bay salt traders also was preserved, if not enhanced during the Esterlings' forced exile from England. Fleets of four or five dozen vessels continued to reach Danzig from Brouage and the Bay from 1468 through 1470. That several of these carriers were actually Holland or Kampen vessels is verified by the Danzig chronicles. In 1470 they brought so much salt to Danzig that the market was glutted and prices fell. Only a single ship 'uth der Baije' is listed in the Danzig records for the following year. However, 24 of 25 vessels 'von Amsterdam' and 'von Campen' brought salt cargoes, and so did seven other carriers from Holland and Zealand.[108] Ports and countries listed in the Danzig accounts apparently do refer to places whence the ships actually departed. Although many shippers from the Bay are easily indentifiable as Hollanders, Zealanders, and Danzigers, there is little doubt that most of them were in fact returning from the Biscay coast. Many other ships identified as coming from Zealand likely weighed anchor at the Bay as well, and had called at Middelburg, Veere, Arnemuiden, Vlissingen, or Zierikzee to revictual and take on additional cargo. Or, alternatively, they refreighted salt already stockpiled at the Zealand quays. The role of the Zealand carriers in Danzig's salt trade was just as significant in 1472, when the Bay fleet, consisting of 29 vessels, was augmented by 26 Zealand or Veere ships also laden at least partly with salt.[109]

The Lowland shippers were the principal non-Hanseatic carriers in the salt trade to the Baltic. It is not surprising that more of the trade should have accrued to them while the Hanse's disputes with England and then with the French disrupted shipping lanes along the Atlantic seaboard. The deployment of Danzig ships against foreign enemies likely reduced the tonnage available on the Bay routes. Moreover, the Franco-Hanseatic dispute, which was not formally resolved until the summer of 1473, must have increased the risks to Baltic skippers in the long-distance carriage trade. By contrast, although the Hollanders and Zealanders were not necessarily safe from French privateers and the likes of Warwick, their access to supply sources for Bay salt was not unduly restricted by extraneous political feuds between the Hanse and the sovereign states.

The extant Danzig records that run from 1468 through 1472 indicate that the Bay ships seldom freighted anything except salt, and the cargoes are merely listed together with the shippers' names. Normally, however, some indication is given of the ownership of salt and mixed cargoes brought to Danzig from the Lowland ports. The vast majority of these salt shipments belonged to prominent Danzig merchants with already clearly discernible Atlantic trade connections.[110] And they continued to be served by some of the agents previously active in trade between the eastern Baltic and England. Of the Esterlings importing both Bay salt and Baltic goods into Zealand by 1472–3, several had been involved in direct Anglo-Baltic trade prior to 1468, and at least two, Danzigers Albrecht Valand and Hans Barenbrock, were refugees from the London Steelyard.[111]

The Hanseatic salt fleet also included a number of Danzig skippers recently displaced from the trade with England. Paul Nymann and Albert Kloffamers, who had freighted cargo to Lynn in the mid-1460s, were hauling salt home from the Lowlands in 1471–2. The next year Nymann offloaded salt in Zealand. Paul Roole also joined the salt ships during the war years and in 1475 he was still traversing the Bay route with Paul Beneke and Derick Schach. Heinrich Schroder and Kersten Kosseler, both of whom had called at English ports prior to the war, also brought salt cargoes to Hansards at Veere in 1473, and were sailing for Brouage again in the spring of 1475. Such was not the case, however, with the two Danzig captains arrested at Hull in 1468. Eler Bokelman had joined the Hanseatic privateers, while his colleague, Martin Happe, withdrew to the relative tranquillity of the Danzig/Stockholm run during the Anglo-Hanseatic hostilities.[112]

The treaty that officially ended those hostilities was concluded in February 1474, and the immediate postwar period, leading up to Cologne's reinstatement as a member of the Hanse in the autumn of 1476, was one of transition for the Anglo-Hanseatic trade, particularly in London. Although merchants from Cologne remained in the English capital, they were required to vacate the London Steelyard within a year. Understandably reluctant to do so, they complained to Danzig, Lübeck, and King Edward, and even threatened economic reprisals of their own. By May of 1475, however, they were preparing to evacuate their charters and books from the Steelyard archive. Cologne was readmitted to the Hanse the following year, but the other Hanseatic merchants in London did not consent to readmit the Cologners to the Steelyard until 1478.[113] The Esterlings themselves evidently did not begin returning to England in significant numbers before late 1474. The merchants of Hamburg were only ready to freight ships to London in the spring of 1475.[114]

The provisions of the Utrecht treaty, and their subsequent implementation – specifically the Hansards' exemption from royal customs and subsidies – afford a unique opportunity to delineate Cologne's contribution to London's foreign trade, as well as the Hanse's role in the regional economies of eastern England and the impact thereon of the Anglo-Hanseatic conflict. Because they had been banished from the Hanse in 1471, the merchants of Cologne were excluded from the exemptions. Hence, customs enrolments for London, where most of the Cologne trade was concentrated, distinguish Cologners from Hansards throughout the late 1470s. For this period, therefore, the volume of the Cologners' cloth exports can easily be determined within the larger 'Hanseatic' total. Furthermore, since the Hansards were excused from paying the petty custom, enrolments also make the distinction between Hanseatic and other alien merchants, both in London and the east-coast ports, in some instances on into the 1490s.[115]

The return of the Esterlings to London in 1474–5 did not compensate immediately for a severe reduction in cloth exports by denizen and Cologne merchants. However, by the following year the cloth trade had rebounded dramatically. Total cloth exports from the capital topped 34,000 units. The combined Cologne/Hanseatic total represented a quarter of the aggregate, and Cologners alone shipped almost 3,000 cloths. Although increases in aggregate 3d custom totals were less startling, it is clear that the Esterlings soon reacquired a large share of London's non-denizen trade in miscellaneous goods as well. The Hanseatic share of petty custom merchandise in the capital soared from 19% in 1474–5 to 30% the following year.[116]

Outside of London, effects of the prolonged dispute varied.[117] During the absence of the Esterlings, the value of merchandise paying the petty custom at Lynn was halved, and cloth exports became insignificant. However, the port's trade was revitalized during the 1474–6 period, as cloth exports quickly rose to prewar levels, with the returning Hansards accounting for 78% of the aggregate volume. Similarly, there was a surge in the value of non-denizen merchandise subject to the 3d custom, and 30% of the trade was Hanseatic.

A rather different story unfolded at Boston. Throughout the period 1468–74, when Lynn's trade was reduced to a trickle, Boston's cloth exports remained relatively constant, averaging about 500 yearly, with other aliens making significant, albeit temporary, inroads. But after 1474 English merchants and non-Hanseatic aliens virtually abandoned Boston's cloth trade to the Hansards, and apparently clung instead to the port's sporadic but as yet not entirely depressed wool trade. Even so, Boston's postwar cloth export trade was greatly reduced. Furthermore, the traffic in miscellaneous merchandise had declined by a full 75% during the war years, and there, too, recovery was by no means immediate or permanent, even though the Hansards accounted for 44% of nearly £1,000 worth of petty custom goods exchanged in 1475–6.

At Ipswich/Colchester, despite some shipments by the free Cologners, the cloth export trade was greatly diminished during the war years. Only in 1475–6 was there a short-lived recovery to the prewar volume, and in that year 63% of total woollen exports were customed to Hansards. The trade in goods subject to the 3d tariff was also devastated by the Anglo-Hanseatic conflict, and except for a temporary surge in 1474–5, no postwar recovery ever materialized.

Far to the north, at Hull, the two years immediately following the Utrecht treaty saw the value of miscellaneous goods traded by Hansards and other aliens average £2,580 – double the prewar average. In the interim it had slipped to under £850 annually. Cloth exports had slumped badly before 1467–8 and had averaged fewer than 700 cloths annually during the hostilities. They now increased threefold, with the Hanseatic share exceeding 44%.[118]

The postwar resumption of trade out of England is also reflected in the Danzig *Pfahlkammerbücher*.[119] In 1474 only two ships voyaged from Hull to Danzig, but the next year saw seven vessels reach the eastern Baltic from England, and in 1476 there were at least twelve. Principal cargoes consisted of cloth, lead, and small consignments of Gascon wine, augmented by salt (including Bay salt) and Spanish wine. However, among the merchants listed with the cargo inventories only a half dozen non-German names appear, and almost all of the major woollen cargoes belonged to Hansards. The only certain English carrier was Lynn skipper Robert Bees, who came to Danzig in 1475 and again the next year. His presence there represents the extent of an apparently modest effort to re-establish direct English participation in the Baltic trade in the mid-1470s. But this is hardly surprising, for the English were placed at a disadvantage almost from the outset. Much of their merchant marine was requisitioned in 1475 for Edward IV's planned invasion of France. This effectively permitted the Esterlings to reassert their dominance of the shipping lanes between England and the Baltic, uncontested. And the timing was crucial, since the resumption of trade to the Baltic after such a prolonged disruption, together with an impending war against the French, augured well for the traffic in wood, iron, and grain.

CHAPTER IV
AFTER UTRECHT: THE TURBULENT 1480s

The war between England and the Hanse in the early 1470s had disrupted English commercial traffic to the Baltic and had led to important modifications within a broad international trade network. This was particularly true with regard to the role of the Zealand quays and the fairs they served at Antwerp and Bergen op Zoom. The permanence of these changes would be tested over the next fifteen years, and their impact mirrored in both the development of English overseas commerce and the emergence of new and distinct patterns within the Hanseatic trade. On the diplomatic front, relations between the English government and the Hanse would remain cordial for a time, only to deteriorate again as the 1480s wore on. Long before then, however, international trade and commerce would feel the effects of other profound political changes on the Continent.

New challenges and old controversies

The great English invasion force crossed to Calais in the summer of 1475. But when the anticipated military support of the Burgundians was not forthcoming, Edward accepted Louis XI's offer of a seven-year truce and a generous pension, and took his army back to England. In January 1477 Duke Charles was slain in battle at Nancy, and with him died the grand schemes for an Anglo-Burgundian military alliance. Nevertheless, a new treaty of mercantile intercourse between England and Burgundy was agreed to the following year.[1] For more than a decade after the duke's death, though, the Burgundian Lowland territories, and especially Flanders, were threatened with French invasion and ravaged by civic revolts against the Hapsburg regent, Archduke Maximilian of Austria. By 1485 the disruptions caused many Hanseatic and Italian merchants in Bruges to evacuate to Antwerp, where the Hanse's extensive trading freedoms had been confirmed for an extended period. Three years later, in an apparently deliberate move to avenge his temporary imprisonment at Bruges in February 1488, Maximilian ordered other foreign merchants to transfer to Antwerp also.[2]

The Hansards' main competitors in the English woollen trade at the Brabant marts were the London and York merchants, who continued to oppose the privileged status of their foreign rivals in England.[3] But in 1480 their repeated complaints about the lack of reciprocal rights in Hanseatic territory failed to gain royal support. Again in December 1482 merchants from York were preparing to seek a 'remede' against the Hansards in the coming Parliament, for, it was claimed, 'the Estyrlyngs cumys in to thys pairts, and has thair fre bying and fre selyng in thys land, and ... ynglish marchaunts cannot so hav in thar cuntreis.'[4] A list of more specific grievances, likely dating from the 1480s and perhaps compiled in support of this initiative in Parliament, accused the Esterlings of taking the profits they earned on their bulk freight out of northern England and not reinvesting in commodities available there. Strangers coming to York were said to deal only with the Esterlings, who allegedly knew every market town and village from Newark to Carlisle. The York men further complained that English merchants in Hanseatic (sic. Baltic) towns were not allowed to do business with strangers or to sell retail, as their German counterparts could do in England.[5] Early in the new year, however, merchants of the Hanse were among those exempted when Parliament granted a subsidy on aliens to help finance war against the Scots. Nor was there any discernible change in the attitude of the Crown following the untimely death of Edward IV in 1483. Richard III reconfirmed Hanseatic privileges, and so, too, did Henry VII in 1486, over the objections of merchants from Hull, York, Lynn, and London.[6]

This round of protests centred specifically on the Hansards' preferential customs and subsidies rates in England, and their dominance of the Bergen and Icelandic fisheries. Additionally, English merchants complained that they were deprived of old privileges and freedoms in Hanseatic towns, especially at Danzig, where they also claimed to have possessed dwellings in times past.[7] While this latter concern was only of indirect significance with regard to commercial traffic over Brabant and thence to eastern markets, the differential tariffs in England were indeed contentious, since they placed denizen merchants at a disadvantage in their own cloth export trade. But neither revocation of the entrenched Hanseatic exemption from poundage nor a reduction in rates applicable to native merchants could be expected from the Crown, so again blame was focused instead on the Hansards themselves. Just how deeply they had come to be resented in some quarters is apparent from one of the contemplated remedies. Little more than a decade after the agreement at Utrecht, aggrieved London mercers evidently viewed the resumption of war as a viable alternative to the status quo: 'so were beter ... to vorsoken de beteringe und remedie hijervan dorch openbayr orloge und strijde, it costete dat rijke van Englande wat it weuld.'[8]

On the high seas, too, the comparative tranquillity of the immediate postwar period faded quickly. Lübeckers and Bristol fishermen skirmished off Iceland, and a Scottish vessel *en route* from Leith to Flanders with a cargo of grain and jewels belonging in part to merchants from Lübeck was taken by English pirates in 1476. That same summer the *Jacob* of Hamburg, bound for London with £600 worth of fish from Iceland, ran aground off Hartlepool and was attacked and destroyed by bandits. A similar incident, involving a Danzig ship stranded near Yarmouth, occurred in 1477.[9] Yet, relative to the apparent bedlam of past decades, and despite quarrels between Holland and the Wendish towns that lingered on until the close of the 1470s,[10] incidents of piracy involving Hanseatic and English ships were at worst sporadic until renewed hostilities with Scotland and Denmark ushered in another sustained disruption of the seaborne trade. In the early 1480s a number of Hanseatic vessels were plundered, some by English warships ostensibly deployed against the Scottish foe.[11] Moreover, in May of 1481 England had acquired yet another enemy when young King John was elected to the Danish throne. The Anglo-Danish truce, so vital to England's Baltic trade aspirations, had been renewed twice during the late 1470s, but Danish attacks on English shipping and John's use of Esterling mercenaries now fuelled antipathy in England and led to new charges of Hanseatic collusion and piracy.[12]

Aside from the increasingly frequent trouble on the northern routes, mercantile shipping in the Narrow Seas also was disrupted from mid-November 1487 until early April 1489 by the first of a series of

English embargoes on direct trade with the Lowlands. It was imposed in the first instance as a punitive response to the involvement of the Burgundian ducal house, and specifically that of dowager Duchess Margaret, in the failed Yorkist rebellion of 1487.[13] Already for more than a year, though, English attempts to negotiate a commercial agreement with the now Emperor-elect Maximilian had been unsuccessful. As early as November 1486, therefore, English merchants had contemplated evacuating from his dominions. Moreover, since that time the English government also had been reinterpreting and enforcing parliamentary statutes to limit the thriving Lowland trade of London's Hanseatic merchants. Despite the intrigue surrounding the Yorkist pretender, Lambert Simnel, and the alleged complicity of some English merchants, members of London's merchant guilds had continued to do business as usual in the Lowlands. Henry therefore ordered them to cease trading to and from the lands of the 'King of Romans' by 15th November.[14] Hanseatic merchants in England also were obliged to comply with the ban, although thinly veiled coercion and restrictions on the export of unshorn English woollens had been hampering their trade since the previous autumn.[15] In any event, the subsequent embargo was imposed at the height of political turmoil in Flanders, with English trade there already compromised. The drapery towns of Bruges and Ghent were in open revolt against Maximilian, and as if marauding bands of mercenaries and the constant threat of French military incursion were not enough to disrupt normal commercial traffic, maritime skirmishes involving English and Flemish vessels provoked additional violence directed specifically at the English merchant community.[16] Though amenable to a new commercial treaty with England, Maximilian was barely holding his own against the rebellious towns, and so lacked the requisite political security for a meaningful trade pact.[17]

Until it was rescinded in the spring of 1489,[18] the restriction virtually closed down England's direct export trade to the Lowlands, and therefore significantly affected not only the English economy but also important sectors of the continental trade. In particular, the Cologners, who normally shipped great quantities of English woollens to Brabant for eastward distribution via Cologne and Frankfurt, were forced to alter their central distribution network. Although the Cologne merchants were still sending English cloth to markets as far off as Venice in 1487, they alone declared lost profits of £1,000 sterling at the Antwerp, Bergen op Zoom, and Frankfurt marts when their shipments from England that year were hindered.[19] Subsequently, they were bound by affidavits submitted to the king's treasurer to stop shipping to Maximilian's Lowland ports. Instead, they had to reroute their consignments far northward over Hamburg, Kampen, and Groningen and cart them south again to interior markets and distribution points.

Another option, and one on which the English merchant adventurers became particularly dependent, was to redirect the woollen trade to Calais. However, while Calais might serve as a continental gateway and attract a range of European buyers for cloth as well as wool, there were obstacles. The protectionist ordinances of Bruges and the Flemish drapery towns restricted the onward movement of English cloth. Only Hanseatic merchants were allowed to transport foreign woollens through the county to inland markets.[20] So the majority of English cloth consignments still had to be trans-shipped coastwise – that is to say, by sea from Calais – to Brabant or elsewhere. Here too, though, the limitations of Calais as a potential entrepôt and transit centre were accentuated by the prevailing political instability in Flanders. Insurrections there periodically made coastal traffic as well as the road to Bruges insecure for those attempting to move merchandise to or from the town.[21] As much as commercial traffic was threatened and obstructed, however, Calais did manage to serve as a conduit for some woollen shipments and for England's import trade. Despite the risks, diverse Hanseatic-owned cargoes of wainscots, hops, and tar were being directed there from Antwerp in 1488 and, in incidents not directly related to the Anglo-Hapsburg feud, Cologners from the Steelyard also had pepper, textiles, thread, and dyestuffs distrained at Calais the following year.[22]

Even with the rerouting of shipments via Calais and the northern Hanseatic ports, there was a reduction of about 20% in aggregate cloth exports from London during the two Exchequer years affected by the ban. Especially hard hit were the English merchants.[23] Consequently, the embargo had the subsidiary effect of rekindling English interest in an alternative overseas market, specifically the Prussian staple at Danzig. So the Baltic trade and, hence, England's relations with Denmark and the Hanse once again demanded the attention of the English government. Since the early 1480s Anglo-Hanseatic relations had been deteriorating steadily, but by the autumn of 1487 the English Crown was floating proposals for a formal conference with Hanseatic representatives. This initiative coincided exactly with the troubles in Flanders and King Henry's Lowland trade embargo.[24] Of special interest to the English at this point was the possibility of expanding their commercial presence in the Baltic. In relation to the overall volume of denizen woollen exports from England, Danzig had become a distant secondary market, and was likely to remain so indefinitely, so long as the Brabantine connection could be maintained. However, the Anglo-Lowland dispute was threatening to disrupt routine traffic in the Narrow Seas for an extended period. Against this backdrop of uncertainty, then, there was a renewed interest in the Baltic – a market that had been of little importance to English woollen exporters throughout most of the preceding decade.

The obstacles in the way of a shift to the Baltic trade were not insuperable, the most obvious hindrance being the escalating cycle of violence in northern waters. This was largely a by-product of King John's demonstrated animosity toward England, together with Anglo-Scottish hostilities that did not abate until a truce was agreed to in 1486. Passage to the Baltic via the Sound, as well as access to the much coveted Icelandic fisheries, ultimately hinged on relations with the Danes. But Danish hostility and King John's use of Esterling mercenaries had provoked considerable bitterness, and inevitably this came to bear on relations with the Hanse. In northern England improprieties by customs and law enforcement officials were augmented with arrests and attacks on Baltic ships. A series of indentures between the Crown and various towns and individuals in 1487 required authorities in all major English ports to arrest the spoils of pirates and ensure that English skippers kept the peace with the king's subjects and allies. With accusations against Esterling mercenaries proliferating in the north, this new delegation of responsibility for sea keeping likely exacerbated the already aggravated relationship with the Baltic Hansards.[25] By early 1488 the hostility at Hull had become so intense that the London *comptoir* felt obliged to prohibit Hansards from going there, as their physical safety could not be guaranteed.[26] Other confrontations at sea, including several with French and Scottish ships, now were occurring with alarming frequency.[27]

The atmosphere in London, where the Steelyard merchants continued to be vexed by statutes restricting the export of unfinished cloth and the trade in Cologne silk, was hardly better.[28] There, too, ships from the Baltic were seized, crew members injured, and cargoes spoiled. Established merchants from Cologne were accused of abetting piracy, and consequently saw their goods attached at Calais. A Hanseatic messenger was assaulted on the road to Dover, and in 1490 Cologners resident at the London Steelyard were waylaid in broad daylight while leaving church. Gerhard van Wesel's younger brother, Peter, was mortally wounded, but the assailants, though identified, went unpunished.[29]

Both of the principal Hanseatic subgroups in England – the Esterling shippers who served the east-coast ports, as well as the merchants from Cologne, Danzig, Hamburg, and various other Hanseatic towns who worked out of the Steelyard – were faced with difficult predicaments stemming in part from their peculiar roles within the commercial network. Passage through the Sound was now crucial to the international trade of the Danzig staple, and was not to be jeopardized wilfully by any careless affront or challenge to the Danish king over his periodic attacks on English shipping or his hiring of mercenaries. With the Danes apt to search any Hanseatic vessel at Helsingor, merchants and shippers could risk possible arrest for freighting goods belonging to Englishmen, so Danzig was understandably reluctant to antagonize King John any further.[30] Paradoxically, the wrath of the discontented merchants of northern England was directed largely at the Baltic skippers, who were endeavouring, albeit in their own interest, to maintain rather than eliminate the tenuous trade link with England. The vulnerability of the Hansards in London was no less acute. It is most unlikely that they were involved directly in the robberies of English ships, since the potential repercussions on the vital London trade would have outweighed by far any possible benefits. Though they enjoyed relative autonomy in affairs pertaining to the Steelyard, they could not do much to affect the demeanour of gangsters on the high seas. They remained at the mercy of the xenophobic element in the capital, which required little enough by way of pretext to vent frustrations against them, in forms ranging from parliamentary lobbying aimed at the curtailment of Hanseatic freedoms, to simple physical intimidation. There was a natural reliance on the Hanseatic leadership, such as it was, to mount a diplomatic defence of the Hansards in England and if possible bring to justice those responsible for the piracies.[31] Unfortunately, so far as the London *comptoir* was concerned, Lübeck, Danzig, and other Hanseatic towns often appeared more interested in the redistribution of English customs rebates than in the precarious position of the Steelyard community itself.[32]

Negotiation of a new Anglo-Danish accord in 1489 appeared to be the first step toward ending the confrontations at sea and lessening tensions in the Anglo-Hanseatic sphere.[33] It permitted the English to trade to Iceland upon obtaining licences every seven years from the Danish Crown. And by guaranteeing mutual freedom of navigation and commerce, it also partially cleared the way for possible English commercial expansion in the Baltic. By the time the accord with Denmark was ratified in 1490 King Henry's Lowland embargo had already been lifted. However, the interruption of the Narrow Seas trade, together with the spiralling disruption of northern routes, had provided the impetus for a successful diplomatic initiative – one that would attempt to lay the foundations of a contingency network for the English woollen export trade. The other essential prerequisite was the articulation and confirmation of English rights at the Prussian staple. To this end pressure on England's Hanseatic community was not eased. Seizures of Hanseatic vessels continued, and the English government turned a deaf ear to Cologne's appeals against attachments of goods. Along with the harassment in London, this was interpreted by Cologne as another deliberate attempt to force her *Englandfahrer* out of the kingdom. In response, the Steelyard archive and treasury were evacuated, and the Lübeck *Hansetag*, which convened in October, recommended an immediate and severe reduction in Hanseatic trade to England. But with crisis looming ever closer, the assembly finally heeded the fears of the beleaguered Steelyard merchants, and consented to a conference with English envoys in the new year.[34]

Following a winter of preparation, talks between English and Hanseatic officials opened rather inauspiciously at Antwerp in late May 1491.[35] The English delegation, led by jurists Edmund Martin and William Warham, was a month late in arriving, and their expressed preference to treat only with delegates from Lübeck, who ostensibly represented the entire Hanse, offended the other assembled emissaries from Hamburg, Danzig, Münster, Deventer, and Nijmegen. Already the contingent of Cologners was unhappy that Lübeck should be heading the Hanseatic delegation in the first place, and made no secret of their displeasure. As far as the more pertinent issues were concerned, it was anticipated within the membership that Hanseatic commercial interests in England would be served well if a conciliatory response could be coaxed from Danzig's representatives regarding familiar English complaints about allegedly unfair restrictions at the Prussian staple.[36]

Detailed summaries of the injuries and transgressions committed during the previous decade – most relating to piracy, robbery, or extortion – were exchanged, but the dominant issue to emerge from the ensuing four weeks of talks was indeed that of English access to Prussia. As a consequence, the onus for any agreement shifted largely to the Danzigers, whose mandate stipulated that English status at the Prussian staple should remain the same as other non-Hansards ('glick anderen copluden uther hanse in gliker wisze').[37] Warham and Martin were reminded that the granting of trading privileges in Prussia technically was not within Danzig's jurisdiction, but rather a matter for the king of Poland and his vassal, the master of the Teutonic knights. In so far as trade in Danzig was concerned, however, the English were offered as much freedom as they were supposed to have had for the past sixty years. This meant that they were welcome to come to the *Artushof*, but like other non-Hansards, their direct commercial contact with foreigners, such as the Russians, Poles, Lithuanians, and native Prussians who also traded at Danzig, would be confined to the *Dominikmart* each summer.

Although the Danzigers did not view them as new concessions, these articles became the basis of a notarial instrument, drafted on 22 June, which ultimately satisfied the English negotiators.[38] The two sides then agreed to curtail open hostility and study other unresolved issues for one year before reconvening discussions. In the interim, although the restrictions on exports of unshorn English cloth were not lifted, all existing Hanseatic privileges and exemptions in England were to be respected. Notwithstanding the manifold grievances of both sides, another extremely volatile situation had been defused. In the end, the Prussian staple was the key to reconciliation, just as it also had been, perhaps, to much of the violence and intimidation that preceded the formal discussions.

A multitude of restrictions, the diligence of local sheriffs, and a pervading air of hostility had made the situation of the Hanseatic *England-fahrer* difficult in the extreme. This, in turn, eventually helped bring about the sessions at Antwerp, where, against a backdrop of continued piracy and harassment,[39] the English envoys succeeded in their goal of obtaining clarification of the status of Englishmen in Prussia. Together with the recent Anglo-Danish accord, this would form the legal foundation of any new commercial initiative in the Baltic. The compromise at Antwerp also alleviated the most serious difficulties of the Hansards in England and so fostered the normalizing of Hanseatic trade to and from the kingdom.

England's Baltic trade

According to the established traditions of English historiography for the period, the Anglo-Hanseatic War and the Treaty of Utrecht were the death knell for English trade to the Baltic in the fifteenth century.[40] Yet, if the absence of the English from the Baltic trade extended beyond the mid-1470s, it must have had a significant effect on the regional economies of eastern England. Moreover, the legal status of Englishmen in Prussia had not been altered by the treaty. So if there was a prolonged English absence from the Baltic, was it the result of protectionist restrictions at Danzig, or might it somehow have been linked to a newly evolving commercial network that had been necessitated, in part, by the recent Anglo-Hanseatic conflict?

In northern England, customs records for Hull and Newcastle, incomplete as they are for the late 1470s and the 1480s, do not suggest a very significant role in direct Anglo-Baltic commerce for local English merchants. It was the Danzigers who exchanged bulk cargo at the Tyne and Humber ports, primarily for coal and lead, and they did not carry freight for indigenous traders. While the York mercers complained of restrictions in Hanseatic towns, the accusations by Hull shippers against Esterling pirates and mercenaries do not imply that vessels from the Humber were attempting to trade to Danzig. The most controversial incident involved English ships returning from southern waters. Other victims were, for the most part, shipping to either Zealand or Iceland.[41] The Icelandic ventures, moreover, would have automatically courted trouble with the Danes and the Esterlings in their service.

Elsewhere, patterns of trade varied. At Boston, English skippers offloaded fish and refreighted cloth for Hansards, but here again the connection likely was with Iceland. For some years during the 1480s no Hanseatic goods at all were customed at Boston, while in others large consignments of Baltic forest products were discharged from Danzig ships exclusively for Hanseatic merchants.[42] This contrasted sharply with the situation at nearby Lynn. In 1475 Lynn merchant/shipper Robert Bees brought cargo to and from Danzig for Esterlings and fellow Norfolk merchants John Belles and John Biston. He also returned to Danzig in 1476. A year later, another English vessel, homeward bound from Prussia, with goods belonging to English and Danzig merchants, was wrecked by storm off the Pomeranian coast. The *Christofer* of Lynn was in Danzig in 1479, and the link was still intact the following year, when two Lynn vessels returned home laden exclusively with Baltic cargo for Lynn and Danzig merchants. A third apparently was pirated *en route*.[43]

For the next half decade there is a paucity of customs evidence, but presumably English shipping to the Baltic was again severely restricted by the Danes. Nevertheless, combined cargoes belonging to Esterlings and denizens, carried by English as well as Hanseatic vessels, attest to the maintenance of the tenuous commercial ties between Lynn and the Danzig staple throughout the 1480s. Bees and indigenous merchant Richard Peper exported cloth from Lynn in the spring of 1484 in a Hamburg ship that also carried cloth for Danzigers. In light of Bees's previous and subsequent involvement in the Baltic trade, it is entirely possible, though not certain, that the cargoes were destined for Danzig, either via Hamburg and Lübeck, or directly via the *Umlandfahrt*. Still other Lynn merchants freighted a cargo of cloth, coverlets, caps, needles, and pins with Danzig skipper Laurence Fredeland, while Lynn captain Roger Petman offloaded a wax consignment for Danziger Albrecht Valand. Again in 1487 Bees freighted both import and export merchandise aboard a ship from Hamburg, and also was one of three indigenous merchants and a pair of Danzigers exporting woollens with Lynn merchant/shipper John Brekersley. The cargo of wood and fish oil with which Brekersley returned to Lynn also belonged to both denizens and Hansards. Before the end of the decade traders from Lynn complained of the robbery of other cargoes shipped from Prussia, but in 1490 and 1491 Brekersley, Bees, and others were still bringing bulk freight to Lynn in Danzig ships.[44] John Belles and fellow merchant Thomas Carter also had a hand in negotiating the new Anglo-Danish mercantile treaty of 1490, which, among other considerations, provided for freedom of navigation for English shipping.[45]

The extent to which Londoners and other merchants from southern

England may have been involved in postwar trade to Danzig is difficult to determine, since very few complete customs particulars survive for the capital or for Ipswich/Colchester. Indigenous merchants did not share in the large bulk cargoes discharged from Hamburg and Danzig ships at southern English ports in the early 1480s, nor again a decade later. It is impossible to say where substantial similar cargoes carried by denizen shippers may have been picked up. It is apparent, though, that Londoners and their colleagues in Essex and Suffolk did not employ Hanseatic carriers to bring bulk freight directly from the Baltic.[46]

From 1475 through 1491 there was, then, a perceptible reorientation of eastern England's overseas commerce vis-à-vis the Hanse. The port of Boston still served the Hanseatic Bergenfahrer, and some English carriers were employed in the fish trade to Norway and Iceland. But active English participation in the Baltic trade apparently reverted to a small nucleus of merchants and skippers from neighbouring Lynn, who used both Hanseatic and English shipping to maintain connections with the Danzig staple. For the merchants of northern England, however, the trend was away from the Baltic routes. The Esterlings continued to supply Hull and Newcastle with essential forest products and iron, while the denizen trading community was drawn more toward the lucrative trade across the Narrow Seas, to Zealand and the Brabant fairs.

An essential consideration in assessing this post-1475 modification of England's overseas trading network and its significance is that the only cloth exporting centre of national importance north of Ipswich/Colchester was Hull. The port served the Yorkshire woollen manufacturers, and as the cloth export industry developed during the second half of the century, merchant adventurers from Beverley, York, and Hull, though still conscious of the Baltic market, were drawn naturally to the great marts at Antwerp and Bergen op Zoom. That they already relied heavily on the Lowland market is reflected in depressed cloth export totals for Hull during the Burgundian embargo on English woollens in the mid-1460s. The ensuing five-year conflict with the Hanse, during which English exporters were cut off totally from the alternative Baltic market, accelerated the shift to Brabant, where English cloth and lead could be exchanged readily for bulk raw materials, luxury goods, and manufactured wares. Commercial links between northern England and the Zealand ports thus became more firmly established during the war years. And after the hostilities between

England and the Hanse had ended there was little incentive to alter the new status quo. True, it no longer was necessary to fetch bulk cargo stockpiled at the Zealand quays, since the Esterlings again supplied Hull directly from Danzig. But the merchants of Yorkshire were now attracted by a diverse range of goods available in Brabant, and what they probably perceived as a more secure and dynamic market for their cloth and lead than the distant Danzig staple. Besides, in the Baltic, English cloth exporters would be forced to compete in a long-distance trade not only with the Hansards, but also with the shippers from Brabant, Zealand, and Holland, who already had achieved a foothold. Numerous varieties of cloth manufactured in Holland were being freighted to Danzig by Amsterdam shippers in the 1480s.[47] The controversies with Denmark, which threatened English access to the Baltic anyway, ensured that the new focus of northern England's export trade would continue to be the Lowlands. In 1486 several hundred of the 1,162 cloths exported from Hull by English merchants were sent to the Cold fair at Bergen op Zoom, where toll collectors made specific reference to the English 'Hulfaerder' and the value of their imports.[48] And, although complete records have not survived, it is logical that the same merchants also shipped substantial quantities to the Antwerp fairs.

The English presence in the Baltic was indeed nominal up to 1491. However, the notion that English merchants were barred by protectionist statutes or hindered by non-observance of the terms of the Utrecht treaty is unconvincing. Quite simply, the export trade of another of England's major regional economies, that of the northern drapery towns, had been siphoned off by the Brabant fairs – a process that had been encouraged by the war between England and the Hanse. After 1475 the Baltic trade was left to the Esterlings themselves and the merchants of Lynn, who did in fact maintain their commercial links with Danzig.

The drastic reduction in annual cloth exports from Hull at the end of the decade illustrates the relative importance of the Hansards there and of the ties with the Brabant fairs. The feud with the Esterlings temporarily reduced the Hanseatic portion of Hull's cloth trade to insignificance. But equally important was Henry VII's prohibition on exports to the Hapsburg Lowlands, which severely restricted denizen exports to Brabant. No doubt the frustration caused by this obstacle also contributed in some measure to the wave of anti-Hanse sentiment in the north. Yorkshire merchants had not been particularly active at the alternative market at Danzig for more than a decade, but now, in addition to specific and legitimate complaints against Esterling mercenaries, there was a coincidental revival of the age-old complaints of restrictions in Hanseatic towns. As in the past, English merchants sought to assign blame for all manner of economic hardship to the foreign merchant community. And once again, the highly visible Baltic skippers, with their great ships riding at anchor off Hull and Scarborough, were easy targets.

England's Hanseatic communities

The Hanseatic contribution to various regional economies in England was by no means static. Nor had it ever been. The volume and, hence, overall importance of Hanseatic trade varied from port to port. In the 1480s, in the wake of the Utrecht agreement, there occurred yet more noticable adjustments in the distribution of the Hanse's English trade. Again, customs records, though not offering a complete picture for the ports concerned, make possible a closer examination of the general nature and broad significance of these developments.[49]

a. The North

The regional character and focus of the overseas commerce of northern England is illustrated in the combined and interrelated trade of Hull and Newcastle. And, although customs evidence is fragmentary for the late fifteenth century, some key facets are discernible, especially so far as the Hanse is concerned.[50] Aggregate cloth exports from Hull averaged 2,247 annually from 1476 through 1484, peaking at 3,709 units in 1480–1. The Hanseatic share rebounded and stabilized during the early 1480s at a consistent 20% to 25% of the yearly totals. The mid-1480s, however, saw the beginning of a severe economic slump from which the port did not fully recover until the turn of the century. The trade was especially devastated during the late 1480s. Commercial traffic at Newcastle is first reflected in quantitative customs evidence contemporaneous with Hull's quarrel with the Esterlings at the end of the decade. Consignments of raw wool, lead, hides, and coal were shipped to foreign markets, including Zealand, but cloth exports from Newcastle were not significant. Fewer than 200 units were taxed for shipment from the end of October 1487 to Michaelmas 1491. During the same period, however, alien merchandise subject to the petty custom tariff was valued at £1,166, and more than half of this was Hanseatic. This trade heavily favoured Hanseatic imports. In the summer of 1481 merchandise exchanged by Hanseatic merchants at Newcastle was valued at only £150, and the ratio of their import to export values was 2.5 to 1. In 1488–9 the value of Hanseatic goods jumped to £473, but the ratio of imports to exports remained unchanged.

At Hull, meanwhile, the Exchequer year 1487–8 saw the lowest aggregate petty custom total since the close of the Anglo-Hanseatic War, and the next year the alien trade in miscellaneous goods was still worth less than £1,000. Initially, then, when the trade at Hull was threatened, the Esterlings apparently turned to Newcastle as an alternative access point to the northern English market. However, alien trade figures at Newcastle are relatively low for the next two years, and totals for Hull, which indicate a resurgence there in 1489–90, misrepresent the volume of voluntary Hanseatic trade. At least one of the five Danzig skippers recorded in the Hull customs particulars had been forcibly diverted to the Humber by disaffected English captains. In addition to royal customs and subsidies, various other sums were extorted from the Hanseatic cargo owners.[51] The ship's intended destination had been Lynn, and there is in fact a marked decrease in the alien trade totals at Lynn for this year. Those for Hull and Newcastle for 1490–1 offer, perhaps, a truer reflection of the situation in the north as the Hanse deliberately reduced trade to England. They show that the alien trade at both ports had been brought to a virtual standstill.

During the periods when the Hanseatic trade in northern England was not totally obstructed, it continued to be based on bulk imports, brought directly from Danzig or across from Hamburg or ports in Zealand, and on exports of lead eventually destined for the Baltic region or Brabant. As at Newcastle, the principal agents in this traffic were the merchants of Danzig and their factors. They offloaded more than £1,400 worth of goods at Hull and Scarborough during the summer of 1483, but refreighted minimal cargoes consisting of a few cloths, coverlets, and alabaster altarpieces. Yet Hanseatic merchants, including those from Danzig, exported more than 100 woollen cloths from Hull, presumably to Zealand, in ships from Veere. The remainder of the Hanseatic cloth exports for 1482–3 must have been shipped prior to 9 April, when surviving particulars of accounts commence. They most assuredly were

Cloth Exports 1476–86

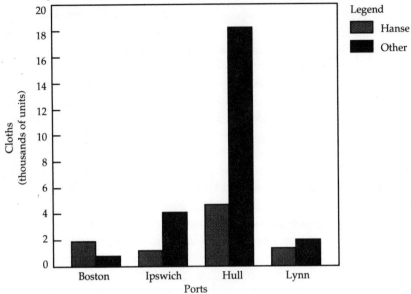

Petty Custom Merchandise 1476–86

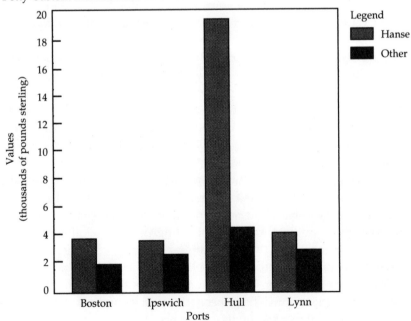

not sent directly to Danzig during the preceding winter months, and therefore the most plausible destination would be Zealand or perhaps Hamburg. At decade's end, in 1489–90, at least half of the £1,495 worth of alien merchandise subject to the petty custom at Hull was carried by Danzig skippers, who in turn refreighted virtually all of the Hanseatic cloth exports, as well as £178 worth of lead.[52]

b. The Ports of the Wash

Although the Hansards maintained a presence in both ports, it is evident that they sustained much stronger commercial links with Lynn than with Boston. Especially important in this respect were the ties with Hamburg and Danzig. Actually, Lynn's importance in the bulk carriage trade from Danzig to the east coast ports north of the capital was surpassed only by that of Hull. And when the Esterlings were unwelcome in the north, Lynn also served as an alternative conduit for their trade. In contrast to Boston also, Lynn began to develop a more diversified export base during the 1470s and 1480s, which compensated, to a degree, for a declining cloth trade. Pewter, hides, and cargoes of lead that had come coastwise from the north frequently augmented the meagre cloth shipments from Lynn. Boston's export trade, on the other hand, continued to be one-dimensional. When the traffic in cloth there was diminished, only the traditional wool fleets to the Lowlands remained.

Except for a brief resurgence in 1478, the cloth export trade out of Boston never recovered to its prewar level, and by the mid-1480s was only marginally significant. However, from Michaelmas 1476 to Michaelmas 1485 £5,791 worth of alien merchandise was exchanged at Boston, and two thirds of it was Hanseatic. During the ensuing twenty-four-month period no merchandise at all was customed to Hansards at Boston, and the value of the alien trade plummeted correspondingly to only £148. There was a partial recovery during the next two years, when the Hansards returned, and a great surge in 1489–90, as 95% of £1,243 worth of petty custom merchandise belonged to Hansards. Their importance to Boston's overseas trade is illustrated equally well in figures for the following year, when their absence caused the value of 3d custom goods to drop to a mere £41. It is clear, therefore, that the Hansards were the principal alien traders at Boston, but that they came there on an intermittent basis, and were not drawn particularly by the cloth export trade.

All of the £210 worth of Hanseatic miscellanea recorded at Boston in the Exchequer year 1483–4 was customed to only three Hanseatic merchants, and consisted entirely of fish and oil imports. The same three Hansards also accounted for all of the 152 Hanseatic cloth exports. Significantly, though, the cargoes – both imported and exported – were freighted with local Boston shippers, as was the £450 worth of fish, osmund, and oil imported in November 1484. This represented the total value of Hanseatic merchandise paying the petty custom in the Exchequer year 1484–5. The only other surviving particulars of accounts for this period, however, show that two years later Danzig ships freighted all of the Hansards' 67 cloth exports and discharged £263 worth of wood, tar, osmund, and bowstaves. This was the aggregate value of Hanseatic 3d merchandise for 1487–8, when the ratio of Hanseatic import to export values, inclusive of cloth exports, would have been almost three to one.[53]

Initially, then, the Hanseatic trade at Boston, though intermittent, was integrated with English commercial interests to the extent that the *Bergenfahrer* employed English carriers to haul fish cargoes. By the late 1480s, however, Boston merchants and shippers evidently had forfeited their role in the Hanseatic trade, which apparently reverted to the Danzigers, who brought bulk freight as well as fish. The trade of the Danzigers was deflected to Boston in part because of the difficulties they were encountering in northern England at the time. Since the beginning of the decade, though, they had also asserted themselves in the Icelandic fish trade.[54] A substantial share of their shipping already served the English and Atlantic seaboard trade, and the port of Boston already was an established distribution centre for stockfish. Perhaps, too, the physical presence of the Hansards generally, and Lübeckers in particular, at Boston was sustained more consistently than trade figures suggest. Only three Hanseatic merchants owned cargo customed there in 1484. A certificate, dated May the following year, which verified the status of Hanseatic merchants for customs officials, also lists only three. In 1487, though, Lübeck merchants were occupied in disposing of the property of one Hans Brinck, a *Bergenfahrer* recently deceased at Boston. The post-mortem inventory of Brinck's belongings in the English port included a pack of leather, eleven kersey cloths, blankets, and stocks of fish, yet no Hanseatic trade was recorded at Boston for this year, and Brinck's name appears on none of the surviving English customs documents.[55]

Elsewhere, at Lynn, cloth export totals for the late 1470s were somewhat lower than those prior to 1468, and there was a severe decline during the mid-1480s, particularly in the denizen sector. By then, annual aggregate cloth exports of around 200 units were usual. There was a spectacular increase to almost 1,000 cloths in 1488–9, with Hansards shipping 80%, but thereafter the trade declined again. From Michaelmas 1487 to Michaelmas 1489 there were also huge increases in the value of petty custom merchandise at Lynn, as Danzig shippers redirected much of their trade at Hull southward. The £3,038 worth of miscellaneous goods customed to the Hansards during this period represented 89% of the total for aliens. Prior to this, the annual total seldom exceeded £1,000, although the Hanseatic share was always significant.

Beginning in 1480–1 there is a wealth of customs particulars for Lynn, and they offer a good indication of the commodity structure, shipping patterns, and main participants in the trade there.[56] In November 1480 two Lynn skippers, in all probability returning from Danzig, offloaded bulk freight for both Danzigers and local English merchants. The following March, the *Godyer* of Hamburg weighed anchor at Lynn with a grain cargo valued at £38. The ship returned in July with osmund, wax, pitch, tar, and boards, and left Lynn again with coverlets, rabbit skins, grain, cheese, and eighteen cloths for Hanseatic clients. Also aboard was similar mixed cargo and 67 cloths customed to four English merchants. Still more bulk freight belonging to Hansards was discharged that summer from a Danzig vessel, which subsequently departed laden with only ten cloths and a few coverlets. A second Hamburg ship carried the remaining 155 Hanseatic cloth exports from Lynn in July, and half that many again customed to denizens. Virtually all of the Hanseatic trade was transacted through the agency of the ships' captains and a half dozen merchants from Hamburg and Danzig. Wax imports also were significant, and on the basis of values entered by customs officials and estimated values for cloth, the ratio of total Hanseatic import to export values was two to one. The pattern was much the same for 1483–4. The carriers were from Lynn, Danzig, or Hamburg, and both Hansards and Englishmen shared in the cargoes. Consignments of Newcastle lead augmented the cloth exports.

By 1486–7, though, only two Hanseatic ships – one each from Hamburg and Danzig – called at Lynn, and except for a few thousand rabbit pelts valued at £18, all of the £256 worth of Hanseatic petty custom merchandise was imported. Again, while the Hanseatic ships carried most of this freight plus additional cargo for indigenous merchants, some Hanseatic consignments also were carried in English ships. Hansards, for example, shipped 40 cloths with John Brekersley of Lynn in May 1487 and also owned part of his return cargo of wood and fish oil. A Calais vessel also brought wainscots, trays, and tar worth £14 for Hamburg merchant/shipper Lutkyn Smyth. The ship from Danzig called in September and did not depart Lynn until 4 October (sic. in the Exchequer year 1487–8). The outbound cargo consisted of three cloths and £34 worth of coverlets and pewter.

The following summer three Danzig captains returned, but except for some ashes, oil, flax, and counters customed to Robert Bees, the bulk cargo they offloaded belonged exclusively to Hansards. While the English role was apparently lessened, rather more Hanseatic merchants, approximately ten in all, now shared petty custom imports valued in excess of £800, and the Hanseatic cloth exports, which reached 280 units for the year. They also shipped almost £200 worth of coverlets, lead, pewter, and hides out of the port. There was little change during the next two years. All Hanseatic petty custom imports, along with small consignments of bulk freight belonging to local merchants, were discharged from Danzig ships. Throughout the 1480s Lynn's Hanseatic trade was carried on by merchants or their factors, whose civic affiliation was either Hamburg or Danzig.

English merchants had become reintegrated into the established network by the end of the decade. Several more indigenous traders had inbound cargo in the ship of Danziger Hans Laurence, who arrived at Lynn in October 1490 and apparently wintered there. The cargo he departed with the following spring also was shared by English as well as Hanseatic merchants, though it was plundered on the return voyage to Danzig by pirates from Honfleur.[57] A Hamburg ship, the only one listed in customs particulars since 1487, also discharged £32 worth of Bay salt, fish, and wood for Hansards in 1491, and another Danzig ship returned in September of that year with a large consignment of bulk freight and £5 worth of flax for John Brekersley. In total, Hanseatic petty custom imports for the year were valued at £436 and exports £147.

Lynn was by no means the only harbour in Norfolk where Esterling ships could be found, but in terms of sustained Hanseatic trade it undoubtedly was the most important. The interest of the Hansards in

Yarmouth, for example, though temporarily spurred by their exemption from royal customs and subsidies, had waned again by the early 1480s. Local customs yield the names of a few Danzigers and Hamburg merchants trading there in the late 1470s, and enrolled accounts record the export of eighty cloths by Hansards in 1479–80. They also received a customs rebate that year of £4 13s 1d for goods that had to have been valued at more than £372. For subsequent years, however, no woollen exports from Yarmouth were customed to Hansards. Nor do the local records suggest the existence of a Hanseatic import trade after 1482. The only exception came in the early 1490s, when Hamburg merchants paid cranage fees for cargoes of wax, beer, and gunpowder. Equally limited was the Hanseatic trade at neighbouring Blakeney. The six pieces of double worsted cloth shipped from there in 1483 were the only recorded Hanseatic exports from that port for the entire decade. Nevertheless, the carrier was Hanseatic, again pointing to the intermittent presence of such shippers along the Norfolk coast.[58]

In accordance with the Utrecht treaty the Hansards were given properties at both Boston and Lynn in the spring of 1475. The working environment in which individuals or groups of Hanseatic merchants subsequently conducted business likely did not vary greatly in the two towns, and the essential characteristics of the Hanseatic houses offer some insight into the day-to-day life of Hansards in the Wash ports. Prior to 1475 Hanseatic merchants had rented these buildings and/or various other gardens, cellars, and waterfront storage facilities. A 1476 memorandum containing a description of the Boston house indicates that the Hansards had been given a very rudimentary structure, comprising ten rooms with seven chimneys. It was in urgent need of repair when the Hansards assumed possession, and its upkeep continued to prove costly well into the next decade. In 1481 both the building and the wharf were so 'bowfellich' [dilapidated] that the *Hansetag* granted the *Bergenfahrer* at Boston £20 from the customs rebates to cover repair costs. A like sum was needed again less than three years later for the same purpose.[59]

Rather more is known of the property at Lynn, just a short distance away, since some of the original buildings have survived. In 1476 they, too, were described as very old and consisting of seven 'huysse' [houses], with ten rooms and eight chimneys. A kitchen, hall, and courtyard are also listed among the other distinguishing attributes. Much of this has endured centuries of flooding and neglect, and some of the original buildings have been altered considerably since their original construction. They occupy a long rectangular site adjoining the south quay on the right bank of the river Ouse. Built around a quadrangle with about 22 metres of frontage on the river, the structure extends a length of 61 metres to its eastern end where the dwelling units were located. The three-storey north wing is constructed of brick, and while much of it was rebuilt in the late sixteenth century, some sections are much older. The long south side of the quadrangle consists of two-storey warehouses constructed of brick and timber. Constant dampness and frequent flooding in times past have ensured that little remains of the original timber work. The west quarter, adjacent to the quay, is also entirely of brick. It contains a small hall with a collar-beam roof, and most likely served as a dining area.[60]

The Hanseatic facility was but one of several commercial houses in the port of Lynn. Together with neighbouring mercantile establishments such as Hampton Court and Clifton House, it is representative of the general character and physical continuity of the waterfront district at the close of the Middle Ages. Here the Hanseatic merchants and factors lived and worked. Within the confines of their houses they took their meals, socialized, slept, stored merchandise, and transacted business. At the wharves along the river ships offloaded lead from northern England, forest products from the Baltic, North Sea stockfish and herring, and diverse products from western Europe. They set sail again laden with English cloth, coverlets, Newcastle lead, pewter, grain, and cheese, as well as wool for the Calais staple. Although the Hanseatic trade to England was inevitably linked to inland market towns, the Esterlings relied heavily on east-coast harbours such as the ports of the Wash, where their business activities came to be centred around newly acquired facilities, especially the one at Lynn. It was counting-house, dwelling unit, warehouse, and distribution centre, and a focal point for the Hanseatic trade to eastern England.

c. Ipswich/Colchester and the London Steelyard

The mention of 'resedencie' at Boston, Lynn, Ipswich, and 'in alle Engelandt' in the Steelyard memorandum of 1476 is a broad reference to communities of Hanseatic merchants outside London. It does not imply the existence of Hanseatic *comptoirs* throughout England during the final quarter of the fifteenth century. Unlike the Wash ports, there is no clear indication that the Hansards maintained a *comptoir* at either Ipswich or Colchester. Evidently merchants from Cologne had maintained their own 'houses' at Colchester in the 1440s,[61] but in later years they may have simply rented dwellings and storage facilities in these towns as the need arose. A suit heard at Chancery in the mid-1460s involved a Hanseatic merchant who had hired storage space for woad in Colchester from a local cloth dealer. In 1491 Hermann van Ae, a Cologne merchant with Steelyard affiliations, boarded in Colchester for a period of eleven or twelve weeks at a house belonging to 'hardwareman' John Ambrose. It is most doubtful he would have needed to do so had the Hansards possessed a facility at Colchester or Ipswich like those at Lynn and Boston.[62]

Aggregate cloth exports from Ipswich/Colchester remained consistently low throughout the 1476–91 period, and never reached the prewar average in any given year. The apparent decline is reflected almost entirely in the severely reduced export trade of the Hansards, whose yearly cloth shipments seldom reached two hundred units in the early 1480s and were still well under a thousand by the end of the decade. However, the Hanseatic traffic in English woollens at Ipswich/Colchester continued to be an extension of the London trade, and the true volume is difficult to determine, since most overseas shipments by the Steelyard Hansards were at least customed in the capital. The value of petty custom merchandise at the Essex and Suffolk ports also saw a decline to half the prewar annual totals or less. Although, as usual, the Hansards' share was always significant – in 1485–6 they were responsible for all of the 3d goods recorded by customs officials – there were drastic fluctuations from year to year, and an overall decline in the value of the trade. There are, however, too few particulars of accounts to permit an estimate of the Hanseatic trade balance over a prolonged period. In 1481–2, with cloth exports static at around two hundred units, the Hanseatic trade would have been in balance. But only a year earlier the Hansards had more than £1,100 worth of 3d merchandise customed, and in all probability most of it consisted of imported goods.[63]

Regardless of the decline in trade, there was a sustained Hanseatic presence at Ipswich/Colchester throughout the late 1470s. Included among those allowed customs rebates were Joris Tack (Duisburg), Heinrich van der Heth (Hamburg), and Hans Stutt (Danzig) – all established Steelyard merchants. From time to time, the London *comptoir* was required to issue certificates for the use of customs officials, verifying the 'Hanseatic' status of merchants. Such a certificate is appended to the 1481–2 particulars of accounts for Ipswich, and fourteen merchants are named. About a dozen individuals actually had merchandise customed.[64] Cologners exported cloth and English cheese, and imported woad, cork, and mixed cargo, often in English ships. A Veere shipper also offloaded wainscots, iron, pitch, wax, salmon, and 'roysonz' for the Hansards. There was one major cargo of bulk commodities, including bowstaves, iron, boards, vast quantities of fish, and 'hedcloth' – a typical import from Hamburg. This cargo was freighted exclusively for Hansards. Hanseatic cloth exports hardly compared to past averages, but still half of the year's total was shipped in August and September of 1482, the usual departure period for sailings to the Brabant fairs.

The only other extant customs records of use for this period are the incomplete and much damaged particulars and controlment of customs and subsidies for 1487–8. They are of some interest, however, as direct shipments to Zealand and Brabant were forbidden at this time. Of the 348 cloths exported from Ipswich/Colchester that year, 187 left aboard two Hanseatic vessels in October 1487. These ships also carried £48 worth of lead, and no cargo was freighted for non-Hanseatic merchants. The ship carrying the greater share of the cloth was captained by Joachim Hommond, whose home port was Hamburg. His arrival in England preceded the start of the 1487–8 Exchequer year, but the profits of his expedition are recorded in the Hamburg chamberlains' accounts. Whether or not his cloth cargo was trans-shipped from the Elbe to either Brabant or the Baltic is impossible to ascertain. However, Hommond's voyage illustrates another increasingly important link in the Anglo-Hanseatic trade, which was being strengthened as cloth shipments were temporarily diverted away from the Lowland ports.[65]

Although the Hansards continued to do business in the ports of Ipswich and Colchester during the final quarter of the century, the focal point of the Hanseatic trade in southern England unquestionably was London. Fifty-three different Hansards were represented at the Steelyard (i.e., had goods customed for export in their names) in 1477–8. At least twenty of them were from Cologne. Others, whose civic affiliations can be determined readily, came from Danzig, Hamburg, Lübeck, Soest, Nijmegen, Duisburg, Münster, Deventer, and Dinant. And, although the

CHART 2 *MAJOR STEELYARD MERCHANTS 1480–1*
[From PRO E122 194/25]*

Merchant & Civic Affiliation	Cloths exported	Value of petty custom exports	Value of petty custom imports	Value of wax imports
Johann van Armesbury	543	£91	£814	–
Tydemann Barck (Lübeck)	504	£65	£562	£230
Hans Culle	594	£116	£675	£570
Albrecht Valand (Danzig)	585	£175	£256	£360
Roger van Feld (Cologne)	544	£55	£825	£214
Matthew Hynkelman (Dorpat)	505	£32	£476	£188
Heinrich Lathusen (Hamburg)	667	£80	£1564	£44
Gerard Lesborn (Kampen ?)	647	£79	£424	£475
Anthony Odyndale (Cologne)	263	£13	£728	–
Lambert Rotard	173	£101	£887	£86
Johann Russynthorp (Cologne)	494	£73	£875	–
Johann Salmer (Dinant)	131	£191	£675	–
William Schaphusen (Soest)	880	£77	£112	£846
Peter Syber (Cologne)	367	£78	£680	–
Arnold van Stalle	213	£42	£912	–
Hans Stutt (Danzig)	1218	£167	£695	£1029

* Printed in *The Overseas Trade of London Exchequer Customs Accounts 1480–1*, ed. H.S Cobb, London Record Society Publications XXVII, 1990.

names of some merchants inevitably disappear from subsequent records, new ones take their places, and the overall composition of the Steelyard community *vis-à-vis* the towns it represented did not drastically change. In any event, the significance of civic affiliations should not be exaggerated with regard to the probable destinations and eventual distribution of export cargoes. Again in 1480–1 five dozen or more Hanseatic merchants had goods shipped either to or from London, and regardless of who actually owned the majority of the woollen shipments, much of the cloth export trade was concentrated in Brabant. While the Cologners formed by far the largest subgroup at the Steelyard and were particularly dependent on the Bergen op Zoom and Antwerp fairs, they by no means completely dominated the Hanseatic traffic out of London. About one third of the combined Cologne/Hanseatic cloth exports from London during the five Exchequer years ending Michaelmas 1479 were customed to Cologne merchants.[66] Of the 14,079 cloths exported by the Hansards during 1480–1, several Cologners shipped between 250 and 400, and others still fewer. Hans Stutt, one of a half dozen Danzigers trading out of London that year, exported well over one thousand cloths. Fellow Danziger Albrecht Valand and Lübeck merchant Tydemann Barck combined for another thousand, and William Schaphusen of Soest/Dortmund, who shipped 880 cloths, was also among the top Hanseatic exporters. Aside from cloth, in which almost every Hansard had an interest, there was some specialization with other commodities, most notably by Johann Salmer and Franck Savage of Dinant, who were the most conspicuous Hanseatic pewter exporters based in London. Among the 'specialist' importers were Anthony Odyndale, dealing in Cologne silk, and Lambert Rotard, who brought in several consignments of steel.[67]

For their trade to Zealand and Brabant the men of the Steelyard hired Hanseatic, English, and Lowland carriers, and also had at least one vessel of their own operating out of London year-round during the early 1480s. Narrow Seas shipping was non-seasonal, but there were peak periods coincidental with the fairs. Six different sailings are recorded for the *Maria de Steleyard*, commanded by Lubert van Boke. The ship sometimes was in port for two weeks or less, and was invariably freighted with woollens and small miscellaneous cargoes when it departed the capital. Its inbound cargoes consisted, just as invariably, of mixed consignments of goods typically available at the Lowland marts. Linens and metalwares were particularly important, and the clientele was not exclusively Hanseatic. Englishmen, Hansards, alien merchants, and even the duchess of Burgundy freighted cargo in this vessel.

At least ten other Hanseatic shippers also called at London in 1480–1. Hamburg was home port for half of them, and four others were from Danzig.[68] They brought large bulk cargoes (wood, osmund, tar, etc.) and left London with cloths, various other woollens, cheese, pewter, and hides. Virtually no cargo was carried in these ships for non-Hansards. Some cloth may have been taken across the Channel, but unlike the mixed ownership of most cargoes bound for Zealand, the large woollen consignments carried in Hamburg and Danzig vessels in September 1481 belonged almost entirely to resident Esterling merchants, and may well have been carried to the Elbe or perhaps Prussia. In the autumn of 1480 two Hamburg ships and one from Danzig offloaded bulk freight exclusively for Hansards. Reladed with cloth, the Hamburg carriers were gone again within a month. The Danzig ship, unable to return to

CHART 3 *COMPOSITE OF HANSEATIC SHIPPING IN LONDON 1480–1*
[From PRO E122 194/25]

Shipper & Civic Affiliation	Date of arrival	Principal cargo	Date of departure	Cloths of assize and other principal cargo*
Lubert van Boke (Steelyard)	02.10.1480	mixed cargo	16.10.1480	52 cloths / mixed cargo
Godard Wrede (Hamburg)	14.10.1480	bulk freight	24.11.1480	367 cloths / straights
Jaspar Boke (Hamburg)	26.10.1480	bulk freight	20.11.1480	236 cloths / pewter
Clays Bylle (Danzig)	13.11.1480	bulk freight	06.04.1481	479 cloths / rabbit skins
Lubert van Boke (Steelyard)	01.12.1480	mixed cargo	09.12.1480	16 cloths / straights
Lubert van Boke (Steelyard)	07.03.1481	mixed cargo	14.03.1481	259 cloths / straights
Matthew Brom			28.03.1481	356 cloths / straights
Lubert van Boke (Steelyard)	14.04.1481	mixed cargo	26.04.1481	367 cloths / russets
Heinrich Castor (Hamburg)	13.05.1481	bulk freight		
Jaspar Boke (Hamburg)	17.05.1481	bulk freight	04.06.1481	735 cloths / russets
Lubert van Boke (Steelyard)	14.16.1481	mixed cargo	04.06.1481	332 cloths / russets
Lubert van Boke (Steelyard)	21.07.1481	mixed / bulk		
Hans Hagen (Hamburg)	21.07.1481	bulk freight	03.09.1481	470 cloths / russets
Clays Bartold (Danzig)	21.07.1481	bulk freight	03.09.1481	603 cloths / pewter
Hans Ruting (Danzig)	21.07.1481	bulk freight	03.09.1481	657 cloths / russets
Jacob Spisholt (Danzig)	28.08.1481	bulk freight	03.09.1481	251 cloths / russets
Detlef Salman (Hamburg)	30.08.1481	fish	22.09.1481	139 cloths / mixed cargo

* Cloth totals for consignments owned by Hansards.

home waters so late in the year, wintered in England, and left London only in April 1481. It carried cloth cargoes for several Esterlings, as well as a small consignment for two denizens. The spring of 1481 also saw two Hamburg ships again in port, offloading bulk freight and relading cloth for Hansards. Over the course of the summer, three Danzig vessels and yet another from the Elbe continued the pattern. The only deviation came a few days before the departure of these four ships in early September, when the *Nicholus* of Hamburg arrived with a cargo consisting entirely of fish and fish oil. It was valued at more than £400 and was customed to a single Hanseatic merchant. By the third week of September this ship, too, had departed London, but with rather small consignments of cloth and mixed cargo for Hansards and a couple of alien merchants. Cargoes of imported salt were insignificant for this particular year, and the Hansards, in any event, were not involved.

Fragmentary customs records for the early 1480s offer no hint of appreciable change in the Hanseatic trade in London. Another ship, the *Julyan de Stileyard*, joined van Boke and the others plying the Narrow Seas, and six vessels from Danzig and Hamburg were in the Thames in the summer of 1483. At least five were there in 1488.[69]

The essential shipping patterns that became established during the 1476–91 period are again easily discernible in London customs records for the Exchequer year 1490–1, notwithstanding a deliberate reduction in the Hanseatic trade in England that year. On 30 September 1490 van Boke and three other Hamburg vessels cleared London with more than 4,000 cloths customed to Steelyard merchants. Shortly thereafter, two Danzig ships discharged bulk cargo at London, and they, too, left with woollen consignments in early November. At the end of October, meanwhile, two more Hanseatic skippers, likely coming from Hamburg, brought in fish and bulk cargo, and another two Danzigers offloaded salt. The latter pair remained in London until well into the new year, when they departed with cloth, but one of the others, Cort Defort, stayed only a fortnight, leaving with a cloth cargo in mid-November. Three of the four shippers who had departed London in September, including van Boke, returned with mixed cargo in mid-December, and all three of them left again in early April, laden with cloth. So, too, did one of the Danzig salt ships that had been in port since the previous autumn, and still another that had arrived with a salt cargo in March. Defort and two more ships, perhaps from Hamburg, were back in the Thames in August 1491, discharging bulk freight, wax, and fish.[70]

It is clear, then, that in addition to the *Maria* of the Steelyard, at least two Hamburg ships were employed year-round on the London/Zealand/Brabant route. Indeed, one of those skippers who left London with

CHART 4 *COMPOSITE OF HANSEATIC SHIPPING IN LONDON 1490–1*
[From PRO E122 78/9]

Shipper & Civic Affiliation	Date of arrival	Principal cargo	Date of departure	Cloths of assize and other principal cargo*
Lubert van Boke (Steelyard)			30.09.1490	452 cloths / russets
Harman Beckman (Hamburg)			30.09.1490	1066 cloths / russets
Hans Merghbrough (Hamburg)			30.09.1490	565 cloths / russets
Jacob Hammod (Hamburg)			30.09.1490	2037 cloths / russets
Laurence Fredeland (Danzig)[1]	31.09.1490	bulk freight	04.11.1490	511 cloths / russets
Ulryk Bernys (Danzig)[1]	31.09.1490	bulk freight	04.11.1490	314 cloths / russets
Cort Defort (Danzig ?)	26.10.1490	fish / bulk	12.11.1490	712 cloths / russets
Hans Rutter	26.10.1490	fish / osmund		
Harman Brogelman (Danzig)	26.10.1490	salt	04.02.1491	62 cloths
Dominic Aalant (Danzig)	26.10.1490	salt	09.03.1491	hides / lead
			11.04.1491[2]	692 cloths / russets
Lubert van Boke (Steelyard)	16.12.1490	mixed cargo	07.04.1491	805 cloths / russets
Hans Merghbrough (Hamburg)[3]	16.12.1490	mixed cargo	11.04.1491	853 cloths / russets
Harman Beckman (Hamburg)	16.12.1490	mixed cargo	11.04.1491	1263 cloths / russets
Hans Mulner (Danzig)[1]	02.03.1491	salt	13.04.1491	1029 cloths / hides
Cort Defort (Danzig ?)	11.08.1491	fish / bulk		
Niclaus Semlond (Hamburg ?)	11.08.1491	fish / bulk		
Derik Plagin (Hamburg ?)	11.08.1491	fish / wax		

* Cloth totals for consignments owned by Hansards.   [1] The Danzigers Fredeland, Bernys, and Mulner were all at Brouage in the summer of 1492. *HUB* XI no. 640.
[2] Aalant was pirated off Walchern a few days later. 'Caspar Weinreichs Danziger Chronik,' *Scriptores Rerum Prussicarum*, ed. T. Hirsch, IV 782.   [3] Merghbrough was pirated *en route* from Zealand to England later in the summer. *HUB* XI no. 505–6.

cloth in early April was pirated on his return voyage from Zealand later in the summer. From among the vessels bringing salt from the Bay or fish and bulk freight from Hamburg a fourth or even fifth ship was added to the cross-Channel run during peak seasons in April and September. In addition, the Steelyard merchants, and especially the Cologners, made regular use of English carriers serving London and the Lowland ports.[71]

The London trade of the Danzig shippers was fully integrated with a wider range of comprehensive interests along the Atlantic seaboard. The Danzig captains who arrived in London in the autumn of 1490 had sailed directly from the Baltic following the *Dominikmarkt* in August. Within a few weeks of their arrival in the capital they discharged their bulk cargoes and refreighted English woollens, likely for transport to Zealand. From there they may well have joined the Bay fleet before eventually heading home. Both of them, as well as a third Danzig captain who called at London during the Exchequer year 1490–1, were at Brouage a year later. Likewise, the Danzig carriers bringing salt to England in midwinter most probably came from the Bay. They reladed woollen cargoes, and their subsequent departures coincided with the fairs in Brabant. Shipper Dominic Aalant left Danzig fully laden in 1490, but arrived in the English capital in October with a cargo of salt. He was pirated off Walchern (Zealand) by mariners serving Philip of Kleves on 17 April 1491, shortly after his departure from England with almost 700 cloths belonging to Steelyard Hansards.[72]

Finally, the shippers who arrived in August represent another principal link in the Hanse's London trade. They could have come from Zealand, but the composition of their cargoes, owned almost exclusively by Hamburg and Danzig merchants, suggests they weighed anchor at Hamburg. They offloaded large fish cargoes, linens of north German manufacture, and Baltic products such as wax, osmund, and wood. Hamburg shippers made regular trips to England in the 1480s and early 1490s, while at the same time securing a major role in the Icelandic fisheries. Up until the late 1480s they could carry Icelandic fish directly to England. Early in 1489, however, in order to protect beer and bread provisioners in Hamburg, the town required all her *Islandfahrer* [traders to Iceland] to revictual in Hamburg prior to any onward journey. Thus, Hamburg's position as a transit point linking the fish trade with England was reinforced, and thereafter a fundamental shipping pattern developed, which endured well into the next century. Skippers returning from Iceland would offload some of their fish cargoes and take on other freight, including linens from the northern German towns and Baltic goods that had reached the Elbe via Lübeck, and then sail to England. Or they could transfer fish cargoes to ships waiting to depart thither. Vessels came back from England laden with cloth, both for domestic consumption in and around Hamburg, and for trans-shipment eastward. This aspect of the trade had been enhanced already, when Hansards were forced to divert English cloth exports over Hamburg during Henry VII's restrictions on direct sailings to Zealand and Brabant in 1487–8. Moreover, the England/Hamburg link could easily accommodate Hanseatic shippers who found it worthwhile to vary their itinerary in Atlantic waters, and not necessarily come as far as London. Cort Defort, for instance, was in England again in January 1492 with another cargo consisting of fish, typical Baltic commodities, and a selection of linens, including varieties manufactured in Osnabrück and Hamburg. He offloaded his cargo not at London, however, but at Ipswich.[73]

The volume of the Hanse's London trade mirrored the course of Anglo-Hanseatic political relations. Aggregate Hanseatic cloth exports from London hovered around 10,000 units for 1490–1, a figure comparable with totals for the 1470s, but not with the significantly higher yearly average for the 1480s.[74] The low total may be attributed to the intentional reduction in the trade, as Hanseatic relations with England reached a low ebb on the eve of the Antwerp diet. Understandably, the only other notable decline in the cloth trade out of the Steelyard came when Hansards were forced to abide by English restrictions on cloth exports. In a 21-month span beginning in December 1486 Hansards shipped only 21,748 cloths from the capital. But the denizen exporters were apparently hit even harder by the Lowland embargo. During the same period they managed to export only about 15,000, which was far fewer than usual.[75]

About four dozen Hansards still traded out of the London Steelyard in 1490–1, and this group included at least eighteen Cologners and ten Danzigers.[76] The cloth exports were relatively evenly distributed. Leading exporters included Danzigers Hans Stagnet, with more than 900 units, and Hans Mulner, with almost 800, but several of the Cologne and Danzig merchants, as well as Tydemann Barck, shipped between

CHART 5 *MAJOR STEELYARD MERCHANTS 1490–1*
[From PRO E122 78/9]

Merchant & Civic Affiliation	Cloths exported	Value of petty custom exports	Value of petty custom imports	Value of wax imports
Tydemann Barck (Lübeck)	566	£26	£85	£100
Hermann Bergentrik (Hamburg)	732	£85	£893	–
Johann Blitterswik (Cologne)	518	£103	£372	–
Dethert Brander (Danzig)	250	£13	£31	£180
Peter Ecksted (Danzig)	422	£146	£289	£86
Johann Greverod (Cologne)	442	£29	£25	–
Arnold Metelar (Danzig)	593	£129	£465	£70
Hans Mulner (Danzig)	791	£104	£82	£232
Hermann Overcamp (Danzig)	510	£103	£191	£22
Hermann Plough (Danzig)	499	£133	£180	£416
Johann Questenberck (Cologne)	449	£77	£329	–
Hermann Rinck (Cologne)	469	£58	£189	–
Berthold van Ryne (Hamburg)	329	£21	£585	–
Peter Sano (Danzig)	496	£64	£300	£42
Johann Symlinck (Cologne)	279	£116	£283	–
Hans Stagnet (Danzig)	944	£138	£250	£126

400 and 600 cloths. Hamburg merchant Hermann Bergentrik also accounted for more than 700.

Fluctuations in the Hanseatic import trade for the 1476–91 period are more difficult to detect than those in the woollen export trade.[77] In 1476–7 the recorded value of Hanseatic 3d merchandise was £7,487. Following a brief decline the next year, it increased steadily and by 1481–2, the last year Hanseatic totals are distinguished from the alien aggregate in the customs enrolments, it had virtually tripled to more than £22,000, and accounted for more than half of the total value of the non-denizen trade. Moreover, Hanseatic wax shipments for that year peaked at 3,560 quintals. Rated at £2 the quintal by the London customers, this wax added another £7,100 to the value of imports. There is no way of assessing the volume of trade during the rest of the 1480s, as the Hanseatic totals are buried in the enrolled figures for aliens, and there are no particulars of accounts on which to base any calculation. However, a breakdown of the 1490–1 particulars shows the value of Hanseatic 3d merchandise was a disappointing £11,554, and constituted only about 30% of the alien trade. The figures also suggest that the clamour in northern England about a severe trade imbalance favouring the Hansards did not apply to the situation in London. Regardless of what reasonable value might be assigned to cloths of assize, the total worth of the Steelyard's export trade (10,074 cloths and £2,223 worth of miscellaneous goods) would have exceeded by a considerable margin that of imports, which totaled £9,331 in petty custom goods and 760 hundredweights of wax valued at £1,520.[78] Even a decade earlier, at the height of a flourishing Hanseatic traffic in London, there is no indication in the customs records that the import trade dominated.[79]

In 1490–1 essentially the same core group of merchants prominent in the cloth trade also accounted for the lion's share of the Steelyard's import trade. Bergentrik and another merchant from Hamburg, Berthold van Ryne, together had almost £1,500 worth of miscellaneous goods customed. Several of the resident Danzigers had between £200 and £400 worth of imported goods, and they still clearly dominated the Hanseatic wax trade as well. Danziger Hermann Plough, for example, imported only about £180 worth of 3d merchandise, but he owned more than 200 quintals of wax, representing a full quarter of the Hanseatic total, with each quintal valued at forty shillings. Another 116 quintals were customed to Hans Mulner. Merchants from Danzig were also key agents in the Hanse's salt import trade. Plough, Peter Ecksted, and Peter Sano of Danzig together owned virtually all of the salt cargoes customed to Hansards. However, in the mid-1480s Cologners, too, had salt freighted to London, only to lose heavily on their investment when the mayor arbitrarily fixed the selling price far below cost. Also, a Hamburg ship was taking salt and other goods to London in the winter of 1485–6 when it was plundered by pirates from Fowey, and only a year before Englishmen had contracted a Danzig skipper to haul salt from the Bay to London.[80]

As was the case with the Esterling merchants, the value of other imports belonging to individual Cologners also varied considerably. The leading Cologner was Johann Blitterswik, with less than £400 worth of petty custom goods. Totals for the leading individuals transacting business through the Steelyard reflect the same trade balance as the aggregate figures. The major cloth exporters, with 250 units or better, appear to have had considerably more invested in English woollens than in the merchandise they imported into London. The combined trade was brought more closely into balance by less prominent merchants, Esterlings and Cologners alike, who were not particularly significant in either the import or export sector, but whose imported goods quite often were valued higher than the merchandise they shipped out of England. The Cologners still offered fustian, steel, thread, wire, cider, madder, and linens, as well as consignments of copperware, 'marbelais plate,' and 'shearmans sherys.' The Esterlings dealt primarily in osmund, linen, wood, canvas, pitch, yarn, bowstaves, and wax.[81]

Business in Brabant

Like their Hanseatic competitors, English merchants also were attracted to the Brabant fairs during the 1470s and 1480s. Most conspicuous among them were Londoners and merchants from Colchester and Ipswich, but there were several northerners as well, from Hull, Beverley, and York.[82] Their business ventures in the Low Countries were spurred on in the late 1470s by the treaty of mercantile intercourse between England and Burgundy concluded in the summer of 1478. For the most part they used English and Lowland shipping to transport their wares, and seldom freighted cargo in Hanseatic vessels. The shipments they brought to Brabant typically consisted of cloths of assize and other English textiles, although cargoes of lead and leather were not unusual. Englishmen laded fish oil, tar, pitch, wood, and iron at the Zealand quays, and also purchased ships there.[83]

Aside from the local Brabantine merchant communities, the most important commercial contacts for the English traders at Antwerp and Bergen op Zoom may well have been the Hansards of the London Steelyard and their associates or factors, since it was common for the obligations of Hanseatic cloth buyers to be paid at the fairs. In 1477 payment for cloth purchased from Colchester merchant William Smyth by Cologner Johann van Dorn was to be made to Smyth's English factor, Richard Russel, at the Bergen op Zoom fairs. Likewise, other Steelyard Cologners, Johann Hardenrode and Heinrich Molhem, were obliged to discharge a debt to London grocer John Brouck at Antwerp in 1485. A transaction between another London grocer, Richard Lendorp, and Hansard Thomas Tack in 1491 for cloth was entrusted to Lendorp's English factor at Antwerp. Still other London merchants employed resident Antwerp burgesses as their agents at the fairs.[84]

A second indispensable component in the expanding trade of Antwerp and Bergen op Zoom were the native Brabantine merchants themselves. Not only did the cross-Channel routes employ many a Lowland mariner during the late fifteenth century, the Brabantine merchant community also carried on a brisk trade with England. The volume of their trade in the kingdom is difficult to estimate, although English customs figures suggest it hardly compared with that of the Hansards in ports where the latter were active. Nevertheless, the merchant citizens of Bergen op Zoom and Antwerp commonly freighted their own cargo to England. The spring of 1480 saw Antwerp merchants shipping hops and iron to distant Newcastle, while others were bringing barley and friezes from England to Bergen op Zoom with London shipper Richard Blackborn.[85]

The traffic to England was, though, but a single aspect of the expanding mercantile interests of the Brabanters. They transacted business with Hansards, Englishmen, Italians, Spaniards, and south Germans at the great fairs, and shipped coastwise also to Amsterdam and the Hanseatic ports of Hamburg and Lübeck.[86] Furthermore, a strong link with the English wool staple at Calais was maintained even during the troubled late 1480s. Records of goods certified for transport to and from Antwerp in 1488 suggest a steady traffic between Calais and Brabant when direct sea transport from England was restricted. Finally, unlike the English, Brabantine merchants contributed significantly to the eastern extension of the burgeoning overland trade. They not only met the Nürnberg, Breslau, and Augsburg merchants at Bergen op Zoom and Antwerp, but also sent cloth, spices, and mixed cargo of their own by cart to Frankfurt and points beyond.[87]

So far as Hanseatic interests were concerned, the Brabant fairs had clearly emerged as an integral part of their vast commercial network. While reliance on Zealand and Brabant had been heightened by the Anglo-Hanseatic War and subsequently by political instability in Flanders, other inducements also contributed to the further expansion of the Hansards' Brabantine trade. In 1477 Bergen op Zoom conveyed a house to them with the right of permanent and free occupation. They already possessed a house at Antwerp, and early in 1481 a twenty-five-year extension of Hanseatic privileges there was confirmed by Maximilian and Duchess Maria of Burgundy.[88]

And so, the temptation to shift Hanseatic commerce away from

Flanders existed even without Maximilian's instructions to the foreign merchants in 1489. The Bruges Hansards routinely attended the fairs at Bergen op Zoom and Antwerp anyway, and as turmoil engulfed Flanders during much of the decade, the flourishing market and comparative security of the Brabantine ports beckoned. Still caught on the treadmill of protectionist restrictions, Bruges could do little to slow the departure of the Hansards. Harbour officials at the outport of Sluis persisted in arresting consignments of English textiles owned by Hanseatic merchants, and the Flemish cloth staple offered few new incentives to Hanseatic buyers.[89]

Together with inbound cloth cargo inventories, the names of several Cologne and Westphalian merchants from the London Steelyard appear in the Zealand/Brabant toll records for the late 1470s. So does that of Johann Salmer, the Steelyard's pewter specialist, who, not surprisingly, brought in quantities of tin as well. The same essential pattern was intact on the eve of the English restrictions on cloth shipments in the autumn of 1486. Leading Steelyard men, among them Tydemann Barck, Hermann Bergentrik, Joris Tack, Salmer, and numerous Cologners, were sending cloth to the Cold fair at Bergen op Zoom.[90]

The Brabant entrepôts and their outports in Zealand were utilized extensively as distribution points for North Sea fish and Baltic imports. Merchants from Lübeck, Hamburg, and Danzig brought beer, copper, stockfish, and lumber coastwise from the Elbe to Zealand, whence cargoes could be taken to Bergen op Zoom and Antwerp, or redirected to England. In 1481 quantities of copper, wax, tar and tallow belonging, in part, to Lübeckers, were seized as false goods in Antwerp and burned.[91] Danzig's fleets also brought grain, salt from the Bay and Lisbon, and English woollens. They sailed home from Zealand laden with textiles, salt, wine, and North Sea herring. Cologners, too, brought herring shipments through Brabant for transport southward to Frankfurt.[92]

Just as the bulk carriage trade of the Baltic Hansards had been deflected to the Zealand outports and thence to the Brabant fairs during the Anglo-Hanseatic War, so also had the conflict fostered a strengthening of the east-west axis of Cologne's trade. Cologners were largely eliminated from Baltic ventures during the hostilities with England, and this was a catalyst not only for the increased traffic in woollens between England and Brabant, but also for the eastward extension of the trade to Frankfurt. During the 1470s Cologne merchants continued to send cartloads of English cloth eastward following the autumn fairs.[93] They sold great quantities of it at Frankfurt, especially to merchants from Nürnberg. In accordance with the restriction on the export of unshorn cloth enforced at the insistence of English cloth shearers, Cologners alone claimed they were obliged to have 13,650 cloths sheared in England between 1485 and 1491. Undoubtedly, most of these shipments were consumed by the Brabant/Cologne/Frankfurt market.[94] Moreover, even as Cologne laboured to extend trade eastward, growing numbers of non-Hanseatic buyers from eastern regions were attracted to the Brabant fairs. Merchants from Nürnberg, Frankfurt, Augsburg, and Leipzig were forging strong direct links with Brabant, expanding both their own specialized trade in precious metals and metalwares and the traffic in woollens.[95]

The eastward extension

The ascendancy of the Brabant fairs and the related strengthening of the Cologne/Frankfurt trade drew a range of responses within the Hanse and prompted certain fundamental shifts in the trade structure of northern Europe. This was because the south Germans not only reached out to Antwerp, they also were drawn toward the markets of the northeast. Already since mid-century cloth, including English varieties, had been reaching Warsaw via Leipzig and Posan or Breslau. Silk from Nürnberg also was brought as far as Thorn. A crucial overland trade artery, the *Vogtländerstrasse*, linked Breslau with south German markets via Görlitz, Dresden, Zwickau, and Bayreuth. In addition, merchants from the southern non-Hanseatic towns extended their trade to the easternmost reaches of the Hanseatic community, tapping the Livonian trade in furs and bulk products. Nürnberg and Leipzig, too, became alternatives to Danzig as outlets for the grain and timber producers in greater Poland.[96]

In 1470 the Hanseatic diet at Lübeck resolved to implement tough protectionist policies, ostensibly aimed at the south Germans trading to Livonia. They restricted the transport of goods from Livonia and Poland westward 'dorch Dutsche lande' [through German lands], and required that all Flemish, Brabantine, and Holland cloth be sent to non-Hanseatic towns only via Antwerp or Bergen op Zoom, or the staple at Bruges.

This was an attempt to consolidate the Hanseatic grip on the east-west trade and prevent circumvention of established routes between Flanders, Brabant, and the eastern regions. It was undermined, of course, by the perseverance of the Cologners and eventually some of their Westphalian colleagues, who would not relinquish their integral commercial connections with Frankfurt and Nürnberg.[97] The successful preservation of this link in the early 1470s produced another important corollary, since the eastward extension of Nürnberg's overland trade hinged, in the first instance, on traffic to and from Silesia and the Hanseatic town of Breslau. Merchants there were well acquainted with cloth manufacturers in the Low Countries, and generally were opposed to the Hanseatic policy of maintaining the Bruges staple. During the 1450s and 1460s Breslau seldom sent delegates to the *Hansetag*, and as the overland trade expanded, the town's role within the Hanse became all the more obscure. Finally, in 1474, Breslau withdrew from the Hanse, citing the confederation's outdated *Stapelpolitik* as a principal reason. Breslau now developed as a vital non-Hanseatic transit point in the trade further eastward to Cracow, creating a link that challenged the established Danzig/Thorn/Cracow connection by drawing the trade of Poland into the east-west overland network. By the late 1480s Cracow also was no longer a member town of the Hanse.[98]

While stringent protectionism was as yet an effective deterrent against the incursion of the south Germans in Livonia, it did not preserve the Hanseatic dominance of overland supply routes that interconnected with the seaborne trade of Danzig. Hence, the Danzigers, too, were obliged to reassess relationships with their southern neighbours. By the mid-1470s Danzig's deliberately lax enforcement of prescribed Hanseatic restrictions on non-Hanseatic merchants signalled at least a limited attempt to accommodate rather than totally inhibit commercial contact. The town even experimented with two new annual fairs open to foreigners in the early 1480s, although evidently at least one of them soon was discontinued.[99]

This rather moderate attitude contrasted sharply with policy in Livonia. Even though Novgorod came under Muscovite control in 1471 and would capitulate completely in 1478, the towns of Dorpat, Riga, Reval, and Narva still formed the established and most viable conduits for Novgorod's trade to the west. They continued to prohibit the transport of cloth, wax, and furs overland via Poland and Lithuania. Even the inevitable expulsion of the Hansards from their Novgorod *comptoir*, postponed as it was through truce and treaty until 1494, did not in itself necessitate an immediate reorientation of trade links with the emporium. Nor did it force any new flexibility in Livonia regarding trade with the south Germans.[100] Joining the Livonian towns in efforts to maintain the Bruges staple and preserve traditional trade routes were the Lübeckers, although they also were not without commercial interests in the south. From Cologne, Nürnberg, and the Frankfurt fairs shipments of weapons, jewels, books, precious metals, wine, Italian embroidery, fine Augsburg cloth, and eastern spices were all funnelled through Lübeck for redistribution in the Baltic region. In return, Lübeck supplied southern markets with stockfish and herring.[101]

This commercial sub-structure within the broader trade framework reveals an underlying concern at the heart of the debate between protectionists and those towns favouring either partial or total deregulation of trade. Within the Hanseatic network the primary role of Lübeck remained that of distribution centre for goods in transit, and therefore the town was especially vulnerable to altered commodity structures and any reorientation of transport links. By contrast, the cornerstone of the trade out of the southern German towns, Cologne, and even Danzig was some sort of industrial or agricultural resource base. The Leipzig market, for example, was a principal outlet for the mines of Saxony. Nürnberg and Frankfurt not only offered exotic luxury wares from Italy and the east, they were, in their own right, key production and supply centres for weaponry, metals, and metalwares. Silk and steel production in and around Cologne also provided that town with a solid industrial base for a potentially dynamic export trade. And, although links to sources were somewhat more tenuous in the eastern Baltic, Danzigers could rely on grain and forest products to sustain their vital seaborne commerce so long as they dominated trade with the Prusso-Polish hinterland.

While the situation of Lübeck with regard to resource industries and agriculture did not compare, it did not necessarily preclude an opportunity for expansion of a shipping industry to serve the long-distance carriage trade along with Hamburg and Danzig. Indeed, the existing intra-Baltic trade connections between Lübeck and Livonia might well have provided the basis for growth in the shipping sector. Yet, by mid-century it was not the Lübeckers, but rather the Hollanders who

were forging important new links in the salt and grain traffic that
linked the Lowlands with the eastern Baltic region. The Icelandic fisheries also offered excellent prospects for further development of Lübeck's
Atlantic and North Sea shipping, especially if the Wendish sector could
have been reintegrated into the Hanse's trade with England. Again,
though, Lübeck seemed bound by a traditional reliance on the Bergen
comptoir and the Norwegian fisheries supplying the Baltic. And the
town remained alienated from or largely indifferent to the English trade
throughout much of the second half of the century.

The strains of disunity

By the beginning of the 1490s the modification of the economic infra-
structure of northern Europe was already placing incalculable stress on
the political viability of the Hanse. Though fuelled by a series of both
economic and political developments, this commercial reorientation and
its repercussions also were rooted, at least partly, in the ebb and flow
of relations between the Hanse and England, commencing with the
crisis of 1468 and Cologne's subsequent refusal to forsake the English
trade. Prior to that, Hansards constituted the principal foreign merchant
group linking England's overseas trade with the northern continental
network. The severing of that link neccessarily had far more complex
consequences than the long-term loss of England's Baltic trade, to which
English historiographical tradition has drawn much attention. It is true
that, except for the merchants of Lynn, English presence at the Prussian
staple remained quite limited during the 1470s and 1480s. Moreover, the
postwar era saw most of the Hanse's English trade outside of London
revert to the Esterlings from Hamburg and Danzig, who had been
England's staunchest adversaries during the conflict. And, by the Treaty
of Utrecht, Hansards did retain all prior rights and privileges in England until the almost systematic harassment began in the late 1480s. But
the war years also had at least two other profound repercussions on the
English seaborne economy. They accelerated the consolidation of the
English cloth export trade in London, which had begun some years
before, and linked it all the more firmly with the Brabant fairs. Also, the
total exclusion of Englishmen from the Baltic during the war years
prompted a complete shift in the focus of the Yorkshire woollen export
industry to Brabant as well. Neither London's importance nor the

concentration of the trade out of northern England diminished following the suspension of hostilities. Throughout the disruption of direct mercantile contact between the Baltic and England, and afterward, the Brabant fairs and the Zealand outports served to integrate England's main commercial interests, as well as the trade of the Esterlings, with vital continental markets.

In addition to the English mercers, the merchants of Cologne were crucial to London's cloth export trade in peacetime, and they, too, played a central role in keeping the trade to Brabant open during the Anglo-Hanseatic War. Just as important, the heightened significance of the Brabant fairs, coupled with the temporary curtailment of Cologne's northern commercial interests, ultimately increased emphasis on the east-west trading axis. In turn, this led to the strengthening and eventual extension of the overland trade eastward. It was coincidental as well with mercantile expansion in the south German regions, and foreshadowed the development during the 1470s and 1480s of an alternative commercial network capable of challenging established Hanseatic monopolies.

The response of various Hanseatic interest groups to the new challenge again highlighted regional particularism and the overall political decrepitude of the confederation, so that by the time the Anglo-Hanseatic conference convened at Antwerp in 1491, there could no longer be any common perception of the Hanse's *raison d'être*. In the first instance, it had been the merchants of Cologne who had strayed furthest from the fold by helping to extend the London/Brabant trade eastward beyond Frankfurt. In this sector Cologners derived no particular benefit from membership in the Hanse. Indeed, 'Hanseatic' policy regarding Bruges and commercial contact with foreigners often was a burden. But their Hanseatic status was of paramount importance in England, if they hoped to maintain their advantage in the woollen trade. That was still crucial, after all, to their mercantile prosperity. Preferential English customs rates and exemptions from subsidies for merchants of the 'Hanse Almain' were indeed all important to the Cologners and their associates.

For the Esterling merchants and shippers from Danzig and Hamburg membership in the Hanse also had become a mixed blessing. They were just as well or perhaps better served by moderate and selective protectionist statutes that could be modified to suit a changing trade framework, as by the blanket restrictions traditionally prescribed by the *Hansetag*. Hamburg and Danzig were, however, still keenly interested in preserving the Hanseatic status of their merchants in England, or at least stable relations with the English, in order to exploit the lucrative English connection in both the cloth and bulk carriage trade. Quite a different set of circumstances confronted Lübeck, though. Lübeckers, by and large, could no longer take full advantage of their Hanseatic status *vis-à-vis* England, since their trade there had ceased to be very significant. Yet they were loath to abandon much of the all-encompassing Hanseatic protectionism that previously had served their entrenched interests outside of England by safeguarding distributive routes vital to the town's static long-distance trade.

Not directly represented at the Antwerp talks, and least of all concerned with Hanseatic privileges in England, were the distant Livonian towns. Aside from the Muscovite military threat, a key concern in Livonia was the south German challenge to established monopolies of regional supply sources and transport routes. Here then, Hanseatic membership was useful, since rigid protectionism, sanctioned by the Hanse, continued to be an effective deterrent.

Notwithstanding the Iberian connections and occasional forays into the Mediterranean, there were as yet three possible avenues for expansion of English overseas trade in the late fifteenth century. In each of them England was confronted by Hanseatic interests. Although the first of these – the Icelandic fisheries – was a sector coveted by Hansards and English alike, England's role would ultimately be determined through Anglo-Danish diplomacy. In any event, while the English did succeed in penetrating this trade, it was really of little benefit to the woollen export industry on which the national economy was so dependent. A second and highly speculative possibility for expansion, therefore, was the trade to Brabant, and the forging of more direct links with south German buyers. But this would necessitate dislodging the Cologners and Westphalians from the trade out of London, and even then the English could scarcely expect to make inroads much beyond the Brabant fairs. Cologne would still be an essential intermediary in both the Rhineland trade and its eastern extension. Besides, the substantial import trade of the Steelyard Cologners and their colleagues furnished England with dyestuffs, metals, and other essentials for which English merchants would be hard pressed to find an alternative source. Finally, there remained the Prussian staple at Danzig – as much a neglected market as an inaccessible one for the better part of a quarter century.

This, then, was at the heart of the Antwerp talks in 1491. The convening of the conference, coming as it did as a direct result of pressures on the Hanseatic community in England, marked the initial success of a new initiative by the government of Henry VII to give English mercantile interests an opportunity to re-establish a presence in the Baltic. But only time would tell if England's merchants would prove themselves equal to the task. And again, as they had had some twenty years earlier, pressures in England had anything but an all-pervasive effect within the Hanse membership. Rather, they once again highlighted the divergent concerns of a number of the key subgroups within the confederation. Now, though, those concerns were all the more clearly defined by a modified and no longer exclusively Hanseatic commercial network in northern continental Europe.

*H*ANSARDS, ENGLISHMEN, AND THE TUDOR-HAPSBURG TRADE WARS

Following the conference at Antwerp in 1491, further talks between English and Hanseatic representatives were postponed repeatedly from year to year, as first one side and then the other managed to delay the reconvening of a formal diet.[1] The confirmation of existing rights and freedoms at the Prussian staple satisfied English mercantile interests temporarily. And, with open hostility toward the Hanseatic community in abeyance, the Steelyard merchants tolerated, though not without protest, the continued enforcement of the statutes restricting exports of unshorn cloth. All in all, relations between the Hansards and the denizen merchant community, at least in southern England, were stable and cordial enough to allow the resumption of normal Anglo-Hanseatic trade. Relations between the Hanse and the English Crown, on the other hand, would be fraught with tension once again within the decade.

The interruption of trade

With the English cloth export trade so heavily concentrated in London and so dependent on the Brabant markets for overseas distribution, the Hansards of the Steelyard, and indeed almost all merchants shipping overseas, remained particularly vulnerable to serious new breaches in Anglo-Hapsburg diplomacy. Just such a rift occurred in 1493, following a summer of political transition in the Lowlands. In August, Maximilian officially succeeded to the imperial dignity. His son, Philip the Fair, was about to be proclaimed of age to assume his ducal responsibilities in the Burgundian territories. Of much greater immediate consequence for the merchant communities in England, though, was a new Yorkist conspiracy and dowager Duchess Margaret's overt support for another false claimant to the English crown, the impostor Perkin Warbeck. As in 1487, a potential dynastic threat now provoked a punitive Tudor response on the commercial front. On 18 September 1493 Henry VII again suspended direct trade to the Low Countries.[2]

Records of the London mercers confirm that the sanction was not instigated by the great merchant fraternities in the capital.[3] By mid-July John Etwell, then governor of the English merchants in the Lowlands, had negotiated a new one-year safe conduct for Englishmen and their goods in Flanders and had sent word to London of the 'syngler good will' of the town of Bruges. While Etwell's correspondence implies that again members of the English fellowship had been having difficulty transiting goods via Flanders, the mercers' assembly in London seemed well enough satisfied with his tidings from Bruges.[4] But there was a sense, as well, of trouble in the offing, as the mayor cautioned that a royal envoy was to be sent overseas and that it would be the king who would decide: 'yf ... we shall Repayre to the said towne [Bruges] havyng fyrst aswell a sure and laufull sauf cundith for us oure Marchaundyses and specially oure clothes for sure passage by the towne and Castell of Sluyse withoute interupcion prejudice or damage of the enhabytantes of the same.'[5] Yet a month later the trading guilds still had heard nothing from King Henry or his chancellor, and so sometime between 26 August and 6 September they sent a delegation to the king's treasurer to seek clarification of the sovereign's wishes respecting the Lowland trade. In a curiously evasive response the merchants were told to check instead with royal customs agents. Promptly doing so, they discovered to their professed amazement that Henry had in fact ordered the suspension of all commercial traffic to and from the Lowland ports of the emperor and Duke Philip. So a decision on the matter had in fact been made at least twelve days to three weeks before the sanction was actually proclaimed, and without consulting denizen merchants who traded overseas. Those merchants were left all the more bewildered and distressed since they, as well as non-denizen traders, had only just recently been issued passports for shipments to the autumn fairs in Brabant.

It is far from clear why Henry VII kept the Londoners at arm's length for so long. Of course he knew full well that his edict was unlikely to be very popular with them in the short term, yet he also could be

reasonably certain of compliance. After all, it was not for loyal subjects
to question his prerogative, and England's merchants remained loyal if
nothing else. They could be counted on to abide by his decision so long
as the prohibition applied to Hansards and other foreigners as well as
Englishmen. On 16 September, though, another delegation from the
merchant fraternities set off hastily for Northampton to voice to the king
their concern about non-denizen rivals. Representatives from the Steelyard had preceded them and already had bound Hanseatic merchants
to the Crown not to ship directly to the restricted territories. Initially,
they were to be permitted to sail from England to the Zuider Zee port
of Kampen, but the Londoners prevailed upon the king to rescind even
this exemption, and further require the Hansards to agree that '... in cas
any Englyshe man wolde do shipp any goodes into any theyre [Hanse]
Shyppes now purposed into theyr Cuntrey he shalbe welcom unto
theym and aswell there entreted amonges theym as they be amonge and
with us here ...'[6] This, then, was the situation on 18 September, when
sheriffs throughout England were issued mandates to publish the
proclamation forbidding trade to or from the restricted territories. By
the end of the month Etwell had been instructed to oversee the evacuation of the English merchants and their communal property from
Antwerp and Bergen op Zoom.

On the whole, the concerns expressed by the merchants of London
were both rational and highly predictable. The Crown, for its part,
easily agreed to the recommendations put forth, and so the entire
exercise at Northampton helped to create the appearance that the
merchant fellowships actually had some input *vis-à-vis* what amounted
to a crucial decision affecting the commercial sector. In truth, though,
it was the king and his advisers who had decided on the ban, and since
the Hansards had not been exempted from a similar one in the late
1480s, it stands to reason that the Crown would not have contemplated
special concessions for them in 1493. Likewise, the principle that Englishmen be allowed to trade freely to Hanseatic ports was not new. It
had been confirmed as recently as two years before by the joint
Anglo-Hanseatic assembly at Antwerp.

Nevertheless, and whatever the king's motives, both the embargo and
the concerns of the London mercers served to bring the Hanseatic trade
into focus once again. Of the main foreign merchant groups in England,
the Flemings and Brabanters were not especially vital to the national

economy. Although the suspension of traffic to and from the Lowlands would affect, to some degree, the substantial trade of Spanish and Italian merchants, it would have its most profound impact on the Hansards. They usually accounted directly for roughly one third of London's overseas trade, not to mention their importance in other places like Hull, Ipswich, and Lynn. Also, the confirmation of the terms of the Utrecht treaty, wrested from the Hanse in 1491, had not in itself provided sufficient incentive for northern expansion of English overseas trade once traffic to the Lowlands had resumed. The new embargo of 1493, though, could not help but test the reciprocal arrangement with the Hanse, by forcing the development and utilization of that alternative market. English merchants were entitled, theoretically at least, to trade freely to Hanseatic ports, and with the Lowland trade again severed it might have been expected that they would be all the more inclined to do so.

The Hanseatic merchants in London had ships laden with cloth and ready to sail by October 14, and at least one English skipper, Steven Bull, offered to accompany them, provided the Londoners would furnish a cargo. But London's mercers were unprepared and hesitant, as if they had never seriously contemplated the option that now presented itself.[7] Adept at voicing complaints to their king about the Hanseatic fellowship and other 'straungers,' they were equally slow to come to grips with the reality of the embargo and adjust their export trade accordingly. As a result, it seemed that their rivals at the Steelyard were poised to gain an advantage. The Hansards were bound for the extortionate sum of £20,000 sterling not to ship directly to the Lowlands, but unlike their English counterparts, they were not about to sit idle while Henry waged his economic war on the Hapsburgs.

In the early-morning hours of October 15 a riotous mob gathered at the gates of the Steelyard. Warehouses were damaged and the mayor had to dispatch an armed contingent to disperse the unruly crowd and arrest the perpetrators. Evidently the trouble was instigated by servants of some London mercers, although the Crown's own tardiness in proclaiming the restraint on the Hansards may also have been partly to blame. Weeks before, the Londoners had complained that if they were restrained 'before that yt were knowen oppenly whether the Esterlynges ... shuld have their passage thider or not' the trade of Englishmen would be damaged greatly, but by mid-October they certainly were aware that 'of late' the Hansards 'dyd bynde theym self' to discontinue shipping to the Lowlands. Nevertheless the royal decree announcing that the Hanseatic merchants were bound for the sum of £20,000 was not actually published until a week after the violence.[8] Following the restoration of order at the Steelyard the chancellor required wardens of the merchant guilds to post a nightly guard at the Hanseatic enclave to ensure the safety of its inhabitants.[9] He further urged the denizen adventurers to take advantage of their opportunity to ship with Hanseatic carriers and trade to Hanseatic ports. But therein lay the dilemma, for the London merchants were, by their own admission, 'not advised or in purpos at this tyme to shipp any goodes with the said Esterlinges.'[10] Instead, they proposed that all shipments by foreigners be banned, on grounds that the Hansards had been buying more cloth than usual and that they 'of lyklyhode' intended to ship it to the lands of Duke Philip and his father. It is questionable whether this recommendation ever reached the chancellor. The last references to it in the mercers' records indicates the fellowship was hedging on a formal petition for fear it might offend the king, who, whether by chance or design, had presented English merchants with as good an opportunity as they were likely to get to penetrate the Hanseatic markets they consistently claimed to be excluded from. In this respect, though, London's cloth exporters appear to have been their own worst enemies.

The merchants of the Hanse were by no means happy with the situation, either. The embargo had been imposed during the annual autumn fair at Antwerp, and they had goods worth several thousand pounds sterling ready for export from the English capital. Those shipments now had to be diverted to Hamburg. When bad weather forced some carriers to seek shelter in Zealand anyway, exasperated Cologne merchants begged the Crown's forbearance, since the cargoes were intended for the mart at Frankfurt. They added that they were prepared to forsake their English trade if any punitive action were taken against them. In this instance the king chose not to force the issue,[11] but otherwise the restrictions were enforced, and the resultant disruptions of sailings to Zealand and Brabant again presented the Steelyard with the necessity of reintegrating their London trade with the east-west axis of the continental network. They did so by diverting seaborne cargoes far northward and funnelling commercial traffic through Hamburg. The Cologners had to rely extensively on the inland network that linked

Hamburg with the Rhineland via Stade, Osnabrück, and Münster. Although extensive use of these routes was not unprecedented, it still depended on the cooperation of numerous bishops, princes, and territorial magnates, including John of Kleves, the bishops of Münster and Osnabrück, and the counts of Teklenburg.[12]

Aware that Henry VII's prohibition was a burden on English cloth manufacturers and merchants as well as those in the Lowlands, Maximilian and Duke Philip resisted the temptation to retaliate immediately. Instead, they engaged in a veritable war of nerves with the English monarch until the following spring. By that time it must have been abundantly clear to King Henry that his English merchants were incapable of sustaining their cloth export trade without a cross-Channel gateway. And so, in April 1494, he took the next logical step open to him by officially declaring a cloth staple and free market at Calais, with commercial freedoms comparable to those offered at the Brabant marts.[13] This forced the hand of the Hapsburgs, who, buoyed by a measure of political stability that had eluded Maximilian a half decade earlier, proclaimed a counter-ban on English cloth throughout their Lowland dominions. Aside from overt action in the shipping lanes they were powerless to prevent English woollens from being carried to and offered for sale at Calais, but they were determined now to make it exceedingly difficult for anyone to move such merchandise to inland markets once it had crossed the Channel.[14]

The subsequent hiatus effectively suspended direct trade between England and the Low Countries for most of the next two years, though how stringently the Hapsburg edict was enforced is open to question. Early on, licences exempting individuals from the restrictions could be purchased, and a threat of increased vigilance in January 1495 suggests that enforcement may have been rather haphazard. Certificates for commercial traffic to and from Antwerp also reflect inconsistencies. A Florentine merchant attempting to bring English cloth coastwise from Calais to Antwerp had his cargo seized at Vlissingen. There were other confiscations as well, and traders from Augsburg, Breslau, and Memmingen, sending textiles to Cologne and Leipzig, made declarations that none of the cloth was English. Yet other agents of Strasbourg merchants did not attempt to conceal their intention to trans-ship English cloth. Certainly by September 1495 the restrictions in the Lowlands were relaxed. But then Duke Philip proclaimed Bergen op Zoom to be the

staple for woollen imports and imposed a heavy tax of one gold florin
– the *Andriesgulden* or St Andrew florin – on each English cloth of assize
offered at the Brabant marts.[15]

The sanctions instituted by Henry VII evidently were observed and
enforced more strictly. The Hansards were held to their £20,000 surety
and shipments intended for Cologne had to be rerouted through northern ports and brought southward again via the inland corridors. Denied
their request to be allowed to import goods of Hanseatic origin from
ports in the Low Countries, the Cologners at the Steelyard were no
more successful in appealing for permission to ship cloth to Kampen.
Throughout 1494 and 1495, this too was refused.[16] And there were other
problems for the Steelyard. In the autumn of 1494 royal customs
searchers in London again impounded a consignment of imported silk
belonging to Cologne merchants. It had been shipped quite legally from
Hamburg, and its seizure ran contrary to what Cologne felt had been
agreed to at Antwerp three years before. But with a new session of
Anglo-Hanseatic negotiations already postponed until the summer of
1495, the Cologners found themselves with little economic leverage.
They contemplated an intentional reduction in their trade to England,
to which both Danzig and Lübeck were agreeable. Yet the Cologners
and their northern colleagues alike knew that a boycott of English trade
would be ineffective unless it had the support of other key member
towns, and in the end, the grievance apparently did not warrant risking
further disruption of the already modified transportation network.[17]

Protracted negotiations eventually brought about the lifting of the
English and Hapsburg embargoes, and culminated in February 1496
with a new treaty, the much heralded *Intercursus Magnus*, which, among
other considerations, also exempted English merchants from any new
tolls or taxes in the Lowlands.[18] Although the accord reopened Brabant,
its potential impact on a return to the old distribution system was not
as immediate as it might have been, principally because the *Andriesgulden* was resisted well into the late 1490s. Moreover, in accordance with Philip's reform edict of 1495 ducal tolls again were levied
on incoming English ships, contrary to the spirit if not the letter of the
new treaty. Ultimately, the English merchants lobbied successfully for
relief from these later in 1496,[19] but the florin of St Andrew was quite
another matter. Henry VII had expressly forbidden Englishmen in the
Lowlands to pay the new tax on their woollen cloths, but when English

merchants indeed refused payment in the spring of 1496 they were arrested forcibly, brought before the lords of the Council of Brabant, and compelled to do so. Informed of this, the furious King Henry ordered the immediate evacuation of English traders from the duke's lands. By September, only a half year after the *Intercursus* had been proclaimed, direct textile shipments to Lowland ports once again were forbidden. Nevertheless, cargoes of English cloth reached the Cold Mart at Bergen op Zoom – some from Calais, and some directly from London.[20]

In the spring of 1497 these measures had to have been taken more seriously. Merchants of the Steelyard again were bound to the royal treasury – this time for the sum of £18,000 – not to ship to the restricted ports. Shippers from Hamburg and Danzig, freighting their vessels at London, were required to procure certificates from towns where they would discharge the cargoes, in order to satisfy the Crown that they were not contravening the sanctions.[21] Renewed negotiations between Burgundian envoys and English officials resulted in the resumption of sailings to the autumn mart at Antwerp, whereupon the merchants of Cologne, at least, were under the impression that collection of Duke Philip's cloth tax was to be suspended. Instead, it was merely reduced – and not until November – to two shillings Flemish money on each cloth, and the Cologners and their civic council were irate when the tariff was collected at Antwerp.[22] As a result, some Hanseatic merchants continued to avoid the Zealand/Brabant corridor by shipping English cloth over Kampen up until a new Anglo-Burgundian treaty was concluded in 1499 and the tax thereby discontinued.[23]

Hence, these serious disagreements, so important to the English, Brabantine, and Hanseatic trade, were not resolved until some three years after the *Intercursus*. Indeed, since 1493 London's cloth exporters had made no real inroads in the Hanseatic sector, relying instead on the commercial lifeline to Calais to sustain their export trade to northern Europe. Henry VII's embargo and the resultant trade war had done virtually nothing to lessen the dependence of the nation's cloth exporters on traditional Lowland markets. Merchants of the Hanse had, to some extent fared rather differently. Brabant still formed the most convenient conduit for their trade from London, and to stay competitive within the expanding international merchant community in the Lowlands they necessarily had to maintain a high profile at the Brabantine entrepôts once normal traffic resumed. But if the trade also depended on getting English cloth to Frankfurt for subsequent distribution – and to a great extent it did – then Hanseatic adventurers proved reasonably adept at adjusting their network to circumvent the Anglo-Lowland dispute. In the process they inevitably enhanced the economic importance of the North Sea and Zuider Zee ports, which already interconnected with the Baltic trade, and strengthened both the coastal trade to these ports and the inland routes that linked them to the Rhineland. Cologners and Lübeckers shipped cloth from Calais to Kampen and Hamburg when the Anglo-Brabantine trade was disrupted, and as late as 1499 some Cologne merchants continued to redirect consignments of English goods southward from Kampen.[24] This was ample demonstration that, notwithstanding the importance of the fairs and finishing industries at Bergen op Zoom and Antwerp, Brabant was not the exclusive transit corridor for an extended continental woollen trade in which the non-Hanseatic market at Frankfurt remained a principal connection.

An unfortunate two-year gap in London's customs enrolments, beginning Michaelmas 1494, makes it especially difficult to assess the impact of the severing of the Brabantine link on overseas commerce from the English capital. A decline in cloth exports during the previous embargo and again during a subsequent interruption points to the probability that the volume of trade was affected adversely during the mid-1490s also.[25] However, during 1493–4, the first year of the embargo, woollen exports were in line with previous annual totals, as a significant though not drastic decline in cloth exports by non-Hanseatic aliens was offset by a corresponding increase in the Hanseatic sector. The creation of the cloth staple and free market at Calais apparently did ease the problems of English exporters as well, but again, without quantitative customs evidence, an assessment of trade over the next two years is not possible. Beginning with the Exchequer year 1496–7, when denizen woollen exports totalled 18,310 units, enrolled customs for London run consecutively, and reflect a steady upward trend with few setbacks in all sectors of the cloth export trade. The greatest surge, however, came only after the collection of the St Andrew florin was discontinued, and the most dramatic improvement was in the denizen sector.[26]

Brabant also was a primary market for the woollen exporters of Yorkshire, who shipped from Hull. That enrolled figures for denizen cloth exports do not reflect a very significant slump during the Lowland embargoes suggests that the potentially negative impact on the export trade of English merchants may have been cushioned fairly effectively by the establishment of the cloth staple and free market at Calais. The same probably was true of the export trade of Newcastle, although the embargoes really were aimed at the traffic in cloth, in which that port played only a very minor role. Newcastle shippers and merchants regularly brought lead, coal, and hides to Zealand and Brabant prior to 1494. Thereafter, in 1495, when the Lowland traffic was disrupted and Calais was the principal link to the continental trade, more than twenty ships from Dieppe, Boulogne, and Calais laded coal and lead at Newcastle.[27] After the Cold Mart of 1493 virtually no English imports were recorded by the toll collectors in Zealand and Brabant until the autumn of 1495, when some cloth and wool again arrived via the Scheldt-Honte. Following the *Intercursus* the English trade was re-established quickly, despite the heavy tax on cloth, and the next year a half dozen carriers from Hull, London, and Calais brought several hundred assize cloths, friezes, and kerseys to Bergen op Zoom's Cold Mart, and departed laden with mixed cargo. Thereafter the Lowlands reassumed their central place in the overseas trade of the northern English ports. For the Exchequer year 1498–9 denizen woollen exports from Hull totalled 963 cloths. Almost half of them (435 cloths) were carried to Veere in early October 1499 in four Hull ships and one from York. There is no reason to doubt that similar shipments were sent earlier in the year to the other major fairs. From Brabant and the quays in Zealand, merchants of Hull, York, and Newcastle shipped a broad range of goods like steel, copperware, soap, madder, tar, sugar, and paper back to England, using English and Lowland carriers.[28]

There was other regional interest in the Anglo-Brabantine trade. East Anglian merchants from Yarmouth and Lynn traded across the Narrow Seas, although neither port was a significant cloth exporting centre, and much of Lynn's cloth trade went to the Baltic anyway. But Norfolk merchants did exploit a modest agricultural resource base to diversify their export trade, and in the Lowlands they found markets for English cheese, beer, meat, and grain. Cheap textiles, hides, and butter were also shipped from the Norfolk ports and from Boston as well.[29]

On the Anglo-Hanseatic diplomatic front, time and again proposals for renewed discussions were put off. Throughout his dispute with the Hapsburgs, Henry VII dismissed suggestions that the talks take place in the Low Countries, and insisted instead on London or Calais. Neither venue suited the Hansards, who sought a more neutral political environment. Early in 1496, though, as the king's negotiations with Burgundian envoys showed promise, he suddenly announced that nothing now appeared to stand in the way of a meeting with Hanseatic officials at Antwerp that same summer. When the *Hansetag* expressed reservations that this was insufficient notice, Henry quickly agreed to another one-year postponement, and later requested yet another, while he made war on Scotland. At Cologne's urging, the *Hansetag* then prevailed upon the English government to send at least a small delegation to Antwerp in the summer of 1497, to address the alleged non-observance of Hanseatic privileges.[30]

A group of four appointed English representatives turned up at Antwerp in June 1497 to hear the concerns of an equally small delegation from Cologne and Lübeck. Point by point the Hansards rehearsed their complaints of price fixing by the mayor of London, extortion and harassment by royal officials, and the enforcement of parliamentary statutes in contravention of the Hanseatic exemption from new ordinances. In addition, there was the matter of pledges to the Crown to cease shipping to the Low Countries – first for the sum of £20,000, then £2,000, then another £1,000, and now £18,000 – all contrary to the Hansards' right to ship to and from wherever they chose.[31] Nothing was resolved. Having fulfilled their mandate to hear the Hansards, the English envoys took their leave. Henry's offer to send them back for another meeting at Calais in the new year merely caused Lübeck to canvass the other principal Hanseatic towns as to the appropriate course of action. In particular, Lübeck now needed to know the wishes of Danzig, whose merchants and shippers had, after all, greater economic interests in England than did the Lübeckers.[32] When pressed on this, it was the Danzigers' turn to hesitate, and it was they who now managed to postpone a full Anglo-Hanseatic diet until 1499.[33]

The new round of discussions finally did convene at Bruges in June of that year. William Warham, now Master of the Rolls, again headed the English contingent that exchanged views with representatives from Lübeck, Hamburg, Cologne, and Danzig. Neither the fundamental issues nor the standard responses to them had changed appreciably over the preceding decade.[34] The Hansards continued to object to English protectionist legislation that prohibited the export of unshorn cloth from England and restricted silk imports. As they saw it, their charters and the 1491 agreement guaranteed immunity from the ordinances in question.[35] On the other side, Danzig's envoys had explicit instructions not to deviate from the articles of the Treaty of Utrecht, which had been reconfirmed in 1491. So the familiar request for expanded English privileges in Prussia met with Danzig's equally familiar reply that unrestricted trade was not negotiable and that English merchants already had the same rights as other non-Hansards who traded there. When Warham revived the old claim that Englishmen had been deprived of the common house they once possessed at the Prussian staple, the Danzigers were again unsympathetic. No one from that town, they said, could recollect the English occupying such a place.[36]

Following a break of several days, which permitted the English delegates to relay the list of Hanseatic complaints to the king and receive instructions regarding Henry's desired response, talks resumed in mid-July. But compromises were not forthcoming, and with no real movement on either side, prolongation of the discussions soon proved pointless. The meetings adjourned, to neither party's particular satisfaction, with a simple reaffirmation of the status quo and Henry VII's offer to treat with the Hansards again in two years.[37]

The Bruges diet was not without at least one interesting and important sidelight, though. A generation earlier the civic fathers of Riga and some neighbouring Livonian towns had declined to ratify the Treaty of Utrecht, and consequently had been excluded from Hanseatic rights and privileges in the English kingdom since that time. In 1498, however, an embassy representing Riga and her neighbours had come to England and concluded an agreement with the Crown that would have granted tariff preferences for English merchants trading to Riga in exchange for Hanseatic rates on Livonian imports into England. Livonian merchants shipping goods out of the kingdom would continue to pay royal customs and subsidies at the alien rate.[38]

This rather sudden initiative was significant on at least two counts. It had to have illustrated to the English government the growing political independence of yet another prominent member of the Hanse, and perforce undermined, to some extent, a consolidated 'Hanseatic' position at the Bruges meetings. Secondly, a pact so blatantly tied to the self-interest of Livonian exporters in the bulk carriage trade constituted a potentially fatal precedent *vis-à-vis* more comprehensive Hanseatic interests in England. This would have a direct bearing on the interests of the Cologne, Westphalian, and Hamburg merchants, who, partly on the basis of their 'Hanseatic' privileges, invested heavily in the English cloth export trade. A separate piecemeal commercial agreement such as this, which parcelled out trade concessions on an individual basis, could not only undermine the fading political credibility of the Hanse as a whole, but also conceivably threaten entrenched Hanseatic franchises in England. In the end, pressure from within the Hanseatic membership forced a delay in the ratification of the pact, and in 1500 Riga endorsed the Utrecht treaty instead.[39] Even so, regional economic particularism, rooted in ready access to a specific resource base, again had come briefly to the fore, as the traditionally protectionist Livonian towns offered to open eastern markets in exchange for special commercial considerations in distant England. And another challenge to the fragile unity of the Hanse had manifested itself in the attitude of a principal member town toward the role of England in the northern European network.

Adjusted trade structures and economic corollaries

Modifications in the Anglo-Hanseatic network, some prompted by the Lowland embargoes and others not, now reflected the basic strengths and limitations of principal interest groups within both the English and Hanseatic trading communities. Further adjustments in the Hanseatic trade in England had an especially profound bearing on the east-coast ports, where, as in the past, a role in Baltic commerce ultimately went a long way in determining the prospects for mercantile prosperity or decline.

Nowhere were the effects of trends in the Anglo-Hanseatic trade more evident than at Boston. Of the port's surviving customs particulars for the 1490s the most complete and useful are those for the Exchequer year 1491–2 – a rather unrepresentative boom year for the alien trade, in which the Hansards were the key participants.[40] Danziger Johann Hadersleff brought his ship to Boston in mid-October 1491, and left again in early November. He and four other Danzig skippers returned the following spring. While none of these ships carried any cargo to or from Boston for indigenous English merchants, they did account for almost all of the Hanseatic trade. The Esterlings used English carriers only to transfer cargo to neighbouring Lynn, although a ship from Haarlem also offloaded another small consignment of litmus and tar for a Hanseatic merchant. The bulk cargo and wax discharged from the Danzig vessels pushed the combined value of Hanseatic imports to well over £1,400. Additionally, the Danzigers refreighted 146 cloths and £191 worth of lead and coverlets. However, this was really the last great surge in the Hanseatic trade at Boston. Cloth exports by Hansards had not topped a hundred units in any one year since the 1480s, and after the last of the Danzig ships weighed anchor in the summer of 1492, the Hanseatic trade virtually disappeared. Indeed the entire cloth export trade of the port, insignificant to begin with, all but evaporated during the final decade of the century. Likewise, the value of alien merchandise subject to the petty custom, which had soared to £1,574 in 1491–2, would struggle to average £100 per annum for the rest of the decade, and the Hanseatic absence was a major factor. Corresponding poundage totals, representative of the combined trade in miscellaneous goods of non-Hanseatic aliens and denizens, also reflect severe economic stagnation in this sector until after 1499.

The departure of the Hansards is not particularly surprising in light of their steadily declining trade at Boston from at least the mid-1470s onward. The woollen export trade was firmly centred in London, and the Hanseatic import trade from Hamburg and the Baltic was served by East Anglian ports. Perhaps, too, the *Bergenfahrer*, who traditionally supplied Boston with fish cargoes, had been eased out as English competitors successfully tapped the Icelandic fisheries. Hansards from Danzig and Hamburg, whose Icelandic ventures were part of a range of comprehensive commercial interests linking the Baltic trade with England and the Atlantic seaboard, apparently had much stronger ties with Lynn than with Boston. The modest alien trade of the port also had felt the effects of the embargo on traffic to and from the Lowlands. In 1493–4 the £42 worth of goods on which a single Hanseatic merchant paid the petty custom represented 80% of the aggregate non-denizen trade in miscellaneous merchandise at Boston. Essentially, this sector of Boston's overseas commerce was dormant until temporarily revived by the *Intercursus* and by the brief return of the Hansards. Though damaged to the extent that cargo values are no longer legible, the surviving particulars of account for 1496–7 show that two Hanseatic ships, both from Danzig, offloaded bulk cargo and reladed lead and a few cloths.

Coincidentally, the value of the non-denizen trade for that year rebounded to £270. Other foreign shippers from Zealand and Holland brought fish and wine cargoes, while most of the English tonnage was confined to fleets carrying wool consignments across the Channel. But again, the resurgence was short-lived. Thenceforth both the aggregate alien trade and the Hanseatic portion of it remained negligible.[41]

For the port of Hull, there are virtually no customs particulars for the 1490s, although the Exchequer enrolments do attest to a consistent and significant Hanseatic presence there.[42] In 1492–3 the Hanseatic merchants accounted for a third of all cloth exports, and the value of their traffic in other goods exceeded that of denizens and non-Hanseatic aliens combined. In four other years for which Hanseatic totals are enrolled separately from others, Hansards were responsible for 54% to 76% of the trade in petty custom goods and one third of the cloth export trade. Moreover, during an eight-year span ending with the Exchequer year 1498–9, they imported 1,250 quintals of wax, which would have added another £2,500 to the value of the Hanseatic trade. The disruption of trade with Zealand and Brabant did not have an obvious impact on the volume of recorded trade, but although cloth exports recovered from the great slump of the 1480s, levels attained during the previous decade were not improved upon. Poundage and petty custom values not only recovered during the 1490s, they were soaring to unprecedented highs by the turn of the century.

The overseas trade of Newcastle was very modest in comparison to Hull's, although the presence of the Hanseatic merchants was perhaps no less significant.[43] Raw wool was a key export commodity for the port, but cloth shipments of only a few dozen units per year were of little importance. Petty custom totals reflect the gradual and fairly consistent growth of the alien and Hanseatic trade through 1499, but even so the annual aggregate value never exceeded £437. For most years it was considerably lower than that. Nevertheless, from March 1494 to Michaelmas 1499 a third of the total value of goods customed to non-denizens at Newcastle belonged to merchants of the Hanse. In 1494–5 the only substantial consignment of bulk freight offloaded there was brought by the *Gabrielle* of Danzig. This ship departed in February 1495 laden with coal, lead, and only two cloths. Both the inbound and outbound cargoes were customed to the ship's master, Hans Laurence, and one other Hansard.

Especially significant in the traffic between England and the Baltic throughout the late fifteenth century was the trade of Lynn. There had been sustained commercial contact between the East Anglian port and Danzig even during the worst of times in the late 1480s, and the active role of denizen merchants was especially important. While Englishmen from other east-coast ports ranted against the Esterlings and shunned the Baltic market in favour of Brabant, a small nucleus of merchants from Lynn strove to build an overseas trade at the Prussian staple by diversifying their limited export base and placing ships on the Baltic route. In both the short term and the long, this stood them in good stead, for as the traffic at Boston declined and the bulk import trade in northern England was left largely to the Esterlings, the established Baltic link was preserved as the cornerstone of Lynn's maritime commerce. With little evidence to suggest that Yorkshire merchants in particular took advantage of their newly confirmed status at Danzig after 1491, the success of Lynn's Baltic trade is all the more noteworthy. It further illustrates that access to the Prussian staple depended not so much on statutes as on secure shipping lanes and the energetic pursuit of mutually beneficial business relationships within the broad commercial network. To a considerable degree the trade between Danzig and Lynn integrated the interests of both the Lynn merchants and their Hanseatic counterparts.

A marked increase in the overseas trade of Lynn during 1492 and 1493 was attributable mainly to the Hanseatic sector. Cloth exports for the two years totaled 962 units, of which 818 belonged to Hansards. By topping £1,370 in both years, the value of petty custom goods also exceeded previous annual averages. For the Exchequer year 1491–2 the Hanseatic share, enrolled separately from that of other non-denizens, constituted 89% of the total. Further, Hanseatic wax imports for this and the following year totalled seventy quintals.[44] After that, a drastic reduction in the overseas traffic foreshadowed a four-year slump in woollen exports, likely exacerbated somewhat by the Lowland embargoes. But by 1494–5, the first full year of the 1490s for which particulars of customs permit a clear delineation of the trade, the traffic in miscellaneous merchandise already had begun to show signs of stabilizing.

In October 1494 a Hamburg ship departed Lynn laden with thirty cloths, plus coal, Suffolk cheese, and coverlets valued at £10 for the shipper and four other Hansards. A Danzig ship also cleared port in mid-May the following year with an outbound cargo of eight cloths and £113 worth of hides, lead, and coverlets for three Hansards, and £8 worth for local merchant Richard Peper. Four more Danzig ships called at Lynn between 19 May and 4 September 1495, each discharging bulk freight and relading export cargo. These ships, from Danzig and Hamburg, carried all of the Hanseatic woollen exports from Lynn, and while the volume was not significant in light of the general disruption of the English cloth trade at this time, the use of these particular carriers again indicates the importance of Lynn's Baltic connections. These same shippers freighted £131 worth of exports and £121 worth of imports, and therefore were responsible for half of the aggregate value of the alien trade in miscellaneous goods for the Exchequer year 1494–5.[45] Worthy of note, too, is the fact that diverse commodities such as lead and coverlets could, in combination with cloth exports, push the Hanseatic trade balance at Lynn in favour of the export trade.

Something else that distinguished the trade of Lynn even further from that of Boston, Hull, and Newcastle was the coalescence of denizen and Hanseatic interests. English merchants shipped fourteen cloths and £15 worth of miscellaneous exports with the Baltic carriers, and although the Hanseatic ships did not carry inbound cargo for denizens, the Lynn merchants almost certainly sent their own vessel to Hamburg or the Baltic in the summer of 1495. William Cufford, master of the *Kateryn* of Lynn, returned home in July carrying osmund, tar, counters, and 'pruse skynnes' belonging to eight different English merchants. Among them were Robert Bees and John Brekersley, who, along with shipper Cufford and at least two other members of the group, had invested in prior commercial ventures to the Baltic. Bees and his colleague Richard Peper, moreover, were among those merchants who exported cloths and other goods in the Danzig ships that same summer.[46]

The degree to which industries in or near Lynn may have depended on Baltic imports is difficult to say. Undoubtedly the small consignments of ashes and dyestuffs helped sustain the middling textile industry, and the local and regional shipyards probably took much of the pitch, tar, lumber, and iron. Other principal imports, flax and hemp, may have been used in linen production, or in the manufacture of rope, cable, and cordage. A local rope and thread industry had existed at Lynn at least since the early fifteenth century. Yarn purchased, if not manufactured there was used to make hawsers for the fleet that Henry

VI inherited in the 1420s. Seventy years later, during the rebuilding of the royal fleet begun under Henry VII, the clerk of the king's ships at Portsmouth was buying 'ropes of dyvers compasses and byggenes of lyne [Lynn] and Normandy makyng.' He also sent an agent to Lynn to purchase cordage for the warship *Regent*. In 1497 his inventory for fitting out a new ship, the *Sweepstake*, also included various cables and a large 'Tye of iiii Strondes' bought at Lynn. The clerk's account shows that most cordage came in fact from Genoa or Normandy, but any that did not was manufactured and/or purchased at Lynn and brought coastwise from there to the new dockyards on the south coast.[47]

The Exchequer year 1496–7 saw both the aggregate value of petty custom merchandise and total woollen exports at Lynn plunge to their lowest levels since the mid-1470s. There was, however, a coincidental and temporary increase in the Hanseatic traffic at Boston. This very unrepresentative year for Lynn's overseas trade is especially significant, though, because it is the first for which the registers of the toll collectors at the Danish Sound survive. The toll records, and particularly those running consecutively during the mid-sixteenth century, are a principal quantitative source for the study of northern trade and shipping. However, in the spring and summer of 1497 at least forty English merchant ships as well as some from the Lowlands were brought into royal service as escort and transport vessels for a renewed military campaign against Scotland. Notwithstanding the potential for disruption of the shipping lanes off the Scottish coast, this likely reduced tonnage available on the northern commercial routes. Therefore, the earliest Sound toll account must be interpreted with considerable caution. No skippers from Lynn or any other English port are listed, but for English shipping and the northern trade this was an untypical year. Lynn was the leading east-coast port in terms of denizen participation in the Anglo-Baltic trade, and the register for 1497 definitely is not a fair barometer of English traffic to and from the Baltic during most of the 1490s.[48] The volume of trade in petty custom goods at Lynn increased substantially after 1497. Cloth exports, both denizen and Hanseatic, also began to recover, and by the turn of the century the trend was one of growth in overseas commerce.

Finally, significant changes to the role of Ipswich and Colchester completed the modification of the Anglo-Hanseatic trade network at the close of the century. Customs particulars for 1491–2 show that of the 209 cloths exported by Hansards that year 50 were shipped by Cologners of the London Steelyard in November 1491. The rest were freighted the following August by shipper Cort Defort, who also took with him £25 worth of lead for indigenous merchant Thomas Drayle. The skipper's destination cannot be determined with certainty, but the cargoes he discharged at London the year before, together with the timing of his arrivals and departures, indicate he was plying the Hamburg route. The cargo he brought to Ipswich/Colchester in June 1492 would tend to substantiate this, for along with consignments of wax, lumber, osmund and fish, it included various linens, 'hedelaken,' 'osnibrygge' (Osnabrück), and 'hombercloth' (Hamburg cloth). It accounted for more than half the total value of Hanseatic petty custom goods. The remainder consisted mainly of fish cargoes brought in by Hanseatic vessels, probably from Iceland via Hamburg.[49]

Subsequent Exchequer enrolments indicate the almost total disappearance of the Hanseatic cloth trade at Ipswich/Colchester after 1492, even though the Hansards continued to do business there on a fairly regular basis. The Lowland embargo was a serious setback for trade in general, but the traffic in miscellaneous goods was stabilizing by the late 1490s, and denizen cloth exports accelerated dramatically in the years following the *Intercursus*. However, petty custom figures are enrolled as combined alien/Hanseatic totals, and therefore reveal little more about the Hanseatic trade. But with Steelyard men no longer trans-shipping much cloth, the traffic in imported goods undoubtedly became the primary focus. There is little doubt, too, that this trade served the English capital as well as the Essex and Suffolk ports. A complaint about the quality of 'Spruse flax' purchased by a London grocer from Colchester clothman Richard Barker in the 1490s suggests that even bulk imports from the Baltic found their way to London via Colchester.[50]

On the other side of the Channel and along the North Sea coast an extensive shipping network linked the busy markets of Zealand, Brabant, and Holland with the Hanseatic port of Hamburg. Shippers from the Elbe hauled bulk freight like wood, ashes, copper, wax, and Hamburg beer coastwise to Zealand, and laded diverse return cargoes that frequently included salt, figs, fruit, and wine.[51] The merchants of Lübeck were important players in the eastward extension of this trade, and they also had wide-ranging business interests in Brabant. Like the Danzigers, they expanded their carriage trade southward to Iberia and hauled salt to Zealand from distant Lisbon. Wool, hides, and salmon from Scotland also reached Lowland ports in Lübeck ships. From Antwerp, Bergen op Zoom, and their outports the Lübeckers sent cloth, spices, and mixed cargo northward for eventual redistribution in the Baltic region. Cloth was the essential commodity. Basing calculations on extant Lübeck port books, W. Stark has estimated that cloth shipments accounted for up to three quarters of the total value of Lübeck's export trade to Danzig in the early 1490s.[52]

The Lübeckers functioned primarily as forwarding agents in this traffic to Prussia, and as Danzig's direct seaborne links to England and the Lowlands carried more and more of the trade toward the end of the century, their services became less vital. Perhaps, too, the presence in the Baltic of the Hollanders and merchants from Lynn began to have an effect. The English in particular had absolutely no established trade at Lübeck, and therefore shipped directly to Danzig. But Lübeckers still supplied many other important Baltic centres, like Stockholm, Riga, and Reval, with a vast array of western cloth manufactured in Flanders, Brabant, Holland, Westphalia, and England. The Lübeckers apparently had relinquished much of their direct role in England at the same time as the Brabant fairs were eclipsing Bruges as the chief market for regionally produced as well as imported fabrics. The traditional Low-lands/Hamburg/Lübeck link was still used, however, for the moving of cloth to the Baltic. Not only had the constraints on the Anglo-Lowland trade necessitated development of the overland corridor from Hamburg to Cologne, they had also meant the strengthening of links in the coastal traffic to the North Sea and Zuider Zee ports that interconnected as well with the Baltic trade. The Lübeckers thus retained their intermediary function in the commercial traffic to the north and east. By the same token, much of what they imported from Danzig and other Baltic towns was transferred to Hamburg and then reshipped to English and Atlantic ports.[53]

London and the Lowland corridor

Despite the many unresolved differences, relations between the Hanse and England were largely without major incident during the final decade of Henry VII's reign. No doubt there were occasional piracies, but the mayhem that often seemed to characterize maritime commerce during the 1480s apparently subsided. The Esterlings from Hamburg and Danzig solidified their grip on the Hanseatic traffic to and from eastern England. English traders, realizing that perhaps their competitive potential at Danzig was not quite so limited as they once had believed, began to venture to the Baltic on a limited but more regular basis. Likewise, the Steelyard merchants still maintained a thriving trade in the English capital, in spite of restrictions on unshorn cloth.

The early years of the new century saw further Anglo-Hanseatic talks deferred yet again. Initially, preparations for the marriages of the king's eldest son, Arthur, and his daughter Margaret took priority. Then, in 1504, tensions in the Baltic, which developed out of the conflict between Denmark and Sweden, caused the Hansards to request postponement.[54] By that time, though, Henry VII's stormy relationship with the Hapsburgs had again assumed a central role on the diplomatic stage. In 1502 there was a new alliance and commercial treaty with Maximilian,[55] but within two years relations had soured, and the cycle of embargoes seemed set to begin all over again according to an all too familiar scenario. Yet another pretender to the English throne – Edmund de la Pole, earl of Suffolk – was in the Low Countries, and when Maximilian deferred repeated requests for his banishment, Henry VII responded with another punitive trade ban. The prohibition on direct sailings to the Lowlands came into effect in late 1504 and was followed by the usual proclamation of the free market at Calais in January 1505. Accordingly, Hanseatic cargoes again were diverted over Hamburg and Kampen. No one was permitted to bring goods to Calais that had originated in the Hapsburg-Burgundian Lowlands.[56]

Prior to this there had been a rather noteworthy compromise with the Hanse. The Bruges meetings between English and Hanseatic officials in 1499 had failed to resolve outstanding differences, including charges that entrenched Hanseatic privileges in the kingdom were being systematically curtailed. So, early in 1504, Henry VII's final Parliament, in a move initiated by the Crown, passed an act that exempted Hanseatic merchants from all statutes that conflicted with their existing charters, notwithstanding certain privileges granted to London regarding retail trade there.[57] The Steelyard merchants thereby gained their long-sought guarantee of rights and freedoms that effectively defined and confirmed their legal status in England.

While recent biographers of Henry VII have not hesitated in labelling this an 'inexplicable action'[58] and an 'acknowledgement of total defeat against the Hansards ... not dictated by economic considerations,'[59] it was actually a quite logical conciliatory gesture given the almost continually unsettled state of Tudor-Hapsburg affairs. Nearly twenty years into a reign punctuated throughout by trade sanctions that responded as often as not to dynastic intrigues rather than mercantile concerns, the foreign trade of Henry VII's England was hardly less dependent on the Lowland markets or the contribution of the Hanseatic merchants than it had been in 1485. In fact, the Hanseatic trade remained crucial to England. The king knew that his on-again-off-again embargoes played havoc with the trade, and was equally aware of the aggravation the embargoes caused the merchants of the Steelyard, who were already annoyed about the inconclusive talks of 1499 and the enforcement of protectionist statutes. While there may be an element of plausibility in the notion that the king and his advisers feared possible Hanseatic support for the fugitive Suffolk, they likely sensed also that the Steelyard fellowship was nearing the end of its tether over existing grievances and the repeated disruptions of trade. Aware, moreover, that his government probably had achieved all it possibly could for Englishmen desiring to trade to the Baltic, the king would have been all the more disinclined to antagonize London's Hanseatic community any further. The new legislation therefore was an attempt to offset the difficulties that the impending resumption of politically motivated trade war would cause the Hanse. The practical implications were, in any event, fairly inconsequential. Even before the new crisis had fully passed, Hansards were again complaining of the zealous enforcement of statutes that hindered their trade.[60] In the absence of what might pass for coherent economic 'policy,' this was entirely consistent with a pattern of ad hoc strategems that still had to accommodate either the Hanseatic trade or the Lowland commercial link at any given time, or else risk England's possible isolation from the northern sector of the European trade.

This last embargo came to an end under unusual circumstances early in 1506. Duke Philip and his wife, Joanna, *en route* to Spain to claim her Castilian inheritance, were forced by rough seas to seek the safety of the Dorset coast. For several weeks thereafter they and their entourage remained in England as the guests of King Henry, and during this time both the extradition of de la Pole and a new commercial treaty were agreed upon.[61] But the resultant *Intercursus Malus* remained unconfirmed by Philip at the time of his death in late September.[62] Margaret of Savoy, regent of the Lowlands during the minority of Philip's son Charles, insisted, furthermore, that any trade pact with the English should do no more than confirm the terms of the 1496 agreement. So it was indeed the *Intercursus Magnus* that formed the basis of a further accord in June 1507[63] – one that determined the status quo in Anglo-Lowland commercial relations for the remainder of Henry VII's reign and the early years of Henry VIII's.

For the Hapsburgs there had been no lack of incentive to end the dispute with England and alleviate the economic hardship it caused. Already in another sector of the Lowland economy – the carriage trade to and from the Baltic – new uncertainty was looming. King John of Denmark was engaged in a trade war of his own against dynastic and political rivals in Sweden. Since 1502 he had been trying to enforce an embargo by arresting ships suspected of trading to Stockholm and by turning loose privateers in the shipping lanes. In an attempt to force Lübeckers to renounce their Swedish trade, the Danes deliberately victimized a number of that town's shippers who plied the routes to Livonia.[64] After Scottish and French mediation resulted in a brief lull in 1507, the quarrel escalated again, and Emperor Maximilian was drawn into the turmoil. At Lübeck's request, he forbade his subjects to trade to Denmark or otherwise support King John. This, however, inevitably had negative implications for Lowland shippers whose trade to the eastern Baltic depended on passage through Danish waters. As a consequence, the prohibition was amended early in 1510. But when Lübeck's privateers then attacked Lowland vessels trying to break the Wendish blockade of the Sound, a state of war between Lübeck and Holland resulted.[65]

By then, Narrow Seas commerce between England and the Low Countries was back to normal. The interruption of that trade in 1505 and 1506 had, however, produced negative economic repercussions on both sides of the Channel. In England, the impact is mirrored in the extant customs enrolments for London. Exports by denizens, which were averaging more than 24,000 cloths annually in the four years prior to the embargo, plummeted to well under 19,000 for each of the two Exchequer years affected by the restrictions. The trade of non-Hanseatic aliens in London also declined, although by contrast the Hanseatic trade, with its alternate network in place on the Continent, remained steady and even indicated slight growth. All three sectors – denizen, alien, and Hanseatic – showed improvement from 1506 onward, and there was a spectacular recovery by English exporters, who sent more than 30,000 cloths overseas from London in the final year of Henry VII's reign. The figures leave little doubt as to the key participants in the trade. From Michaelmas 1505 through Michaelmas 1509 denizens accounted for half of London's cloth exports, and merchants of the Hanse a full 36%.[66]

The interaction of Londoners and other merchants from southern England with merchants in the Lowlands was an essential element in this trade. Englishmen shipped cheese and beer to the marts, shopped for precious metals, and offered their quality cloth to Brabantine dealers and finishers. South Germans also bought English wares in Brabant, and so too did Italian merchants. The Brabanters, for their part, contracted English agents to deliver cloth at the fairs, bought and sold it at Bergen op Zoom or Antwerp, and sent consignments onward to Cologne. A diverse range of commodities could be offered in exchange, including copperware from Dinant, or metal ores brought from Saxony or points east. Antwerp merchants shipped copper and other metals from Bergen op Zoom to Calais, and exchanged 'batteryware' for English cloth at the Antwerp fairs.[67] As might be expected, however, from time to time relations between the Brabanters and their English counterparts were less than amiable. Notwithstanding the common complaints about unfulfilled obligations and disagreements with tax and toll collectors on both sides of the Channel, there were instances when dislike and distrust of Englishmen in the Lowlands seem to have run rather deep. An example was the inquiry in 1501 into the demeanour of some Kentish merchants in Bergen op Zoom, who were accused not only of engaging in unfair and illegal business practices, but also of uttering scurrilous remarks against Duke Philip. Their accusers were merchants from Antwerp.[68]

Eastern England and the Hanseatic network

At Hull, the rejuvenated cloth trade of the post-1497 period was set back again by the new interruptions in the Anglo-Lowland traffic. Cloth exports of 3,951 units in 1503–4 surpassed totals even for the previous peak years of the early 1480s, but in 1505–6 they were halved, and for the rest of the decade hovered around 2,000 cloths per year. The trade in petty custom merchandise followed a similar pattern, although it recovered in 1506–7 and was reasonably stable thereafter. There is little evidence to suggest that the merchants of northern England made much of an attempt to offset the disruption of the Lowland trade with new initiatives in the Baltic. A Hull merchant by the name of Basell claimed that he laded a ship with osmund and flax at Danzig in July 1497, only to see the cargo spoiled by pirates before it left the Vistula. No English ships passed through the Danish Sound in either direction that year, and Danzig's delegates to the Bruges talks in 1499 denied any knowledge of the alleged incident. Nor did their English counterparts press the matter. Of the ten or eleven different English shippers who did clear the Sound in 1503, none was from Hull or Newcastle.[69]

Hanseatic activity at Newcastle was not inconsiderable. All of the Hanseatic merchandise recorded there between Michaelmas 1499 and Michaelmas 1502 was carried by a total of only four ships – three from the Baltic and one from Hamburg. The value of the imports was £254 and that of the exports, excluding thirteen cloths, was £152. In the summer of 1506, though, three Danzig ships carried £396 worth of freight for Hansards, but more than half this value was assigned to their lead exports. The inbound freight, as well as the cargoes loaded for export in the Danzig vessels, was customed only to Hansards. The corresponding Danzig *Pfahlkammerbücher* also confirm that ownership of the lead cargoes subsequently discharged from these ships was confined to the Esterlings themselves, who evidently controlled much of the trade between Newcastle and the Prussian staple.[70]

To the south, the Hansards had long since given up their trade at Boston. After 1502 they did not ship any cloth from the port, and the woollen trade there ceased to be of any importance. The extant customs particulars for 1502–3 contain no references to Hanseatic trade of any description. This, in itself, is not particularly unusual; a number of fifteenth-century accounts make no mention of Hansards, while still others do. But other factors confirm that by the early sixteenth century the Hanseatic absence was permanent. In the summer of 1505 the London Steelyard again paid for extensive repairs to the Boston *comptoir*, and requested Lübeck to encourage the *Bergenfahrer* to resume trading there. The implication was that the place had fallen into disuse.

Yet the English, it was claimed, had begun to use the Bergen/England route extensively. But the refurbished facility and the Steelyard's assurance that Hansards using it would not be obliged to absorb the recent expenditures were not enough to lure the *Bergenfahrer* back. Nor was an assurance from the king's mother, Lady Margaret, promising fair and indeed favourable treatment of Hansards coming to Boston. Again in 1506–7 no Hanseatic trade was recorded in the customs particulars, and the absence of such trade is confirmed again by the accounts for 1514–15. Although enrolments for the petty custom continued to use the rubric 'alien and Hanse,' all indications are that Hansards in fact no longer figured in the non-denizen trade at Boston.[71]

And there were other changes elsewhere. Ipswich and Colchester, once busy outports for the Steelyard's cloth export trade, were now, in so far as the Hansards were concerned, merely depots for bulk freight brought in by the Esterlings. The surviving particulars of accounts for 1505–6 and the Danzig books are instructive. A single Danzig captain, Urban Some, offloaded a standard Baltic cargo of clapholts, wainscots, bowstaves, and wax in May 1506. He returned home on three separate occasions, each time laden with cloth for Danzig merchants. Yet Hansards shipped no cloth from Ipswich/Colchester that year, and indeed Some's departure from there is not recorded. Nor did he call at London or Newcastle. If the cloth he took back to the Baltic was from England – and this is not certain – then it almost had to have been picked up at Hull and/or Lynn, the only other English ports where Hansards had woollens customed for export. Urban Some was no stranger to Lynn, having called there two years previously, although the size of the cargoes he discharged at Danzig suggests they may have been loaded at Hull, where the volume of Hanseatic trade was much greater. Of course, they may just as well have come from the Lowlands. In any case Ipswich and Colchester were no longer significant cloth exporting centres within the Anglo-Hanseatic network, and now served the Hanseatic trade primarily as clearing stations for bulk imports.[72] Possibly this trend stimulated some local interest in the Baltic, for the following year an apprentice of Ipswich merchant John Caldwell was alleged to have purchased nearly £200 worth of goods at the Prussian staple through the agency of Danzig merchant Hans Stendell. Stendell later claimed that Caldwell's man, Thomas Bradde, had not paid for the merchandise and that he also owed £4 for board and lodging in Danzig.

Bradde was arrested there, but his master denied any knowledge of the business.[73] To what degree the interests of Suffolk merchants in Prussia may have been set back by this incident is impossible to tell, given the unknown extent of their trade there. Needless to say, however, it could have done little to enhance short-term prospects for an increased share in the Baltic market.

Eastern England's main link to Danzig was in fact maintained by the merchants of Lynn, as evidenced by customs particulars for 1503–4. They show aggregate cloth exports consistent with a general upward trend and the volume of petty custom goods higher than the average for the first decade of the century, but not unrepresentative for the period.[74] In November 1503 William Sanderson, one of six Lynn skippers to pass through the Sound that calendar year,[75] returned to his home port with a typical Baltic cargo of rafters, eels, platters, and Prussian chests belonging to four local merchants. In the spring three more English ships departed Lynn laden with cloths, coverlets, hides, and lead for Hanseatic as well as denizen merchants.[76] They arrived home together at the end of July, and their bulk cargoes, also shared by a Hanseatic agent, strongly suggest that they, too, were returning from the Baltic. No fewer than seven Hanseatic ships from Danzig also called at Lynn during the summer. On their outward voyage the English vessels had carried 190 cloths, or a full 43% of denizen woollen exports for the Exchequer year. Moreover, the £428 worth of miscellaneous imports and exports freighted by the English merchants in the Lynn and Danzig ships constituted 23% of the denizen trade in miscellanea. So far as the Hanseatic merchants were concerned, all of their cloth shipments, totaling 123 units, were sent with these Lynn and Danzig carriers. The value of other goods, which consisted mainly though not exclusively of imports in the Danzig ships, amounted to half the alien trade for the year. The Hansards also owned an additional fifty quintals of wax.

Skipper Sanderson's indisputable presence at the Sound in the autumn of 1503, together with the complete particulars of account for the subsequent summer, which indicate with relative certainty that at least three more Lynn ships made return voyages to Danzig, permit an approximate evaluation of the overall importance of that distant market to Lynn's overseas trade. Cloth exports from Lynn during the Exchequer year 1503–4 totaled 572 units, and the shippers from Lynn and Danzig who sailed to the Baltic carried 313 of them. The combined

Baltic shipments of English and Esterling merchants therefore accounted for 55% of Lynn's woollen export trade. The value of other denizen and Hanseatic goods shipped to or from Lynn in these ships was £974, while the overseas trade of the port as a whole was £2,879.[77] Hence, the Baltic connection also drew 34% of Lynn's aggregate overseas trade in goods other than cloth, wool and wine. In all, twenty-four Lynn merchants or ships' masters were involved, while the Hanseatic participation was left to the skippers of the Danzig ships and a half dozen other Esterlings. Regrettably, the customs particulars for 1503–4 are the only ones to have survived for the first decade of the sixteenth century. Nevertheless, interpreted in context with the enrolled trade statistics for the period, they may be taken as fairly representative of both the structure and volume of Lynn's Baltic trade at this time.[78]

Relations between the denizen business community and the Hansards likely were amiable, for the most part. Of those numerous local merchants who traded to the Baltic, many were or later became prominent Lynn burgesses. They dealt routinely with a small community of resident Esterlings with whom they had undoubtedly become well acquainted over a period of several years. By the early sixteenth century the Hanseatic depot on the river Ouse – called the 'Stylehoffe' after the great London *comptoir* – had as its governor Hamburg merchant/shipper Lutkyn Smyth. He had been a familiar face in the Wash ports for more than thirty years. Of course, the integrated commercial interests of the two merchants' groups did not mean that the Esterlings and the citizens of Lynn coexisted in perfect harmony. Occasionally old personal feuds surfaced, as when an action of trespass and battery resulted in the arrest of Danzig skipper Lutkyn Molner. Claiming that the plaintiff had for a long time harboured 'grete males' against him, Molner appealed to the chancellor to intervene on his behalf, since he was 'a straunger and unknowen' in Lynn, and therefore not allowed to plead his case fairly there. In 1497 Lynn merchants accused the Hanseatic *Bergenfahrer* of the deliberate drowning of fishermen from Cromer and Blakeney, and a couple of years later a Danzig captain's attempt to defraud customs agents at Lynn also embarrassed the Hanseatic merchants there.[79]

The port's commerce to and from Danzig suffered no serious disruption during the remainder of Henry VII's reign. This was not the case, though, in the years that followed. Beginning in 1512 Atlantic and

North Sea shipping was disrupted by England's naval war against
France and Scotland. Some months before, the equally vicious maritime
conflict between Denmark and towns of the Hanse's Wendish sector
had claimed at least one vessel from Lynn. Hanseatic trade there declined temporarily, and it is possible that Lynn's captains avoided the
Baltic route for a time. Towards the end of the decade some of the
town's merchants still had not been compensated for damages inflicted
by privateers from Stralsund, and the Crown tried to exploit the situation in an attempt to intimidate the Steelyard fellowship in London. By
then, however, skippers from Lynn were again offloading typical Baltic
cargoes, and Danzigers were once more freighting cloth for Englishmen.[80]

The Steelyard

Other than the ships from Lynn, the only English vessels passing
through the Sound in 1503 were recorded as being 'aff Lunden i England.' Four or perhaps five London skippers are listed in the toll register, yet only two of them appear in the corresponding particulars of
customs for London. It is possible that the others cleared the Thames in
ballast or actually departed from some other port. William Sayer sailed
to the Baltic twice in 1503, departing London each time with modest
cloth cargoes for English merchants. The other captain, John Scott, also
carried a denizen woollen cargo. Unlike the Lynn merchants, Londoners
do not appear to have utilized Hanseatic carriers on the Baltic route.
Huge consignments of bulk freight and enormous quantities of wax
were offloaded in London from Hanseatic ships likely coming directly
from Danzig and Hamburg, yet virtually none of these cargoes was
customed to Englishmen.[81]

The same pattern held true for Danzig-bound ships, whose arrivals
there are listed in the extant shipping records for 1506. Hanseatic
shippers did freight some cloth for denizen English merchants, but it
was rare for an Esterling to employ an English carrier. Consignments
of Gascon wine were also carried in the English ships, and several
dozen London merchants may have had interests in the Baltic ventures.[82] The transactions at Danzig, however, likely were entrusted to a
handful of English agents in Prussia or to those who travelled there
with the ships. It is entirely plausible, too, that the Londoners used

some of the same Hanseatic factors who served merchants of the Steelyard.

During the first decade of the sixteenth century the value of petty custom goods recorded in London increased dramatically. But with no extant particulars of customs except for the Exchequer years 1502–3 and 1505–6, fluctuations in the Hanseatic and non-Hanseatic share of this trade cannot be traced. Nor is it possible to determine if the increases were general or attributable to either the import or export sector. Moreover, although the Hansards had £15,793 worth of miscellaneous merchandise customed at London in 1502–3, and therefore accounted for one-third of the non-denizen trade, the aggregate for this year is low and perhaps even untypical for the period. In 1509–10 it was £77,253, and already had topped £84,000 once in the interim. Particulars of accounts show that the Hanseatic 3d goods were valued at almost £18,000, or 30% of the total eventually enrolled for that year.[83]

At the Steelyard, regional representation within the non-transient Hanseatic fellowship naturally lent itself to a degree of specialization, particularly in the import trade. In 1503, for example, some Hanseatic grain was brought to London, and virtually all of it belonged to Hamburg or Danzig men. Dinanter Johann Salmer continued as the Steelyard's pre-eminent metalwares dealer, exporting tin and pewter and importing several hundred pounds sterling worth of copperware. A handful of Esterlings, Hermann Plough among them, monopolized wax imports, which in most years now added between £8,000 and £9,000 to the value of the Hanseatic import trade.[84]

The advancing technology of warfare, coupled with modest naval and military expansion under the early Tudors, undoubtedly enhanced economic opportunities for the Hansards in London as well. Much of the royal arsenal was stocked with weapons and armour from continental Europe, procured through Italian agents, but as England developed its own weapons industry other purveyors of war materials, including Hansards from the Steelyard, found a ready market for their wares. Although little is known of the royal armoury in the fifteenth century, purchases for ordnance in the first few years of Henry VIII's reign give some indication of the Hansards' role, and their involvement need not have been new or temporary. In all likelihood they assisted in the development of Henry VII's arsenal as well. In October 1509 alone more than twenty tons of copper was purchased by the Crown for the king's gunfounders. Half of it was supplied by Esterling merchant Cort van Sight, and was brought from the Steelyard to the Tower in carts. Van Sight had been doing business in London as early as 1503, when he imported wax, linen, and iron from the Baltic, and it is not clear from the scant records that have survived just how regularly he sold copper to agents of the Crown. Within a few years, however, he was succeeded by a small group of fellow Steelyard merchants who consistently supplied war materials to Henry VIII's armourers. One of them was Hermann Baghragh, who sold vast quantities of saltpetre for the making of gunpowder, and others included Egar van Kempen and Jeromyas Dolwyn, purveyors of bowstaves and copper.[85]

Cologne and Westphalian merchants – the Blitterswiks and Questenbercks, Johann van der Besen, and others active in the Lowland trade – offered, as they had throughout the late fifteenth century, a range of merchandise distinct from that in which most of the Baltic Hansards usually dealt. Many of their shipments of fustian, thread, silk, dyestuffs, and steel came, like Salmer's 'batteryware,' either from the Low Countries or the lower Rhineland, or originated in the non-Hanseatic regions of western Europe. More often than not English and Lowland carriers were hired to haul these goods to London, and the Hansards shared cargo space with English and alien merchants.[86] The export trade from the capital was keyed to English textile suppliers and a circle of business contacts in diverse regions of the country, from Hampshire to the Midlands. While there was still a traditional reliance on the weavers in Gloucestershire and Somerset, Steelyard merchants also did business with Wiltshire merchants and with John Burnet, a 'cotonman' from Manchester.[87]

The volume of Hanseatic trade at London was considerably greater than it had been a quarter of a century before. About three dozen Hansards, including ships' masters, had cloth customed for export from the English capital in 1506, and a few more than that shared the import cargoes. Much of the trade from Hamburg was managed in the name of Lutkyn Buring and Hans van Tynsen. Hermann Plough, Albrecht Gyse, and Tydemann Blanck were among the more prominent Danzigers. The severely damaged particulars of accounts for 1507–8 also show about thirty-six different Hansards exporting cloth from the Steelyard.[88]

Change and stability

A gradual restructuring of the Anglo-Hanseatic trade, precipitated initially by the war in the 1470s, and inextricably bound up with the subsequent ascendancy of the Brabantine entrepôts and the expansion and modification of continental routes, was in a large measure complete by the second decade of the sixteenth century. In terms of the value of goods exchanged there, Hull remained the most important single link in the Anglo-Hanseatic trade outside of London. And, even though the Esterlings were not well liked in northern England, it was the merchants of Danzig and Hamburg who sustained the Hanseatic trade there, exchanging bulk imports for English cloth and lead. At Newcastle, too, lead provided an export base to balance a modest Hanseatic import trade also controlled exclusively by the Esterlings. To the south, in Lincolnshire, the port of Boston was dropped entirely from the Hanseatic shipping routes, and the aggregate value of overseas trade there declined correspondingly. But the port of Lynn emerged as the focal point of both the import and export trade of the Hansards in East Anglia. The Prussian staple was the crucial connection, and the involvement of denizen merchants in Lynn's Baltic trade was especially important. The other East Anglian ports – Ipswich and Colchester – ceased to be of any consequence in so far as Hanseatic woollen exports were concerned, but they continued to be utilized as points of entry for Hanseatic imports from the Baltic and elsewhere. Finally, the Hanseatic traffic in woollens from southern England was concentrated entirely in the English capital, which also was the largest market by far for Hanseatic imports. The London Steelyard clearly relied on two principal overseas connections: the staple at Danzig and the great marts in Brabant.

With the exception of the London *comptoir*, where merchants from diverse regions of the Hanse were active, the Hanseatic trade in England remained rather narrowly confined to the Esterlings, and more especially to the merchants and shippers of Hamburg and Danzig. Lübeckers and other Wendish merchants were still intermediaries in the traffic to and from the Baltic, and some of them owned shares in the ships trading to England. However, by their own admission, the Lübeckers had scarcely four or five men engaged in direct trade to

England by the end of the fifteenth century.[89] Their traditional commercial link with eastern England, the fish trade at Boston, had been all but abandoned by the late 1490s, as English fleets and those of Hamburg and Danzig took advantage of the Icelandic fisheries.

The withdrawal of the *Bergen/Englandfahrer* from Boston and the elimination of the Hanseatic cloth export trade at Ipswich and Colchester streamlined the Hanseatic presence in England in terms of both the distribution network and the central participants. Hull in the north and London in the south provided most woollen exports, while Lynn and Newcastle had enough of a subsidiary trade in lead, hides, and other miscellanea to attract the Hansards as well. Only these four ports, together with Ipswich/Colchester, were of any importance to the Hanseatic import trade by the end of the fifteenth century. And except in the case of London, the import trade of the Hansards was by then almost synonymous with the bulk carriage trade from Danzig and Hamburg.

A number of circumstances had contributed to the ascendancy of Hamburg's merchants and shippers in the Anglo-Hanseatic sphere. To begin with they successfully competed with the English for a share of the Icelandic fish trade, and by integrating it with existing commercial links with the kingdom, largely eclipsed the role of the *Bergenfahrer* in England. The Wendish merchants kept the Bergen *comptoir* and maintained a steady though somewhat less secure trade in stockfish and herring to south German markets,[90] but Lübeckers showed little interest in bringing their fish to England. In addition to their Iceland/ Hamburg/England connection, Hamburg shippers were tied to the east-west commercial axis of the Anglo-Lowland trade through their coastal traffic to and from the Low Countries. They also provided extra tonnage for the Narrow Seas routes between Brabant and the London Steelyard. Moreover, Hamburg's trade and shipping along the Atlantic seaboard remained a vital extension of the vast Baltic network that supplied many essential bulk materials. Hamburg's fish and bulk carriage trade was augmented by grain exports and inexpensive textiles supplied by local and regional industries.[91] Cloth manufactured in Hamburg, Hannover, Osnabrück, Münster, and Saltzwedel reached England via Brabant, but also was taken there directly in Hamburg ships. The diverting of Hanseatic exports of English cloth from London and Calais in the 1490s further strengthened Hamburg's direct commercial links with England in addition to the coastal trade and inland routes that connected the North Sea port with the lower Rhineland.

While the role of the east-coast ports had been revised and the merchants of Hamburg had supplanted the Lübeckers in the English trade, the other two principal Hanseatic subgroups remained firmly entrenched. Danzig skippers maintained their place as the foremost foreign suppliers of bulk forest products to London and eastern England. Indeed, the basic orientation of the Danzigers' seaborne trade was now clearly a western one. They, too, tapped the Icelandic fish reserves, shipped bulk freight extensively to England and the Lowlands, purchased cloth there, and stretched their commercial network along its Atlantic axis as far as Lisbon, where imported Baltic timber helped build the ships for Iberian maritime expansion.[92] The other group – the Cologners and their associates from the lower Rhineland and Westphalia – maintained an English trade concentrated almost totally at the London Steelyard, but tied to a broad network of resource bases and retail centres across western Europe. In this trade the Brabant fair towns and their outports, of great commercial importance in their own right, also served as vital though not exclusive transit points connecting Cologne's London trade with the eastern inland network.

CHAPTER VI

CONCLUSION

The institutional decay of the German Hanse in the late fifteenth century, as seen in context with the confederation's economic and political relationship with England, is closely tied to significant changes in the Anglo-Hanseatic trade. Commercial interests inevitably influenced political allegiances within the Hanseatic confederation, and by the first decade of the sixteenth century the trade network that linked the seaborne economies of Hanseatic and English towns was appreciably different from the one that had existed three generations earlier.

Throughout the 1450–1510 period the merchants of Hamburg and the Baltic maintained a largely itinerant import trade in fish and bulk cargo along England's east coast, from Lynn to Newcastle. This trade underwent at least one important modification, however, for by the end of the century Lübeck's *Bergenfahrer* – once the most prominent Hanseatic fish importers, with a particularly significant trade at Boston – were scarcely a factor. They had been supplanted by the merchants and shippers of Hamburg and Danzig, who brought fish consignments from Iceland in addition to typical cargoes of flax, wood, iron, tar, and linen. This group now dominated the Hanseatic trade to ports north of London.

In southern England the focus of a much more diversified Hanseatic trade was and ever had been the London Steelyard, where a more closely balanced traffic in woollen exports and various imports, ranging from silk to dyestuffs and bulk raw materials, was maintained by a resident Hanseatic community. Within the Steelyard fellowship two principal subgroups – the Esterlings from Hamburg and the Baltic, and the Cologners, Westphalians, and merchants from the lower Rhineland – depended on two essential overseas connections: the northern trade to and from Danzig and Hamburg, and the cross-Channel traffic to and from the Lowlands. Both of these trade links were interconnected, in turn, with the north-south commercial axis of the Atlantic network, which by the end of the fifteenth century extended from the northernmost Hanseatic ports to Lisbon. The Anglo-Hanseatic War (1469–74) and its aftermath saw the Hanseatic woollen trade in southern England, like the English cloth export trade as a whole, become concentrated almost exclusively in London and highly dependent on the fair towns of Brabant for continental distribution. By the 1490s the once thriving outports for the Steelyard – Ipswich and Colchester – would cease to be of any relevance in this sector of the Hanseatic trade.

In fact, the suspension of Anglo-Baltic commerce and the Hanseatic embargo on English cloth during the war years set in motion a number of crucial changes within the European trade structure. The trade of denizen cloth exporters, from both northern England and London, became almost wholly dependent on the Lowland market, and the Baltic Hansards were obliged to redirect much of their seaborne traffic there as well. This not only benefited the Lowland cloth manufacturers and exporters, who, in the absence of English competition in the northern Hanseatic sphere, had the non-Hanseatic share of the Baltic market much to themselves for a time. It also contributed to the ascendancy of the Brabantine entrepôts and their outports in Zealand. With access to alternative markets restricted, a continental gateway for the English woollen trade became all the more essential for English exporters and the merchants of Cologne. Protectionist statutes in Flanders were offset by comparatively liberal trade policies at Antwerp and Bergen op Zoom, making Brabant the logical conduit. So, in addition to the political turmoil in Flanders that weakened the trade of Bruges after the death of Duke Charles, the strengthening of the London/Zealand/Brabant corridor from 1469 through 1474, coupled with the increased dependence of the Baltic Hansards on the Zealand quays, also helped pave the way for subsequent expansion of the Brabantine market. The Cologners, moreover, not only preserved their trade between the Steelyard and Brabant in the early 1470s, they of necessity expanded lucrative commercial links eastward to non-Hanseatic regions. Thenceforth, the extension of the east-west overland network through Silesia challenged the protectionist policies of Prussian and Polish towns and their established control of trade to the west via Danzig.

Economic developments to some degree shaped political attitudes. Likewise, key adjustments in the commercial network reflect many of the trends and crises in Anglo-Hanseatic diplomacy. An obvious prelude to the diminished presence of the *Bergenfahrer* in England, for instance, was the severe and prolonged breach in relations between Lübeck and England following the attacks on the Wendish salt ships in 1449 and 1458. Next, the Anglo-Hanseatic War of the early 1470s eliminated the Lübeckers entirely from the English trade for the better part of half a decade. Their peaceful departure was assured in the years that followed, as fleets from England, Danzig, and Hamburg successfully exploited the Icelandic fisheries and lessened English dependence on the Bergen *comptoir*. The main residual effect was that Lübeck, though still capable of wielding considerable political influence within the Hanseatic community, was left with no significant trading interests in the English kingdom. This situation ultimately contributed to political polarization within the Hanse, for unlike Lübeck's now nominal trade with England, that of Cologne was vital; so much so that the town willingly forfeited membership in the Hanse in order to preserve that trade when Anglo-Hanseatic relations reached their lowest ebb in 1468. Notwithstanding the ongoing controversy regarding the Bruges *comptoir*, then, one of the most serious and obtrusive rifts to develop within the Hanse in the late medieval period stemmed directly from Anglo-Hanseatic relations between 1450 and 1468.

Cologne's temporary defection from the Hanse, together with the range of other responses to England's challenge, clearly delineated a number of special interest groups within the Hanseatic confederation, and thus exemplified the disunity that weakened the Hanse as a political entity. Yet, although it contributed to a gradual institutional paralysis, particularism within the Hanse was not a new development, and by the same token Hanseatic political solidarity or lack of it was not a barometer for the mercantile prosperity of individual member towns. That now depended very much on adaptability to the evolving trade structure. The modifications in the northern European commercial network, triggered in part by Anglo-Hanseatic crises, certainly reinforced Cologne's integral position along the east-west axis of the burgeoning cloth trade from London and the Low Countries. And, in the face of competition from the extended overland routes, the Danzigers energetically expanded their seaborne traffic to western markets. In the final quarter of the century they, too, gained a foothold in the Icelandic fisheries, and extended their long-distance carriage trade to Iberia. They also played an increasingly important role at the Steelyard, and controlled much of the non-denizen overseas trade in ports north of London. Hamburg also integrated her Baltic connections and the Icelandic fish trade with English and Lowland markets, and provided shipping for coastal and Channel traffic. Later in the century the Anglo-Lowland trade wars undoubtedly enhanced Hamburg's prospects for mercantile growth as well, when much of the Hanse's English cloth trade had to be redirected to Hamburg.

The Anglo-Hanseatic talks at Antwerp in 1491, precipitated by a steady worsening of relations between the two parties, further accentuated diverse interests within the Hanse. Lübeck was represented as the nominal head of the Hanseatic delegation, and the Cologners were intensely involved, but the real negotiations were between the English envoys and the Danzigers. The main issues were recognition of Hanseatic privileges in England – a joint concern of Danzig, Hamburg, and Cologne, but hardly for Lübeck and the distant Livonian towns – and English status at the Prussian staple.

Throughout much of the fifteenth century English access to the Baltic market, and more specifically to the Danzig staple, was a predominant issue in Anglo-Hanseatic affairs. Inevitably, then, historians attempting to delineate and explain commercial trends have been drawn to the two major Anglo-Hanseatic treaties that dealt with that issue. Postan, for one, was of the mind that the Utrecht accord of 1474 effectively stymied English interests in the Baltic for the rest of the century.[1] Yet a recent textual analysis of that treaty shows that clauses pertaining to the status of Englishmen in Hanseatic territory hardly differ at all from those contained in the earlier agreement. Indeed, the Treaty of Utrecht did nothing to alter the legal position of English merchants in Prussia.[2] Even so, another equally current study continues to link the fate of England's Baltic trade to this accord; the English *Vorstoss* [thrust] in the region was not blocked by the 1437 treaty, but instead was brought to an end in 1474 – by one that reiterated the terms of its predecessor. In the interim, and indeed prior to 1437, policies adopted by the Teutonic knights and Danzig were not devised to protect the meagre Prussian share of Anglo-Baltic trade so much as to undermine the English preponderance in that sector.[3] Yet if perceived restrictions failed to prevent the English from monopolizing trade between the kingdom and the Prussian staple, then why was there such an incessant clamour for 'reciprocal' privileges at Danzig? Perhaps, after all, too much credit has been given to English entrepreneurs who had commercial interests in Prussia during the middle decades of the century and rather too little to those who kept the trade alive thereafter.

There was some English commercial traffic to and from Danzig between 1450 and 1468. From time to time it was disrupted by political crises that more often than not affected freedom of navigation and actual physical access to the eastern Baltic. Paramount among these were England's strained relations with Lübeck, the hostility of the Danes, and also the war between Poland and the Order. Then in the early 1470s, England's Baltic trade was shut down entirely by the Anglo-Hanseatic War. But the Treaty of Utrecht subsequently reopened the region, and once again English ships – and especially those from Lynn – made their way to Danzig. During the next three decades the trade continued to be affected by the ebb and flow of Anglo-Danish relations and also by attitudes toward Hansards in England, particularly at Hull. The English merchant community as a whole, however, had become all the more dependent on the trade to Brabant during the war years. Except for the merchants of Lynn, who obviously found it profitable to sustain commercial links with Danzig, Englishmen who engaged in overseas commerce remained somewhat preoccupied with the Lowland trade until new crises arose in the late 1480s and early 1490s. Even then, they were slow to respond to the Baltic alternative, despite the explicit confirmation of their status in 1491. They were then, as they had been in the past, on an equal footing at Danzig with all other non-Hansards. By and large their mercantile achievements were not equal to those of the government on the Anglo-Hanseatic diplomatic front. Indeed the inability of England's merchants to penetrate alternative markets during the early 1490s muted the effectiveness of royal policy regarding the Hanse and the Low Countries. During his trade wars with the Hapsburgs, Henry VII had little choice but to open Calais as a free market and declare it the staple for English cloth, in order to preserve England's woollen export trade. And the inertia of the English merchant community vis-à-vis the Baltic continued through the early years of Henry VIII's reign. Englishmen still had a share of the Anglo-Baltic trade, although in the cloth export sector at least, it was a far cry from that of the Hansards. The Dano-Wendish sea war that erupted in the spring of 1510 played havoc with commercial traffic and necessarily had an impact on English and Hanseatic trade. Having given advance notice that passage through Danish waters would not be tolerated, Wendish captains vigorously blockaded the Sound throughout the summer of 1510, seizing vessels from the Low Countries, England, and several from Danzig. There can be little doubt that under these circumstances both denizen and Hanseatic exporters in England held back cloth shipments to the Baltic. Hanseatic woollen exports dropped drastically in the Exchequer year 1509–10. Those of denizens, whose share in the Baltic trade was small, fell off slightly. Attacks on neutral shipping in the western Baltic continued over the next three years. Even so, after Danzig succeeded in negotiating an exemption from the blockade in the summer of 1511 for ships from Danzig, Hamburg, and England, the English cloth export trade rebounded accordingly.

In England the overall importance of the Hansards is mirrored in the impact of disruptions in the Anglo-Hanseatic trade on various regional economies. In most years for which evidence survives, Hansards in the east-coast ports of Lynn, Hull, and probably Newcastle accounted for 33% to 75% of the trade in miscellaneous goods other than cloth and wool, and were the only foreigners of any significance in the woollen export trade. Their absence during the war years 1469–74 resulted in a precipitous decline in the overseas trade of the East Anglian towns and ports to the north. Again in 1490, when antipathy at Hull was such that the Hansards were reluctant to go there, the foreign overseas trade of the port was virtually closed down. Also, as the *Bergenfahrer* gradually abandoned the port of Boston during the waning years of the century that port's seaborne trade, already in decline since the 1450s, faded dramatically. Similarly, when the Steelyard Hansards did not resume their cloth shipments from Ipswich/Colchester after the 1470s there was an appreciable decline there. In London, woollen exports by the free Cologners during the Anglo-Hanseatic War amounted to only about half of the usual Hanseatic aggregate in any one year. However, both before and after the conflict Hanseatic merchants accounted for one third of the cloth export trade and at least that much of the foreign import trade. Collectively, they remained an essential component in London's overseas commerce.

NOTES

Preface

1 E. Pitz, 'Steigende und fallende Tendenzen in Politik und Wirtschafts-leben der Hanse,' discusses many interesting aspects of this question, though primarily for the sixteenth century.

Chapter 1

1 The following is a brief outline of the principal aspects of Anglo-Han-seatic politics and trade up to the mid-fifteenth century, and is not intended as a comprehensive treatment of the subject. S. Jenks, *England, die Hanse und Preussen*, II 474–678 and T.H. Lloyd, *England and the German Hanse, 1157–1611*, 109–83 provide thorough and up-to-date analysis for this period, and no attempt will be made to duplicate these works here. Unless specifically indicated, references to Anglo-Hanseatic diplomacy are based on these two studies and on the following older works: E. Daenell, *Die Blütezeit der deutschen Hanse*; K. Engel, 'Die Organisation der deutsch-hansischen Kaufleute in England im 14. und 15. Jahrhundert'; M.M. Postan, 'The Economic and Political Relations of England and the Hanse from 1400 to 1475,' W. Stein, 'Die Hanse und England beim Ausgang des hundertjährigen Krieges' and *Die Hanse und England: Ein hansisch-englischer Seekrieg im 15. Jahrhundert*.
2 K. Fritze, *Am Wendepunkt der Hanse*, 55–9.
3 Ibid, 70–1.
4 Ibid, 71–3. Also M. Malowist, *Croissance et régression en Europe XIVe–XVIIe siècles*, 98–122; F. Vollbehr, *Die Holländer und die deutsche Hanse*, 26–46; K. Spading, 'Zu den Ursachen für das Eindringen der Holländer in das hansische Zwischenhandelsmonopol im 15. Jahrhundert.'
5 For the *Carta Mercatoria* see Jenks, 'Die "Carta Mercatoria." Ein hansisches Privileg.'

6 D. Keene, 'New Discoveries at the Hanseatic Steelyard in London'; *HUB* II no. 31; *Urkundliche Geschichte*, ed. J.M. Lappenberg, 3–56.

7 The English standard of measurement was the 'cloth of assize', a double-width cloth twenty-four yards long. Shorter cloths of standard quality also were exported, but were converted to cloth of assize equivalents for customs calculations. *England's Export Trade*, 13; G.P.H. Chorley, 'The English Assize of Cloth.'

8 *England's Export Trade*, 14–15, 199.

9 N.S.B. Gras, *The Early English Customs System*, 112; M. Oppenheim, *A History of the Administration of the Royal Navy*, 10. The suggestion of E.M. Carus-Wilson and O. Coleman in *England's Export Trade* that, except for wine, other imports are 'inextricably mixed with miscellaneous exports, since all were subject to poundage,' is perhaps misleading, especially for the post-1437 period. From 1437 the poundage subsidy was not normally paid by Hansards, except when relations with the Crown were extremely strained. Nor was wax – a principal Hanseatic import – subject to poundage.

10 Although according to the *Carta Mercatoria* the charge on wax was not *ad valorem*, customs officials consistently assigned a value to wax of 40s per quintal. PRO E356/21–4. Both tunnage (a specific duty) and poundage (an *ad valorem* duty) were parliamentary subsidies. They usually were granted together.

11 Recent summaries of fifteenth-century customs and subsidies and how they were collected are to be found in *The Customs Accounts of Hull 1453–1490*, ed. W.R. Childs, XI–XVIII and *The Overseas Trade of London Exchequer Customs Accounts 1480–1*, ed. H.S. Cobb, XI–XIV. Values and prices are discussed in context with estimated trade balances in the next chapter.

12 In 1388 merchants from Lynn, Yarmouth, Norwich, Boston, Hull, and London complained that men of the Wendish towns had arrested their servants and goods. However, subsequent arrests in England were not confined to traders from the Wendish sector. Several of those detained were from Cologne and Dortmund. All were released after promising that Englishmen would not be harassed in the Wendish towns. *CPMR 1381–1412*: 143–4, 149–50. A similar situation arose again in 1397. *CPR 1396–9*: 309–10.

13 T. Hirsch, *Danzigs Handels- und Gewerbsgeschichte unter der Herrschaft des Deutschen Ordens*, 99–101; F. Schulz, *Die Hanse und England von Eduards III. bis auf Heinrichs VIII. Zeit*, 49–50; K.-H. Ruffmann, 'Engländer und Schotten in den Seestädten Ost- und Westpreussens,' 21.

14 Schulz, 50–1.

15 *CPR 1401–5*: 424, 432, 433, 508, 509; *CPR 1405–8*: 59, 60.

16 R. Hakluyt, ed., *Voyages*, I 136–62; *CPR 1405–8*: 153. This episode in Anglo-Prussian diplomacy is reviewed in J.L. Kirby, 'Sir William Sturmy's Embassy to Germany in 1405–06.'

17 The commission to hear disputes involving Hansards was appointed in summer 1406. *CPR 1405–8*: 234. Merchants from Hull and Lynn were arrested, and restitution ordered for the robbery of ships from Lübeck and Greifswald. Ibid, 230, 232, 236, 302, 305. Within a year, however, merchants from the east-coast ports were being sought in connection with the capture of a ship from Hamburg. Ibid, 352–3.

18 Hakluyt, I 163–70; *CPMR 1413–37*: 70–1; *CPR 1408–13*: 383–5; *CLB* (I) 1400–22: 95–6, 198; *Foedera*, VIII 700–1, 722–5, IX 325–6.

19 Ruffmann, 22–3; J.S. Roskell, *The Commons and Their Speakers in English Parliaments 1376–1523*, 183, 186 and *The Commons in the Parliament of 1422*, 51–3, 125–9; *Rot. Parl.* IV 193, 348, V 65.

20 *Rot. Parl.* IV 192, 348, 403; *CCR 1422–9*: 49–50, 53, 140, 192, 257, 311; *Akten*, I no. 385, 387, 484. But apparently the English merchants in Danzig still had 'Olderlude' [Aldermen] there in 1431. Hirsch, 106, n. 156. For the restrictions encountered by English merchants in the 1420s and 1430s: Jenks, *England, die Hanse und Preussen*, I 124–38 and II 550–71.

21 *CCR 1429–35*: 55.

22 *CPR 1429–36*: 220, 357, 519; *CCR 1429–35*: 155; *Rot. Parl.* IV 369, 390, 493. For the negotiations between English officials and representatives of Hanseatic towns and the Grand Master: *Foedera*, X 605, 627–8; *HR.* (2) I no. 321#4, 383, 385, 386, 407, 421, 429–38, 459, 501, 508–11, 524, 559, 561–3.

23 *HR* (2) I no. 319, 321#1–5, 357#17–27, 361.

24 *HUB* VII no. 44; G. Schanz, *Englische Handelspolitik gegen Ende des Mittelalters*, II no. 171; *HR* (2) I no. 321#1–5. Protectionist measures against English cloth had been extended to include Holland and Zealand in 1428, but up until 1434 the town of Middelburg had managed to secure exemption. J.A. van Houtte, *An Economic History of the Low Countries 800–1800*, 107. The Anglo-Burgundian trade resumed in 1439. M.R. Thielemans, *Bourgogne et Angleterre*, 133, 437. English access to markets in Holland and Zealand was confirmed by treaty in 1445. *Bronnen*, ed. H.J. Smit (1) II no. 1288, 1296, 1298.

25 *Proceedings*, IV, 239.

26 Lloyd, 'A Reconsideration of Two Anglo-Hanseatic Treaties of the Fifteenth Century,' 916–33.

27 *HR* (2) II no. 16–92; *Urkundliche Geschichte*, 57–8 (no. LXXVI–LXXVII); H. Buszello, 'Die auswärtige Handelspolitik der englischen Krone im 15. Jahrhundert,' 71–3; *Foedera*, X 667–70; *CPR 1436–41*: 62; J. Ferguson, *English Diplomacy 1442–1461*, 96; Hirsch, 113–14; *Akten*, II no. 37, 40. Some economic repercussions of the conflict between England and Burgundy are reviewed in N.J.M. Kerling, *Commercial Relations of Holland and Zealand with England from the late 15th Century to the Close of the Middle Ages*, 48–50.

28 C.F. Richmond, 'The Keeping of the Seas during the Hundred Years War 1422–1440,' 285–90 and *Royal Administration and the Keeping of the Seas*,

1422–1485, 31–66; *CPR* 1429–36: 509–12, 515, 603. A summary of the relevant statutes is contained in *Documents relating to Law and Custom of the Sea*, ed. R.G. Marsden, 115–18.

29 Richmond, 'The Keeping of the Seas,' 295 and C.L. Kingsford, *Prejudice and Promise in Fifteenth-Century England*, 77–8.

30 *CPR* 1436–41: 85, 86, 90, 202, 270, 408, 409.

31 *CCR* 1435–41: 310–12; *Rot. Parl.* V 6; Roskell, *The Commons and Their Speakers*, 220.

32 *HR* (2) II no. 318, 346, 380, 539, 644, 647; *Rot. Parl.* V 64–5; *Foedera*, X 753–5.

33 *Akten*, II no. 87, 332, 370. England's Baltic trade in the 1450s and 1460s is outlined in chapter 3.

34 *Akten*, III no. 11, 13–18. Minutes of the Council for 19 March 1447 indicate that the Hansards were to be accorded a new three-year safe conduct so that they would not be troubled by any letters of marque granted or to be granted. Yet by the end of April one Henry Spyser of Derby, with the assistance of the duke of Buckingham, had used a letter of marque to have three Cologners arrested in Colchester. He attempted to extort £600 damages from them for an alleged piracy dating back to the war between Holland and the Wendish towns. *Proceedings*, VI 61; *HR* (2) III no. 281, 286, 287, VII no. 488#11; *Quellen*, ed. B. Kuske, I no. 1155. The *Hansetag* that convened at Lübeck in May discussed a possible prohibition on English trade in Prussia, but the Grand Master sent envoys to England instead. *HR* (2) III no. 289, 293–4, 308.

35 *HR* (2) III no. 283, 286–7, 295, 316#6, 318#1. Also Schulz, 89.

36 *HR* (2) III no. 503–5; *LUB* VIII no. 334, 411; *Akten*, III no. 51. In January 1447 there had been another Burgundian embargo on English cloth. *Bronnen*, ed. Smit (1) II no. 1311; Schanz, II no. 173. After meeting the Hanseatic representatives at Lübeck, the English delegation moved on to Copenhagen. The Danes had been harassing English shipping in retaliation for violations of trade restrictions in Iceland. Caunton succeeded in arranging a truce, but it lapsed two years later. *Diplomatarium Christierni Primi*, ed. C.F. Wegener, no. 8.

37 *Rot. Parl.* V 142.

38 A.R. Bridbury, *England and the Salt Trade in the Later Middle Ages*, 90–1; A. Agats, *Der hansische Baienhandel*, 76–8; *HR* (2) III no. 530–1, VII no. 34#24; *HUB* VIII no. 84, 215; Richmond, *Royal Administration*, 193–7. Wenyngton was a merchant and shipowner at Dartmouth, who had already been pardoned for piracy and murder in 1445–6 and was commissioned to serve in the keeping of the sea in April 1449. *CPR* 1446–52: 270; J. Wedgwood, ed., *History of Parliament* I, Biographies of the Members of the House of Commons 1439–1509, 934. He was mayor of Dartmouth, 1447–8, and a member of Parliament, 1449–50. In 1452 he was pardoned for the attack on the salt fleet, and he was mayor of Dartmouth again in 1456–7. For his own report of the capture see 'Robert

Wenyngton to Thomas Daniel – 25 May 1449' in *The Paston Letters*, ed. J. Gairdner, I 84–6. The Bay salt trade and some of the shipping routes with which it was integrated are discussed in the next chapter.

Chapter 2

1 Ferguson, 101. Both Lloyd and Richmond reject the notion that the English government instigated the attack, but suggest that some members of the Council did profit by it. Lloyd, *England and the German Hanse*, 181–2 and Richmond, *Royal Administration*, 197–202. See also Thielemans, 337.
2 *HR* (2) III no. 536, 555#2; *HUB* VIII no. 84, 215. English merchants were arrested and held in Danzig. *HR* (2) III no. 571–3. Richard Caunton, by now at Copenhagen, assured Lübeck that Wenyngton's actions were contrary to the king's will, and anticipated that the perpetrators would suffer the death penalty. *HR* (2) VII no. 516.
3 *Akten*, III no. 73; *HR* (2) III no. 608–12.
4 *HR* (2) III no. 567.
5 Ibid, no. 570.
6 For the English deputation: *CFR* 383–4; *Foedera*, XI 272–3; *CPR* 1446–52: 330; *HR* (2) III no. 561, 593#4, 594#2–3, 604, 608; PRO E364/86. It was financed with a loan of £400 from English merchants, *CCR* 1447–54: 148, and was captured on 25 July 1450. 'Die Ratschronik von 1438–1482,' *Die Chroniken der niedersächsischen Städte IV: Lübeck*, ed. F. Bruns, IV 107–10. The subsequent worsening of relations between Lübeck and the English government, as well as Lübeck's growing isolation within the Hanse, are discussed at length in Jenks, *England, die Hanse und Preussen*, II 678–93 and Lloyd, 186–94.
7 *Akten*, III no. 75; *HR* (2) III no. 647, 654, 666, 667. In early September 1450 bailiffs in Lynn, London, Ipswich, and Colchester were instructed to arrest Hansards and their goods. *CPR* 1446–52: 330–2. By November the Hansards had been released on a promise not to leave England. *HR* (2) III no. 669–70. Lübeckers, however, were again or still in custody in 1453. *CPR* 1452–61: 123. Merchants from Wismar, Stralsund, and Braunschweig, granted safe conducts to visit England in 1453, were arrested as Lübeckers upon their arrival in Lynn on grounds that men from Lübeck were still in possession of property belonging to the English envoys. PRO C76/135 m.5; *CPR* 1452–61: 119.
8 Stocker was allowed to leave Lübeck on 17 March 1451 to arrange talks between English and Hanseatic envoys at Utrecht, and Kent apparently was to stay in Lübeck as a guarantee that he would do so. Both men were in Utrecht by 26 May. *HUB* VIII no. 40; *LUB* IX no. 11; *HR* (2) III no. 702, 709#8ff. The behaviour of 'truwelos' Kent and Stocker profoundly offended and embittered the Lübeckers. *HR* (2) IV no. 14, 23, 127.
9 *CPR* 1446–52: 445. Also *Foedera*, XI 281–2.

10 *Akten*, III no. 103–5, 131, 149, 164; *HR* (2) III no. 651, 693#1, 694#1–3, 10,
    696–726; PRO C47/30/10(7); *Urkundliche Geschichte*, 76–86 (no. XCIV). For
    the piracies see *CPR* 1446–52: 434–6, 438–42; *HR* (2) III no. 626; *HUB* VIII
    no. 33, 101, 415; StA Köln Hanse III. K. 2. Bl.136–7, 168, 186, 194, 206.
11 Lübeck and the Danes blocked the passage of English ships and wares
    through the Sound in early 1452. Lübeck also banned the transport of
    English goods through the town. Malowist, 123–4; *HUB* VIII no. 140, 159,
    160, 171, 178, 227, 250, 261, 264, 293, 305, 307; *HR* (2) IV no. 71, 80–2, 152.
    For the reaction of the Cologners see *HUB* VIII no. 92–3.
12 W. Stark, *Lübeck und Danzig in der zweiten Hälfte des 15. Jahrhunderts*,
    183–9; E. Weise, 'Die Hanse, England und die Merchant Adventurers:
    Das Zusammenwirken von Köln und Danzig,' 151–3; Jenks, II 656–7. For
    the earlier, more traditional interpretation that Lübeck held the Hanse
    together by taking a firm line against England: P. Dollinger, *The German
    Hansa*, 302–5 or *Die Hanse*, 4th ed., 394–5; W. Stein, *Die Hanse und Eng-
    land: Ein hansisch-englischer Seekrieg im 15. Jahrhundert*, 17–22, and Schulz,
    99.
13 *Akten*, III no. 164, 285; *CPR* 1452–61: 123; *HUB* VIII no. 280–5, 289, 380,
    446; *HR* (2) III no. 670, IV no. 7, 168–70, 176–7, 235–6, 355, 364, 399–401,
    450; PRO SC1/57/75; Jenks, I 33.
14 H. Rosenberg, 'The Rise of the Junkers in Brandenburg Prussia
    1410–1653'; M. Biskup, 'Der preussische Bund 1440–1454'; P. Simson,
    'Danzig im 13. jährigen Krieg, 1454–1466.' For more comprehensive
    analyses of the Prussian League and the decline of the Order in the fif-
    teenth century see M. Burleigh, *Prussian Society and the German Order*,
    esp. 111–73; K.E. Murawski, *Zwischen Tannenberg und Thorn*, and Weise,
    *Das Widerstandsrecht im Ordenslande Preussen und das mittelalterliche
    Europa*. Lübeck's role in the dispute is reviewed in Biskup, 'Das Reich,
    die wendische Hanse und die preussische Frage um die Mitte des 15.
    Jahrhunderts,' 341–57.
15 There was considerable disruption of intra-Baltic shipping from the out-
    set of the war. *HR* (2) IV no. 323–6, 377; *HUB* VII no. 498, 513, 524, 528,
    538, 554, 563. In 1455 part of the salt fleet from Holland attempted to run
    Danzig's blockade of Memel and Königsberg. When ships from Amster-
    dam were distrained, the duke of Burgundy authorized the arrest of
    Danzig ships in his Lowland ports. Relations between Danzig and Hol-
    land remained strained for several years. Ibid, no. 410, 412, 487–8, 498,
    608, 656, 663. Danzig issued safe conducts to three English ships in 1457,
    but Englishmen were by no means safe from Lübeck's raiders. Ibid, no.
    574, 622–9; Malowist, 124–7; *LUB* IX no. 510, 520, X no. 85, 381. More-
    over, Danzig's captains were at liberty to attack 'enemy' shipping, and
    scores of confrontations ensued in the late 1450s, many of them involv-
    ing Wendish ships allegedly trying to continue trade to Livonia. *HUB*
    VIII no. 674–5, 684–5, 687, 692–5, 697–9, 702, 704, 707–15, 989; *HR* (2) IV

no. 559, 590–1, 603, 687, 700–4. In 1459 Danzig alleged that the Danes were distraining Prussian ships for carrying English goods, and so the chaos continued into the 1460s. Ibid, no. 497; *LUB* X no. 33–5, 38, 41, 162, 173, 283, 354. Lübeckers captured another English ship off Bornholm in 1463. Ibid, no. 381.

16 *CPR* 1452–61: 174, 179, 221, 223. Also *HUB* VIII no. 297, 363; *HR* (2) IV no. 279.

17 *CPR* 1452–1461: 299. A linen cargo belonging to Hamburg merchants in Ipswich also had been seized, taken to Harwich, and exposed for sale. Ibid, 311. There was also considerable hostility directed against Italians in England at this time. See R. Flenley, 'London and Foreign Merchants in the Reign of Henry VI.'

18 *HR* (2) IV no. 666–7, V no. 169; *HUB* VIII no. 769, IX no. 196#3; *CPR* 1452–61: 436–43; *CPR* 1461–7: 231–2, 349–50.

19 *HR* (2) V no. 147, 166–80, 263#4–7, 9, 282–5; *CPR* 1461–7: 109, 261, 276–7.

20 *HR* (2) V no. 263#8–47, 583; Stark, 191; *LUB* X no. 653; *Urkundliche Geschichte*, 126 (no. CX); *HUB* IX no. 196; PRO E30/1381. See also Lloyd, 196–200 and Jenks, I 700–9.

21 *English Historical Documents*, ed. A.R. Myers, IV 1042–3.

22 *Rot. Parl.* V 565–6; PRO C49/35/23; Stein, 'Die Merchant Adventurers in Utrecht 1464–1467.'

23 *HR* (2) V no. 642–744; *HUB* IX no. 196, 211–12, 245. Later in December that year, however, some Cologners had goods seized by London customs agents, who attempted to charge the poundage subsidy on Hanseatic merchandise contrary to the exemption. *HUB* XI no. 1275.

24 *Diplomatarium Christierni Primi*, no. 124.

25 The importance of Danzig's English trade in relation to Lübeck's was demonstrated in 1468, with the arrest of Hansards and their merchandise in England. Of the funds rebated to those affected (Cologne was not included), Danzig claimed 40% and Lübeck 14%. *HR* (3) I no. 163.

26 *HUB* IX no. 304, 305, 308–10.

27 *HUB* IX no. 350, 387, 415; *HR* (2) VI no. 53–4.

28 Thielemans, 411–24; PRO E30/522, 1073(1), 1608(4).

29 *HUB* IX no. 433–4.

30 *Foedera*, XI 551; Carus-Wilson, 'The Icelandic Trade,' 179–80; *45th Report of the Deputy Keeper of the Public Records, appendix 2*, 5.

31 *HUB* IX no. 519#4, 7, 8. In all, seven English ships were taken. Three others had already cleared the Sound and reached Danzig. They returned safely to England later in the year.

32 *HUB* IX no. 519#4. Also *HUB* IX no. 468, 471, 476, 478, 495, 520#1–3 and 5–19, 523; 'Caspar Weinreichs Danziger Chronik,' *Scriptores Rerum Prussicarum*, ed. T. Hirsch, IV 730; *HR* (2) VI no. 95, 97, 102, 108, 115.

33 *HUB* IX no. 471, 523#9.

34 PRO E122 10/9, 10/10, 97/9.

35 *HUB* IX no. 519; StA Köln Hanse III. K. 15. Bl.1, 2, 10, 11, 70, 91, 95.

36 *HUB* IX no. 478.
37 The testimony of Thomas Roger, *HUB* IX no. 519.
38 *CPR* 1446–52: 380. PRO E122 9/68; 52/42–5; 61/71; 62/1, 3–7, 10; 96/37, 40, 41; 97/2, 4, 6, 7, 9; 194/11.
39 For the trade in English wool see E. Power, 'The Wool Trade in the Fifteenth Century.'
40 'Handelsbriefe aus Riga und Königsberg von 1458 und 1461,' ed. Stein, letter 27; Hirsch, 251–3.
41 Jenks, 'Das Schreiberbuch des Johann Thorpe und der hansische Handel in London 1457–59'; *HUB* IX no. 525; StA Köln Hanse Urkunden. U. 2. Bl.133; Appendix A.3.1; CLRO MC1/3/192, 200, 209, 214, 224, 225, 235, 236, 241, 244, 347, 364, MC1/3A/1, 48, 67, 113, 116–18, 136, 210–12, 263.
42 R.H. Britnell, *Growth and Decline in Colchester, 1300–1525*, 172–3, citing Colchester borough court rolls.
43 The *Hansetag* of May 1447 authorized the discontinuance of trade to Southampton and Yarmouth because local tolls there were higher than in other English ports. *HR* (2) III no. 288#78.
44 *England's Export Trade* and H.L. Gray, 'English Foreign Trade from 1446 to 1482,' 1–38.
45 G.V. Scammell, 'English Merchant Shipping at the end of the Middle Ages,' 328–31; H. Clarke, 'King's Lynn and East Coast Trade in the Middle Ages,' 277–90; D. Burwash, *English Merchant Shipping 1460–1540*, 151–58; P. Heath, 'North Sea Fishing in the Fifteenth Century: The Scarborough Fleet,' 53–69.
46 PRO E122 particulars of accounts for Hull, Boston, Lynn, Ipswich and London.
47 'Ouch ist in Prussen und kumpt us Prussen di meiste war, di si hir in desen landen [England] durffen.' *HR* (2) III no. 670.
48 *Quellen*, ed. B. Kuske, I no. 1169, II no. 393; PRO E122 particulars of accounts; F. Irsigler, *Die wirtschaftliche Stellung der Stadt Köln im 14. und 15. Jahrhundert*, 60–61, 184–200.
49 Pre-1483 petty custom figures are printed in *Studies*, 330–60. Post-1482 totals for Lynn, Ipswich, Hull, Newcastle and Boston are appended to this study. See Appendix A.1.1 and also A.1.3. There are some discrepancies in the cloth export figures in *Studies* and those compiled by E.M. Carus-Wilson and O. Coleman in *England's Export Trade*. The published totals are not usually representative of calendar years, but rather of Exchequer years running from Michaelmas to Michaelmas (i.e., 1450 = 29.09.1449 to 28.09.1450). However, totals and percentages have been computed here for the period Michaelmas 1449 to Michaelmas 1467, rather than for individual years, because although some annual totals do not correspond to Exchequer years, they are, unless noted, continuous without major gaps.
50 Appendix A.1.1; *Studies*, 348; PRO E122 96/37, 40, 41; 97/1–4, 6–9; E356/21. The particulars of account for 1464–5 (PRO E122 97/4) are published

in *The Making of King's Lynn*, ed. D.M. Owen, 366–78; those for 1466–7 (PRO E122 97/8) are published in Gras, 606–24.

51 Jenks, *England, die Hanse und Preussen*, II 675.

52 *CPR* 1446–52: 156, 430; *CFR* 385, 386, 395, 405, 408, 427, 437, 438, 441, 442, 448, 449.

53 Appendix A.1.1; *Studies*, 331; PRO E122 9/53, 54, 56, 59, 65, 68; 10/1, 4, 6–10; E356/21. There is a gap in the enrolments from Michaelmas 1458 to 5 December 1459. For the seizures at Helsingor see *HUB* IX no. 519#12–14. Lübeckers were still freighting goods from Danzig to England early in 1462, using Danzig skippers. *LUB* X no. 124.

54 There is a gap, however, in the enrolled customs figures for Hull from 12 August 1460 to 11 April 1461.

55 Appendix A.1.1; *Studies*, 342; PRO E122 61/71, 75; 62/1, 3–10; E356/21. Particulars of accounts for Hull have been edited and published by W.R. Childs in *The Customs Accounts of Hull 1453–1490*. For the English ships taken in 1468 and the subsequent arrests at Hull see *HUB* IX no. 519, 520, 541. For the trade in raw iron: Childs, 'England's Iron Trade in the Fifteenth Century,' 37. The Hansards also traded to Newcastle, but customs records for the 1450s and 1460s are too fragmentary to permit a quantitative evaluation.

56 Appendix A.1.1; *Studies*, 340; PRO E122 52/42–9; E356/21.

57 Appendix A.2.2; StA Köln Hanse III. K. 15. Bl.103. The importance of Dover and Sandwich as outports for London's cloth export trade in the 1430s and 1440s is reviewed in Lloyd, 220–1.

58 *Studies*, 345–6; PRO E122 76/48; 194/11, 12; E356/21.

59 PRO E122 19/5; *Studies*, 335.

60 PRO E122 152/5, 7; *Studies*, 360.

61 PRO E122 142/2, 3; *Studies*, 358.

62 PRO E122 128/2, 8, 9; *Studies*, 356.

63 Even at the cloth exporting centre of Ipswich in 1465–6, Hansards shipped 2,339 cloths 'sine grano,' but only one whole cloth and 9 ells 'in grano,' together with 32 worsteds. PRO E122 52/48.

64 PRO E122 10/8; 52/54, 55; 62/10; 97/3, 8, 9; Gray, 9. The enrolment for London in 1472 does show a value of £2 per cloth for woollen exports belonging to Cologners. PRO E356/21 m.10d.

65 For examples of retail prices: Appendix A.4.1; PRO C1/31/495–6, C1/149/49, C1/186/66, C1/326/52.

66 Appendix A.1.3. Jenks also suggests (I 264) a value of £1 6s 8d for cloths exported from ports other than London and £1 13s 4d for those shipped from the capital.

67 PRO E122 194/11; *Urkundliche Geschichte*, 110–11 (no. CVI); *HUB* IX no. 482, 541; Appendix A.5.5.

68 APG 300.19/1, 3. Also H. Samsonowicz, *Untersuchungen über das Danziger Bürgerkapital in der zweiten Hälfte des 15. Jahrhunderts*, 33–46.

69 APG 300.19/1.

70 APG 300.19/3.
71 APG 300.19/2.
72 Malowist, 'A Certain Trade Technique in the Baltic Countries in the 15th–17th Centuries,' 103–12.
73 O. Rackham, *Ancient Woodland*, 151; L.F. Salzman, *Building England down to 1540*, 245–8; R.W. Symonds, 'Furniture: Post Roman,' 244; Stark, 96–105; *LUB* X no. 124; *HUB* VIII no. 222; Stark, 'Die Danziger Pfahlkammerbücher (1468–1476),' 71.
74 Malowist, 108–12; Stark, *Lübeck und Danzig*, 113–26.
75 APG 300.19/3 4r, 21v; PRO E122 97/9. See Appendix A.2.1.
76 *HUB* IX no. 519#1, 2.
77 APG 300.19/1 2r; PRO E122 96/41.
78 APG 300.19/1 32v; PRO E122 96/41.
79 APG 300.19/3 23v; PRO E122 62/10.
80 *HUB* VIII no. 21, 84, 215, 538; *HR* (2) IV no. 666–71. Also Bridbury, 76–93.
81 *LUB* X no. 173, 283; *CPR* 1452–61: 118; APG 300.19/3 20r–9r. For the Hollanders trading to Prussia and Livonia see *HUB* VIII no. 412, 415 and *Bronnen*, ed. Poelman (1) II no. 2278.
82 PRO E122 151/69, 70; 76/42, 46 (Hans Schomaker), E122 52/43, 44 (Heyne Yake bringing salt to Ipswich in May 1462), and E122 52/46 (Deryk Berne, Thomas Jonnesson, and Walter Hermansson bringing salt to Ipswich in May 1464).
83 PRO C1/26/193. Sculte's undated petition to Chancery is addressed to the bishop of Winchester, who was chancellor during the late 1450s. See Appendix A.4.2. Gasper Sculte is listed in the debt register for Dowgate ward dated 24 October 1457. Jenks, 'Das Schreiberbuch,' 94. He also freighted forty-eight charges of Bay salt to London for John Warnes on 16 December 1457. PRO E122 203/4.
84 O. Lienau, 'Danziger Schiffahrt und Schiffbau in der zweiten Hälfte des 15. Jahrhunderts,' 72–5; Hirsch, 263–4; H. Winter, *Das Hanseschiff im ausgehenden 15. Jahrhundert*, 1–33; R.M. Nance, 'A Hanseatic Bergentrader of 1489'; 'Caspar Weinreichs Danziger Chronik,' 768; W. Stieda, 'Schiffahrtsregister.' For the joint ownership of vessels, the Bay fleet losses of 1449 provide a good example: *HUB* VIII no. 215. A valuable study of English ships of this period is D. Burwash. See also A. McGowen, *Tiller and Whipstaff: The Development of the Sailing Ship 1400–1700*, 3–17, and R.W. Unger, *The Ship in the Medieval Economy 600–1600*, esp. 161–71, 222–4.
85 Although Daenell advanced the notion some eighty years ago that this so-called *Winterlage* was intended to protect shipping from the winter elements, Jenks attributes the idea to Dollinger, and takes great pains to refute it. According to Jenks, the risks of the winter voyage 'spielte dagegen keine Rolle,' and by the 1420s this shipping hiatus was intended to ensure that foreign carriers did not reach port ahead of Hanseatic

ships. Daenell, 'The Policy of the German Hanseatic League respecting the Mercantile Marine,' 50–1; Dollinger, *Die Hanse*, 192–6; Jenks, I 305–20.

86 Irsigler, 89–90, 97–8; G. Asaert, 'Handel in kleurstoffen op de Antwerpse markt tijdens de XVe eeuw,' 380–3, 392–3, 399–400.

87 Irsigler, esp. 12–20, 32–6, 60–1, 184–92, 200, 266–73; F. Rülke, *Die Verlagerung der Handelswege zwischen 1450 und 1550 und ihre Rückwirkung auf die deutsche Hanse*, 150–5; Kuske, 'Die Kölner Handelsbeziehungen im 15. Jahrhundert.'

88 *Quellen*, ed. Kuske, II no. 23–4, 36–7, 64, 69, 607; *HUB* VIII no. 147–8, 159, 174, 176; *LUB* XI no. 367; A. Simsch, *Die Handelsbeziehungen zwischen Nürnberg und Posen im europäischen Wirtschaftsverkehr des 15. und 16. Jahrhunderts*, esp. 90–5.

89 PRO E122 52/42.

90 G. Asaert, 'Antwerp Ships in English Harbours in the Fifteenth Century,' 30–34.

91 G. Asaert, *De Antwerpse Scheepvaart in de XVe Eeuw (1394–1480)*, 154, 248–54, 411; SAA SR 57, ff. 153r, 256v, 257r.

92 *HUB* VIII no. 250; APG 300.19/3.

93 J. Munro, 'Bruges and the Abortive Staple in English Cloth'; H. Van der Wee, *The Growth of the Antwerp Market and the European Economy*, II 70–83; R. Davis, 'The Rise of Antwerp and Its English Connection 1406–1510,' 4–11; C. Wehrmann, 'Die Gründung des hanseatischen Hauses zu Antwerpen,' esp. 84–7. Hansards refused to abandon their trade at Antwerp or Bergen op Zoom in 1454 or use Utrecht in 1456. *HR* (2) IV no. 247#31–41, 414. Cologners objecting to taxes in Bruges were given extended privileges by Antwerp in 1466. *HUB* IX no. 286.

94 SAA SR 43–72. I gratefully acknowledge the assistance of Dr G. Asaert, who kindly pointed out many of the numerous references to foreign merchants in the Antwerp registers that are cited specifically elsewhere in this text.

95 Stein, 'Die Merchant Adventurers in Utrecht 1464–1467.' For the fellowship of merchant adventurers at Antwerp and Bergen op Zoom in the fifteenth century see also Weise, 'Die Hanse, England und die Merchant Adventurers,' 156–8 and O. de Smedt, *De Engelse Natie te Antwerpen in de 16e Eeuw*, I 60–135.

96 SAA SR 45, ff. 173r, 274v; 46, f. 130v; 50, f. 316v; 51, f. 132r; 61, ff. 48v, 357r; 63, ff. 38v, 200r, 245v; 68, ff. 128r, 309r.

97 PRO E122 52/42–6; 76/42, 48; 194/11.

98 Davis, 4–6; *HUB* VIII no. 244; *HR* (2) IV no. 52; S.T. Bindoff, *The Scheldt Question to 1839*, 34.

99 *HUB* VIII no. 655; Bindoff, 52–6. From the mid-1460s onward collection of the main ducal toll on shipping through the Scheldt-Honte channels (the Honte watch of the Iersekeroord toll collectors) was suspended due to protracted litigation, and this undoubtedly enhanced Antwerp's foreign trade prospects still further.

Chapter 3

1 Affected merchants came from Hull, York, Lynn, Boston, and London. *HUB* IX no. 478, 520.

2 *Acts of Court*, 63–138; C. Ross, *Edward IV*, 353–5; S.L. Thrupp, *The Merchant Class of Medieval London 1300–1500*, 56–9, 83–4; M.S. Giuseppi, 'Alien Merchants in England in the Fifteenth Century,' 75–98.

3 Ross, 356–65; *Urkundliche Geschichte*, 127–9 (no. CXI–CXIV); *Rot. Parl.* V 508–9; PRO C49/35/23; *CLB* (L) Edward IV – Henry VII. 18; *CPR* 1461–7: 109, 261, 276–7. In the summer of 1461, at the instigation of London, Hanseatic privileges in England were initially confirmed only until the following February. This caused much anxiety among the Cologne and Danzig merchants, who lobbied successfully for an extension. *HR* (2) V no. 147, 166–80, 263#3, 4, 30, 284. For the king's involvement in overseas trade see Power, 'The English Wool Trade in the Reign of Edward IV,' 23. London's charter: *CChR*, VI 189.

4 P.M. Kendall, *Warwick the Kingmaker*, 250–4.

5 K.A. Fowler, 'English Diplomacy and the Peace of Utrecht,' 12–13; Ross, 365; *HUB* IX no. 478, 482, 520. Wenlock was a councillor in Warwick's circle. J.R. Lander, 'Council, Administration and Councillors 1461 to 1485,' 160.

6 *HR* (2) III no. 288#6, 350, IV no. 161#6, 621–42.

7 *Rot. Parl.* V 64–5.

8 The following outline of the arrests of the Hansards and the subsequent release of the Cologners is based on the depositions of the Cologne merchants and of Gerhard van Wesel, then governor of the Steelyard fellowship. *HUB* IX no. 467, 482, 490. Thereto also *HR* (2) VI no. 119; Appendices A.5.1 through A.5.5, and H. Buszello, 'Köln und England 1468–1509,' 437.

9 The depositions of the imprisoned Esterlings contradict the official story of the Cologners and suggest considerable collusion between English officials and Cologne's merchants. *HR* (2) VII no. 42, 338#81–101.

10 *HUB* IX no. 507, 526–8, 530–3, 548–9, XI no. 1310; *HR* (2) VI no. 121–4, VII no. 34. A partial inventory of property seizures in England includes everything from stock merchandise to small household items. StA Köln Hanse IV. 68. Bl.47–64.

11 For the not particularly persuasive suggestion that England needed Cologners for their shipping interests, see F.R. Salter, 'The Hanse, Cologne and the Crisis of 1468.'

12 The following interpretation of England's Baltic trade in the 1450s and 1460s is based primarily on direct references to English activity at Danzig. It does not adhere to the model constructed by Jenks, which offers the premiss that virtually all denizen cloth exports from Boston, Yarmouth, Lynn, and Hull went exclusively to northern and eastern markets (Iceland, Hamburg, Prussia). It therefore does not reflect that author's

conclusion that denizens from these ports actually monopolized England's cloth trade to the Baltic at the expense of their Hanseatic counterparts. Jenks, *England, die Hanse und Preussen*. I, esp. 156–8 and 217–24. The limitations of the construct ultimately lead to inconsistencies, especially with regard to the port of Hull, which maintained 'traditionell weitverzweigten Handelskontakte' with Bordeaux, Calais, and Spain. If 91.37% of denizen cloth exports from Hull in 1464–5 went to Bordeaux and Spain (ibid, 221, n. 59), then presumably 100% of them did not go to the 'Ostseeregion' (ibid, 218).

13 *HUB* VIII no. 45; *Quellen*, ed. Kuske, I no. 1169, 1193. For the *Artushof*: Simson, *Der Artushof in Danzig und seine Brüderschaften die Banken*, esp. 1–66.

14 *HUB* VIII no. 46; PRO C1/19/295; *Bronnen*, ed. Smit (1) II no. 1357.

15 *HUB* VIII no. 122, 123, 128. The 'Berinckhem' of these letters was Lynn merchant Henry Bermingham, who, together with Robert Stocker's brother John, was part of Thomas Kent's delegation in 1450–1. *HR* (2) III no. 637; *CFR* 384.

16 *CPR* 1446–52: 160; *HUB* VIII no. 354, 393. Barry, William Henry Hancock, James Frecht, and one Richard Brown of Norwich owned cloth and tin aboard two Danzig-bound ships seized by the Lübeckers in 1453. The vessels operated out of Arnemuiden and Antwerp, but their cargoes, which were also shared by merchants from Cologne, Nijmegen, Antwerp, and Danzig, were apparently freighted in London and/or Colchester. *HUB* VIII no. 244, 249. For Hancock see also *HUB* VIII no. 293.

17 *HUB* VIII no. 574, 639. Although most of the cargo offloaded from four Danzig ships at Hull in the summer of 1453 belonged to Hansards, £94 worth of wainscots, boards, linen, and bowstaves also were carried for indigenous English merchants, including Katerina Ratclyff and William Gaunte. PRO E122 61/71.

18 PRO E122 96/37, shipper Thomas Clerkson, 13 September 1456.

19 APG 300.19/1 2r, 3v, 41v, 42v. All four ships arriving in Danzig from England in 1460 were Hanseatic. The notations 'uth Engelant,' 'von Lub[eck]' etc. in the Danzig *Pfahlkammerbücher* most likely indicate the place or port of origin. If, however, they refer to the last port of call, then it is conceivable that ships coming from Lübeck or even anywhere along the Atlantic seaboard could have carried goods for Englishmen. But none of the skippers or merchants listed with these vessels is English either. Also, English merchants imported typical Baltic goods (tar, iron, lumber) into Lynn and Hull in the early 1460s, but the arrival and departure times rule out long direct voyages to and from the Baltic, and suggest instead that this merchandise was picked up at ports in the Lowlands or perhaps at Hamburg. PRO E122 9/68; 10/4; 62/1, 3, 4, 5; 96/41; 97/1, 2. From Michaelmas 1459 to March 1461 Danzig shippers calling at Lynn carried some cargo for Englishmen, but with a total value of less than £15. PRO E122 96/41.

20 *LUB* X no. 85, 381. Already in the summer of 1459 Danzig ships had been detained by the Danes at the Sound for allegedly carrying English goods. *HR* (2) IV no. 497.

21 *HR* (2) IV no. 568#3, V no. 60; 'Handelsbriefe,' ed. Stein, letters 10, 12, 18, 27. English cloth was previously available in Reval as well. *Kämmereibuch der Stadt Reval 1432–1463*, ed. R. Vogelsang, I no. 117, 693, 772, II no. 1190; *Kämmereibuch der Stadt Reval 1463–1507*, ed. R. Vogelsang, I no. 1337.

22 *HUB* IX no. 162. Moreover, though seven Hanseatic ships brought more than £600 worth of bulk freight to Lynn that year, none of it was customed to Englishmen. Nor did the Baltic ships carry any cloth exports for denizens. PRO E122 97/4. The following year indigenous merchant John Stokys shipped twenty cloths in a Danzig vessel. PRO E122 97/6, 7. (shipper Eler Bokelman, leaving Lynn on 28 September 1466).

23 'Caspar Weinreichs Danziger Chronik,' 729.

24 *CPR* 1467–77: 101, 168–9; *HUB* IX no. 519#8. A 1464 statute prohibiting Englishmen from using foreign carriers applied only if sufficient denizen ships were available, and so had no real impact on the Anglo-Baltic trade. *Statutes of the Realm*, II 394–5 (3 Ed. IV c.1). A similar statute was introduced in the reign of Henry VII. Ibid, II, 535 (4 Hen. VII c.10). A cargo brought to Hull by Danzig shipper Derick Schach in June 1467 included pitch, tar, wainscots, and iron worth £33 belonging to denizen Thomas Nelson. PRO E122 62/10. Schach's outbound cargo consisted of lead and woollens, including twenty-four cloths customed to indigenous merchant John Mitchell. But the English did use their own ships as well. In 1466 Thomas Howard had hired John Yonge at Deptford to captain his ship on a voyage to Prussia. M.A.S. Hickmore, *The Shipbuilding Industry on the East and South Coasts of England in the Fifteenth Century*, 33, citing records of the Howards' household.

25 *HUB* IX no. 541. A draft petition denying Danzig's culpability lists nine ships taken: one each at Newcastle, Hull, Scarborough, Southwold, and Ipswich, and two each at London and Lynn. StA Köln Hanse III. K. 15. Bl.1.

26 *LUB* XI no. 515; 'Die Chronik Christians von Geren,' *Die Lübecker Bergenfahrer und ihre Chronistik*, 357.

27 The *Mary* and the *James* of Lynn and the *Christopher* of Boston left Lynn on 2 May. PRO E122 97/9. The *Christopher* picked up cloth at Boston and departed there together with the *Gabrielle* and the *George* of Boston on 6 May. PRO E122 10/9, 10. Also *HUB* IX no. 478.

28 PRO E122 97/9: the *James* of Lynn and the *Christopher* of Boston. *HUB* IX no. 541#VIII.

29 *HUB* IX no. 478, 519, 520.

30 F. Ketner, *Handel en Scheepvaart van Amsterdam in de vijftiende Eeuw*, 116–18; *Bronnen*, ed. Poelman (1) II no. 2050–1, 2073, 2104, 2281.

31 *HR* (2) III no. 694#5–6, IV no. 26–8, 64–5, 250, 414; *HUB* VIII no. 64, 203, 209, 376, 378, 395.

32 Vollbehr, 54–61; *HUB* VIII no. 499, 508, 579, 630; W. Friccius, *Der Wirtschaftskrieg als Mittel hansischer Politik im 14. und 15. Jahrhundert*, 52–82.

33 *Akten*, IV no. 367; *HUB* VIII no. 563; Rosenberg, 235.

34 *Akten*, IV no. 367. Danzig and the Order had been trying to restrict the trading activities of foreigners for at least half a century. Jenks, I 588–710.

35 J. Müller, 'Handel und Verkehr Bremens im Mittelalter,' 48–9; *HR* (2) V no. 319.

36 *Die Zolltarife der Stadt Hamburg*, ed. Pitz, no. 57–79; *LUB* X no. 425, 439.

37 The ordinances and staple regulations of these Hanseatic towns are reviewed in Stein, *Beiträge zur Geschichte der deutschen Hanse*, 41–3, 123–41. For Riga see G. Hollihn, 'Die Stapel- und Gästepolitik Rigas in der Ordenzeit 1201–1561,' particularly 113–36 and 165–76; *HR* (2) IV no. 758, 764–8. For Hamburg: Pitz, ed. and *Hamburgische Bursprachen 1346–1594*, ed. J. Bollard, II, 15/1, 17/5, 17/34, 22/1, 24/1–2, 42/16–17, 45/6, 54/5, 54/31. See also Malowist, 'Poland, Russia and Western Trade in the Fifteenth and Sixteenth Century'; *LUB* XI no. 368.

38 *HUB* IX no. 491, 494, 517; *HR* (2) VI no. 100, 114–15; StA Köln Hanse Urkunden. U. 2. Bl.251.

39 It is not surprising, therefore, that Lübeck's old nemesis, Thomas Kent, was among those appointed to investigate Warwick's attack on the Hanseatic salt fleet in 1458. *Foedera*, XI 415–16.

40 *HUB* IX no. 495, 501–6, 509; StA Köln Hanse III. K. 15. Bl.47.

41 *HUB* IX no. 541#I-a-4. [... so together we prisoners wrote to all the clothmakers in the land to come to London and assist us ...]

42 *Ibid* no. 525. A similar complaint was drafted by the clothmakers 'withyn the townes of Bristowe, Bathe, Wellys, Glastynbury, Shepton, Malette, Coscombe, Trowebrigge, Bradeford, ffrome Bekyngton and Warmyster in the countees of Bristowe, Somerset and Wiltshire'. StA Köln Hanse III. K. 15. Bl.49. See Appendix A.5.2. There may be yet a third document of this sort. Jenks also refers to a hitherto unknown petition, but provides no further details (II 717, n. 100).

43 *HUB* IX no. 467, 541#VI-b-5, XI-2, 555; StA Köln Hanse III. K. 7. Bl.17–18, Hanse III. K. 15. Bl.83.

44 *HUB* IX no. 511, 542–5, 549, 554, p. 431 n. 1; PRO E30/529.

45 *HUB* IX no. 569–70.

46 *HUB* IX no. 497, 540#103–60.

47 *HR* (2) VI no. 124, VII no. 42; *HUB* IX no. 555, XI no. 444#2.

48 *HUB* IX no. 585, 639#47.

49 *Ibid*, no. 584–5, 588.

50 'Caspar Weinreichs Danziger Chronik,' 731; Simson, *Geschichte der Stadt Danzig bis 1626*, I 288.

51 *Ibid*, 289; Lienau, 74. But already since 1447 all Hanseatic merchant ships

were supposed to be armed in order to ward off pirates. Daenell, 'The Policy of the German Hanseatic League,' 49.

52 'Caspar Weinreichs Danziger Chronik,' 731–2; *HR* (2) VI no. 314; *HUB* IX no. 539, 541.

53 Richmond, *Royal Administration*, 348; 'Caspar Weinreichs Danziger Chronik,' 733; 'Die Chronik Christians von Geren,' 360.

54 *HR* (2) VI no. 161, 202, 249#12, 283, 356#61–73, 360–1, 418–20. For the campaign of 1470 see also H. Fiedler, 'Danzig und England: Die Handelsbestrebungen der Engländer vom Ende des 14. bis zum Anfang des 17. Jahrhunderts,' 95.

55 *HR* (2) VI no. 316, 347, 352; *Quellen*, ed. Kuske, II no. 513; *HUB* IX no. 691, 796. For Cologne: *HR* (2) VI no. 356#61–73, 106, 114–15, 358.

56 A.R. Myers, 'The Outbreak of War between England and Burgundy in February 1471'; 'Caspar Weinreichs Danziger Chronik,' 733; 'Die Chronik Christians von Geren,' 359.

57 *CPR 1467–77*: 272; *Urkundliche Geschichte*, 134 (no. CXVII).

58 'Caspar Weinreichs Danziger Chronik,' 733; *Bronnen*, ed. Smit (1) II no. 1612.

59 Ibid, 731, 733; Lienau, 72–80; Fiedler, 95–6. *HR* (2) VI no. 529–59 consists of a series of letters written by Pawest while he commanded the *Grosse Kraweel*. They provide much insight into the manifold difficulties he and the other Hanseatic privateers encountered during 1471–2. See also *Caspar Weinreichs Danziger Chronik*, ed. T. Hirsch and F.A. Vossberg, 93–117. In the early spring of 1472 Pawest cruised along the south coast of England as far as Plymouth, then crossed to Pointe de Saint Mathieu in Brittany and then back to Sluis, but had no English prizes to show for his efforts. Ibid, 109–11.

60 F. Rörig, 'Ein Hamburger Kapervertrag vom Jahre 1471.' For the costs of outfitting privateers in Hamburg, and an indication of the booty taken: *Kämmereirechnungen der Stadt Hamburg*, ed. Koppmann, III 55–6.

61 *HR* (2) VI no. 507, 524–6, 548; 'Die Chronik Christians von Geren,' 360; *HUB* X no. 109.

62 Richmond, *Royal Administration*, 349–50; *CPR 1467–77*: 299, 355; *HR* (2) VI no. 534, 557–8. According to the chronicler Weinreich, the English had twenty-three warships. 'Caspar Weinreichs Danziger Chronik,' 734–5. Also 'Die Chronik Christians von Geren,' 360; 'Die Ratschronik von 1438–1482,' 99–100.

63 *CSP Milan*, I 166–67, 170; *HUB* IX no. 691, X no. 192, 218.

64 As early as March 1472 English ambassadors had been empowered to treat with the Hansards. PRO E30/1073 (12–13).

65 *HUB* X no. 166; 'Caspar Weinreichs Danziger Chronik,' 735.

66 *HR* (2) VI no. 642–3; 'Caspar Weinreichs Danziger Chronik,' 736. For Valand's and Nederhoff's losses in England in 1468: *HUB* IX no. 541.

67 *HR* (2) VII no. 41; *HR* (3) III no. 176, 183; 'Caspar Weinreichs Danziger Chronik,' 736; F.E. de Roover, 'A Prize of War: A Painting of Fifteenth

Century Merchants'; Simson, *Geschichte der Stadt Danzig*, I 291–4. It was also a lucrative summer for Hamburg's privateers. *Kämmereirechnungen der Stadt Hamburg*, III 93–8; 'Ein kort Uttoch der Wendeschen Chronicon von 801–1535,' *Hamburgische Chroniken in niedersächsischer Sprache*, ed. Lappenberg, 258.

68 *HR* (2) VII no. 135; Lienau, 72–80. English efforts to gain restitution are outlined in *Acts of Court*, 68–76. For the Italian reaction see de Roover, 3–12 and O. Meltzing, 'Tommaso Portinari und sein Konflikt mit der Hanse,' and for the misgivings of Hamburg and Lübeck, *HR* (2) VII no. 69; Stark, 201; 'Die Ratschronik von 1438–1482,' 118.

69 *HUB* X no. 218, 242; *Bronnen*, ed. Smit (1) II no. 1707.

70 *HR* (2) VI no. 470#5, 483–5, 589; *HUB* X no. 122.

71 *HR* (2) VII no. 22, 34#6. The earliest commissions of the English envoys are dated 4 March 1472, 10 December 1472, and 7 March 1473. PRO E30/548, E30/1073 (12), E30/1605 (2, 3, 5). A truce extending from 10 June until 1 October was proclaimed in May 1473, although it evidently had little effect on the privateers. PRO E30/1605 (4, 6). The truce with Denmark is dated 1 May 1473, and was renewed for two years in 1476, and again in 1479. *Diplomatarium Christierni Primi*, no. 186, 204; *45th Report of the Deputy Keeper of the Public Records*, appendix 2, 5; PRO E30/1096 (1–5). For the peace initiatives of England and the Hanse see H. Buszello, 'Die auswärtige Handelspolitik'; Fowler; and G. Neumann, 'Hansische Politik und Politiker bei den Utrechter Friedensverhandlungen,' 25–9.

72 The report of the English ambassadors is contained in *HUB* X no. 241.

73 Ibid, no. 241#67.

74 Ibid, no. 241#92; *HR* (2) VII no. 44.

75 *HUB* X no. 241#86.

76 *HR* (2) VII no. 142. Hatclyff's final instructions, dated 20 December 1473, are printed in Schanz, II no. 82. Thereto: PRO E30/1604, E30/1605 (7, 8, 9, 11). Ratifications were exchanged by 4 September 1475. PRO E30/554. See also Lloyd, 'A Reconsideration,' 925–8.

77 Carus-Wilson, 'The Icelandic Trade,' 180; C.F. Richmond, *Royal Administration*, 335–45.

78 See Stein, 'Die Hanse und England: Ein hansisch- englischer Seekrieg im 15. Jahrhundert,' 29; Schulz, 113; Postan, 134; Dollinger, *The German Hansa*, 305–10; Stark's partial reassessment of the Hanseatic victory, 182–211.

79 Kendall, 295–302.

80 Ibid, 303–13.

81 *HUB* X no. 111.

82 'Caspar Weinreichs Danziger Chronik,' 735; *CSP Milan*, I 167. A ten-year Franco-Hanseatic truce was proclaimed on 23 August 1473. *HR* (2) VII no. 45; *HUB* X no. 236. The negotiations leading up to this agreement had been of concern to the English, and undoubtedly helped to spur on the Anglo-Hanseatic peace talks at Utrecht.

83 Postan, 134.
84 *HR* (2) VI no. 435, 436; *HR* (3) I 2#3, 65#1–2, 83#4, 202#1, IV no. 278; *HUB* XI no. 1295, 1296.
85 Neumann, 58, n. 140; *LUB* XI no. 433–4, 438–44, 448–51, 469, 473, 482, 490.
86 *HR* (2) VI no. 283; Stark, *Lübeck und Danzig*, 201.
87 *HR* (2) VI no. 524, VII no. 34#136, 141, 143. For Bremen: Müller, 48; Asaert, *De Antwerpse Scheepvaart*, 308–11.
88 *HUB* IX no. 541. For Danzig's continued determination to limit English intrusion into the Baltic see *HR* (2) VII no. 63, 131–3.
89 *HR* (2) VI no. 356#62, 73, 418, 483#1, 484–5, 589; *LUB* XI no. 659.
90 Schulz, 113.
91 Postan, 134.
92 *CPR* 1467–77: 445; StA Köln Hanse III. K. 9. Bl.62–83, 88; *Urkundliche Geschichte*, 152–7 (no. CXXXV); *HUB* X no. 528, 534, XI no. 603#10; PRO E30/1342; *HR* (2) VII no. 151, 409; *HR* (3) I no. 169. Danzig's objections to the terms of the treaty were intentionally de-emphasized by the Hanseatic secretary in London in order to allay the concern of the chancellor. *HR* (2) VII no. 259.
93 Appendix A.1.2; PRO E122 194/20. The figures for 1469–70 published in *England's Export Trade* are correct, although the 828 cloths exported by the Cologners from November to February have been calculated in the alien total. The totals printed in *Studies*, 356 do not correspond with those in the Exchequer enrolment.
94 *HUB* X no. 111, 144; *Quellen*, ed. Kuske, II no. 560, 577.
95 *HUB* IX no. 698#3.
96 PRO E122 52/52, Coppyn Welle (Ipswich, 21 August 1470), 194/19 Jan de Zeelander and Peter de Wale (London, 11 November 1472), Mathijs Valke (13 March 1473), Adrian van Polfiete and Jan de Zeelander (28 July 1473). Transcriptions of the entries for these Antwerp shippers are printed in *Documenten*, ed. Asaert, 46–7, 142–9. See also *Quellen*, ed. Kuske, II no. 563.
97 PRO E122 62/13, Claus van Cucke (Hull, 18 March 1471); *Documenten*, ed. Asaert, 41.
98 The accounts of the collectors of the Zealand water toll at Iersekeroord, Middelburg, Veere, and Arnemuiden between October 1472 and 1473 are published in *Iersekeroord*, ed. W.S. Unger, 235–333. For the offloading of Baltic cargo see especially 280–1, 306–7, 314, 330, and for its refreighting by English carriers 262, 287, 300–3. Some Baltic cargo also reached Zealand via Holland or through the agency of Holland merchants. Ibid, 249–52, 259. Certificates for consignments of Cologne thread, wainscots, and Prussian chests shipped from Zealand are included in PRO E101 129/1,2.
99 *Bronnen*, ed. Smit (1) II no. 1657, 1668, 1684, 1711–12, 1741–2.
100 Ibid, no. 1643; *CPR* 1467–77: 282.

101 *Bronnen*, ed. Smit (1) II no. 1381, 1418, 1456, 1497, 1538, 1544, 1549, 1587, 1597, 1602; *HUB* VIII no. 244, 260.
102 Appendix A.1.1 and *Studies*, 331, 340, 342, 346, 348. For the Hull and Newcastle shippers in Zealand: *Iersekeroord*, ed. Unger, 264, 270, 272, 287, 293, 298–301, 303, 308. Zealand skippers also freighted lumber, tar, and osmund for Englishmen. Ibid, 266, 317, 326.
103 Ibid, 266.
104 APG 300.19/3 53r, shipper Johann Segersson. For Esterlings shipping cloth in Zealand: *Iersekeroord*, ed. Unger, 246, 261, 277–9, 284, 286.
105 APG 300.19/3 186r–187v. For some of the major shipments arriving in Danzig from Lübeck: Ibid, 48v, 54r, 64v, 67v, 71v, 96r, 97v, 100r, 107v, 114v, 123r, 144r, 150r, 166r, and varieties of cloth from the Lowlands: Ibid, 123r (Amsterdam), 136r (Kampen), 135v (Hoorn), 99v and 172r (Dordrecht), 131v (Leiden), 131v and 92v (Deventer), 99v and 171v (Flemish).
106 'Caspar Weinreichs Danziger Chronik,' 736.
107 *Iersekeroord*, ed. Unger, 298; APG 300.19/3 135v, 171v, 172r; PRO E122 62/7, 97/4, Heinrich Schroder hauling bulk freight for Danzigers to Hull (10 May 1465) and Lynn (10 September 1465). It is Jenks's contention that England's trade to the Baltic continued through the war years (I 222).
108 'Caspar Weinreichs Danziger Chronik,' 733; APG 300.19/3 20r–9r, 54r–66v, 98v–105v, 131r, 135v, 136r, 136v, 137r, 139v, 146r, 147v, 149v, 150r, 153r, 153v, 154r, 155r, 155v, 156v, 157r, 158r, 158v, 159r, 161r, 162v, 167r.
109 Ibid, 177r–180v, 181r, 186r–188r. Many were laden exclusively with salt, as were the nine ships reaching Danzig 'uth Amsterdam.' Ibid, 179r–182v. For Hansards hauling salt cargoes to and from the Zealand ports see *Iersekeroord*, ed. Unger, 310–11, 325.
110 Peter Kosseler, Rolf Velsted, Tydemann Valand, Peter Monk, Jacob Wulff, Gerd Overram, Tews Pelz, Peter Biscop, Jacob van Fechten, Thomas Sukow, Johann Winckeldorp, Arndt Apsthagen, Reynold Kerkhorde, Jacob Grene, Cord Schele, Johann Sidinghusen, Hans Tutting, Dirk Gunther, Jurgen Erik, Heinrich Eggerd.
111 *Iersekeroord*, ed. Unger, 280–1, 291, 294 306–7, 314, 316, 320.
112 Ibid, 310–11, 316; APG 300.19/3 118v, 139v, 158r, 158v, 159v, 171r, 179r, 179v; 300.19/5 54, 56, 295; 300.19/5a 12, 13; 'Christoph Beyers des ältern Danziger Chronik,' *Scriptores Rerum Prussicarum*, ed. T. Hirsch et al., V 443.
113 *HR* (2) VII no. 110, 111, 113, 214, 408, 409; *HR* (3) I no. 169.
114 *HR* (2) VII no. 281.
115 As there was a ceiling of £10,000 on Hanseatic customs exemptions, it was necessary, for administrative purposes, to record values and tariffs applicable under normal circumstances. The actual revenues, however, were transferred to the London Steelyard for redistribution to those affected by the arrests in 1468.
116 Appendix A.1.2. The 'Hanseatic' export totals for the war years printed

in *Studies* and in *England's Export Trade* actually apply only to Cologne merchants. Those for the next two years represent combined Cologne/ Hanseatic figures, because although the Crown had regranted Hanseatic privileges to Cologne, *Rot. Parl.* VI 81, the town was not readmitted to the Hanse until 1476.

117 For the east-coast ports see Appendix A.1.1.

118 It has been suggested by Jenks (I 221–2) that during the war years the lion's share of denizen cloth exports from Hull was directed to the Brabant marts, but substantial quantities continued to be shipped to Prussia as well, notwithstanding the Hanseatic boycott and the other risks involved. If this were true, one might expect the corresponding Danzig *Pfahlkammerbücher* (APG 300.19/3) to yield the names of some English skippers and/or merchants who operated out of Hull from 1469 to 1472 (PRO E122 62/12–17). This is not the case.

119 APG 300.19/5 esp. 81, 121–3, 130, 137, 186, 206, 249, 256–7, 279, 281, 289–90, 297, 299, 304. The Danzig records for the period 1474 through 1476 are edited in V. Lauffer, 'Danzigs Schiffs- und Waarenverkehr am Ende des 15. Jahrhunderts.' However, the published totals, at least for the English trade, appear to contain a number of errors. See revised figures in Appendix A.1.4.

Chapter 4

1 PRO E30/561, 568.

2 Munro, 'Bruges and the Abortive Staple,' 1146–9; For the extension of Hanseatic privileges at Antwerp: *HUB* X no. 861, 886; ARA CC. Cartons series I, 1–4, no. 189.

3 *Acts of Court*, 136–7.

4 *York Civic Records*, ed. A. Raine, 66.

5 *The York Mercers and Merchant Adventurers 1356–1917*, ed. M. Sellers, 107–8. Also *HUB* XI no. 19.

6 *HUB* X no. 1149–50; *HR* (3) II no. 30–3; *CPR* 1476–85: 353; *Urkundliche Geschichte*, 160–2 (no. CXXXIX, CXLI, CXLIV).

7 *HUB* XI no. 18 (esp. #2, 4, 6, 8), 19.

8 From the Steelyard secretary's summary of the English complaints, *HUB* XI no. 18#10. [so it would be better ... to seek the improvement and remedy through open war and conflict, whatever the cost to the kingdom of England ...] The condemnation of the Hansards was by no means unanimous, though, as once again the clothmen of Bristol rallied to their support. *Acts of Court*, 294–5.

9 For piratical encounters of the 1470s see *CPR* 1467–77: 605 and 1476–85: 23, 49; *HUB* X no. 489, 526; 'Die Chronik Christians von Geren,' 372; R. Meissner, 'Eine isländische Urkunde'; PRO E30/557, 560.

10 For the Wendish disputes with Holland: *HR* (3) I no. 7–18, 216–30; *HUB* X no. 537, 539, 545, 616.

11 *HUB* X no. 975, 988, 994, XI no. 1303; *HR* (3) I no. 435#7, II no. 509#37, 510#4–27.
12 *HUB* XI no. 24, 79; *45th Report of the Deputy Keeper of the Public Records,* appendix 2, 5.
13 Margaret of York and her agents had contributed about 1,500 German and Swiss mercenaries to the Yorkist invasion force that departed the Lowlands for Ireland in mid-April, crossed to England, and was routed by the king's troops at the battle of Stoke in June. M. Bennett, *Lambert Simnel and the Battle of Stoke,* 60–3.
14 *Acts of Court,* 299–303. Confronted with uncertain prospects for an Anglo–Burgundian accord, the mercers' fellowship in London already had advised members in the Lowlands to 'sett all your charges of goodes and dettes in suretie unto ye have certen knowlege of a good and sure Entercours betwix bothe Prynces' in November 1486. Ibid, 297.
15 *HUB* XI no. 183; *HR* (3) II no. 109–10.
16 *The Cely Letters,* ed. A. Hanham, 235–6.
17 By early 1488 the English government had reopened trade talks, but Maximilian had not yet subdued Ghent. Ibid, 227, 242; *The Reign of Henry VII from Contemporary Sources,* ed. A.F. Pollard, I 282–5; *Letters and Papers,* II 52–4; *Materials for a History of the Reign of Henry VII,* ed. W. Campbell, II 247–8, 284.
18 *Tudor Royal Proclamations,* ed. P.L. Hughes and J.F. Larkin, II no. 18. Articles of the new Anglo–Hapsburg treaty apparently were being drafted as early as December 1488, by which time Henry VII already had granted licences to several shippers from Holland to resume trading to England. *Materials,* II 356, 359, 362, 377–78, 440–41.
19 *HUB* XI no. 183, 233, 243; *HR* (3) II no. 228–33; *Quellen,* ed. Kuske, II no. 1055, 1206#32.
20 The protectionist regulations in Flanders are outlined in Munro, 'Industrial Protectionism in Medieval Flanders.'
21 *Cely Letters,* 236–42; *HUB* XI no. 331; *Quellen,* ed. Kuske, II no. 1206#22.
22 SAA Cert I, ff.2r, 16r; *HUB* XI no. 292–3, 299; *Bronnen,* ed. Smit (2) I no. 39; *Quellen,* ed. Kuske, II no. 1206#8, 29, 39. Meanwhile the king's embargo also was felt within England's import trade, as Hanseatic merchants complained of customs searchers confiscating cargoes as 'verbuert goet ... in des roemschen konincks land gelaeden' [forbidden goods ... laded in the land of the Roman king]. Ibid, 1206#12, 14, 26.
23 *England's Export Trade,* 109–10.
24 *HR* (3) II no. 188–90, 212.
25 PRO E101 55/17, E163 9/37.
26 *HR* (3) II no. 161#12, 193, 217#20, 28, 220, 223, 224, 509; PRO C1/59/302, C1/64/1105; Appendix A.3.2. There had been several incidents of Esterlings being harassed at Hull since the mid–1450s. E. Gillet and K.A. MacMahon, *A History of Hull,* 54, 75, 76, 79. The arrest of Danzigers

Johann Slagetin and George Timmerman in 1489 for alleged participation in a Danish attack on Hull ships is instructive in view of the threats issued by Hull against Prussian shipping, and reports of the forced sale of Hanseatic goods there. Much indignation was aroused among the Esterlings, because the two men were imprisoned for an inordinately long period despite the sworn testimony of at least two dozen Danzig burgesses that they were not serving with the Danes at the time of the robbery. The pair claimed to have been set ashore at the Humber from a Danzig merchant ship to hire a pilot to guide the vessel to Lynn. They insisted that their arrest had come only after the local authorities realized that the ship did not intend to put in at Hull. They were still in custody in the summer of 1490, when another Danzig captain, Nicholaus Klinckabel, was forcibly diverted to Hull from his intended destination of Lynn. PRO C1/172/16; HR (3) II no. 309, 342–3, 359, 509#69, 83, 510#36, 42; HUB XI no. 636.

27 CPR 1476–85: 425, 1485–94: 105; HR (3) II no. 117–18, 205#6, 226, 509–11; HUB X no. 1201, 1225, XI no. 131, 187, 236, 265, 393, 443; Bronnen, ed. Smit, (2) I no. 9; Bronnen, ed. Z.W. Sneller and W.S. Unger, I no. 354–55, 361–4, 366, 369, 374; BL Additional 15505 f. 21. Also, a fierce privateering campaign waged against Lowland and Hanseatic shippers by Philip of Kleves endangered Hanseatic trade still further. A ship bound from Boston to Danzig was seized in 1490 and the following year at least two more Hanseatic vessels plying the London/Zealand route were pirated as well. HUB XI no. 505–6; 'Caspar Weinreichs Danziger Chronik,' 782.

28 HUB XI no. 126–7, 594; HR (3) II no. 109–10, 161#10, 298–300; Quellen, ed. Kuske, II no. 1054, 1206#6, 27, 28, 33–5; Statutes of the Realm, II 506 (1 Hen. VII c.9), 520 (3 Hen. VII c.12). A summary of the various restrictions is contained in Schulz, 139–41.

29 PRO C1/64/71; HUB XI no. 292–3, 295, 299, 333; HR (3) II no. 302–3, 306–8, 311, 313, 387, 508#35, 509#1–27; 'Caspar Weinreichs Danziger Chronik,' 780. For the harassment of the Cologners see Quellen, ed. Kuske, II no. 1206, and for the attack on Peter van Wesel et al., ibid, no. 1206#42.

30 As early as 1482 the Danes were stopping Danzig ships and searching them for English cargoes, and at least one vessel was distrained. King John offered to release it only if Danzig would agree to discontinue trade to England. HUB X no. 997, 1003, 1028, 1036–37, 1047, 1112; HR (3) I no. 546#165, 178, 180, 547#36, 38, 550#14–20, 554#8; 'Caspar Weinreichs Danziger Chronik,' 745. The trade continued, of course, and apparently the ship still was in Danish custody in March 1484.

31 HR (3) II no. 106.

32 HR (3) I no. 129, 205, 264–5, 299, 346–7, 383, 441, 609, II no. 114–24.

33 CPR 1485–94: 321; Tudor Royal Proclamations, I no. 21; 45th Report of the Deputy Keeper of the Public Records, appendix 2, 5–6.

34 HR (3) II no. 339–41, 345, 357, 360, 374–86, 399, 406–7; HUB XI no. 292–3,

333–4. For attacks on Hanseatic shipping in 1490 see *HR* (3) II no.
510#40–6, and for the evacuation of the Steelyard archive, Irsigler, 'Die
Lübecker Veckinchusen und die Kölner Rinck,' 324.

35 Unless specifically noted, the following summary of the Antwerp negotiations is based on the Hanseatic records of the diet in *HR* (3) II no.
496–511.

36 *HR* (3) II no. 496#267–70; Schulz, 142.

37 *HR* (3) II no. 502#3–7.

38 *HR* (3) II no. 504; *Caspar Weinreichs Danziger Chronik,* ed. Hirsch and
Vossberg, 123–4; Schulz, 143; Lloyd, *England and the German Hanse,
1157–1611,* 244–5. With regard to the past status of Englishmen at the
Artushof, if they had been denied access, it was only for a brief time, as
Schulz suggested. Citing the early membership register of one of the
fellowships (*Banken*) who met at the *Artushof,* P. Simson confirmed that
Englishmen were indeed welcomed there soon after 1483: '... von aus-
serhalb des Reiches stellten sich schon früh Gäste ein, die ebenfalls als
vollberechtigte Mitglieder in die Banken eintraten: ... 1483 bei der Rein-
holdsbank je zwei Stockholmer und Aalborger, bald auch Engländer und
Russen.' Simson, *Der Artushof in Danzig und seine Brüderschaften, die
Banken,* 43. Anyway, although the *Artushof* was by this time a central
meeting place for merchants in Danzig, foreigners must not have relied
too much on actual physical admittance to the hall. That was not auto-
matic. Furthermore, the *Artushof* was destroyed by fire in December
1476, and its reconstruction took the better part of five years. Yet this did
not seem to inhibit the merchants of Lynn trading to Danzig, to say
nothing of the Danzigers themselves.

39 Even as the talks were in session English captains were attacking Hanseatic salt ships returning from Brouage. 'Caspar Weinreichs Danziger
Chronik,' 783.

40 Postan, 101, 138; J.L. Bolton, *The Medieval English Economy,* 310; J.D.
Mackie, *The Earlier Tudors 1485–1558,* 221. Thereto: Jenks, I 253. Lloyd's
recent reassessment: Lloyd, 214, 284–6.

41 *HR* (3) II no. 511#24–61; PRO E122 63/1,2,8; 107/61; 108/2.

42 PRO E122 10/22, 24, 25, 26; 11/2, 3, 4, 6.

43 APG 300.19/5 123, 206, 300.19/5a 57; PRO C1/32/356 (see Appendices
A.1.4 and A.4.3); PRO E122 97/17,18: shippers John Melborn and
William Passheley coming to Lynn in mid–November 1480. See also
HUB X no. 595, 1139.

44 PRO E122 98/1,2 (shipper Elryk Crewer, April 1484), 98/5 (shipper John
Brekersley, May and August 1487, and Lutkyn Smyth, May 1487), 98/7,
8 (shipper Laurence Fredeland, May and July 1488), 98/9 (Hans
Laurence, May and June 1489), 98/10 (Hans Laurence, May and June
1490), 98/11 (Hans Laurence, October 1490 and April 1491, Clays Mors,
September 1491); *HR* (3) II no. 511#1–8, 15, 18–20.

45 *45th Report of the Deputy Keeper of the Public Records,* appendix 2, 5–6.

Belles and Carter are identified in this document as merchants from Lynn. The former most probably is the same John Belles of Norwich, who also had business interests in the Low Countries. *Bronnen*, ed. Smit, (1) II no. 1794.

46 PRO E122 52/58; 53/3, 4, 6; 78/9; 194/24, 25. However, according to the Danzig chronicle of Caspar Weinreich, the ship taken by the Danes in 1482 for allegedly attempting to smuggle an English merchant and his goods through the Sound was bound for London. Perhaps, then, the merchant in question was a Londoner. 'Caspar Weinreichs Danziger Chronik,' 745. Thereto: *HUB* X no. 997, 1003, 1036–7, 1112.

47 *De Oosterse Handel te Amsterdam*, ed. N.W. Posthumus, 255–336.

48 *Iersekeroord*, ed. Unger, 349–51.

49 The contribution (based on customs records) of the Hansards to the overseas trade of Boston, Lynn, Ipswich, and Hull, during the period 1476–86, is illustrated in chart 1.

50 Appendix A.1.1 and A.1.3; PRO E122 63/1, 2, 8; 107/61; 108/1, 2, 3.

51 *HR* (3) II no. 509#83, 510#42; PRO E122 63/8 (shipper Nicholaus Klinckabel, September 1490). In Hull the Hansards also dealt with merchants from York. *York Civic Records*, 163; Gillet and MacMahon, 76.

52 PRO E122 63/1, 2, 8.

53 Appendices A.1.1 and A.1.3; PRO E122 10/22, 24, 25, 26; 11/2, 3, 4, 6. Another Danzig ship sailed directly to Boston in the spring of 1490 and left again with lead, cloth, and ballast. *HUB* XI no. 539.

54 'Caspar Weinreichs Danziger Chronik,' 742.

55 *Die Lübecker Bergenfahrer und ihre Chronistik*, ed. F. Bruns, 183–4.

56 Appendices A.1.1 and A.1.3; PRO E122 97/17, 18; 98/1, 2, 5, 7, 8, 9, 10, 11.

57 *HUB* XI no. 433.

58 PRO E122 152/12; *HUB* X no. 438#27; *Studies*, 360; *England's Export Trade*, 106–10. Specific references to merchants from Danzig, Hamburg, and 'le Stelyard' occur in the local customs for Yarmouth, appended to the Borough Court Rolls: Norfolk Record Office Y/C4/181 8d; 183 13d; 184 9d; 185 14d,15; 186 13,13d; 195 9; 196 8d,10. There are extant Yarmouth customs particulars for 1485–6: PRO E122 152/17,18. They make no mention of Hanseatic trade.

59 *HUB* X no. 477#56–8; *HR* (3) I no. 347#9, 501#51.

60 *Urkundliche Geschichte*, 209–12 (no. V–VII); *CPR* 1467–77: 519, 540; *HUB* X no. 407, 477#56–8; D. Purcell, 'Der hansische "Steelyard" in King's Lynn, Norfolk, England'; W.A. Pantin, 'The Merchants' Houses and Warehouses of King's Lynn.' The history of the property at Lynn, which came into Hanseatic possession in 1475, is reviewed in Jenks, 'Die "Liber Lynne" und die Besitzgeschichte des hansischen Stahlhofs zu Lynn.'

61 Lloyd, 164; Jenks, *England, die Hanse und Preussen*, I 386, II 655.

62 *HUB* X no. 477#18, XI no. 545, 548; PRO C1/31/494–8; *Quellen*, ed. Kuske, I no. 1276.

63 Appendices A.1.1 and A.1.3; PRO E122 52/58.
64 Ibid; *HUB* X no. 438.
65 PRO E122 52/58, 53/3, 4; *Kämmereirechnungen der Stadt Hamburg*, III 528.
66 Appendix A.1.2.
67 PRO E122 194/22–5. For the leading Steelyard merchants see chart 2. The controlment of the customs particulars (PRO E122 194/25) is printed in *The Overseas Trade of London Exchequer Customs Accounts 1480–1*, ed. J.S. Cobb, 1–164. Salmer and Savage dealt directly with tin and pewter manufacturers in southwestern England. Jenks, I 288, n. 34.
68 PRO E122 194/22–5 and chart 3. Shipper Matthew Brom, departing London on 28 March 1481, is also identified as a Hansard, but his home port is not given, nor is his arrival in London recorded.
69 PRO E122 73/41; 78/3; 194/26; *HR* (3) II no. 228–31.
70 PRO E122 78/9; chart 4.
71 PRO E122 78/9; *HUB* XI no. 505–6.
72 PRO E122 78/9; *HUB* XI no. 640; APG 300.19/7 43v. For Aalant see ibid, 10v and 'Caspar Weinreichs Danziger Chronik,' 782. Danzigers also had interests in two ships taken *en route* from Zealand to England by the French in June 1487. *Acta Statuum Prussiae Regalis*, ed. K. Gorski and M. Biskup, I no. 250; BL Additional 15505 f. 21. Another Danzig skipper, Peter Harder, also had come to London in 1488, his cargo consisting partly of a consignment of flax for one Gregor Matern, also of Danzig. A dispute between the two men over water damage to the cargo was carried on until both of them were back in Danzig two years later. When Matern then did not obtain the justice he sought from the civic authorities he embarked on a new career of kidnapping, murder, mutilation, and arson, and thus became one of the most notorious criminals in Prussia. 'Christoph Beyers des ältern Danziger Chronik,' 445–50.
73 *Kämmereirechnungen der Stadt Hamburg*, III 528, 596, IV 154; *HR* (3) II no. 228–30; *HUB* XI no. 275; PRO E122 53/8, 9; 78/9; Friedland, 'Hamburger Englandfahrer 1512–1557,' 8–14.
74 Although the controlment of the cloth and petty custom for 1490–1 (PRO E122 78/9) apparently extends to the end of the Exchequer year, the last recorded Hanseatic cloth shipments were in June 1491 and the last imports in August. The absence of shipments, especially cloth consignments, from mid–August through late September is quite extraordinary if, in fact, the account is accurate and complete, since the intentional reduction in Hanseatic trade to England presumably would have ended when the Antwerp conference concluded at the end of June.
75 *England's Export Trade*, 106–10.
76 PRO E122 78/9. Leading Steelyard merchants for 1490–1 are listed in chart 5.
77 PRO E122 78/3; 78/9; 194/24–6; E356/22 m.36–8.
78 Appendix A.1.2.
79 PRO E122 194/25.

80 *Quellen,* ed. Kuske, II no. 1206#36; *CPR* 1485–94: 105; *HUB* X no. 1130; chart 5.

81 PRO E122 78/9; *Quellen,* ed. Kuske, II no. 1206#37.

82 SAA SR 89 f. 58r, SR 92 ff. 16r, 16v, 48r, 195v, SR 93 f. 78r, SR 94 f. 45r, SR 96, ff. 123v, 128v, 215r, 240v; *Etudes,* ed. R. Doehaerd, II no. 238, III no. 2944.

83 PRO E122 78/3; 78/9; 194/24–26; *Iersekeroord,* ed. Unger, 348–50. For the Anglo–Burgundian treaty: PRO E30/561, 566, 568, 1097.

84 *Etudes,* ed. Doehaerd, III no. 2918, 2952; *Bronnen,* ed. Smit, (1) II no. 1823, (2) I no. 7.

85 *Documenten,* ed. Asaert, 16, 23, 40, 150–68, 173; *Etudes,* ed. Doehaerd, II no. 156, 160.

86 *Etudes,* ed. Doehaerd, II no. 39, 395.

87 Ibid, II 1ff.

88 *HUB* X no. 569–70, 865–9, 886; ARA CC. Cartons series I, 1–4, no. 189.

89 *HUB* X no. 562. For Bruges Hansards at the Brabant fairs see ibid, no. 509, 694, 736, 870, 911. 1012.

90 ARA CC. 49833 3v, 4r; *Iersekeroord,* ed. Unger, 334–49, 363–8; *Bronnen,* ed. Smit (1) II no. 1999, (2) I no. 9; *Quellen,* ed. Kuske, II no. 1206#23, 41. The contention of W. Brulez, 'Bruges and Antwerp in the 15th and 16th Centuries: An Antithesis?,' 23, that since English cloth was finished in Brabant, Cologne merchants purchased it from English and Brabantine merchants at Antwerp, is not supported by English customs records. Particulars of accounts clearly show that the Cologners themselves, as well as other Hansards, shipped vast quantities of English woollens from London with Zealand, Brabantine, and Hanseatic carriers. Furthermore, not only would the Cologners likely pay a lower wholesale price for English cloth in London than in Brabant, they also could ship it to the fairs more cheaply, since they paid lower customs duties than English merchants. So far as the final processing of cloth at Antwerp is concerned, under Henry VII the English government severely restricted the export of unfinished cloth at the insistence of denizen cloth shearers.

91 Correspondence relating to this incident implies that the Hanseatic merchants at Antwerp were quite scandalized by it. *HUB* X no. 911.

92 *CPR* 1476–85: 425; *HUB* X no. 680, 827, XI no. 505–6; *Etudes,* ed. Doehaerd, II no. 158; *Bronnen,* ed. Poelman (1) II no. 2821; 'Caspar Weinreichs Danziger Chronik,' 743–4.

93 ARA CC. 49833 4r and 4v; Rülke, 83; Irsigler, *Die wirtschaftliche Stellung der Stadt Köln,* 303–5.

94 *Quellen,* ed. Kuske, II no. 1055, 1206#3, 9, 22, 23, 27, 32, 35, 41.

95 SAA Cert I ff. 10r, 11v, 27r, 31v, 64r, 67v, 69r; SR 90, ff. 218v, 239r, 289v; 91, ff. 181r, 262v, 290v; SR 92, f.143v; SR 93, f.257v; SR 96, f.202r; SR 99, f.90r; *Etudes,* ed. Doehaerd, II no. 36, 242, 246.

96 Simsch, 25–9, 90–5.

97 Rülke, 114–19; *HR* (2) VI no. 356, 483.

98 Rülke, 52, 126–31; *HR* (2) VII 181#5.
99 *HR* (2) VII no. 367, 379; 'Caspar Weinreichs Danziger Chronik,' 744, 754.
100 *HR* (2) VII no. 338#210ff; *HR* (3) II no. 136; *HUB* X no. 938, XI no. 102.
101 *LUB* X no. 112, 227, 292, 308, XI no. 318, 367, 397; *HR* (2) VII no. 81#7, 368, 388#141, 159; Rülke, 94–109.

Chapter 5

1 StA Köln Hanse III. K. 11. Bl.5, 32, 35, 36, 48, 80, 86, 88, 101.
2 *Tudor Royal Proclamations*, I no. 31; *CPR* 1485–94: 475. For Margaret of York's complicity in the Perkin Warbeck intrigue: C. Weightman, *Margaret of York Duchess of Burgundy 1446–1503*, 170–7. Maximilian subsequently supported the imposter as well in 1494–5. *CSP Venice*, I no. 644, 648–52, 664, 667.
3 Unless specifically noted, the following account of events leading up to the imposition of the embargo in September 1493 is based on records of the London mercers printed in *Acts of Court*, 572ff.
4 Ibid, 572–4.
5 Ibid, 575.
6 Ibid, 583.
7 Ibid, 587. Bull was an established London carrier. In 1491 he was one of several captains commissioned by the Crown to impress mariners and soldiers for his ship, the *Margaret* of Dieppe. Similar commissions given in 1497 indicate he had at least three ships. *Letters and Papers*, II 372, 376. See also *Naval Accounts and Inventories of the reign of Henry VII, 1485–8 and 1495–7*, 128–9.
8 *Acts of Court*, 580, 587–90; Schanz, II no. 85; *The Reign of Henry VII from Contemporary Sources*, I 96–7. It is important to note that the insurrection came after the Hansards had bound themselves to abide by the prohibitions, in order not to suppose that the riot caused the king to include the Hansards in the ban. It prompted the Crown only to proclaim the status quo that had existed since the discussions with the Hanseatic delegation at Northampton in September.
9 *Acts of Court*, 589; *HR* (3) III no. 259. A passage from the Drapers' Wardens rolls cited in A.H. Johnson, *The History of the Worshipful Company of the Drapers of London*, I 141–2, indicates the watch at the Steelyard lasted seven days, although the date given for the riot (cited from Grafton's Chronicle) is incorrect.
10 *Acts of Court*, 590.
11 *HUB* XI no. 710, 723; *HR* (3) III no. 285–9, 291–2, 353#61. Nine Hanseatic ships left the Thames in October 1493. Steelyard merchants declared that all the cargoes were bound for either Hamburg or Danzig, and that they would not be offloaded in Burgundian territory. The intended destination of the shippers who ended up in Zealand was Hamburg. They were freighting cloth for Cologners.

12 HUB XI no. 713, 715, 743, 769, 781, 783, 784, 835; *Quellen*, ed. Kuske, II no. 1335, 1405; *HR* (3) III no. 290a, 333, 415–19; 422.

13 *CPR* 1485–94: 477; *HUB* XI no. 729.

14 *Bronnen*, ed. Smit (2) I no. 82; *Tudor Economic Documents*, ed. Power and Tawney, II 6–9.

15 Munro, 'Bruges and the Abortive Staple,' 1150–2; Schanz, II no. 6; *Bronnen*, ed. Smit (2) I no. 92 n. 2; *Etudes*, ed. Doehaerd, II 925, 1006, 1020, 1042–3, 1053, 1116. The tax applied to other cheaper English textiles as well, although they paid proportionately less: friezes and kerseys 3s each, stockbreds 1s 3d, and 'huls' or 'hulse laken' 6s Flemish money. ARA CC. 23250.

16 StA Köln Hanse III. K. 11. Bl.48, 49, 84, 111, 121, 162; *HR* (3) III no. 279, 333, 358, 399–402, 416.

17 *HR* (3) III no. 381, 383, 385; *HUB* XI no. 777, 786.

18 *Tudor Economic Documents*, II, 11–15; *Bronnen*, ed. Smit (2) I no. 96. According to Francis Bacon, writing more than a century later, the name *Intercursus Magnus* was popularized in the Low Countries: 'This is that treaty which the Flemings call intercursus magnus ... chiefly to give it a difference from the treaty that followed in the one and twentieth year of the king, which they call intercursus malus.' Bacon, *The History of the Reign of Henry the Seventh*, ed. F.J. Levy, 185.

19 Bindoff, 52–7; *Acts of Court*, 609–10; ARA CC. Cartons series I, 1–4, no. 103–4; *Letters and Papers*, II 69–72, 377.

20 *Acts of Court*, 599–618; *Bronnen*, ed. Smit (2) I no. 111.

21 *HUB* XI no. 994; *Antient Kalendars and Inventories of the Treasury of His Majesty's Exchequer*, ed. F. Palgrave, III 58.

22 *Bronnen*, ed. Smit (2) I no. 96–134; *HUB* XI no. 972, 981, 991, 1019, 1033, 1046; *Acts of Court*, 633–4; StA Köln Hanse III. K. 12. Bl.72, 74; *HR* (3) IV no. 56, 57.

23 *Quellen*, ed. Kuske, II no. 1425, 1459, 1505#33; *HUB* XI no. 1072, 1129; Munro, 'Bruges and the Abortive Staple,' 1154; Schanz, II no. 7–14. The new treaty was proclaimed in England on 18 May 1499. *Tudor Royal Proclamations*, I no. 45.

24 *HUB* XI no. 904, 910, 1129.

25 A different conclusion, based on 'estimated' cloth export figures, is offered in P. Ramsey, 'Overseas Trade in the Reign of Henry VII.'

26 *England's Export Trade*, 110–11.

27 Appendix A.1.1; PRO E122 108/8

28 Appendix A.1.1; *Iersekeroord*, ed. Unger, 441–94, 508, 511, 513–16; *Etudes*, ed. Doehaerd, II no. 882; *Bronnen*, ed. Smit (2) I no. 87.

29 *Iersekeroord*, ed. Unger, 505, 513–15.

30 *HR* (3) III no. 232–40, 265, 269–71, 278, 379, 573–7, 581–5, 724, 726–8, 731, 748.

31 *HR* (3) III no. 6–24. For the Hanseatic allegations: ibid, no. 14 esp.#4–8, 14–18.

32 *HR* (3) IV no. 61: 'nachdeme denne desset juw [Danzig] und de juwen, so de mercklike handelinge in Engelant hebben, mer dan uns [Lübeck] belanget.' Also ibid, no. 58–60.

33 Ibid, no. 82, 83, 85, 109.

34 Hanseatic records of the Bruges meetings are printed in *HR* (3) IV no. 127–212. See also Schulz, 146–9; Schanz, II no. 89–94.

35 *HR* (3) IV no. 150–3, 180 esp.#16–22.

36 Ibid, no. 79#231–6, 160 esp.#1, 4 and 165–6.

37 Ibid, no. 155, 174, 180–1.

38 *The Reign of Henry VII from Contemporary Sources*, II 311–13; *HR* (3) IV no. 128–32.

39 *HR* (3) IV no. 143–4, 150#78, 151#16–18, 153#6, 195, 278–80, 295, 460.

40 PRO E122 11/8. There is no obvious explanation for the increased Hanseatic presence at Boston (and Lynn) in 1492. Perhaps the trade at Hull, much diminished during the late 1480s, had not yet normalized, thereby prompting the continued diversion of some Baltic cargoes to the Wash ports. Not until 1492–93 did the value of the alien trade at Hull reach levels previously attained during the early 1480s.

41 PRO E122 11/14, E356/24 m.8–9d; *England's Export Trade*, 110–11; Appendix A.1.1.

42 PRO E356/23 m.31–31d, E356/24 m.25–7; *England's Export Trade*, 110–11; Appendix A.1.1.

43 For Newcastle: PRO E122 108/8, E356/24 m.57–8; *England's Export Trade*, 110–11; Appendix A.1.1.

44 Appendix A.1.1; PRO E122 98/12, 13, and E356/23 m.49.

45 Appendix A.1.1; PRO E122 98/14 and E356/23 m.49.

46 Ibid. For prior Baltic ventures involving these Lynn merchants see, for example *HR* (3) II no. 511#8, 18, 19. Peper also did business in the Lowlands. *Bronnen*, ed. Smit (2) I no. 87.

47 *Naval Accounts and Inventories*, 243–4, 246–7, 251–2, 281, 298; Hickmore, 93–6. Purchases for the fleet in the 1420s included Lynn, Bordeaux, Normandy, Holland, and Dutch yarn. *The Navy of the Lancastrian Kings. Accounts and Inventories of William Soper, Keeper of the King's Ships, 1422–1427*, ed. S. Rose, 136–206. Notwithstanding that the types are distinguished one from another, Rose contends that the Lynn cordage was actually of Baltic origin. Ibid, 270–1, n. 215. For the regional cultivation and use of flax and hemp see N. Evans, *The East Anglian Linen Industry*, 1–55.

48 Rigsarkivet Øresundstoldregnskaber 1497; N.E. Bang, *Tabeller over Skibsfart og Varentransport gennem Øresund 1497–1660*, I 2–3; *Naval Accounts and Inventories*, 82–102, 280–1, 341–3. The petty custom figure for Lynn in 1497 is enrolled as a combined alien/Hanseatic aggregate. A small quantity of wax, which was a typical Baltic import, was customed to denizens. PRO E356/23 m.50.

49 PRO E122 53/8–9.

50 PRO E356/23 m.23–35, C1/206/16; Appendix A.1.1.

51 *Iersekeroord*, ed. Unger, 380–9, 482, 484, 491–3, 506–7, 515–16.

52 Stark, *Lübeck und Danzig*, 34–8.

53 Ibid, 86–9, 219–24; *Iersekeroord*, ed. Unger, 504, 508, 511; F. Bruns, 'Die Lübeckischen Pfundzollbücher von 1492–1496.'

54 *HR* (3) IV no. 279, 368, 484–5; Buszello, 'Köln und England 1468–1509,' 464.

55 *Tudor Royal Proclamations*, I no. 52; PRO E30/686.

56 *Tudor Royal Proclamations*, I no. 56; *Letters and Papers*, I 186–222, II 379; *CPR 1494–1509*: 404–6; *HR* (3) V no. 29, 105#335–9.

57 *The Reign of Henry VII from Contemporary Sources*, II 272–3; *Statutes of the Realm*, II 665 (19 Hen. VII c.22); *HR* (3) IV no. 180–1, V no. 22.

58 R. Lockyer, *Henry VII*, 74.

59 S.B. Chrimes, *Henry VII* 236. It is also considered a 'sacrifice of English commercial interests' in J.R. Lander, *Government and Community: England, 1450–1509*, 29.

60 *HR* (3) V no. 45, 115.

61 *Letters and Papers*, II 155–64.

62 *The Reign of Henry VII from Contemporary Sources*, II 322–3. For the popular usage of the term *Intercursus Malus* see Bacon, 185, 235.

63 *The Reign of Henry VII from Contemporary Sources*, II 324; *Letters and Papers*, I 327–37.

64 *HR* (3) IV no. 349–64, 383–90, 394–407, V no. 43, 58, 64. By 1506 Danzig ships also had been seized. *HR* (3) V no. 119–34.

65 Ibid, no. 344–7, 406–9, 564–7, 607, 613. By late 1509 King John was seeking English support for his cause against Lübeck. Henry VIII, who had succeeded his father in April of that year, prudently declined to become involved. Ibid, no. 518, 533; *45th Report of the Deputy Keeper of the Public Records, appendix 2*, 6.

66 *England's Export Trade*, 112–13.

67 PRO C1/272/54; *Etudes*, ed. Doehaerd, II no. 1031, 1332, 1354, 1398, 1460, 1604, 1606, 1613, 1619, 1623, 1631, 1721, 1773, 1800–1, 1823, 1848, 1850, 1870, 1999, 2020, 2068, 2095, 2107; *Iersekeroord*, ed. Unger, 517, 527.

68 ARA CC. Cartons series I, 1–4, no. 106. Whether true or not, such allegations were sure to draw the attention of local authorities. Some years before, another English merchant had been jailed briefly at Bergen op Zoom after a Lombard falsely accused him of slandering Maximilian. A Hanham, *The Celys and Their World*, 25.

69 Rigsarkivet Øresundstøldregnskaber 1497, 1503. The English documents relating to Basell's claim are quite vague and inconsistent: Schanz, II no. 94; *HR* (3) IV no. 165#5, 166#7.

70 PRO E122 108/6, 7, 9, 12.

71 PRO E122 11/17, 18, 20, 12/1; *HR* (3) V no. 58.

72 PRO E122 53/17, 18; Appendix A.1.1; APG 300.19/9 119v, 155r, 155v.

73 PRO C1/160/5–8.

74 PRO E122 98/16, also printed in Gras, 647–84.
75 Rigsarkivet Øresundstoldregnskaber 1503; Bang I 2–3.
76 PRO E122 98/16. The *Balynger* or *Peter*, the *Trinite*, and the *John* of Lynn, captained by William Chamberleyn, Robert Sanderson, and William Davyson, all left Lynn on 23 April 1504 and returned on 31 July.
77 The aggregate value of Lynn's trade in miscellaneous goods other than cloth, wool, and wine has been calculated by starting with the £2,333 worth of merchandise on which poundage was paid by both non-Hanseatic aliens and denizens: PRO E356/23 m.55d. To this has been added the value of Hanseatic goods (£446) subject to the petty custom, as derived from the particulars of account. The alien share of 3d custom merchandise is omitted, since non-Hanseatic aliens also paid poundage, and therefore the value of this trade is already included in the poundage totals. Finally, the value of Hanseatic wax imports (50 quintals, i.e., £100) is added to the aggregate. Indigenous merchants did import some wax as well, but the value is included in the poundage figures. Appendix A.1.3.
78 A list of Hanseatic merchants and skippers appended to the particulars of account contains twelve names, but not that of the leader of the Hanseatic community, Lutkyn Smyth, who exported eighty cloths in English ships. PRO E122 98/16.
79 *HUB* XI no. 1229; PRO C1/267/16; *45th Report of the Deputy Keeper of the Public Records, appendix 2*, 6; *Urkundliche Geschichte*, 212 (no. VIII). Of the Lynn merchants in the Baltic trade, William Trewe was a member of the Commons in the Parliament of 1504, and others, such as Richard Amphles, Richard Peper, Christopher Brodbank, Richard Harde, and Humphry Wolle, were important civic figures. *Historical Manuscripts Commission 11th Report*, 171–2.
80 PRO E122 99/2, 3, 4, 5, 6, 8, 9, 11, 12; *HR* (3) V no. 607, VI no. 188#54, 196#109, 203, VII no. 110#7, 203, 252.
81 Rigsarkivet Øresundstoldregnskaber 1503; PRO E122 80/2. Sayer left London on 13 March and again on 19 June. John Scott left with cloth cargoes on 22 March and 8 July. His name is entered late in the Sound toll book for 1503, which suggests only a single voyage to Danzig. However, a London skipper with the surname Scott also is listed twice (i.e., entering and leaving the Sound) much earlier in the year, so perhaps both Sayer and Scott sailed twice to the Baltic that summer.
82 For some of the shippers on the London/Danzig route: PRO E122 79/12 (John Hubard leaving London on 16 July, Thomas Oldehoff on 10 May and 12 August, Simon Merkenbeck and Jacob Timmermann on 10 September, and Tydemann Blanck on 8 July); APG 300.19/9 18v, 65r, 82r, 100v, 118r, 137v, 153v.
83 PRO E122 79/12, 80/2, 5, E356/24 m.47–50d; Appendix A.1.2.
84 Ibid.
85 PRO C1/308/71, E122 79/12; 80/2; *Letters and Papers Foreign and Domes-*

tic of the Reign of Henry VIII, ed. J.S. Brewer, I (1) 640, (2) 1164–5, 1229–32, 1552.

86 PRO E122 79/12, 80/2.

87 PRO C1/277/20, C1/302/50, C1/316/58.

88 PRO E122 79/12; 80/5.

89 *Caspar Weinreichs Danziger Chronik*, ed. Hirsch and Vossberg, XI: 'Ock werenn bynnen erer Stede [Lübeck] küme iiii eft v de der Engelschenn Reyse todoende hedden.'

90 StA Lübeck Niederstadtsbuch Konzept 1506–1510, 189r, 212v, 225r, 262v, 362v, 366r, 366v.

91 *Die Zolltarife der Stadt Hamburg*, ed. Pitz, no. 66, 75, 78; K. Friedland, 'Hamburger Englandfahrer 1512–1557,' 9–10.

92 *HUB* XI no. 413–14; *Caspar Weinreichs Danziger Chronik*, ed. Hirsch and Vossberg, VIII.

Chapter 6

1 Postan, 'The Economic and Political Relations of England and the Hanse from 1400 to 1475,' *Studies*, 91–153.

2 Lloyd, 'A Reconsideration,' and *England and the German Hanse, 1157-1611*, 214-16, 284.

3 Jenks, *England, die Hanse und Preussen*, esp. I 219, 253–7 and II 735–6.

APPENDICES

The following series of appendices, consisting of statistical compilations, composites, and transcripts of notarial records, illustrates various facets of Anglo-Hanseatic trade during the second half of the fifteenth century.

Appendix A.1.1 utilizes (a) cloth export totals published in E.M. Carus-Wilson and O. Coleman, *England's Export Trade 1275–1547* and *Studies in English Trade in the Fifteenth Century*, ed. M.M. Postan and E. Power, and (b) petty custom statistics up to 1482 in *Studies* plus figures for subsequent years gleaned from PRO E356 KR. enrolled customs accounts. The figures for Hull, up to 1500, are from *The Customs Accounts of Hull 1453–1490*, ed. W.R. Childs, 226–9. Further breakdowns of the Hanseatic trade have been calculated from the surviving particulars of accounts of the cloth and petty custom for various individual ports, specifically:
Boston: PRO E122 9/53, 54, 56, 59, 65, 68; 10/1, 3, 4, 5, 6, 7, 8, 9, 10, 22, 24, 25, 26; 11/2, 3, 4, 6, 8, 14, 17, 18, 20
Hull: PRO E122 61/71, 75; 62/1, 3, 4, 5, 6, 7, 9, 10, 11, 13, 14; 63/1, 2, 8, 13
Ipswich: PRO E122 52/42, 43, 44, 45, 46, 47, 48, 49, 52, 54, 55, 58; 53/3, 4, 6, 8, 9, 11, 17, 18
Lynn: PRO E122 96/37, 40, 41; 97/1, 2, 3, 4, 6, 7, 8, 9, 17, 18; 98/1, 2, 5, 7, 8, 9, 10, 11, 12, 13, 14, 15, 16
Newcastle: PRO E122 107/53, 61; 108/1, 2, 3, 4, 5, 6, 7, 8, 9, 12.

Appendix A.1.2 has been compiled from PRO E122 78/9, 80/2 and E356/21 10–11d, E356/22 34–8. Hanseatic trade balances computed for Appendix A.1.3 are based on actual values for miscellaneous goods given in the accounts and an estimated value for cloths of assize outlined in chapter 3. The archival sources for appendices A.1.4 through A.5.5 are noted with the corresponding transcripts. Original spellings have been maintained, although all figures have been changed from Roman to Arabic numerals. Short definitions of many terms encountered in the transcripts are included in the glossary.

A.1 TRADE STATISTICS

A.1.1 *BOSTON*	Cloths exported				Value of petty custom mdse (£ sterling)	
Date	Deniz.	Hanse	Alien	Total	Total	Hanse
01.09.1460/28.09.1461	188	346	nil	534	563	532
29.09.1461/28.09.1462	135	636	nil	771	1042	
29.09.1462/20.07.1463	189	nil	nil	189	1593	
20.07.1463/25.02.1465	278	279	9	566	1002	519[2]
25.02.1465/28.09.1465	54	450	4	508	281	4[2]
29.09.1465/25.03.1467	387	95	144	626	[1340]	713[2]
25.03.1467/06.03.1468	185	42	1	228	452	328
06.03.1468/25.12.1468	576	56	1	633	228	
25.12.1468/28.09.1469	397	5	166	568	313	nil
29.09.1469/13.11.1470[1]	623	nil	4	627	100	nil
26.10.1470/28.09.1471	273	nil	30	303	166	nil
29.09.1471/08.10.1472	372	nil	43	415	160	nil
08.10.1472/08.10.1473	479	nil	149	628	237	nil
08.10.1473/02.11.1474	337	nil	206	543	444	nil
02.11.1474/28.09.1475	169	31	170	370	53	1
29.09.1475/28.09.1476	12	283	4	299	998	436
29.09.1476/28.09.1477	84	nil	6	90	543	nil
29.09.1477/28.09.1478	107	548	6	661	1100	682
29.09.1478/28.09.1479	204	195	21	420	596	377
29.09.1479/28.09.1480	68	265	nil	333	439	314
29.09.1480/28.09.1481	41	241	nil	282	535	417
29.09.1481/28.09.1482	152	62	7	221	948	815
29.09.1482/28.09.1483	91	214	11	316	792	546
29.09.1483/28.09.1484	66	152	nil	218	353	210
29.09.1484/28.09.1485	54	283	nil	337	85	458
29.09.1485/28.09.1486	51	nil	nil	51	76	nil
29.09.1486/28.09.1487	99	nil	nil	99	62	nil
29.09.1487/28.09.1488	88	67	nil	155	309	263
29.09.1488/28.09.1489	30	32	nil	62	394	394
29.09.1489/28.09.1490	89	31	nil	120	1243	1177
29.09.1490/28.09.1491	50	nil	nil	50	41	nil
29.09.1491/28.09.1492	9	146	nil	155	1574	1512
29.09.1492/28.09.1493	38	nil	nil	38	35	nil
29.09.1493/28.09.1494	53	nil	nil	53	51	42
29.09.1494/28.09.1495	81	5	nil	86	50	
29.09.1495/28.09.1496	50	nil	nil	50	42	nil
29.09.1496/28.09.1497	22	15	18	55	270	
29.09.1497/28.09.1498	71	nil	nil	71	160	
29.09.1498/28.09.1499	42	1	nil	43	62	27
29.09.1499/28.09.1500	56	7	8	71	113	94

29.09.1500/28.09.1501	123	nil	7	130	131	nil
29.09.1501/28.09.1502	103	6	7	116	325	
29.09.1502/28.09.1503	54	nil	7	61	432	nil
29.09.1503/28.09.1504	6	nil	11	17	520	
29.09.1504/28.09.1505	11	nil	6	17	161	nil
29.09.1505/28.09.1506	9	nil	29	38	158	nil
29.09.1506/28.09.1507	25	nil	59	84	312	nil
29.09.1507/28.09.1508	28	nil	24	52	315	nil
29.09.1508/28.09.1509	5	nil	2	7	147	nil
29.09.1509/28.09.1510	11	nil	4	15	250	nil

[1] Overlap   [2] Minimum

A.1.1   HULL

	Cloths exported				Value of petty custom mdse (£ sterling)	
Date	Deniz.	Hanse	Alien	Total	Total	Hanse
11.04.1461/28.09.1461	629	115	16	760	716	171[2]
29.09.1461/28.09.1462	2065	101	nil	2166	997	
29.09.1462/06.10.1463	1616	252	nil	1868	1990	645[2]
06.10.1463/28.09.1464	928	507	1	1436	1102	
29.09.1464/28.09.1465	730	93	75	898	1027	471[2]
29.09.1465/28.09.1466	125	134	4	263	1365	
29.09.1466/28.09.1467	326	32	17	375	1026	253[2]
29.09.1467/28.09.1468	1449	189	25	1663	1415	272[2]
29.09.1468/28.09.1469	738	36	3	777	651	
29.09.1469/05.11.1470	480	nil	nil	480	50	nil
05.11.1470/28.09.1471	577	nil	nil	577	431	43[3]
29.09.1471/28.09.1472	839	nil	1	840	606	nil
29.09.1472/28.09.1473	699	nil	91	790	1357	nil
29.09.1473/22.08.1474	699	nil	17	716	2119	
22.08.1474/08.08.1475	784	444	22	1250	2817	1115
08.08.1475/28.09.1476	2074	438	102	2614	2578	1183
29.09.1476/28.09.1477	1938	435	80	2453	2423	1532
29.09.1477/28.09.1478	2623	208	21	2852	1025	397
29.09.1478/28.09.1479	1872	232	44	2148	2396	1671
29.09.1479/28.09.1480	2354	791	67	3212	2227	1610
29.09.1480/28.09.1481	2724	915	70	3709	3054	2485
29.09.1481/28.09.1482	2069	690	14	2773	4256	3907
29.09.1482/28.09.1483	1397	387	28	1812	2729	2036
29.09.1483/28.09.1484	1042	334	45	1421	2698	1902
29.09.1484/22.08.1485[1]	620	291	90	1001	2934	2158
22.08.1485/28.09.1486	1163	337	1	1501	2194	1693
29.09.1486/28.09.1487	304	68	20	392	2848	2497
29.09.1487/28.09.1488	342	116	16	474	557	319

Date	Deniz.	Hanse	Alien	Total	Total	Hanse
29.09.1488/28.09.1489	780	43	1	824	970	
29.09.1489/28.09.1490	888	105	11	1004	1495	1193
29.09.1490/28.09.1491	1549	nil	3	1552	322	
29.09.1491/28.09.1492	1212	148	82	1442	2146	
29.09.1492/28.09.1493	1249	619	10	1878	3212	3037
29.09.1493/28.09.1494	1368	444	37	1849	4290	3246
29.09.1494/28.09.1495	1202	548	13	1763	4746	
29.09.1495/28.09.1496	1286	392	52	1730	4992	3671
29.09.1496/28.09.1497	1578	926	85	2589	5828	
29.09.1497/28.09.1498	1269	676	69	2014	5883	2716[2]
29.09.1498/28.09.1499	963	547	102	1612	6775	3673
29.09.1499/28.09.1500	1604	642	71	2317	4152	
29.09.1500/28.09.1501	2457	415	107	2979	4955	
29.09.1501/28.09.1502	2511	782	104	3397	8518	
29.09.1502/28.09.1503	2160	1024	173	3357	7161	4805
29.09.1503/28.09.1504	3023	880	48	3951	7206	
29.09.1504/28.09.1505	1627	438	228	2293	5640	
29.09.1505/28.09.1506	1101	353	35	1489	4266	
29.09.1506/28.09.1507	1611	630	83	2324	8558	
29.09.1507/28.09.1508	1383	580	84	2047	7086	
29.09.1508/28.09.1509	1193	648	47	1888	5217	
29.09.1509/28.09.1510	758	77	47	[1882]	[1048]	

[1] Gap   [2] Minimum   [3] Cologne merchants

A.1.1   *IPSWICH*

	Cloths exported				Value of petty custom mdse (£ sterling)	
Date	Deniz.	Hanse	Alien	Total	Total	Hanse
29.09.1460/28.09.1461	313	1844	2	2149	3934	
29.09.1461/16.10.1462	313	1373	1	1687	2443	730[2]
16.10.1462/10.07.1463	106	1022	51	1179	1184	
10.07.1463/31.08.1464	118	501	31	650	1738	
31.08.1464/28.09.1465	63	1167	82	1312	1561	
29.09.1465/28.09.1466	159	4525	43	4727	3148	2706
29.09.1466/28.09.1467	520	606	115	1241	1494	
29.09.1467/28.09.1468	460	852	63	1375	1300	
29.09.1468/02.04.1469[1]	476	132[3]	16	624	513	
01.09.1469/09.10.1470	388	nil	nil	388	238	80[3,2]
09.10.1470/30.09.1471	595	184[3]	20	799	352	166[3,2]
30.09.1471/28.09.1472	287	242[3]	18	547	775	
29.09.1472/28.09.1473	328	50[3]	35	413	668	
29.09.1473/28.09.1474	337	nil	1	338	491	
29.09.1474/08.11.1475	115	349	5	469	1968	1469
08.11.1475/08.11.1476	460	851	30	1341	786	496

08.11.1476/08.11.1477	648	40	8	696	632	301
08.11.1477/08.11.1478	355	158	6	519	249	55
08.11.1478/14.10.1479	458	155	2	615	339	255
14.10.1479/14.10.1480	532	194	6	732	497	251
14.10.1480/28.09.1481	515	146	16	677	2089	1148
29.09.1481/28.09.1482	391	228	13	632	778	317
29.09.1482/28.09.1483	124	35	2	161	515	336
29.09.1483/28.09.1484	266	nil	nil	266	92	nil
29.09.1484/22.08.1485[1]	455	273	nil	728	873	642
29.09.1485/28.09.1486	401	7	1	409	367	367
29.09.1486/28.09.1487	411	348	6	765	1443	1129
29.09.1487/28.09.1488	233	736	2	971	778	501[2]
09.09.1488/28.09.1489	140	320	3	463	608	
29.09.1489/28.09.1490	235	504	6	745	1637	
29.09.1490/28.09.1491	388	721	17	1126	842	
29.09.1491/28.09.1492	354	209	nil	563	1008	603
29.09.1492/28.09.1493	262	nil	13	275	526	
29.09.1493/28.09.1494	355	31	21	407	674	
29.09.1494/28.09.1495	617	nil	14	631	309	
29.09.1495/28.09.1496	493	nil	27	520	306	69
29.09.1496/28.09.1497	504	nil	7	511	313	
29.09.1497/28.09.1498	515	nil	28	543	1220	509
29.09.1498/28.09.1499	911	79	57	1047	1013	
29.09.1499/28.09.1500	1002	nil	83	1085	855	nil
29.09.1500/28.09.1501	1258	nil	85	1343	1012	72
29.09.1501/28.09.1502	1730	nil	79	1809	915	nil
29.09.1502/28.09.1503	1204	5	35	1244	787	
29.09.1503/28.09.1504	1307	nil	26	1333	862	
29.09.1504/28.09.1505	841	2	63	906	814	
29.09.1505/28.09.1506	1401	nil	95	1496	387	47[2]
29.09.1506/28.09.1507	1447	nil	64	1511	621	
29.09.1507/28.09.1508	2313	nil	142	2455	2246	nil
29.09.1508/28.09.1509	2535	1	128	2664	1760	nil
29.09.1509/28.09.1510	2263	nil	200	2463	2000	16

[1] Gap   [2] Minimum   [3] Cologne merchants

A.1.1 *LYNN*

Date	Cloths exported				Value of petty custom mdse (£ sterling)	
	Deniz.	Hanse	Alien	Total	Total	Hanse
06.08.1460/24.11.1461	330	47	nil	377	1026	707[2]
24.11.1461/28.08.1462	180	31	nil	211	467	
29.08.1462/12.07.1463	297	27	nil	324	296	
12.07.1463/19.11.1464	561	72	nil	633	954	

Period					
19.11.1464/19.11.1465	125	502	nil	627	742	648
19.11.1465/02.11.1466	277	150	nil	427	979	651[2]
02.11.1466/02.11.1467	217	145	nil	362	748	386
02.11.1467/02.11.1468	911	52	nil	963	497	309
02.11.1468/17.09.1469	63	nil	nil	63	508	nil
17.09.1469/16.05.1470	19	nil	nil	19	260	nil
03.11.1470/13.11.1471[1]	29	nil	nil	29	214	nil
13.11.1471/13.11.1472	56	nil	nil	56	271	nil
13.11.1472/13.11.1473	92	nil	nil	92	325	nil
13.11.1473/13.11.1474	6	nil	nil	6	646	
13.11.1474/13.11.1475	25	270	1	296	929	136
13.11.1475/13.11.1476	108	308	24	430	731	528
13.11.1476/13.11.1477	250	84	1	335	615	177
13.11.1477/13.11.1478	432	129	nil	561	821	477
13.11.1478/13.11.1479	471	187	nil	658	556	237
13.11.1479/13.11.1480	132	183	1	316	588	411
13.11.1480/28.09.1481	182	184	35	401	997	294
29.09.1481/28.09.1482	217	181	nil	398	1247	895
29.09.1482/28.09.1483	129	79	4	212	520	317
29.09.1483/28.09.1484	68	89	nil	157	613	424
29.09.1484/22.08.1485[1]	68	145	nil	213	775	662
17.09.1485/28.09.1486	63	145	nil	208	382	244
29.09.1486/28.09.1487	81	46	3	130	444	256
29.09.1487/28.09.1488	nil	280	12	292	1196	1032
29.09.1488/28.09.1489	191	777	nil	968	2202	2006
29.09.1489/28.09.1490	85	32	1	118	799	466
29.09.1490/28.09.1491	103	30	4	137	866	582[2]
29.09.1491/28.09.1492	89	338	nil	427	1371	1226
29.09.1492/28.09.1493	55	480	nil	535	1371	
29.09.1493/28.09.1494	156	17	nil	173	327	308
29.09.1494/28.09.1495	69	47	nil	116	498	252
29.09.1495/28.09.1496	129	74	nil	203	922	580
29.09.1496/28.09.1497	10	6	nil	16	328	
29.09.1497/28.09.1498	173	101	13	287	1133	
29.09.1498/28.09.1499	229	52	3	284	913	553
29.09.1499/28.09.1500	152	315	6	473	479	
29.09.1500/28.09.1501	241	104	12	357	706	
29.09.1501/28.09.1502	345	98	1	444	[170]	
29.09.1502/28.09.1503	479	73	1	553	938	
29.09.1503/28.09.1504	444	123	5	572	886	446
29.09.1504/28.09.1505	915	84	10	1009	410	113
29.09.1505/28.09.1506	737	71	2	810	442	
29.09.1506/28.09.1507	1121	80	9	1210	618	289
29.09.1507/28.09.1508	823	110	11	944	971	
29.09.1508/21.04.1509[1]	706	nil	9	715	[199]	
21.11.1509/28.09.1510	465	nil	5	470	670	

[1] Gap   [2] Minimum

A.1.1 *NEWCASTLE*	Cloths exported				Value of petty custom mdse (£ sterling)	
Date	Deniz.	Hanse	Alien	Total	Total	Hanse
24.12.1459/20.09.1460[1]	nil	nil	nil	nil	27	
10.05.1461/18.02.1462	11	nil	nil	11	85	
18.02.1462/01.08.1463	nil	nil	6	nil	416	
01.08.1463/03.05.1464	nil	nil	nil	nil	111	
03.05.1464/04.03.1465	2	nil	nil	2	342	
04.03.1465/11.04.1466[1]	16	nil	12	28	590	
18.03.1467/28.03.1468[1]	11	nil	nil	11	521	
19.12.1468/03.09.1469[1]	15	nil	nil	15	239	
03.09.1469/30.03.1476*						
30.03.1476/17.06.1476	nil	nil	nil	nil	24	
17.06.1476/01.06.1477	nil	2	nil	2	89	
01.06.1477/01.06.1478[1]	28	8	nil	36	110	85
01.11.1478/28.09.1480	3	nil	nil	3	97	
29.09.1480/16.11.1486*						
16.11.1486/28.10.1487	nil	nil	nil	nil		
28.10.1487/28.10.1488	110	1	14	125	181	93
28.10.1488/28.09.1489	nil	9	4	13	550	473
29.09.1489/28.09.1490	7	1	17	25	315	9
29.09.1490/28.09.1491	22	nil	7	29	120	65
29.09.1491/12.03.1494*						
12.03.1494/02.12.1495	52	2	7	61	206	78
02.12.1495/28.09.1496	3	12	nil	15	343	280
29.09.1496/28.09.1497	8	nil	1	9	217	
29.09.1497/28.09.1498	1	nil	2	3	294	54
29.09.1498/28.09.1499	6	nil	5	11	437	153
29.09.1499/28.09.1500	29	12	4	45	447	229
29.09.1500/28.09.1501	40	1	5	46	425	121
29.09.1501/28.09.1502	22	nil	3	25	254	55
29.09.1502/28.09.1503	51	nil	6	57	188	
29.09.1503/28.09.1504	43	nil	4	47	437	
29.09.1504/28.09.1505[1]	30	nil	nil	30	658	
29.09.1505/28.09.1506	5	5	2	12	866	396
29.09.1506/28.09.1507	13	nil	nil	13	1102	
29.09.1507/28.09.1508	36	nil	7	43	666	25
29.09.1508/28.09.1509	13	nil	3	16	601	
29.09.1509/28.09.1510	8	nil	5	13	492	

[1] Gap   * No account

A.1.2 LONDON

Date	Cloths exported					Value of petty custom merchandise			Hundredweights of wax imported	
	Deniz.	Hanse	Cologne	Alien	Total	Total	Hanse	Cologne	Total	Hanse
29.09.1468/06.11.1469	24489	695	*	2961	28145	£26196	nil	?	[13]	13[3]
06.11.1469/09.10.1470	10679	nil	4900	1033	16612	£19293	nil	?		
06.06.1471/28.09.1471	13383	nil	3158	690	17231	£11639	nil	?		
29.09.1471/04.08.1472[1]	8657	nil	2960	1671	13288	£28825	nil	£2132	7	nil
04.08.1472/28.09.1473	17917	nil	4037	7035	28989	£35591	nil	?	108	
29.09.1473/28.09.1474	16432	nil	1949	15913	34294	£20758	?	?	106	
29.09.1474/28.09.1475	11959	1623	1472	7341	22395	£22789	£4288	nil	417	294
29.09.1475/28.09.1476	19239	5274	2999	6855	34367	£26385	£7908	£127	1299	1158
29.09.1476/20.11.1477	15305	5379	2926	10925	34535	£33464	£7487	nil	1204	1169
20.11.1477/09.07.1478	12923	3003	2260	3330	21516	£23268	£6539	nil	850	821
09.07.1478/28.09.1479	28724	0570	880	9827	50001	£33867	£14921	£1288	1356	1342[4]
29.09.1479/28.09.1480	20748	10068	*	9694	40510	£24235	£16701	*	1636	1628
29.09.1480/28.09.1481	23115	14079	*	7558	44752	£43857	£22281	*	2859	2839
29.09.1481/28.09.1482	20558	13386	*	7254	41198	£38411	£22534	*	3564	3560
29.09.1490/28.09.1491	15370	10074	*	11926	37370	£37933	£11554	*	778	760
29.09.1502/28.09.1503	25119	15374	*	8335	48828	£46889[5]	£15793	*	3430	3405
29.09.1505/28.09.1506	23314	15745	*	6539	45598	£58177	£17896[2]	*	4278	4275

*Included in Hanse total.

[1] Gap
[2] Minimum
[3] Cologne merchants
[4] Includes 12 belonging to Cologne merchants.
[5] PRO E122 79/2: £46889, PRO E356 24 m.48: £48889

A.1.3   *HANSEATIC TRADE BALANCES 1450–68*

Port and Date	Est. val. of cloth exports[1]	Val. of petty custom exports	Total value of exports	Total value of imports	Val. of petty custom imports	Val. of wax imports[2]	Ratio of export to import values
BOSTON							
15.12.1459/28.09.1461	£1721	£46*	£1767*	£1583*	£1583*		1.1 : 1
25.02.1465/25.03.1467	£725	nil	£725*	£717*	£717*		1 : 1
25.03.1467/25.12.1468	£130	£4	£134	£324	£324		1 : 2.4
HULL							
02.10.1452/28.09.1453	£527	nil	£527*	£364*	£364*		1.4 : 1
11.04.1461/28.09.1461	£153	nil	£153	£171*	£171*		1 : 1.1
29.09.1464/28.09.1465	£124	£4	£128	£466*	£466*		1 : 3.6
29.09.1466/28.09.1467	£41	£44	£85	£209*	£209*		1 : 2.5
29.09.1467/28.09.1468	£251		£251*	£272*	£272*		1 : 1.1
IPSWICH							
29.09.1458/28.09.1459	£1645	£31	£1676	£1006	£999	£7	1.7 : 1
29.09.1465/28.09.1466	£6018	£172	£6190	£2592	£2534	£58	2.4 : 1
LYNN							
13.06.1455/24.01.1457	£242	£211*	£453*	£449*	£449*		1 : 1
29.09.1459/24.11.1461	£147	£20	£167	£1146	£1146		1 : 6.7
19.11.1464/19.11.1465	£667	£30	£697	£618	£618		1.1 : 1
19.11.1465/02.11.1466	£200	£64*	£264*	£587*	£587*		1 : 2.2
02.11.1466/02.11.1467	£193	£40	£233	£346	£346	£16	1 : 1.5
02.11.1467/02.11.1468	£69	£28	£97	£281	£281		1 : 2.9

[1] Based on a value of £1 6s 8d per cloth.   [2] Based on a value of 40s per hundredweight.
* Minimum. Although totals for cloth exports are complete for the entire period, particulars of 3d customs accounts, which distinguish Hanseatic exports from imports, are fragmentary and sometimes do not coincide with complete Exchequer years. In these instances the Hanseatic total for 3d imports and exports is shown as a minimum for the period indicated.

A.1.3   *HANSEATIC TRADE BALANCES 1474–91*

Port and Date	Est. val. of cloth exports[1]	Val. of petty custom exports	Total value of exports	Total value of imports	Val. of petty custom imports	Val. of wax imports[2]	Ratio of export to import values
BOSTON							
29.09.1487/28.09.1488	£89	£1	£90	£262	£262		1 : 2.9
IPSWICH							
29.09.1481/28.09.1482	£303	£13	£316	£317	£304	£13	1 : 1

LYNN

13.11.1480/28.09.1481	£245	£94	£339	£288	£200	£88	1.2 : 1
29.09.1483/28.09.1484	£118	£103	£221	£349	£321	£28	1 : 1.6
29.09.1486/28.09.1487	£61	£56	£117	£204	£200	£4	1 : 1.7
29.09.1487/28.09.1488	£372	£193	£565	£938	£838	£100	1 : 1.6
29.09.1498/28.09.1490	£43	£166	£209	£300	£300		1 : 1.4
29.09.1490/28.09.1491	£40	£147	£187	£544	£436	£108	1 : 2.9

NEWCASTLE

28.10.1488/28.09.1489	£12	£131	£143	£342	£342		1 : 2.4

A.1.3 HANSEATIC TRADE BALANCES 1492–1510

Port and Date	Est. val. of cloth exports[1]	Val. of petty custom exports	Total value of exports	Total value of imports	Val. of petty custom imports	Val. of wax imports[2]	Ratio of export to import values
BOSTON							
29.09.1491/28.09.1492	£194	£191	£385	£1469	£1321	£148	1 : 3.8
IPSWICH							
29.09.1491/28.09.1492	£278	nil	£278	£647	£603	£44	1 : 2.3
29.09.1505/28.09.1506	nil	nil	nil	£161	£47	£114	1 : 161
LYNN							
29.09.1494/28.09.1495	£63	£131	£194	£121	£121		1.6 : 1
29.09.1503/28.09.1504	£164	£3	£167	£443	£443		1 : 2.6
NEWCASTLE							
29.09.1499/28.09.1500	£16	£85	£101	£146	£144	£2	1 : 1.4
29.09.1500/28.09.1501	£1	£66	£67	£55	£55	1.2 : 1	
29.09.1505/28.09.1506	£7	£216	£223	£186	£180	£6	1.2 : 1

[1] Based on a value of £1 6s 8d per cloth.   [2] Based on a value of 40s per hundredweight.

A.1.4   DANZIG'S ENGLISH IMPORT TRADE 1474–76*

Ships and Cargoes		1474	1475	1476
'uth Engelant'[1]	Ships / Laden Ships	–	2/2	12/11
Cloth	Terling	–	5.5	30
	Pack	–	–	1
	Single	–	5	30
Lead	Foder	–	–	6
	Centner	–	–	31.5
	'Stuck'	–	6	

Salt	Hundredweight	–	–	3.5
Wine (Gascon)	Pipe	–	–	2
(Red)	Hogshead	–	–	7
Herring Last		–	–	6
'von Lunden'[2]	Ships / Laden Ships	–	1/1	–
Cloth	Terling	–	7.5	–
	Pack	–	–	–
	Single	–	–	–
Salt	Hundredweight	–	2	–
'von Lindn'[3]	Ships / Laden Ships	–	1/1	1/1
Cloth	Terling	–	3	1.5
	Pack	–	6	3
	Single	–	2	–
'Fygn'	'Stuck'	–	30	–
Wine ('Romanie')	Vat	–	2	–
('Hispanisch')	'Stuck'	–	2	–
('Bastert')	Pipe	–	1	–
(Unspecified)	Pipe	–	–	4
'Decken'	Pack	–	–	1
Rabbit Pelts	Pack	–	–	2
Salt	Last	–	5	–
'von Holl'[4]	Ships / Laden Ships	2/2	2/1	–
Cloth	Terling	1.5	–	–
	Pack	–	1	–
	Single	28	–	–
Lead	'Stuck'	8	–	–
Unidentified	'Paxken'	2	–	–
	'Pynak'	6	–	–
	'Berdel'	2	–	–
'von Sandewyk'[5]	Ships / Laden Ships	–	1/0	–
'von Nucastel'[6]	Ships / Laden Ships	–	–	1/1
Wine (Gascon)	'Stuck'	–	–	4

[1] APG 300.19/5 137,186,249,256,279,281,289,290,297,299,304.   [2] Ibid, 121.
[3] Ibid, 123,206.   [4] Ibid, 81,130.   [5] Ibid, 122.   [6] Ibid, 257.
* Damage to the manuscript (APG 300.19/5) renders some entries for 1476 illegible. These figures summarize only those entries that unquestionably refer to ships arriving from England, and therefore actually represent minimum totals.

A . 2 SHIPPING AND MOVEMENT OF CARGO

A.2.1 Composite of the cargoes freighted by shipper Paul Roole between Danzig and England, December 1467 – August 1468. PRO E122 97/9, APG 300.19/3 4r,21v, *HUB* IX no. 519.

In Navi Paul Roole intrante [Lynn] xi die Decembris [1467]
de eodem magistro de Hansa pro di last olii valoris 50s item pro 1 nest counters valoris 10s
item pro una cista cum 6 scok trenchours 3 dussenis pruse skynnes et 300 uln prusie de Inderland valoris
£4 item pro 2 cistis cum 20 scok de trenchours et doubz pecis lewent continente 100 uln valoris 40s
summa valoris in toto £9 --- custuma 2s 3d

In Navi Pauli Roole exeunte [Lynn] xxviii die Februarii [1468]
de eodem magistro de Hansa pro 10 pannis curtis sine grano ------------ custuma 10s
de Hennyng Buryng de Hansa pro 10 pannis curtis sine grano ----------- custuma 10s

    uth Engelant [Danzig, 1468]
    schipper Paul Roel syn schip
    item eyn paxken laken [40] mrc item 4 last laken [5 mrc]
    Peter Schomaker eyn paxken laken £10
    Hans van Plauen eyn paxken laken 50 mrc'

In Navi Pauli Roole de Hansa intrante [Lynn] x die Maii [1468]
de eodem magistro de Hansa pro 2000 waynscots valoris £20 item pro 1 last clapholt
valoris 40s item pro 200 remis valoris 40s item pro 2 lastis asshes valoris 40s
item pro 1 last et di osmondi valoris £6 item pro uno nest counters valoris 10s
item pro 4 bunches de botulf iron valoris 40s item pro 6 pecis lewent course valoris 40s
summa valoris in toto £36 10s -- custuma 9s 1d ob
de Hans van Plaughe de Hansa pro 1 last lini valoris £6 item pro 8 lastis trane valoris £8
item pro di last osmundi valoris 40s item pro doubz nest counters valoris 20s
item pro una cista cum 5 scok trenchours 2 doubz wyre 6 paris pruse gloves et pro
1 last baste valoris 20s item pro 1 scok pruse platers valoris 20d
summa valoris in toto £18 20d --- custuma 4s 6d

    [Helsingor, 1468 – Whitsuntide, 4-7 June]

    uth Engelant [Danzig, 1468]
    schipper Paul Roel syn schip invorpalt coustat 60 mrc'
    item eyn paxken laken und 6 last laken £12 item 2 last [molt']
    Jacob Wulf eyn paxken laken £3

Navi Pauli Role intrante [Lynn] xi Augusti [1468]
de eodem magistro de Hansa pro 1200 waynscots valoris £12 item pro 1 last clapholt valoris 20s
item pro 30 ores valoris 5s item pro 4 nest counters valoris 40s item pro 11 cistis cum
118 scokke trenches valoris 46s 8d item pro 2 douden pair playng tables valoris 10s
item pro uno scok tromp' glasses valoris 5s item pro 4 fethirbedde cum 6 drinkyng cannes
et pro 6 peper quernes valoris 20s item pro uno last pic valoris 20s item pro una douden
tankards pro 26 uln lewent et pro 8 scokke w[...]nyng valoris 20s
summa valoris in toto £21 6s 20d -- custuma 6s 4d
de Simon Pigot indigena pro 1000 waynscots valoris £10 item pro di last clapholt valoris 10s
item pro di last barell hed' valoris 6s 8d item pro di lastis pich et tar valoris 40s
item pro 2 lastis woode asshes valoris 40s item pro 3 bundell de botulph iron valoris 30s
item pro di last flex valoris 50s item pro doubz peciis cere valoris 10s
item pro doubz barellis olii valoris 10s
summa valoris in toto £20 6s 8d -- subsidium 20s

A.2.2   Record of cloth exports customed to Cologners in London, for shipment overseas from Dover. Undated. [ca. 1469] StA Köln Hanse III. K. 15. Bl.103-103v.

Names of dyvers marchauntes of Coleyn that hath sent certeyn bales of cloth by watir
fro London to Gravesende and so forth to be caried by lande to Dover and there to
have ben reshipped over the See which yit passid not Cauntirbury but there ben still
the which clothes were custumed in the seid porte of London as folowith.

De Hans Langerman viii die Februarii 1 bal cum 15 pannis sine grano 34 god'
pannis striet wall' 1 bal cum 16 pannis sine grano 48 god' pannis striet wall'.
Item xviii die Februarii 1 bal cum 19 pannis di sine grano 50 god' pannis striet
wall' 1 bal cum 15 pannis 4 virgis sine grano 7 virgis violet in grano 65 god'
pannis striet wall'.

De Johanne Berkam xx die Februarii 1 bal cum 18 pannis sine grano 30 god'
pannis striet wall'.

De Everardo Clippynge xviii die Februarii 1 bal cum 18 pannis 9 virgis sine
grano 30 god' striet wall'.

i bal secundo die Marcii cum 20 pannis sine grano 25 god' pannis striet wall'.

De Hans Herderote tercio die Februarii 1 bal cum 18 pannis sine grano 33 god'
striet wall' 1 roll frises wall' Item secundo die Marcii 1 bal cum 18 pannis sine
grano 26 god' pannis streit wall' 1 roll frises wall'.

De Reginaldo Lobryht secundo die Marcii 1 bal cum 19 pannis sine grano 40
god' pannis striet wall'.

De Petro Cangheter secundo die Marcii 20 pannis sine grano 50 god' pannis
striet wall' 1 bal cum 20 pannis sine grano 40 god' pannis striet wall'.

De Johanne van Brele secundo die Marcii 1 bal cum 18 pannis sine grano 80
god' pannis striet wall'.

De Johanne van Dorn secundo die Marcii 1 bal cum 17 pannis sine grano 30
god' pannis striet wall' 1 bal cum 16 pannis 8 virgis sine grano 50 god' pannis
striet wall' 1 bal cum 18 pannis sine grano 20 god' striet wall' 1 bal cum 17
pannis sine grano 20 god' pannis striet wall'.

De Johanne Fernam secundo die Marcii 1 bal cum 18 pannis sine grano 50 god'
pannis striet wall' 1 bal cum 18 pannis sine grano 36 god' pannis striet wall'.

De Johanne van A secundo die Marcii 2 bal cum 36 pannis sine grano 18 god'
pannis striet wall'.

De Goswyn Sherell secundo die Marcii 2 bal cum 36 pannis sine grano 80 god'
striet wall' Item 2 bal cum 37 pannis sine grano 80 god' pannis striet wall'

The bales folowyng were not shipped nethir leyden in the Watir but leid in cartes to
be caried by lande to Dover and there to be custumed the which bales went no further
than Cauntirbury and there yet lien stylle.

De Goswyn Shorell viii die Marcii 1 bal cum 20 pannis sine grano 1 panni skarlet qt' 33 virgis di 40 god' pannis striet wall'.
De Hans Harderote 1 bal cum 19 pannis 6 virgis sine grano 1 gros poyntes 1 double bonett 2 roll fris 40 god' pannis striet wall'.
De Petro Cangheter 1 bal cum 20 pannis sine grano 50 god' pannis striet wall'.
De Johanne Stomell 1 bal cum 22 pannis sine grano 30 god' striet wall'.
De Johanne Fernam 1 bal cum 17 pannis di sine grano 4 virgis di skarlet 4 god' pannis striet wall' 1 bal cum 20 pannis sine grano 1 pecia 3 virgis worsted 61 god' pannis striet wall'.

A.3 LITIGATION

A.3.1 Complaint of Richard Penevel, clothmaker, regarding the balance due for cloth purchased by Niclas Wulff of Danzig, heard by the aldermen of the Steelyard. 1449. StA Köln Hanse Urkunden U. 2. Bl.133.

Allen den ghennen de dessen unsen breeff sullen seyn off hoeren leesen don wy Alderman und ghemene Copman van der Duetschen Hense nu to London in Englant wesende na unse vrondlike grote kentliken apenbarliken met dessem breve tughende Dat upten dagh datum desses breves vor uns es komen de bescheden Ritzart Penevel lakenmaker uns geven to kennende wudanne wijs dat Niclas Wulff van Dantzeke eme van rechter schult schuldich sii van laken de de selve Niclas van eme ghekofft hedde Twintich Engelsche nobelen eme to betalende up sunte Johans dagh to myddensomer de gheleden es int jair uns heren Duysentverhundert sevenundvertich van welker summen he nicht meer untfangen hedde dan Sess nobelen Warvan he uns toghede eyne billen eme van deme vorscreven Niclas dar up ghegeven beseghelt beneden upt Spac[...] myt Roden wasse war inne blickede sodanne merck 本 de wy heel und ghans und ungheserighet in allen eren deelen hebben gheseyn und hoeren leesen ludende van worden to worden alse hijr na gescreven steyt
Item bekenne ick Niclas Wulff dat ick Ritzart Penevel hebbe affghekofft eyn fesses und eyn graw ellick laken vor Teyn nobelen up Sunte Johans dagh to betalende over eyn jaer und den derden pennynck rede desse lakene koffte ick van eme int jaer Sessundvertich hijr up hebbe ick eme ghegeven Twe punt Und want dan de vorscreven Ritzart ume noet sake willen alse he secht nicht van senden en es sick ane zee to voeghen ume de vorscreven anerighe summen to manende So hevet he in der bester formen und wysse alse he van rechte doen solde unde mochte vor unse ghekaren ghesat und gheordinert tot synen vulmechtighen procuratore und honet man den bechedenen Roloff Veltstede van Brunswyck wijser desses breves gevende eme vullenkomen macht de vorscreven anerighe summen to seggende verteyn Engelsche nobelen van deme vorscreven Niclas to manende uptoborende und to untfangende enen twe eder dre vortan to mechtigen off des van no den es de ock hebben de vullenkomen macht dar bij to doende und to latende Quitancien dar van to gevende ghelyck off he selffs dar jeghenwordich und vor oghen w[er] und so wes se samentliken offte bijsunder dar bij doende offte latende werden dat hevet de selve Ritzart vor uns ghelavet stede und vast to haldende to ewighen tyden in kennisse der warheyt so hebbe wy Alderman und ghemene Copman vorscreven uns seghel to Rugge up dessen breeff don drucken int jaer uns heren duysentverhundertneghenundvertich upten sessundtwintichsten dagh van dem Maen de Februarius.

A.3.2 Petition to Chancery by Danziger Hans Schulte for a writ of *corpus cum causa* in response to actions taken against him by merchants of Hull. ca. 1475-80 or 1483–5. PRO C1/64/1105.

To the Right reverend Fader in god Bysshopp of Lincoln Chaunceller of England

Mekely besechith youre good lordshipp Hanse Schulte of Dansk in Pruce and William Croyer maister of a shipp of Dansk aforesaid that where the said shipp beyng lade

aswell with dyvers goodez and merchaundisez of dyvers merchauntez of Dansk
aforsaid as with other goodez and merchaundisez of oon John Nappet of Kyngeston
uppon Hull and of other merchauntez of the same towne commyng uppon the See
hederwerd in to this Realme a shipp of Werre of oon Yongker Gerard beyng in here
dyvers pyratez and men of Werre bourdid and entrid the said Shipp of Dansk and
toke oute of the same shipp agenst the will of youre seid besechers suche goodez and
merchaundisez as pleasid theym aswell of the goodez of the seid merchauntez of
Dansk as of the goodez of the said John Nappet and other merchauntez englissh And
after that your seid besechers with the same shipp of Dansk departyd with the residue
of the goodez and merchaundisez beyng in here and came to the port of the seid
towne of Kyngeston uppon Hull Where the said John Nappet and other persones of
the same towne by colour of the takyng of the said goodez by the said pyratez have
takyn dyvers actionz agenst youre said besechers afore the maire and sherif of the said
town and have theym arrest and gretely trouble and vexe theym by the same And
how be it that noon defaute is in theym as knowith god And also the said takyng was
doon uppon the See oute of the Jurisdiction of the seid towne Yet they entende to
condempne youre seid besechers and recovere agenst theym amendes for their seid
goodez so taken And the same youre besechers have noo knowlech socour nor help be
cause they ben strangers and therfor likly to be undon agenst all right and good conscience Without youre good lordshipp be shewed to theym in this behalf it please
therfor your seid lordshipp the premyssez tenderly to considre and theruppon to
graunte a corpus cum causa directe to the maire and sherif of the seid Towne of
Kyngeston uppon Hull commaundyng theym and everych of theym by the same to
have the bodyes of youre seid besechers and everych of them [which] causez of their
arrest afore the kyng in his chauncerie at a certeyn day ther the seid cause and mater
to be examined and directe accordyng to right and conscience And this for the love of
god and in way of charite.

A.3.3 Petition to Chancery by Steelyard merchant Hermann Rinck for a writ of *certiorari* in response to an action of trespass brought against him. ca. 1486–93. PRO
C1/158/47.

To the moste reverende fadre in god the Archiebischop of Caunterbury
primate of al England and Chaunceller of the same

Sheweth and lamentably complaineth unto your grace your daily Oratour Herman
Ryng merchaunt how that where as he but late ago was occupied in the Stilyard in
feate of merchaundise ther cam thidre unto him one Johane White senglewoman
Which Johane as it appereth by hir owne confession made in writing before credible
personnes was wont to daunce and make revells in hir maisters hous som tyme in
mannys clothing and somtyme naked offering her self unto your said Oratour tobe at
his commaundement and he seeing hir boldnesse mystrusted hir and charged hir to
avoide from him Wherwith she toke a disdeyn and displeasure and wold nat departe
unto tyme that he caused one of his servants to geve hir 2 or 3 stripes and therby
made hir to avoide awey from him Wherupon one Stephan Regate hir maister which is
a nedy man and a combrons to dele withal beeing prive of hir comyng to your said
Oratour as it semed and consenting therunto to thentent to finde a mean of action

ageinst him for to make him to lose money in the like wise as he deleth with many
other men folowed after the said myshyving woman and awaited upon hir comyng
out of the said place And for because he herd by hir confession wher and with whome
she had been and how she was delt withal as above said he of his malicioux dis-
posicion without eny other grounde cause or matier commensed an action of trespasse
ageinst your said Oratour before the Shirifs of London surmitting that he had taken
awey his servant to his damage of £20 Unto which action your said Oratour appered
and according to the trouth pleted nat gilty so that thei wer at an issue of 12 men to
trye the same And wher as your said Oratour beeing a straunger had medietate lingue
as the [custumn] is thei wer so tryed out by the grete meanes and labour of the said
Stephen and other of his affinitie to whome thei wer neghtbours that the whole Enquest was made of commone Jurrers at his [.......] Which Enquest appered at the furst
calling and never wold examyn the matier nor [.....] her eny Evidence geven for the
partie defendaunt nat fering god nor shame of the world without deliberacion contrare
to al trouth founde your said Oratour gilty of trespas and gave damage £3 or
theraboute besides the costs of the courte ageinst al right and good conscience to his
grete prejudice rebouke and hurt Wherupon gracioux lord the Juge of the Courte there
havyng enformation of the trouth of the matier and of the wilfull perjury of the said
Jury of his conscience respited to geve Jugement of and upon the premysses to
thentent that your grace myght have the matier examined before the same Wherby the
trouth myght be perfitely understanded please it your grace in consideracion of the
premysses with the circumstaunce to graunt herupon a Certiorari directed to the
Shirifs of London commaunding theim by the same to certifie the cause of therreste of
your said Oratour before the king in his Chauncerie at a certayn day by you tobe
lymyted ther tobe examined as right and conscience shal require At the reverence of
god and in wey of charite And he shal pray specially for your good and gracious long
prosperite.

A.3.4 Petition to Chancery by London merchants Nicholas Wylde and William Wyl-
cokks for writs of *sub poena* to be directed to the alderman and council of the
Steelyard regarding the alleged debt of Dinant merchants. ca. 1486–93.* PRO
C1/111/49.

To the right reverent Fadre in god John Archebisshopp of Caunterbury and
Chaunceler of Englond

In the moost humble wise shewith unto your good lordship your daily Oratours Nicholas Wylde and William Wylcokks of London merchaunts where oon Francke Savage
and William Carpentar merchaunts of Denaunt ben indettyd and owe unto your said
oratours the some of £175 sterling in the which some the said Francke Savage and
William Carpenter by ther obligacions ben bounden to the said Nicholas Wylde as
wele to thuse of the said William asof the said Nicholas. And bifore that ther dayes of
payment were expired and past the same Francke and William Carpentar and ther
attorneys avoyded out of this Realme of Englond not contentyng your said oratours of
the said some nor any parte therof. After whos avoydeng the noble prince of good
memory king Edwarde the 4th graunted unto the hole Feliship of merchaunts of the

Stiliard within the cite of London £10000 for restitucion of certein injuries to theym comytted Which Feliship ordeyned a cheste in the Stiliard and 6 keyes therto and enacted ther a mong theym that the said £10000 shuld be put in the same cheste as it shuld growe and shuld never be taken owte till the hole some were fully growyn and that 6 merchaunts shuld have 6 keyes of the same cheste for the said entent Which £10000 was fully growen 2 yeres past and the Felaship aforsaid allowed therof unto the forsaid Towne of Denaunt £1014 for ther parte. Wherof was allowed unto the said Francke Savage and William Carpentar for such goods as they loste £500 sterling and your said oratours havyng knowlache of the same allowance the said Nicholas affermed a pleynt of dette of £175 before the Maire of London agenst the said Francke Savage and William Carpentar and attached the said £500 in the handez of Herman Plough then alderman of Stiliard and the same Harman ys now discharged of beyng alderman so that the said attachement ys avoyded and oon John Grevererd newlye chosen alderman which with the said Feliship in to this day hath in kepynge the said £500 in the owne propre handes for ther discharge. How be yt that your said oratours by course of the commen lawe can have no recovere therof bycause the forsaid Feliship yerly chesith a new aldirman Please it therfore your good lordship of your blessed dispocion the premisses tenderly considered to graunt unto your said oratours severall writtes of sub pena to be directed unto the said John Grevererd now alderman of the Feliship aforsaid and to the counsell of the Stiliard to appere byfore your lordship at a certeyn day and uppon ther apperaunces to examyne theym in whose handes the forsaid £500 remayneth and furthermor to ordeyne and see by your blessed meanes a wey by the which your said oratours may attayne unto the recovere of ther duyte accordyng to right and good conscience. And thys at the reverence of god and in wey of charite.

Plegii de prosequendo   Thomas Lamberd de London yoman

Johannes White de eadem Bruer

---

* Johann Greverod and the Steelyard fellowship denied that either £500 or any of Carpenter's or Savage's goods had been attached as alleged, and Wylcokks and Wylde were prosecuted by writ of *sub poena*. On 8 November 1492 Wylcokks and the widow and executrix of Wylde released and gave quitclaim of any sequestrations of money held by Hermann Plough and the debts of Carpenter and Savage, totaling £219 10s, by reason of bonds dated 8 March 1478 and 26 May 1479. PRO C1/111/50, *CCR* 1485–1500: 189.

A.4 CONTRACTS AND LOANS

A.4.1 Bond for the purchase of cloth by Hanseatic merchant Henry van Echte from John Stede of Colchester. 1463.* PRO C1/31/495.

Item I Henry van Eghte have bought of John Stede 22 clothes everich cloth for £3 Summe £66 herfore I shall geve him 6 C[wt] wex everich C for 7 nobles and oon Bale of mader the C 16s and 6d 6000 litmose every C for 7s and 6d 400 [hulsom] everch C for 5 mrc and whatsoever the overpluse drawith to pay in money the oon halff at Whitsontyde and that other halff at Mighelmas anno 63 the friday afore palmyssonday.

* The bond was presented as evidence in support of a request by van Eghte for a writ of *sub poena* against Stede, who, claiming non-payment of the obligation, took possession of 98 quarters of woad that van Eghte had stored with him in Colchester. PRO C1/31/494, 496–8.

A.4.2 Proceedings in Chancery concerning ownership of a cargo of Bay salt brought to England by Danzig captain Gasper Sculte. ca. 1456–60. PRO C1/26/193.

To the wurshipful and reverent Fadir in god the Bisshop of Wynchestre Chaunceler of Ingland

Mekely besechen your pour bedmen Gasper Sculte Maister and owner of a hulk callid le Beriet of Dansk in Almaigne Nicholas Sculte and Thomas Byman that where as it was late acorded bytwene the seid Gasper and on John Frenssh of Wynchelsee that the seid John shuld freight 70 charge salt 22 for 20 in the seid hulk in the Baye as sone tobe laden and redy to saile as other shippes of his felauship then ther beyng and the seid salt tobe delivered atte Wynchelsee or atte Yepyswich paiyng for the freight of every charge 17s 6d and when the seid Gasper was comen into the Baye with the seid hulk the seid John had noe good in merchaundise nor by wey of eschaunge to bey any salt to furnyssh the seid freight and wherby the seid Gasper taried in the seid Baye behynd thothir seid shippes 8 wikes to his gret perell and inpartie. And ther the seid John labored to Ambrose Lomylyne merchaunte of Jene ... the which Ambrose by the suretee of your seid besechers lent and toke to the seid John 94 mrc sterlyng with the which he purveied salt and charged it in the same hulk to be caried to London And your seid besechers bonde them and eche of them were plegges and bounden in the Courte of the Baye to paye the seid 94 mrc to John Lomelyne or to his certain attorney atte the Cite of London upon the adventure of the see fro port of Colette unto the Ryver of Themse withyn 30 dayes after the seid hulk arived in the seid Ryver and the seid John in the seid court permitted and bonde hymseff to save and aquite your seid besechers harmeles agayn the seid Lomelyne and that he shuld not take nor receyve any of the seid salt into the tyme that he hade discharged your seid besechers agayn the seid Lomelyne and paid the seid Gasper of his seid freight as in certain lettres therof made in the seid court sealed with the seale for contractis ther ordeyned more pleynly it apereth and when the seid Gasper was comen with the seid hulk into the seid Ryver and had been beden there 24 daies and more the seid John Frenssh came not for to aquite your seid besechers agayn the seid Lomelyne of their seid bondes and obligacions or to pay the seid freight to the seid Gasper but oon William Long with whome the seid Gasper never spake byfore came to London and ther surmittyng that the seid salt soe charged by the seid John Frenssh shuld be the good of the seid William entrid and playnt byfor the Shireves of London agayn the seid Gasper surmittyng by the same that your seid besecher shuld have take a wey with force in London 70 charge of salt to the value of £200 and aftirward oon Thomas Hoo Squier made another plaint agayn the seid Gasper for the same salt and how be it that the seid Gasper prefered and prefereth to the seid William and Thomas Hoo that if thei will discharge your seid besechers agayn the seid Lomelyne and pay the freight to the seid Gasper and fynde hym surete tobe saved harmelesse and tobe quiet agayn the seid John Frenssh the seid Gasper will deliver to them all the salt by the seid John Frenssh charged in the seid hulk yet netheles the seid Gasper is thus vexed and trobled to thentent that he shuld ... delivere the seid salt without any freight therfor to be paid to the seid Gasper or any discharge of the seid bondes and obligacions agayn the seid Lomelyne into his gret hurt by the which vexacion he is like to abide behynd other hulkes of his contre in grete perell and inpartie of hymself and of his seid hulk and all his goodis Please it your gracious lordship to considere the premisses and to send for the seid William and Thomas Hoo to apere byfor your seid gracious lordship ther tobe examined and ruled in the premisses as right and reson will desire so that your seid besechers maybe discharged agayn the seid Lomelyne and the seid Gasper paid of his freight and discharged agayn the seid John Frenssh for the love of god and in wey of charite.

A.4.3 Proceedings in Chancery regarding a loan by Danzig merchant Tydemann Valand for the repair and revictualling of an English ship at Danzig. 1479. PRO C1/32/356.

To the most reverend Fader in god Archbisshepp of Yorke
Chaunceler off England

Mekely besechith your godd lordshipp Tedman Foland of Danske in Pruse that where in August the 19th yere of the Kyng our sovereyne lord oon Thomas Selman then purser of a shipp callid the Cristofer of Lenne wherof oon Thomas Wright of Lenne and John Tyge of the same then were owners and proprietares for the same shipp then beyng att Danske aforeseid in necessite aswell for vitayle and reparacion as other necessaries there borowed and hadd by eschaunge of your seid besecher 74 mrc pruce to the behauf and use of the said shipp and owners were to pay for every mrc pruce 3s 4d Englyssh at the comyng home of the said shipp in sauftye or withyn a moneth after the same your besecher to bere the adventure of the said money in the said shipp as in several bylles therof by the said purser made redy to be shewyd more playnly shall apper And the which payment well and trewly to be fulfilled and doon the said purser by the said bylles bonde the said shipp Which said 74 mrc pruce drawith in money Englissh after the said rate to the some of £12 6s 8d and came to the use and behofe of the said shipp and owners And how be it that after that the same shipp came home from Danske aforesaid to Lenne in saftie and theruppon the said owners have payed £6 of the said some of £12 6s 8d to the attorney and factor of your said

besecher in this behalfe yet the said owners nor purser althow they oft tymes have
been required £6 6s 8d residue of the said some of £12 6s 8d have not payed nor yet
woll butt vaerly refuse to pay it agenst all right and good conscience Wherfor
forasmoch as your said besecher hath no remedy by the common lawe in this behalfe
it please your good lordshipp the premisses tenderly considerid to graunt writtes of
suo pena severally directe to the said Thomas Wright and John Tyge commaundyng
theym by the same to apper afore the Kyng in his Chauncerye att a certeyn day ther to
aunswere to the premisses and over that to do and receyve as right and conscience
shall require in this behalfe And this for the love of god.

Plegii de prosequendo   Willelmus Crabbe de London yoman

Thomas Hauke de eadem yoman

A.4.4 Proceedings in Chancery regarding alleged non-payment for cloth purchased by
Hanseatic merchant Lutkyn Buring from London draper Peers Starke. 1502-3.*
PRO C1/357/65.

To the moste reverent Fader in God William Archebisshop of Caunterbury
and Chaunceler of Englond

Mekely be sechith youre good lordshipp youre daily Oratoure Peers Starke Citezyn
and draper of London that where oon Lutkyn Buryng marchaunt of Almayn now
abydyng among the Esterlyngs at Stylyarde in London bought of youre seyd
Suppliaunt in London the 24th daye of Maye the 18th yere of oure soveraynge lorde
reygn' kyng Henry the 7th 24 yerdys of Wolleyn cloth for £12 sterling that ys to wete
12 yerdys therof of vyolett in grayn and other 12 yerds of crymsyn in grayn and when
the seyd Lutkyn hadde receyvyd the seyd clothe he de[s]yred youre seyd suppliaunt to
take an obligacion [....] oon John Wayffer of Frome Selwode stode bounden to hym in
£8 for payment of [£]8 parcel of the seyd £12 and also to giff hym respite of the seyd
residue unto the Fest of the Natyvite of Seynt John Baptist than next ensuyng
Wherunto your seyd Supplyaunt was agreable uppon this condicion that the seyd
Lutkyn shuld bryng the seyd John Wayffer afore youre seyd Supplyaunt afore the seyd
Natyvite to [...] [c]onfesse that oblygacion ffor hys dede and duete and then become
dettour to your seyd Suppliaunt for the seyd £8 Whych Lutkyn promysed so to do all
be it he afterwards contentyd and payed your seyd Suppliaunt the sayd £4 but as to
the seyd £8 the same Lutkyn in no wyse woll pay ne yer bryng to your seyd
Supplyaunt the sayd John Wayffer to confesse the seyd oblygacion to be his dede and
duetye accordyng to his promyse and [covenent] but denyeth his duety and promyse
and so by his subtell and untrew meanes wold defraude your seyd Supplyaunte of the
seyd £8 contrary to all ryght and good conscience in consyderacion wherof and also
that youre seyd suppliaunt hath no specialte in wrytyng of the seyd Lutkyn for the
seyd £8 Wherfore that ys thought that the seyd Lutkyn wold wage his lawe yf your
seyd Supplyaunt shuld sue hym by the comen law hit wold therfore please youre good
lordship the premysses consyderyd to graunt a writte of sub pena to be dyrectyd to
the seyd Lutky[n] commaundyng hym by the same to apere afore the kyng in his

chauncery att a certeyn day by your seyd lordship to be lymettyd ther to answere to the premysses accordyng to ryght and goo[d] conscience.

Plegii de prosequendo   Willelmus Gaston de London gent'

Ricardus Lambert de eadem gent'

---

* Buring claimed the obligation of John Wayffer was indeed transferred to Starke as part payment for the cloth, and denied he had agreed to bring Wayffer to Starke to confess the debt. Though protesting that the dispute was a matter of common law and therefore not the concern of Chancery, Buring nevertheless countered with a petition to the chancellor for a writ of *certiorari* against Starke. PRO C1/258/77.

A.5 THE CRISIS OF 1468

A.5.1 Copy of a petition from the Steelyard to the king on behalf of imprisoned Hansards. Undated. [ca. August–October 1468] StA Köln Hanse III. K. 15. Bl.47.

> To the most highest and myghty pryncekyng of England and of Fraunce
> and lord of Irland oure right good and graceous lord

Shewith in the most humble wyse Gerard Wessell Petyr Bodemclopp Arnold Wynkels
and other merchauntez of the Hanse of Almayn beyng in this your realme some borne
in Coleyn some in Dynaunt some in Mynster some in Nemeigh some in Darpmond
and some in dyvers other places in Almayn mekely besechyng your good grace that
where it is compleyned agenst theym by dyvers your suggetts certeyn Englissh shipps
goodes and merchaundisez to ben taken spoiled and robbed in Denmark by the
procuryng [steryng] and abbettyng of your seid besechers and theruppon desirid your
seid besechers to be compellid to make satisfaction to your seid suggetts Where as
your seid besechers be not gylty in dede of the seid procuryng steryng or abbettyng it
please your good grace tenderly to considre the old lege amyte and intercurse of
merchaundise bitwene this your realme and the parties of the Hanse of Almayn and
how your noble pregenitour kyng Edward the second by his graceous lettres patentez
among other thynges graunted unto the merchauntez of the Hanse of Almayn then
beyng and to their successours that they nor their goodes no merchaundisez shold be
arrested or attached for otheris dette or trespas which graunte by your noble
pregenitour kyng Edward the third and king Richard the seconde and by your
highnesse is ratefied graunted and confermed by their and your graceous lettres
patentez and which libertee the seid merchauntez and their predecessours have usid
hadd and enjoied and ben entretid accordyng to the same graunte without interuption
as by dyvers precedentes of recorde therof to your good grace more plenely may
appere And also how it is ordeigned by estatut made the 27th yere of the full noble
reigne of your noble pregenitour aforeseid kyng Edward the third that the merchauntez estraungers shall not be empledid or empeched for otheris trespas or otheris
dette and that it is ordeigned in the 5th yere of your noble pregenitour Richard the
seconde aforeseid that merchauntez estraunges beyng of your amyte shall frely come
abide and merchaundise withyn this your realme and shall under the protection and
savegard of your highness with all their goodes and merchaundise and in leke wyse
your noble pregenitour aforeseid and your highnesse by their and your seid lettres
patentez taken your seid besechers in to your protection and defence and how by virtue of the same grauntez statutz and libertees aforeseid said uppon confidence therof
your seid besechers have more boldly usid and exercisid to come into this your realme
trustyng the sid libertees and grauntez made unto theym as is aforeseid to be good
and effectuell and to have theffecte therof accordyng to the same grauntez by the
[power] of your highness defence and protection aswell as by your lawes and these
premisses graceously considerid it please your hightness of your most benyngne grace
that your seid besechers be not compelled to aunswer nor to satesfye for otheris
offence and trespas and that they mey be entretid accordyng to their innocencis in
dede and accordyng to the seid grauntez statutz and libertees and as they have ben
entretid by force of the same afore this tyme and this for the love of god and they shall
ever pray to god for your most roiall estate.

A.5.2 Copy of a petition by West Country clothmakers on behalf of imprisoned
Hansards. Undated. [ca. October 1468] StA Köln Hanse III. K. 15. Bl.49.

Pyteouslye complaynen un to youre goode lordeshippe youre pore and humble
besechers ocupiyng and exercisyng the makynge of clothe and also the utterers of the
same beyng inhabitauntes withyn the Townes of Bristowe Bathe Wellys Glastynbury
Shepton Malette Coscombe Trowebrigge Bradeford ffrome Bekyngton and Warmyster
yn the countees of Bristowe Somerset and Wiltshire and within the contrayes to the
same adjioynyng That where youre saide pore besechers yn greete nombre have been
greetlye ocupyed afore this tyme and have hadde theyre speciall meanys of theyr
lyving and weele yn makynge of clothe and utterynge of the same yn greet substaunce
and value yerelye to marchauntys Esterlinges of Almayn resortyng and beyng withyn
this Realme and greetly soo coraged to contynue yn theire laboure of cloth makynge
by cause that the saide marchauntes Esterlinges have soo trewly and lovynglye delt by
waye of merchaundise with youre saide pore besechers yn suere and redy paiements
and contentacion of theyre saide cloth to the greet relief and comfort of youre saide
pore besechers as it is openly knowen and undirstoud to alle the saide marchauntis
and contrayes aforesayde entendyng the commie weele of the same Un to that nowe of
late tyme that the saide marchauntes Esterlinges by the kyngis moost high
commaundement have been restrayned of their liberte by occasion wherof youre saide
pore besechers been right grevouslye hurte lakkyng utteraunce and saale of theyre
clothe yn greet value and by that meane thoo that weere utterers of the same clothe be
not of power to fynde and ocupie youre saide pore suppliauntez stondynge therefore
nowe as people dismayde for lakke of ocupacion yn ydelnesse the which is the verry
occasion and bygynnyng of alle vices and mysgovernaunce and soo likly to growe to
the extreme poverte and utter undoyng for youre saide pore besechers And that they
shalle not mowe to be able ne of power by mannys reason to doo ne live ne paie
theyre dewtees accordyng to goddis lawes and the kyngis withouten youre moost
discreete and favorable assistence for theym un to the kyngis highnesse for sume gracious provision to be hadde for theym yn this behalffe Ytt maye please therfore un to
youre fulle noble and gracious lordeshippe consideringge by youre high and mooste
discreete prudence the greet desolacion discomfort and undoyng of youre rehersyd
pore besechers and of many other for lakke of ocupacion of cloth makynge and
utteraunce of the same the which soo contynued also by proces for nown power might
growe to the great hurte and damages un to the kingis moost dradde highnesse for
nown paiement of suche dewetees as of right belongith unto the same his highnesse
and also to the greet hurte and withdrawyng of the commie weele of this Realme to
calle un to youre moost gracious and discrete remembraunce the premisses and to
provide the weele and remedye of youre saide suppliauntez beyng yn this great
hevynesse and perplexite And over this that it maye like youre gracious lordeshippe
that the saide marchauntes Esterlinges no verry proves beyng made agenst theym for
any suche cause of restraynte maye by youre gracious and blessid meanys be to the
kyngis moost noble grace acceptable and yn favorable wise entretid as frendys havyng
their liberte accordyng to the moost oldyst amyte and liege of this his noble Realme yn
as spedy season as shalle mowe like his goode grace and as they maye have the more
corage hereafter to bye the saide cloth soo made and uttered as ys aforesaid as they
have hadde yn tyme passed to the greete weele and meanys of lyvynge by ocupacion
of youre rehersed pore besechers the kingis trewe liege people and subgettys And they
shall praye almyghty god for the weele of youre right noble astate.

A.5.3 Partial summary of confiscations in England. Undated. [ca. August–October
1468] StA Köln Hanse IV. 68. Bl.63v.

This be the names of every towne where the esterlings hath any goodz and the
Retourne acordynge at folowith

Furst in London	£1887 17s 7d ob
Yorcke	£13 6s 8d
Newcastell	£56
Hull	£274 19s 10d
Boston	£297 17s [5d]
Cambruge	£28 17s 3d ob
Lynne	£380 7s 1d ob
Bramidon'Ferei	£34
Ypeswich	£24 8s
Colchester	£65 13s 6d
Braybruke	£18

Some to all the Retournes by cerificattz
£3554 17s ob

Some to all off the Schyppz and goudz that the merchants englisshe complenisth of is
£12606 2s 4d

For my lord part of northumbrlond
in the first for his good Shippe the valentynn	£600
for his freeht	£300
for his merchandise	£140 6s 6d
for his damaige	£14
Some of my lord part	£1054 6s 6d

A.5.4 Copy of an order authorizing the release of cloths belonging to Cologne
merchants. Undated. [ca. August–October 1468?] StA Köln Hanse III. K. 15.
Bl.62.

Ryght worshipfull and welbelovyd in god etc. I rekommend me unto you And where
as 31 Byles of cloth belongyng to certayn merchauntez of Coleyn whiche ben in your
kepynge were of late for certayn causes by the kynges comaundment restreyned and
the seid merchauntez put from the libertee of theym it ys so that the kyng by thadvyse
of his councell hath deuly herd and excused the causez and mater of the seid restreynt
wheryn noo defaute is founde in the seid merchauntez nor merchaundisez Wherfor he
woll that the seid merchauntez have delyveraunce of the seid cloth to conveye and
dispose it at their wille any comaundement to the contrare not withstonding Wherfor y
wills you in the kynges name that you delyvere or make to be delyvered unto the seid
merchauntez their factors or attorneys in this behalfe the seid Byles and every percell

theroff beyng in your kepyng any cause you movyng the contrarie notwithstandyng.
geven at London.

And this our writing shalbe to you at alle
[...] sufficiant warrant and discharge

[dorse] To Gerard Wesell att Stileyerd
To the aldyrman of the Stelyarde in London this be delivered

A.5.5 Partial summary of goods sold to pay expenses of Hanseatic merchants.
Undated. [ca. September 1468]* StA Köln Hanse III. K. 15. Bl.73–73v.

[left margin] hyer affter folowyn the names off the merchants off almayne whiche
desiron to selle [...] off ther goddes and merchandise for to paye ther
freght and expences

Jesus

Arnold Wynkensson 34 balles off madder 6 packs off lynecloth 7 rolles off boultcloth
3 pec' off wex 10 sacs off lycmos ffor ffreght preuiage loidmanage licht'age kraneage
and porterage sauff the Kynges custume £15
Item ffor expences for hem and hys two men from the 29th day of August last past tel
the octava off michelmas next comyng summa £18

Summa totalis £33

Gerard Wesel for John Farnham 3 packs and 1 ffardel of lynecloth ffor freght puiage
loidmanage [lichtage] kranage and portage sauff the Kynges custume £4 10s
Item ffor expences ffor hem and the servant of the place the tyme afforsaid £16

Summa £20 10s

Herry Houwyser and John Ruschendorp the servans of Herman Ryng merchans of
coleyn ffor 9 barells styel 11 balles of madder 1 pipe woode 1 straw wex for uncostes
as is afforsaid £7
Item for the expences off the said Herry and John £12

Summa totalis £19

Matheu van der Schuren for hem and John van A 2 packs and 2 ffardels with lyncloth
12 sacs of [heupp] 2 last off soope 2 pypes 2 bales of madder and a pack off colleyn
threede £6 12s
Item for expences off the said Matheu Peter Berlynhusen and Derik Boule servant to
John van A merchans off coleyn £18

Summa totalis £24 12s

Arnold Seller for 1 pack colenthred and 1 fardel 10s Item for hys costes £6

Summa £6 10s

Herry Foget for expences £6
Herry Rutko and Gerard van Grove for ther expences £12
John Warenthorp 1 ffat of peltrye 2 packs 2 rolles and 1 basket off lynecloth and 4
bales of madder £5
Item ffor hem and Bernard Warenthorp and 2 men expences £20

Summa £25

Jorge Tacke 6 bales off madder 3 [...] oyle 1 pack and 1 fardel off lynecloth 4 barel
soope £5 10s

Item ffor expences ffor hem and hys man £12

Summa £17 10s

Reynold Lobbrech and Peter Sledelman 9 barell styel 6 balles mader 4 bales fustain £4
12s.

Item ffor hys expences £6

Summa £10 12s

John Stockem and John Berchem ffor 6 packs off coleyn threde £2

Item ffor hys expences £6

Summa £9

Herman Slotke ffor expences £6

John Barenbrouk for expences £6

William Schaphusen for expences £6

Johan Langeman ffor 21 fat and di of styel £9 18s. Item for expences £6

Summa £15 18s

Arnold Moldick ffor 3 packs and 1 fardel off lynecloth 1 pack coleynthred 2 last and
7 barells off soope £4

Item ffor expences £6

Summa £10

Richard van Alffter the servand of John van Dorn merchand of coleyn 8 packs off
coleynthrede 5 balle off madder 2 tonne off olye £5

Item for hys expences £6

Summa £11

Herry Breckerfeld ffor 1 pack off lynecloth 4 sacks off [...] 6 sacs of fedders £3 10s.

Item ffor hys expences £6

Summa £9 10s

Reynold Kerchhord for 1 pack lynecloth and 12 barells off potasches for uncostes and
werpyng in the see £2 10s.

Item ffor expences for hem and hys man £12

Summa £14 10s

Albrecht Gyse for 3 last and 7 barells of tran 5 lastes and 10 fat asches 3 last and di
terr 1 last off byer and 200 waynscotte ffor uncostes and werpyng in the see £17 10s

Item ffor expences for hym and hys man £12

Summa £29 10s

Albrecht Valant 7 packs off flax 1 pack of lynecloth 1 straw off wex a half a last off
trane for uncostes and werping in the see £7

Item ffor hys expences £6

Summa £13

Lenard Amelong 5 packs off flax ffor uncostes and werpyng in the see £12

Item for expences £6

Summa £18

Mateus [Katto] 4 packs off flex ffor uncostes and castyng in the see £7

Item for expences £6

Summa £13

[Urgh'] Swartewolt 200 waynscotte 2 last and di off terr and 1 last off asches for
uncostes and castyng in the see £7 4s.

Item for expences £6

Summa £13 4s

Nicolas Steffan 200 off waynscotte 2 last off terr and 2 lastes of asche ferr uncostes and castyng in the see £6 8s.

Item for expences £6

Summa £12 8s

---

* On 20 September 1468 Edward IV granted the Hanseatic merchants permission to sell off goods to the value of 2,000 marks. *HUB* IX no. 509. However, the arrested merchants subsequently complained that the mayor of London and 'his Bretherne' restrained them from selling 'what goodes ... necessary ... for their expenses and other necessaries.' StA Köln Hanse III. K. 15. Bl.100.

GLOSSARY

Bal (Bale): a unit of weight varying according to the commodity; a package varying in size and content.

Barrel (Barellum): a cask; a unit of liquid measure for wine, beer, and ale. 1 barrel = 31.25 gallons.

Batteryware: copperware; i.e., pots and pans.

Bergenfahrer: Hansards working the Norwegian fisheries and/or trading to and from the *comptoir* at Bergen. Primarily merchants and shippers from Lübeck and other Wendish ports.

Cade: a cask for fish, holding 600 herring. 20 cades = 1 last.

Certiorari: a writ directing that a court be informed on some matter, particularly on the record of a case heard in an inferior court.

Chalder (Calder): a unit of weight for coal and grindstones, equal to 1 ton; i.e., 1 chalder = 2,000 lb (c. 907 kg); 20 chalders = 1 keel.

Charge: a unit of weight for salt, usually equal to 5/4 of a hundredweight; i.e., 1 charge = 140 lb (c. 65 kg).

Cist (Cista): a wooden box or chest.

Clapholts (Klappholz): short boards for barrels and general carpentry.

Colenthread (fil colen; colleyn threede): heavy yarn, usually dyed blue.

Corpus cum causa: a writ ordering the production in court of someone committed to prison, especially for debt, together with a record of his/her case.

Deles (Dielenholz): broad flooring planks, freighted by the last. 1 last = 60 deles.

Dicker: a unit of quantitative measure for hides, gloves, horseshoes, etc. 1 dicker = 10 pieces; 20 dickers = 1 last.

Dolium: a cask for wine; a unit of capacity equal to 1 tun (250 gallons) for wine, but varying for other commodities.

Dozen: a unit of quantitative measure equal to 12. The term *dozen* also applied to various types of single-width English (i.e., Welsh) cloth measuring 12 English ells and 12 inches in length.

Ell (Ulna): a unit of linear measure for woollens, linens, and canvas. 1

Danzig ell = 57.1 cm; 1 Cologne ell = 57.6 cm; 1 Flemish ell = 27 inches = 68.5 cm; 1 English ell = 45 inches = 114.3 cm.

Englandfahrer: Hansards trading to and from England.

Fardel: a package of cloth varying in size and content.

Foder: a unit of measure for lead, usually equal to 2,100 lb (c. 952 kg).

Frieze (Frise): a coarse single-width English cloth.

Fustian: a coarse cloth made with cotton and flax.

Gallon: an English unit of liquid measure for wine, beer, and ale, equal to 3.78 litres. 31.25 gallons = 1 barrel; 50 gallons = 1 aume; 62.5 gallons = 1 hogshead (2 barrels); 125 gallons = 1 pipe; 250 gallons = 1 tun.

Goad (God): a unit of linear measure for cloth equal to 4.5 yards (4.1 metres).

Granum (Grain): a red dyestuff made from the dried bodies of the kermes insect, which is found in the small evergreen oak trees of the Mediterranean region. Thus, *pannus in grano* = cloth dyed with grain; *pannus sine grano* = cloth without grain.

Gross: a unit of quantitative measure equal to 12 dozen (144) pieces, for items such as laces, knives, balls, strings, purses, etc.

Hogshead: an English unit of liquid measure for wine, beer, etc., equal to 2 barrels.

Hundredweight: a unit of weight equal to 112 lb or 100 lb, depending on the commodity. Tin, lead, copper, iron, steel, wax, woad, alum, madder, flax, hemp, rope, thread, tallow: 1 hundredweight (cwt) = 112 lb (c. 50 kg); pepper, cloves, ginger, etc.: 1 hundredweight = 100 lb (c. 45 kg).

Inch: an English unit of linear measure equal to 1/36 of a yard.

Islandfahrer: Hansards working the Icelandic fisheries and trading to and from Iceland.

Keel: a unit of weight for coal, equal to 20 tons or 'chalders.'

Kersey (Carsey): a coarse single-width English cloth, not completely felted, 28 yards long by 1 yard wide.

Last: a unit of capacity or weight varying according to the commodity. Hides: 1 last = 200 pieces; Tar, pitch, soap, tran, stockfish, herring, osmund: 1 last = 12 barrels; Bowstaves: 1 last = 600 pieces.

Letter of marque: a commission authorizing private action against enemy ships.

Lb. (English pound): a unit of weight equal to .45 kg.

Lewent (Lewant): canvas.

Litmus (Litmose, licmos): blue dye, obtained from various lichens.

Long hundred (C): a unit of quantity equal to 120 pieces.

Madder (Mader): red dye, obtained from the roots of several Rubia species, dried and crushed to powder.

Nest: a set of objects one inside the other (i.e., counters, coffers, etc.).

Osmund: Swedish bog iron.

Pack (Pac): a quantity of cloth, canvas, linen, etc. 1 pack = 10 cloths.

Piece (Pecia): a unit of linear measure for textiles. Buckram: 1 piece = 40 yards; fustian: 1 piece = 30 yards.

Pipe: a cask, a unit of capacity or weight, equal to a half tun for wine, oil, and fruit, but varying for other commodities.

Poke (Pok): a measure for wool equal to half a sack; also a unit of weight or capacity (indeterminate) for litmus, madder, hops, etc.

Quarter (Quarterium): a unit of weight equal to one quarter of a hundredweight. Thus, 1 quarter = 28 lb (c. 12.7 kg).

Quintal (Quintallus): a unit of weight for wax, equal to a single hundredweight of 112 lb (c. 51 kg).

Remes (Remeholz): oars.

Roll: a unit of linear measure for textiles. Friezes: 1 roll = 40 yards (or more); Cornwall and Devonshire cloth: 1 roll = 15 yards. Also a term (rotula) used to identify pieces of wax weighing less than a quintal.

Sack (Sac): a unit of weight varying according to commodity. Wool: 1 sack = 364 lb (c. 164 kg); Hemp: 1 sack = 300 lb (c. 135 kg).

Schippund (Schiffspfund, ship pound): a Prussian unit of weight equal to 251 English lb (c. 114 kg), for wax, copper, and all types of iron.

Scok (Stok): a unit of quantity equal to 60 pieces, for items such as dishes, platters, and trenchours.

Short hundred: a unit of quantity equal to 100 pieces.

Straight (strait, Striet wall', stricti wall': Welsh straights): a type of single-width English (i.e., Welsh) woollen cloth sold by the 'dozen' (12 yards and 12 inches long by 1 yard wide). Also called cotton russets.

Strawe (Stro): a piece of wax, of indeterminate weight (i.e., 6–14 quintals), not exceeding 5 or 6 schippund.

Sub pena (Sub poena): a writ ordering the appearance of a person in court, under a specified penalty for failure to appear.

Terling (Terlinck, Terlink): a package of cloths.
English cloths of assize: 1 terling = 18-20 cloths. Various cloths manufactured in the Low Countries: 1 terling = max. 26 cloths.

Timber: a unit of quantity equal to 40 pieces, for pelts (sable, ermine, fox, squirrel, beaver, etc.).

Ton: (Cartload): a unit of weight equal to 2,000 lb (c. 907 kg).

Tran (Trane): fish (liver) oil, used for lamp fuel and in leather finishing.

Trenchour (Trencher): a wooden board or plate on which food was cut or served.

Umlandfahrt: the direct shipping route between the Baltic and the North Sea around Denmark, i.e., via the Kattegat and Skagerrak.

Vat: a unit of capacity or weight for various commodities.
Flax and hemp: 1 vat = max. 4 Schippund. Stockfish: 1 vat = 6 schippund.

Wainscots (Wagenchoss): boards, 3 to 5 metres long, used extensively for wall and ceiling panels; freighted by the long hundred and the last. 1 last = 240 wainscots.

Waw: a measure of quantity or weight for glass. 1 waw = 40 'bunches.'

Wendish towns: towns of the so-called 'Wendish' sector of the Hanse: Lübeck, Lüneburg, Hamburg, Stralsund, Wismar, Rostock.

Wey: a unit of weight. Salt: 1 wey = 1 charge = 140 lb. (c. 65 kg); lead: 1 wey
= 182 lb (c. 82 kg). Also used as a measure for tallow, cheese, etc.

Woad: blue dye, obtained from the leaves of the woad plant, milled to pulp,
formed into balls and crushed to powder.

Worsted: a type of English cloth made from long staple wool. Single
worsted: 1.25 yards by 6 yards. Double worsted: 1.25 yards by 10 yards.

Yard (Verga, virga): an English unit of linear measure for textiles equal to
91.4 cm. 1.25 yards = 1 English ell; .75 yard = 1 Flemish ell; 15 yards = 1
dozen English ells; 9 yards = 1 dozen Flemish ells.

BIBLIOGRAPHY

Abbreviations

Acts of Court: *Acts of Court of the Mercers' Company 1453–1527*
Akten: *Akten der Ständetage Preussens unter der Herrschaft des Deutschen Ordens*
APG: Archiwum Państwowe w Gdańsku
ARA: Algemeen Rijksarchief
BL: British Library
Bronnen:
    Bronnen tot de geschiedenis van den Oostzeehandel, ed. H.A. Poelman
    Bronnen tot de geschiedenis van den Handel met England, Schotland en Ierland, ed. H.J. Smit
    Bronnen tot de geschiedenis van Middelburg in den Landesheerlichen Tijd, ed. W.S. Unger
Bronnen tot de geschiedenis van den Handel met Frankrijk, ed. Z.W. Sneller and W.S. Unger
CChR: *Calendar of Charter Rolls*
CCR: *Calendar of Close Rolls*
CFR: *Calendar of French Rolls*
CLB: *Calendar of Letter Books of the City of London*
CLRO: *Corporation of London Record Office*
CPMR: *Calendar of Plea and Memoranda Rolls of the City of London*
CPR: *Calendar of Patent Rolls*
CSP Milan: *Calendar of State Papers – Milan*
CSP Venice: *Calendar of State Papers – Venice*
Documenten: *Documenten voor de Geschiedenis van de Antwerpse Scheepvaart*, ed. G. Asaert
England's Export Trade: *England's Export Trade 1275–1547*
EcHR: *Economic History Review*
Etudes: *Etudes Anversoises : Documents sur la commerce international à Anvers 1488–1514*, ed. R. Doehaerd
Foedera: *Foedera, conventiones, literae, etc.*

HGbll: *Hansische Geschichtsblätter*
HR: *Hanserecesse*
HUB: *Hansisches Urkundenbuch*
Iersekeroord: *De tol van Iersekeroord*, ed. W.S. Unger
Letters and Papers: *Letters and Papers Illustrative of the Reigns of Richard III and Henry VII*
LUB: *Codex Diplomaticus Lubecensis*
PRO: Public Record Office
Proceedings: *Proceedings and Ordinances of the Privy Council*
Quellen: *Quellen zur Geschichte des Kölner Handels und Verkehrs im Mittelalter*, ed. B. Kuske
Rot. Parl: *Rotuli Parliamentorum*
SAA: Stadsarchief Antwerpen
StA Köln: Historisches Archiv der Stadt Köln
StA Lübeck: Archiv der Hansestadt Lübeck
Studies: *Studies in English Trade in the Fifteenth Century*
Urkundliche Geschichte: *Urkundliche Geschichte des hansischen Stahlhofes zu London*, ed. J.M. Lappenberg

Manuscript Sources

Belgium
Antwerp: *Stadsarchief Antwerpen*
   Certificatieboeken: Cert. 1, 2, 3
   Schepenregisters: SR 43–96.
Brussels: *Algemeen Rijksarchief*
   Chambres des Comptes: CC. 22361–62, 23249–51, 49833, 49850–55; CC. Cartons series I, 1–4, no. 31, 48, 103–10, 114, 185–6, 189, 191–9.

Denmark
Copenhagen: *Rigsarkivet*
   Øresundstoldregnskaber 1497, 1503.

Germany
Cologne: *Historisches Archiv der Stadt Köln*
   Hanse III. K. 2–26, 75; Hanse IV. 68; Hanse Urkunden. U.1. Bl.211, U.2. Bl.133, U.2. Bl.251.
Lübeck: *Archiv der Hansestadt Lübeck*
   Niederstadtbuch Konzept 1506–10.

Great Britain
London: *British Library*
   Additional 15505 f. 21, 30158; Additional Charters 40731, 40680; Cotton Nero B II f. 36, IX ff. 19–22; Cotton Vesp. E IX ff. 86–110; Lansdowne 139.42 f. 631, 154.1–20.

Corporation of London Record Office
Mayors Court Original Bills: MC1/3/129, 131, 134, 156, 160, 192, 200, 209, 214, 224, 225, 235, 236, 241, 244, 347, 364; MC1/3a/1, 14, 15, 48, 67, 113, 116, 117, 118, 136, 210, 211, 212, 263.
Journals of the Court of the Common Council: JOR 7–10.
Public Record Office
Chancery: C1 Early Proceedings; C47 Miscellanea; C49 Parliamentary and Council Proceedings; C76 Treaty Rolls; C241 Certificates of the Statute Merchant and Statute Staple.
Chancery and Exchequer: SC1 Ancient Correspondence; SC8 Ancient Petitions.
Exchequer: E30 Treasury of Receipt Diplomatic Documents; E101 Various Accounts; E122 KR. Customs Accounts; E163 KR. Miscellanea; E175 Parliamentary and Council Proceedings; E315 Augmentation Office Miscellaneous Books; E356 LTR. Enrolled Customs Accounts; E364 LTR. Foreign Accounts.
Norwich: *Norfolk Record Office*
Yarmouth Borough Court Rolls: Y/C4/180–211.

Poland
Gdańsk: *Archiwum Państwowe w Gdańsku*
Pfahlkammerbücher 300.19/1, 2, 2a, 3, 4, 5, 5a, 7, 8, 9, 10 (microfilm).

Printed Sources

Acta Statuum Terrarum Prussiae Regalis, vols. 1–4.2, ed. K. Gorski and M. Biskup, Torun, 1955–1967.
Acts of Court of the Mercers' Company 1453–1527, ed. L. Lyell and F.D. Watney, Cambridge, 1936.
Akten der Ständetage Preussens unter der Herrschaft des Deutschen Ordens, ed. M. Töppen, 5 vols. Leipzig, 1878–86 (Aalen, 1973–74).
Akten der Ständetage Preussens, Königliche Anteils, vol. 1, ed. F. Thunert, Danzig, 1896 (Aalen, 1979).
Antient Kalendars and Inventories of the Treasury of His Majesty's Exchequer, ed. F. Palgrave, 3 vols. London, 1836.
Bronnen tot de geschiedenis van den Oostzeehandel, ed. H.A. Poelman, 2 vols. Rijks Geschiedkundige Publicatien 35, 36, 's-Gravenhage, 1917.
Bronnen tot de geschiedenis van den Handel met England, Schotland en Ierland, ed. H.J. Smit, 4 vols. Rijks Geschiedkundige Publicatien 65, 66, 86, 91, 's-Gravenhage, 1928–1950.
Bronnen tot de geschiedenis van Middelburg in den Landsheerlijken Tijd, ed. W.S. Unger, 3 vols. Rijks Geschiedkundige Publicatien 54, 61, 75, 's-Gravenhage, 1923–1950. 3 vols.

Bronnen tot de geschiedenis van den Handel met Frankrijk, ed. Z.W. Sneller and W.S. Unger, 's-Gravenhage, 1930.

Calendar of Charter Rolls, vol. 6, 1427–1516, London, 1927.

Calendar of Close Rolls, Henry V vol. 2, 1419–22, London, 1932; Henry VI vols. 1–6, 1422–61, London, 1933–47; Edward IV vols. 1–2, 1461–76, London, 1949–53; Edward IV – Edward V – Richard III, 1476–85, London, 1954; Henry VII vols. 1–2, 1485–1509, London, 1955–63.

Calendar of French Rolls – Henry VI: 48th Report of the Deputy Keeper of the Public Records, appendix 2, London, 1887.

Calendar of Letter Books of the City of London, vol. I, 1400–22; vol. K, Henry VI; vol. L, Edward IV – Henry VII, ed. R.R. Sharpe, London, 1909–12.

Calendar of Patent Rolls 1396–1509, 16 vols. London, 1897–1916.

Calendar of Plea and Memoranda Rolls of the City of London vols. 3–6, 1381–1482, ed. A.H. Thomas and P.E. Jones, London, 1932–61.

Calendar of State Papers and Manuscripts existing in the Archives and Collections of Milan, vol. 1, 1385–1618, ed. A.B. Hinds, London, 1912.

Calendar of State Papers and Manuscripts existing in the Archives and Collections of Venice, vol. 1, 1202–1509; vol. 2, 1509–19, ed. R. Brown, London, 1864–7.

Caspar Weinreichs Danziger Chronik, ed. T. Hirsch and F.A. Vossberg, Berlin, 1855.

The Cely Letters, ed. A. Hanham, Oxford, 1975.

Die Chroniken der niedersächsischen Städte IV: Lübeck, ed. F. Bruns, Leipzig, 1910.

Codex Diplomaticus Lubecensis: Urkundenbuch der Stadt Lübeck, 11 vols. Lübeck, 1843–1932.

The Customs Accounts of Hull 1453–1490, ed. W.R. Childs, Yorkshire Archaeological Society Records Series CXLIV (1986).

Diplomatarium Christierni Primi, ed. C.F. Wegener, Copenhagen, 1856.

Documenten voor de Geschiedenis van de Antwerpse Scheepvaart voornamelijk de Englandvaart, ed. G. Asaert, Brussels, 1985.

Documents relating to Law and Custom of the Sea, vol. 1, ed. R.G. Marsden, Publications of the Navy Records Society XLIX (1915).

The Early Yorkshire Woollen Trade, ed. J. Lister, Yorkshire Archaeological Society Record Series LXIV (1923).

English Historical Documents, vol. 4, ed. A.R. Myers, London, 1969.

Etudes Anversoises: Documents sur le commerce international à Anvers 1488–1514, ed. R. Doehaerd, 3 vols. Paris, 1962.

'Financial Memoranda of the Reign of Edward V. Longleat Miscellaneous Manuscript Book II,' ed. R. Horrox, *Camden Miscellany* XXIX (1987), 197–244.

Foedera, conventiones, literae, et cujuscunque generis acta publica inter reges Angliae, ed. T. Rymer, 20 vols. London, 1726–35.

45th Report of the Deputy Keeper of the Public Records, appendix 2, London, 1885.

Hamburgische Burspraken 1346–1594, ed. J. Bollard, 2 vols. Hamburg, 1960.

Hamburgische Chroniken, ed. J.M. Lappenberg, Hamburg, 1851.

Hamburgische Chroniken in niedersächsischer Sprache, ed. J.M. Lappenberg, Hamburg, 1861.

'Handelsbriefe aus Riga und Königsberg von 1458 und 1461,' ed. W. Stein, *HGbll*, IX (1898), 59–125.

Hanserecesse, Series 1, 1250–1430, ed. K. Koppmann; series 2, 1431–76, ed. G. von der Ropp; series 3, 1477–1530, ed. D. Schäfer, 24 vols. Leipzig, 1870–1913.

Hansisches Urkundenbuch, ed. K. Höhlbaum, K. Kunze, W. Stein, 11 vols. Halle/Leipzig, 1876–1916.

Historical Manuscripts Commission 9th Report, London, 1885.

Historical Manuscripts Commission 11th Report, London, 1887.

Kämmereibuch der Stadt Reval 1432–1463, ed. R. Vogelsang, 2 vols. Köln/Wien, 1976.

Kämmereibuch der Stadt Reval 1463–1507, ed. R. Vogelsang, 2 vols. Köln/Wien, 1983.

Kämmereirechnungen der Stadt Hamburg, ed. K. Koppmann, 7 vols. Hamburg, 1869–94.

Ledger of Andrew Halyburton conservator of the privileges of the Scotch nation in the Netherlands 1492–1503, ed. C. Innes, Edinburgh, 1867.

Letters and Papers Foreign and Domestic of the Reign of Henry VIII, vol. 1, 1509–14, ed. J.S. Brewer, London, 1920.

Letters and Papers illustrative of the reigns of Richard III and Henry VII, ed. J. Gairdner, 2 vols. London, 1861–3.

Libelle of Englyshe Polycye, ed. G. Warner, Oxford, 1926.

Die Lübecker Bergenfahrer und ihre Chronistik, ed. F. Bruns, Berlin, 1900.

Lübecker Ratsurteile, ed. W. Ebel, 4 vols. Göttingen, 1955–67.

The Making of King's Lynn: A Documentary Survey, ed. D.M. Owen, London, 1984.

Materials for a History of the Reign of Henry VII, ed. W. Campbell, 2 vols. London, 1873–7.

Naval Accounts and Inventories of the Reign of Henry VII, 1485–8 and 1495–7, ed. M. Oppenheim, Publications of the Navy Records Society VIII (1896).

The Navy of the Lancastrian Kings: Accounts and Inventories of William Soper, Keeper of the King's Ships, 1422–1427, ed. S. Rose, Publications of the Navy Records Society CXXIII (1982).

De Oosterse Handel te Amsterdam, ed. N.W. Posthumus, Leiden, 1953.

The Overseas Trade of London Exchequer Customs Accounts 1480–1, ed. H.S. Cobb, London Record Society Publications XXVII (1990).

The Paston Letters, ed. J. Gairdner, 4 vols. Edinburgh, 1910.

Political Poems and Songs relating to English History, vol. 2, ed. T. Wright, London, 1861.

Proceedings and Ordinances of the Privy Council, ed. N.H. Nicolas, 7 vols. London, 1834–3.

Quellen zur Geschichte des Kölner Handels und Verkehrs im Mittelalter, ed. B. Kuske, 4 vols. Bonn, 1917–34.

Regesten zur Geschichte des Harburger Raumes 1059 bis 1527, ed. D. Kausche, Hamburg, 1976.
The Reign of Henry VII from Contemporary Sources, ed. A.F. Pollard, 3 vols. London, 1913–14.
Rotuli Parliamentorum 1287–1503, ed. J. Starchey, J. Pridden, E. Upham, 6 vols. London, 1767–77.
Scriptores Rerum Prussicarum: Die Geschichtsquellen der Preussischen Vorzeit, ed. T. Hirsch, M. Töppen, E. Strehlke, 5 vols. Leipzig, 1861–74 (Frankfurt, 1965–8).
Select Cases in the Exchequer Chamber 1377–1461, ed. E. Hemmant, Publications of the Selden Society LI (1933).
Statutes of the Realm, ed. A. Luders, T.E. Tomlins, J.F. France et al., 11 vols. London, 1810–28.
De tol van Iersekeroord. Documenten en rekeningen 1312–1572, ed. W.S. Unger, Rijks Geschiedkundige Publicatien, klein serie 29, 's-Gravenhage, 1939.
Tudor Economic Documents, ed. E. Power and R.H. Tawney, 3 vols. London, 1924.
Tudor Royal Proclamations, vol. 1, 1485–1553, ed. P.L. Hughes and J.F. Larkin, New Haven, Conn., 1964.
Urkundliche Geschichte des hansischen Stahlhofes zu London, ed. J.M. Lappenberg, Hamburg, 1851 (Osnabrück, 1967).
York Civic Records, ed. A. Raine, Yorkshire Archaeological Society Record Series XCVII (1938), CIII (1940).
The York Mercers and Merchant Adventurers 1356–1917, ed. M. Sellers, Surtees Society Publications CXXIX (1918).
Die Zolltarife der Stadt Hamburg, ed. E. Pitz, Wiesbaden, 1961.
Zwei Stralsundische Chroniken des fünfzehnten Jahrhunderts, ed. R. Baier, Stralsund, 1893.

Secondary Sources

Agats, A. *Der hansische Baienhandel*, Heidelberger Abhandlungen zur mittleren und neueren Geschichte V, 1904.
Ammann, H. 'Deutschland und die Tuchindustrie Nordwesteuropas im Mittelalter,' *HGbll*, LXXII (1954), 1–63.
Asaert, G. 'Handel in kleurstoffen op de Antwerpse markt tijdens de XVe eeuw,' *Bijdragen en mededelingen betreffende de geschiedenis der Nederlanden*, LXXXVIII (1973), 377–402.
– *De Antwerpse Scheepvaart in de XVe Eeuw (1394–1480)*, Brussels, 1973.
– 'Antwerp Ships in English Harbours in the Fifteenth Century,' *Acta Historiae Neerlandicae*, XII (1979), 29–47.
Bacon, F. *The History of the Reign of King Henry the Seventh*, ed. F.J. Levy, New York, 1972.
Bang, N.E. *Tabeller over Skibsfart og Varentransport gennem Øresund 1497–1660*, 2 vols. Leipzig, 1906, 1932.

Bennett, M. *Lambert Simnel and the Battle of Stoke*, New York, 1987.

Bindoff, S.T. *The Scheldt Question to 1839*, London, 1945.

Biskup, M. 'Die polnisch-preussischen Handelsbeziehungen in der ersten Hälfte des 15. Jahrhunderts,' *Hansische Studien*, ed. G. Heitz and M. Unger, Forschungen zur mittelalterlichen Geschichte VIII, Berlin, 1961, 1–6.

– 'Das Reich, die wendische Hanse und die preussische Frage um die Mitte des 15. Jahrhunderts,' *Neue Hansische Studien*, ed. E. Müller-Mertens, J. Schildhauer, E. Voigt, Berlin, 1970, 341–57.

– 'Der preussische Bund 1440–1454,' *Hansische Studien III*, ed. K. Fritze, E. Müller-Mertens, J. Schildhauer, Weimar, 1975, 210–29.

Bolton, J.L. *Alien Merchants in England in the Reign of Henry VI, 1422–61*, unpublished B. Litt. thesis, Oxford, 1971.

– *The Medieval English Economy*, London, 1980.

Bourne, H.R. Fox. *English Merchants*, London, 1866 (New York, 1969).

Bracker, J. ed., *Die Hanse. Lebenswirklichkeit und Mythos*, 2 vols. Hamburg, 1989.

Bridbury, A.R. *England and the Salt Trade in the Later Middle Ages*, Oxford, 1955.

Britnell, R.H. *Growth and Decline in Colchester, 1300–1525*, Cambridge, 1986.

Brulez, W. 'Bruges and Antwerp in the 15th and 16th Centuries: An Antithesis?,' *Acta Historiae Neerlandicae*, VI (1973), 1–26.

Bruns, F. 'Die Lübeckischen Pfundzollbücher von 1492–1496,' *HGbll*, XI (1904–5), 109–31; XIII (1907), 457–99; XIV (1908), 357–407.

Bruns, F. and Weczerka, H. *Hansische Handelstrassen*, 3 vols. Köln, 1962.

Burleigh, M. *Prussian Society and the German Order*, Cambridge, 1984.

Burwash, D. *English Merchant Shipping 1460–1540*, Toronto, 1947.

Buszello, H. 'Köln und England 1468–1509,' *Mitteilungen aus dem Stadtarchiv von Köln*, LX (1971), 431–67.

– 'Die auswärtige Handelspolitik der englischen Krone im 15. Jahrhundert,' *Frühformen englisch-deutscher Handelspartnerschaft*, ed. K. Friedland, Köln/Wien, 1976, 64–86.

Carus-Wilson, E.M. 'The Icelandic Trade,' *Studies in English Trade in the Fifteenth Century*, ed. M.M. Postan and E. Power, London, 1933, 155–82.

– *Medieval Merchant Adventurers*, London, 1967.

– 'The Oversea Trade of Late Medieval Coventry,' *Economies et Sociétés au Moyen Age, Mélanges offerts à Edouard Perroy*, Publications de la Sorbonne, Série 'Etudes,' Tome V, Paris, 1973, 371–81.

– 'The German Hanse in the Economy of Medieval England,' *Aspects of Anglo-German Relations through the Centuries*, ed. P. Kluke and P. Alter, Stuttgart, 1978, 14–23.

Carus-Wilson, E.M. and Coleman, O. *England's Export Trade 1275–1547*, Oxford, 1967.

Chartes, J.A. *Internal Trade in England 1500–1700*, London, 1977.

Childs, W.R. 'England's Iron Trade in the Fifteenth Century,' *EcHR*, 2nd series XXXIV (1981), 25–47.

Chorley, G.P.H. 'The English Assize of Cloth: A Note,' *Bulletin of the Institute of Historical Research*, LIX (1986), 125–30.

Chrimes, S.B. *Henry VII*, London, 1972.

Clarke, H. 'King's Lynn and East Coast Trade in the Middle Ages,' *Marine Archaeology*, ed. D.J. Blackman, Proceedings of the twentythird Symposium of the Colston Research Society, London, 1973, 277–90.

Cobb, H.S. 'Cloth Exports from London and Southampton in the Later Fifteenth and Early Sixteenth Centuries: A Revision,' *EcHR*, 2nd series XXXI (1978), 601–9.

Cowie, L.W. 'The Steelyard of London,' *History Today*, XXV (1976), 776–81.

Daenell, E. *Die Blütezeit der deutschen Hanse*, 2 vols. Berlin, 1905–6. (Berlin/ New York, 1973).

– 'The Policy of the German Hanseatic League respecting the Mercantile Marine,' *American Historical Review*, XV (1909–10), 48–53.

Davis, R. 'The Rise of Antwerp and Its English Connection 1406–1510,' *Trade, Government and Economy in Pre-Industrial England*, ed. D.C Coleman and A.H. John, London, 1976, 2–20.

de Roover, F.E. 'A Prize of War: A Painting of Fifteenth Century Merchants,' *Bulletin of the Business Historical Society*, XIX (1945), 3–12.

de Smedt, O. *De Engelse Natie te Antwerpen in de 16e Eeuw*, 2 vols. Antwerpen, 1950.

Dobson, R.B. 'Urban Decline in Late Medieval England,' *Transactions of the Royal Historical Society*, 5th series XXVII (1977), 1–22.

Dollinger, P. *The German Hansa*, ed. and trans. D. Ault and S.H. Steinberg, London, 1970.

– *Die Hanse*, 4th ed., Stuttgart, 1989.

Endres, F. *Geschichte der freien und Hansestadt Lübeck*, Lübeck, 1926.

Engel, K. 'Die Organisation der deutsch-hansischen Kaufleute in England im 14. und 15. Jahrhundert bis zum Utrechter Frieden von 1474,' *HGbll*, XIX (1913), 445–517; XX (1914), 173–225.

Evans, N. *The East Anglian Linen Industry*, Aldershot, Hants, 1985.

Ferguson, J. *English Diplomacy 1422–1461*, Oxford, 1972.

Fiedler, H. 'Danzig und England: Die Handelsbestrebungen der Engländer vom Ende des 14. bis zum Anfang des 17. Jahrhunderts,' *Zeitschrift des Westpreussischen Geschichtsvereins*, LXVIII (1928), 63–125.

Flenley, R. 'London and Foreign Merchants in the reign of Henry VI,' *English Historical Review*, XXV (1910), 644–55.

Fowler, K.A. 'English Diplomacy and the Peace of Utrecht,' *Frühformen englisch-deutscher Handelspartnerschaft*, ed. K. Friedland, Köln/Wien, 1976, 9–24.

Friccius, W. *Der Wirtschaftskrieg als Mittel hansischer Politik im 14. und 15. Jahrhundert*, Lübeck, 1932.

Friedland, K. 'Hamburger Englandfahrer 1512–1557,' *Zeitschrift des Vereins für Hamburgische Geschichte*, XLVI (1960), 1–47.

Friedland, K. ed. *Frühformen englisch-deutscher Handelspartnerschaft*, Köln/ Wein, 1976.

Fritze, K. 'Die Finanzpolitik Lübecks im Krieg gegen Dänemark 1426–1433,' *Hansische Studien*, ed. G. Heitz and M. Unger, Forschungen zur mittelalterlichen Geschichte VIII, Berlin, 1961, 82–9.
– *Am Wendepunkt der Hanse*, Berlin, 1967.
Frost, C. *Notices relative to the Early History of the Town and Port of Hull*, London, 1827.
Fudge, J. 'Anglo-Baltic Trade and Hanseatic Commercial Systems in the Late Fifteenth Century,' *Britain and the Northern Seas*, ed. W. Minchinton, Pontefract, 1988, 11–19.
– 'Supply and Distribution of Foodstuffs in Northern Europe 1450–1500,' *The Northern Seas: Politics, Economics and Culture*, ed. W. Minchinton, Pontefract, 1989, 29–39.
Gelsinger, B.E. *Icelandic Enterprise*, Columbia, SC, 1981.
Gillet, E. *A History of Grimsby*, London, 1970.
Gillet, E. and MacMahon, K.A. *A History of Hull*, Oxford, 1980.
Giuseppi, M.S. 'Alien Merchants in England in the fifteenth Century,' *Transactions of the Royal Historical Society*, new series IX (1895), 75–98.
Goetze, J. 'Hansische Schiffahrtswege in der Ostsee,' *HGbll*, XCIII (1975), 71–88.
Gramulla, G.S. *Handelsbeziehungen Kölner Kaufleute zwischen 1500 und 1650*, Köln/Wien, 1972.
Gras, N.S.B. *The Early English Customs System*, Cambridge, Mass., 1918.
Gray, H.L. 'English Foreign Trade from 1446 to 1482,' *Studies in English Trade in the Fifteenth Century*, ed. M.M. Postan and E. Power, London, 1933, 1–38.
Gross, C. *A Bibliography of British Municipal History including Gilds and Parliamentary Representation*, New York, 1897.
Hakluyt, R. ed. *Voyages*, intro. J. Masefield, 8 vols. London 1907.
Hanham, A. 'Foreign Exchange and the English Wool Merchant in the Late Fifteenth Century,' *Bulletin of the Institute of Historical Research*, XLVI (1973), 160–75.
– *The Celys and Their World*, Cambridge, 1985.
Haward, W.I. 'Economic Aspects of the Wars of the Roses in East Anglia,' *English Historical Review*, XLI (1926), 170–89.
– 'The Trade of Boston in the 15th Century,' *Lincolnshire Architectural and Archaeological Society Reports and Papers*, XLI (1936), 169–78.
Heath, P. 'North Sea Fishing in the Fifteenth Century: The Scarborough Fleet,' *Northern History*, III (1968), 53–69.
Heaton, H. *The Yorkshire Woollen and Worsted Industries*, Oxford, 1920.
Henn, V. 'Wachsende Spannungen in den hansisch-niederländischen Beziehungen,' *Die Hanse. Lebenswirklichkeit und Mythos*, ed. J. Bracker, Hamburg, 1989, vol. 1, 73–9.
Hickmore, M.A.S. *The Shipbuilding Industry on the East and South Coasts of England in the Fifteenth Century*, unpublished M.A. thesis, London, 1937.
Hirsch, T. *Danzigs Handels- und Gewerbsgeschichte unter der Herrschaft des Deutschen Ordens*, Leipzig, 1858 (Stuttgart, 1969)

Hollihn, G. 'Die Stapel- und Gästepolitik Rigas in der Ordenzeit 1201–1561,' *HGbll*, LX (1935), 91–217.

Holmes, G.A. 'The Libel of English Policy,' *English Historical Review*, LXXVI (1961), 193–216.

Irsigler, F. 'Die Lübecker Vechinchusen und die Kölner Rinck,' *Hanse in Europa: Brücke zwischen den Märkten 12.–17. Jahrhundert*, Köln, 1973, 303–27.

– 'Hansischer Kupferhandel im 15. und in der ersten Hälfte des 16. Jahrhunderts,' *HGbll*, XCVII (1979), 15–35.

– *Die wirtschaftliche Stellung der Stadt Köln im 14. und 15. Jahrhundert*, Köln, 1979.

Jacob, E.F. *The Fifteenth Century 1399–1485*, Oxford History of England, vol. 6, Oxford, 1961.

Jalland, P. 'The 'Revolution' in Northern Borough Representation in Mid-Fifteenth Century England,' *Northern History*, XI (1976), 27–57.

Jansma, T.J. 'Phillipe le Bon et le guerre hollando-wende,' *Revue du Nord*, XIII (1960), 5–18.

Jarvis, R.C. 'The Early Customs and Customs Houses in the Port of London,' *Transactions of the London and Middlesex Archaeological Society*, XXVII (1976), 271–9.

Jenks, S. 'Das Schreiberbuch des John Thorpe und der hansische Handel in London 1457/59,' *HGbll*, CI (1983), 67–113.

– 'Hansische Vermächtnisse in London,' *HGbll*, CIV (1986), 35–111.

– 'Der "Liber Lynne" und die Besitzgeschichte des hansischen Stahlhofs zu Lynn,' *Zeitschrift des Vereins für Lübeckische Geschichte und Altertumskunde*, LXVIII (1988), 21–81.

– 'Hartgeld und Wechsel im hansisch-englischen Handel des 15. Jahrhunderts,' *Geldumlauf, Währungssysteme und Zahlungsverkehr in Nordwesteuropa 1300–1800*, ed. M. North, Köln/Wien, 1989, 127–56.

– 'Der Englandhandel: Erfolge und Rückschläge,' *Die Hanse. Lebenswirklichkeit und Mythos*, ed. J. Bracker, Hamburg, 1989, vol. 1, 68–73.

– 'Köln – Lübeck – Danzig. Von der Unvereinbarkeit der Interessen im Englandhandel,' *Die Hanse. Lebenswirklichkeit und Mythos*, ed. J. Bracker, Hamburg, 1989, vol. 1, 106–11.

– 'Die "Carta Mercatoria." Ein hansisches Privileg,' *HGbll*, CVIII (1990), 45–86.

– *England, die Hanse und Preussen: Handel und Diplomatie 1377–1474*, 3 vols. Köln/Wien, 1992.

Johansen, P. *Deutsch und Undeutsch im mittelalterlichen und frühneuzeitlichen Reval*, Köln/Wien, 1973.

Johnson, A.H. *The History of the Worshipful Company of the Drapers of London*, 2 vols. Oxford, 1914–15.

Keene, D. 'New Discoveries at the Hanseatic Steelyard in London,' *HGbll*, CVII (1989), 15–25.

– 'Die deutsche Guildhall und ihre Umgebung,' *Die Hanse. Lebenswirklichkeit und Mythos*, ed. J. Bracker, Hamburg, 1989, vol. 1, 149–56.

Kendall, P.M. *Warwick the Kingmaker*, New York, 1957.

Kerling, N.J.M. *Commercial Relations of Holland and Zealand with England from the Late 15th Century to the Close of the Middle Ages*, Leiden, 1954.

- 'Relations of English Merchants with Bergen op Zoom, 1480–81,' *Bulletin of the Institute of Historical Research*, XXXI (1958), 130–40.

- 'Aliens in the County of Norfolk 1436–1485,' *Norfolk Archaeology*, XXXIII (1965), 200–12.

Kermode, J.I. 'Merchants, Overseas Trade, and Urban Decline: York, Beverley and Hull c. 1380–1500,' *Northern History*, XXII (1987), 51–73.

Ketner, F. *Handel en Scheepvaart van Amsterdam in de vijftiende Eeuw*, Leiden, 1946.

Kingsford, C.L. 'The Beginnings of English Maritime Enterprise in the Fifteenth Century,' *History*, XIII (1928–9), 97–106, 193–203.

- *Prejudice and Promise in Fifteenth-Century England*, London, 1962.

Kirby, J.L. 'Sir William Sturmy's Embassy to Germany in 1405–06,' *History Today*, XV (1965), 39–47.

Kirchner, W. *Commercial Relations between Russia and Europe 1400–1800*, Bloomington, Ind., 1966.

Kuske, B. 'Die Kölner Handelsbeziehungen im 15. Jahrhundert,' *Vierteljahrschrift für Sozial- und Wirtschaftsgeschichte*, VII (1909), 296–308.

Lander, J.R. 'Council, Administration and Councillors 1461 to 1485,' *Bulletin of the Institute of Historical Research*, XXXII (1959), 138–80.

- *Government and Community: England, 1450–1509*, Cambridge, Mass., 1980.

Lauffer, V. 'Danzigs Schiffs- und Waarenverkehr am Ende des 15. Jahrhunderts,' *Zeitschrift des Westpreussischen Geschichtsvereins*, XXXIII (1894), 1–44.

Lienau, O. 'Danziger Schiffahrt und Schiffbau in der zweiten Hälfte des 15. Jahrhunderts,' *Zeitschrift des Westpreussischen Geschichtsvereins*, LXX (1930), 71–83.

Lloyd, T.H. *Alien Merchants in England in the High Middle Ages*, London, 1982.

- 'A Reconsideration of Two Anglo-Hanseatic Treaties of the Fifteenth Century,' *English Historical Review*, CII (1987), 916–33.

- *England and the German Hanse, 1157–1611: A Study of Their Trade and Commercial Diplomacy*, Cambridge, 1991.

Lockyer, R. *Henry VII*, London, 1974.

Mackie, J.D. *The Earlier Tudors 1485–1558*, Oxford History of England, vol. 7, Oxford, 1952.

Malowist, M. 'Poland, Russia and Western Trade in the Fifteenth and Sixteenth Century,' *Past and Present*, XIII (1958), 26–41.

- 'A Certain Trade Technique in the Baltic Countries in the 15th–17th Centuries,' *Poland at the XIth International Congress of Historical Sciences in Stockholm*, Warszawa, 1960, 103–16.

- *Croissance et régression en Europe XIVe–XVIIe siècles*, Ecole Pratique des Hautes Etudes. Cahiers des Annales 34. Paris, 1972.

Manship, H. *A Booke of the Foundacion and Antiquitye of the Towne of Greate Yermouthe*, ed. C.J. Palmer, Great Yarmouth, 1847.

– *The History of Great Yarmouth*, ed. C.J. Palmer, Great Yarmouth, 1854.

Marcus, G.J. *A Naval History of England*, vol. I, Boston, 1961.

McGowan, A. *Tiller and Whipstaff: The Development of the Sailing Ship 1400–1700*, London, 1981.

McKisack, M. 'The Parliamentary Representation of King's Lynn before 1500,' *English Historical Review*, XLII (1927), 583–9.

Meissner, R. 'Eine isländische Urkunde,' *HGbll*, XIII (1907), 245–64.

Meltzing, O. 'Tommaso Portinari und sein Konflikt mit der Hanse,' *HGbll*, XII (1906), 101–23.

Millack, W. 'Danzigs Handelsbeziehungen zu England,' *Danzigs Handel in Vergangenheit und Gegenwart*, ed. H. Bauer and W. Millack, Danzig, 1925, 80–97.

Müller, J. 'Handel und Verkehr Bremens im Mittelalter: Teil 2,' *Bremisches Jahrbuch*, XXX (1927), 1–107.

Munro, J.H. 'Bruges and the Abortive Staple in English Cloth: An Incident in the Shift of Commerce from Bruges to Antwerp in the Late Fifteenth Century,' *Revue Belge de philologie et d'histoire*, XLIV (1966), 1137–59.

– 'The costs of Anglo-Burgundian Interdependence,' *Revue Belge de philologie et d'histoire*, XLVI (1968), 1228–38.

– 'An Economic Aspect of the Collapse of the Anglo-Burgundian Alliance 1428–1442,' *English Historical Review*, CCCXXXV (1970), 225–44.

– *Wool, Cloth, and Gold: The Struggle for Bullion in the Anglo-Burgundian Trade, 1340–1478*, Toronto, 1972.

– 'Industrial Protectionism in Medieval Flanders: Urban or National?' *The Medieval City*, ed. H.A. Miskimin, D. Herlihy, and A.L. Udovitch, New Haven, 1977, 229–68.

Murawski, K.E. *Zwischen Tannenberg und Thorn*, Göttingen, 1953.

Myers, A.R. 'Parliamentary Petitions in the Fifteenth Century,' *English Historical Review*, LII (1937), 385–405, 590–613.

– 'The Outbreak of War between England and Burgundy in February 1471,' *Bulletin of the Institute of Historical Research*, XXXIII (1960), 114–15.

Nance, R.M. 'A Hanseatic Bergentrader of 1489,' *Mariner's Mirror*, III (1913), 161–7.

Neumann, G. 'Hansische Politik und Politiker bei den Utrechter Friedensverhandlungen,' *Frühformen englisch-deutscher Handelspartnerschaft*, ed. K. Friedland, Köln/Wien, 1976, 25–59.

Oppenheim, M. *A History of the Administration of the Royal Navy*. London, 1896 (Hamden, Conn., 1961).

Pagal, K. *Die Hanse*, 2nd ed., Braunschweig, 1963.

Pantin, W.A. 'The Merchants' Houses and Warehouses of King's Lynn,' *Medieval Archaeology*, VI–VII (1962), 173–81.

Pauli, R. 'Die Haltung der Hansestädte in den Rosen-Kriegen,' *HGbll*, 1874 (1875), 75–105.

– 'Der Hansische Stahlhof in London,' *Bilder aus Alt-England*, 2nd ed., Gotha, 1876, 168–91.

Pitz, E. 'Steigende und fallende Tendenzen in Politik und Wirtschaftsleben der Hanse im 16. Jahrhundert,' *HGbll.*, CII (1984), 39–78.

Ponting, K.G. *The Woollen Industry of South-west England*, Bath, 1971.

Postal, R. 'Der Niedergang der Hanse,' *Die Hanse. Lebenswirklichkeit und Mythos*, ed. J. Bracker, Hamburg, 1989, vol.1, 124–41.

Postan, M.M. *Medieval Trade and Finance*, Cambridge, 1973.

– 'The Economic and Political Relations of England and the Hanse from 1400 to 1475,' *Studies in English Trade in the Fifteenth Century*, ed. M.M. Postan and E. Power, London, 1933, 91–153.

Postan, M.M. and Power, E. eds. *Studies in English Trade in the Fifteenth Century*, London, 1933.

Power, E. 'The Wool Trade in the Fifteenth Century,' *Studies in English Trade in the Fifteenth Century*, ed. M.M. Postan and E. Power, London, 1933, 39–90.

– 'The English Wool Trade in the Reign of Edward IV,' *Cambridge Historical Journal*, II (1926), 17–25.

Puhle, M. *Die Politik der Stadt Braunschweig innerhalb des Sächsischen Städtebundes und der Hanse im späten Mittelalter*, Braunschweig, 1985.

Purcell, D. 'Der hansische "Steelyard" in King's Lynn, Norfolk, England,' *Hanse in Europa: Brücke zwischen den Märkten 12.–17. Jahrhundert*, Köln, 1973, 108–12.

Rackham, O. *Ancient Woodland*, London, 1980.

Ramsay, G.D. *English Overseas Trade during the Centuries of Emergence*, London, 1957.

Ramsey, P. 'Overseas Trade in the Reign of Henry VII,' *EcHR*, 2nd series VI (1953), 173–82.

Richards, W. *The History of Lynn, Civil, Ecclesiastical, Political, Commercial, Biographical, Municipal, and Military, from the Earliest Accounts to the Present Time*, 2 vols. Lynn, 1812.

Richmond, C.F. *Royal Administration and the Keeping of the Seas, 1422–1485*, unpublished D.Phil. thesis, Oxford, 1963.

– 'The Keeping of the Seas during the Hundred Years War 1422–40,' *History*, XLIX (1964), 283–98.

– 'English Naval Power in the Fifteenth Century,' *History*, LII (1967), 1–15.

Rörig, F. 'Ein Hamburger Kapervertrag vom Jahre 1471,' *HGbll*, XXIII (1917), 411–19.

– *Wirtschaftskräfte im Mittelalter*, Köln, 1959.

Rosenberg, H. 'The Rise of the Junkers in Brandenburg Prussia 1410–1653,' *American Historical Review*, XLIX (1943), 1–22, (1944), 228–42.

Roskell, J.S. 'The Social Composition of the Commons in a Fifteenth Century Parliament,' *Bulletin of the Institute of Historical Research*, XXIV (1951), 152–72.

– *The Commons in the Parliament of 1422*, Manchester, 1954.

– *The Commons and Their Speakers in English Parliaments 1376–1523*, Manchester, 1965.

Ross, C. *Edward IV*, Los Angeles, 1974.

Ruffmann, K.-H. 'Engländer und Schotten in den Seestädten Ost- und West-preussens,' *Zeitschrift für Ostforschung*, VII (1958), 17–39.

Rülke, F. *Die Verlagerung der Handelswege zwischen 1450 und 1550 und ihre Rückwirkung auf die deutsche Hanse*, D.Phil. thesis, Hannover, 1971.

Salter, F.R. 'The Hanse, Cologne and the Crisis of 1468,' *EcHR*, III (1931), 93–101.

Salzman, L.F. *English Industries of the Middle Ages*, Oxford, 1923.

– *English Trade in the Middle Ages*, London, 1964.

– *Building England down to 1540*, 2nd ed., Oxford, 1967.

Samsonowicz, H. *Untersuchungen über das Danziger Bürgerkapital in der zweiten Hälfte des 15. Jahrhunderts*, Weimar, 1969.

– 'Engländer und Schotten in Danzig im Spätmittelalter: Zwei Formen der Handelstätigkeit,' *Seehandel und Wirtschaftswege Nordeuropas im 17. und 18. Jahrhundert*, ed. K. Friedland and F. Irsigler, Ostfildern, 1981, 48–58.

Scammell, G.V. 'English Merchant Shipping at the End of the Middle Ages: Some East Coast Evidence,' *EcHR*, 2nd series XIII (1961), 327–41.

– 'Shipowning in England 1450–1550,' *Transactions of the Royal Historical Society*, 5th series XII (1962), 105–22.

Schäfer, D. *Die Hanse und ihre Handelspolitik*, Jena, 1885.

– *Die deutsche Hanse*, Leipzig, 1914.

Schanz, G. *Englische Handelspolitik gegen Ende des Mittelalters*, 2 vols. Leipzig, 1881.

Schildhauer, J., K. Fritze, and W. Stark, *Die Hanse*, 4th ed., Berlin, 1981.

Schnurmann, C. *Kommerz und Klüngel: Der Englandhandel Kölner Kaufleute im 16. Jahrhundert*, Göttingen, 1991.

Schulz, F. *Die Hanse und England: von Eduards III. bis auf Heinrichs VIII. Zeit.* Abhandlungen zur Verkehrs- und Seegeschichte V, Berlin, 1911.

Seifert, D. 'Alte Bindungen, neue Zwänge: Die Krise der niederländischen Hansepolitik,' *Die Hanse. Lebenswirklichkeit und Mythos*, ed. J. Bracker, Hamburg, 1989, vol. 1, 112–18.

Simsch, A. *Die Handelsbeziehungen zwischen Nürnberg und Posen im europäischen Wirtschaftsverkehr des 15. und 16. Jahrhunderts*, Wiesbaden, 1970.

Simson, P. *Geschichte der Stadt Danzig bis 1626*, 3 vols. Danzig, 1913–24 (Aalen, 1967).

– *Der Artushof in Danzig und seine Brüderschaften, die Banken*, Danzig, 1900 (Aalen, 1969).

– 'Danzig im 13. jährigen Krieg, 1454–1466,' *Zeitschrift des Westpreussischen Geschichtsvereins*, XXIX (1891), 1–132.

Smolarek, P. 'Gdańsk, sein Handel und seine Schiffahrt vom 14. bis 17. Jahrhundert,' *Hanse in Europa: Brücke zwischen den Märkten 12.–17. Jahrhundert*, Köln, 1973, 235–50.

Spading, K. 'Zu den Ursachen für das Eindringen der Holländer in das hansische Zwischenhandelsmonopol im 15. Jahrhundert,' *Neue Hansische Studien*, ed. K. Fritze, E. Müller-Mertens, E. Voigt, Berlin, 1970, 227–42.

– *Holland und die Hanse im 15. Jahrhundert*, Weimar, 1973.
Sprandel, R. 'Die Konkurrenzfähigkeit der Hanse im Spätmittelalter,' *HGbll*, CII (1984), 21–38.
Stark, W. 'Die Danziger Pfahlkammerbücher (1468–1476) als Quelle für den Schiffs- und Warenverkehr zwischen den wendischen Hansestädten und Danzig,' *Rostocker Beiträge*, N.F. I, Regionalgeschichtliches Jahrbuch der Mecklenburgischen Seestädte, Rostock, 1967.
– 'Der Utrechter Frieden von 1474 zwischen der Hanse und England,' *Zeitschrift für Geschichtswissenschaft*, XIX (1971), 891–903.
– *Lübeck und Danzig in der zweiten Hälfte des 15. Jahrhunderts*, Weimar, 1973.
Stein, W. 'Die Merchant Adventurers in Utrecht 1464–1467,' *HGbll*, IX (1899), 179–89.
– *Beiträge zur Geschichte der deutschen Hanse*, Giessen, 1900.
– *Die Hanse und England: Ein hansisch-englischer Seekrieg im 15. Jahrhundert*, Pfingstblätter des hansischen Geschichtsvereins I, 1905.
– 'Die Hanse und England beim Ausgang des hundertjährigen Krieges,' *HGbll*, XLVI (1921), 27–126.
Stieda, W. 'Schiffahrtsregister,' *HGbll*, 1884 (1885), 77–115.
Symonds, R.W. 'Furniture: Post-Roman,' *History of Technology*, ed. C. Singer, Oxford, 1956, vol. 2, 240–59.
Thielemans, M.R. *Bourgogne et Angleterre: Relations politiques et economiques entre les Pays-Bas Bourguignons et l'Angleterre, 1435–1467*, Brussels, 1966.
Thierfelder, H. 'Köln und die Hanse,' *Kölner Vorträge zur Sozial- und Wirtschaftsgeschichte*, VII (1970), 1–25.
Thompson, P. *The History of the Antiquities of Boston*, Boston, 1856.
Thrupp, S. *The Merchant Class of Medieval London 1300–1500*, Chicago, 1948.
– 'Aliens in and around London in the Fifteenth Century,' *Studies in London History*, ed. A.E.J. Hollaender and W. Kellaway, London, 1969, 251–72.
Unger, R.W. *The Ship in the Medieval Economy 600–1600*, Montreal, 1980.
Van Houtte, J.A. 'Quantitative Quellen zur Geschichte des Antwerpener Handels im 15. und 16. Jahrhundert,' *Beiträge zur Wirtschafts- und Stadtgeschichte: Festschift für Hektor Ammann*, ed. H. Aubin, Wiesbaden, 1965, 193–204.
– 'Die Beziehungen zwischen Köln und den Niederlanden vom Hochmittelalter bis zum Beginn des Industriezeitalters,' *Kölner Vorträge zur Sozial- und Wirtschaftsgeshichte*, vol. 1 (1969), 5–26.
– *An Economic History of the Low Countries 800–1800*, New York, 1977.
Van der Wee, H. *The Growth of the Antwerp Market and the European Economy*, 3 vols. 's-Gravenhage, 1963.
Van Werveke, H. *Miscellanea Mediaevalia*, Gent, 1968.
– 'Structural Changes in European Long-distance Trade, and particularly in the Re-export Trade from South to North, 1350–1750,' *The Rise of Merchant Empires*, ed. J.D. Tracy, Cambridge, 1990, 14–33.
Vollbehr, F. *Die Holländer und die deutsche Hanse*, Pfingstblätter des hansischen Geschichtsvereins XXI, 1930.

Wedgwood, J. ed. *History of Parliament*, vol. 1, Biographies of the Members of the House of Commons 1439–1509, London, 1936.

Wegg, J. *Antwerp 1477–1559*, London, 1916.

Wehrmann, C. 'Die Gründung des hanseatischen Hauses zu Antwerpen,' *HGbll*, 1873 (1874), 77–106.

Weightman, C. *Margaret of York Duchess of Burgundy 1446–1503*, New York, 1989.

Weinbaum, M. 'Die Stellung des Fremden im mittelalterlichen England,' *Zeitschrift für vergleichende Rechtswissenschaft*, XLVI (1931), 360–78.

Weise, E. *Das Widerstandsrecht im Ordenslande Preussen und das mittelalterliche Europa*, Göttingen, 1955.

– 'Die Hanse, England und die Merchant Adventurers. Das Zusammenwirken von Köln und Danzig,' *Jahrbuch des Kölnischen Geschichtsvereins*, XXXI–XXXII (1956–7), 137–64.

Werner, T.G. 'Der Stalhof der deutschen Hanse in London in wirtschafts- und kunsthistorischen Bildwerken,' *Scripta Mercaturae*, II (1973), 1–127.

Williams, C.H. 'A Norfolk Parliamentary Election 1461,' *English Historical Review*, XL (1925), 79–86.

Winter, H. *Das Hanseschiff im ausgehenden 15. Jahrhundert*, Rostock, 1961.

Wodderspoon, J. *Memorials of the Ancient Town of Ipswich, in the County of Suffolk*, Ipswich, 1850.

ZUSAMMENFASSUNG

Diese Untersuchung befaßt sich mit den wirtschaftlichen und politischen Wechselbeziehungen zwischen England und der deutschen Hanse in der zweiten Hälfte des 15. Jahrhunderts und zeigt auf, in welchem Masse die Umorientierung des englisch-hanseatischen Verkehrs im breiteren Rahmen des europäischen Handelsnetzes sich auf die institutionelle Stabilität der Hanse sowie auf die merkantile Entwicklung ihrer führenden Mitgliedstädte auswirkte. Ferner ermöglicht die Beschreibung der kommerziellen Infrastruktur eine Bewertung des hanseatischen Handels einzelner englischer Häfen wie auch der wirtschaftlichen Auswirkungen verschiedener Unterbrechungen dieses Handels.

Die wirtschaftlichen Interessen der Kaufmannskreise, die in Zusammenhang mit der sich verändernden Handelslage und dem schwankenden Kurs der englisch-hanseatischen Diplomatie gesehen werden, liefern die Grundlage für eine Analyse des politischen Verhaltens der Hansestädte einander gegenüber. Ein durchgängiges Element der Uneinigkeit innerhalb der hanseatischen Gemeinschaft zeigt sich in den weitgefächerten Reaktionen auf das Kapern der hanseatischen Baienflotte durch englische Freibeuter 1449, erst recht in der langfristigen Absonderung Lübecks vom Englandhandel. Zwei Jahrzehnte später gipfelte die immer weiter um sich greifende maritime Gewalt in dem völligen Zusammenbruch der englisch-hanseatischen Diplomatie und in einem Versuch seitens der Kölner Kaufleute, sich von der übrigen hanseatischen Gemeinschaft in England abzusetzen. Die daraus resultierende Zerschlagung des Handels zwischen England und den Ostseeländern in den folgenden fünf Jahren, zusammen mit der Entschlossenheit der Kölner, den Kanalverkehr mit London aufrechtzuerhalten, förderte die Rolle der Zeelandhäfen bei der Abwicklung des englischen und des hanseatischen Seehandels und leistete dem Aufstieg der Marktstädte Brabants im letzten Viertel des Jahrhunderts Vorschub. Die Tatsache, daß die Kölner sich dabei auf Handelswege nach Süd- und Osteuropa stützten, hatte selbstverständlich eine Ausdehnung des Binnenhandelsnetzes zur Folge, die ihrerseits wieder weitreichende Folgen für verschiedene Sektoren der Hanse hatte.

Ferner wurde der Überseehandel der ostenglischen Häfen von der Unterbrechung des englisch-hanseatischen Verkehrs sowohl in dem Zeitraum 1469–1474 als auch in den späten 8oer Jahren schwer betroffen, obwohl dies auf lange Sicht nicht alleine entscheidend war für das Ausmaß der englischen Beteiligung am Ostseehandel. Als mit Ende des Jahrhunderts die englisch-hanseatischen politischen Beziehungen sich wieder stabilisiert hatten, brachten schliesslich die englisch-niederländischen Handelskriege nach 1490 weitere, wenn auch weniger dauerhafte, Umstellungen des Handelssystems mit sich. Dabei treten die Stärken und Schwächen verschiedenster hanseatischer Interessengruppen sowie die im ganzen gesehen mangelnde Festigkeit der Hanse als lebensfähiger politischer Größe deutlich zutage.

INDEX